THE ARCHAEOLOGY
OF
EARLY MAN

THE ARCHAEOLOGY
OF
EARLY MAN

J. M. Coles and E. S. Higgs

FREDERICK A. PRAEGER

Publishers

New York · Washington

BOOKS THAT MATTER

Published in the United States of America in 1969
by Frederick A. Praeger, Inc., Publishers
111 Fourth Avenue, New York, N.Y. 10003

Library of Congress Catalog Card Number: 76–91855

Printed in Great Britain

Preface

THIS book attempts to describe the evidence for some aspects of human behaviour over the greater part of the last three million years. The record, as it is at present known, is fragmentary and obscure. It is all that we have to enable us to pursue that primary concern of archaeology, to give our own behaviour a perspective in time. At present, long-standing concepts of interpretation are under keen criticism and new ones arising in consequence of the development of new or more refined techniques have not yet been fully developed.

Nowhere have we attempted to give a comprehensive account. We have tried to select, to integrate, and to make more easily accessible some of the basic data in order to give a lead to those who wish to go beyond the popular literature and make a first step towards a serious study of the Old Stone Age.

We have leant heavily upon the publications of many prehistorians whose work provides the primary data. We acknowledge our debt to them. We thank Professor J. Desmond Clark, Professor Hallam Movius Jr., Dr Charles McBurney, Mrs Ann Sieveking and Professor Phillip Tobias for permission to use illustrations direct from their publications, Patricia Vinnicombe and Mr Pat Carter for tracings and photographs of South African rock art, and Mr W. Shawcross, Professor Tobias and Mr Rhys Jones for their helpful advice. Most of the illustrations have been redrawn for publication by Miss M. O. Miller and Miss J. Ogden, to whom we are indebted. We also thank Mr L. P. Morley and Miss A. C. Allan of the University Museum of Archaeology and Ethnology, Cambridge, for assistance in photographic work and typing.

J.M.C. & E.S.H.

1 *February* 1968

Contents

CONTENTS

List of Plates

List of Figures

LIST OF FIGURES

LIST OF FIGURES

LIST OF FIGURES

LIST OF FIGURES

Introduction

BIOLOGICALLY, man is an animal and a member of the primates, as are the great apes (gorilla, chimpanzee and orangutan). Physically he is less well-endowed in some characteristics than are many other animals, but it is likely that his lack of physical specialization and his adaptability were conducive to survival in a variety of situations. About two million years ago he appears to have begun to make tools. Other animals use wood and stone objects for immediate purposes, but man is the only animal who can make tools to a standard pattern for future use. It is because of this repetition in tool forms that we are able to recognize them as the products of deliberate manufacture.

A prerequisite for making such tools, or at least their diversification of form and shape, was probably a development in communication, speech, whereby knowledge and experience could be handed down more successfully, and over a wider field, to a succeeding generation. Of this we can only guess, for there is no record.

The first known man-made tools are found in Africa and are dated to an early part of the geological period known as the Pleistocene. Apparently man co-evolved for many millennia with other animals who were physically comparable but who could not make tools. No doubt, crude as the first recognizable tools were, they gave man some small advantage over his competitors in the exploitation of his environment.

Of man's economy at this early time we have little information, but apparently already he may have differed from other primates by his greater reliance on animal protein. This may in fact be the first indication of man's ability to diversify methods of exploiting his environment as a gatherer and hunter, in establishing symbiotic relationships with other animals and plants. This first phase of human development, with man apparently more or less confined to his African homeland, lasted for several hundreds of thousands of years. The archaeologist studying this phase relies to a great extent upon dating by geological formations (p. 26), faunal assemblages (p. 45), and recently developed methods of obtaining dates in terms of 'years ago' (p. 35), and these tend to emphasize the slow evolution of the stone equipment of early man. Although we lack much evidence that man's ability to obtain his living successfully had increased during this time, it is likely that the growing knowledge of the territory available to him enabled him to augment his food supplies, add to his numbers and gradually to extend his range.

From Africa, perhaps slow-moving yet persistent movements of people spread into Europe and southern Asia, and by a quarter of a million years ago large expanses of territory were occupied in the Old World, the northern limit of habitation controlled in part by the ice sheets that periodically advanced from the highlands of the north, from Scandinavia and the Himalayas in particular. The type of man represented in the Old World at this time is called *Homo erectus*.

Through the increasingly detailed knowledge of dating and distributions, many minor episodes in the development of the stone industries of early man can be distinguished by the prehistorian, but an overview of the early phases of stone tool-making appears, superficially at least, to show that only two great industrial traditions existed in the Old World during this early phase of human movements, a handaxe tradition in Africa, western Europe and the Near East, and a pebble and flake tradition in the Far East. This, however, is to take an oversimplified view of the range, and there is no doubt that, in due time, any broad uniformity in tools and in man himself had disappeared, as increasing isolation and specialization led to the development of new cultural traditions and physical beings. One of the latter was *Homo sapiens*, now the only surviving species of *Homo*.

By technological inventions a greater range of equipment was made available to *Homo sapiens*. His occupation was extended into northern latitudes, where he could cope with glacial conditions, and territory expansions eventually took him as far north as the Arctic Circle, and into the New World. In tropical Africa and the Far East, it is possible that the absence of major climatic or even emphatic seasonal changes did not stimulate the processes of challenge leading to cultural development as much as did the northern environment.

In terms of major cultural achievements, perhaps the most important of late glacial times was the sudden emergence of a belief in a life after death, which is recorded for the prehistorian in the many burials of the dead with accompanying clothing, decoration, food and weapons. This tradition of burial is first in evidence about 50,000 years ago, and opened the way to a fuller appreciation of the mysteries of life and death, which in western Europe may have stimulated the development of the earliest mural art in the world. Other societies also participated in art as a form of commemorative or symbolic expression, but the glacial art of Europe remains a prime source of information about the concepts of early man.

Our knowledge about the prehistory of human behaviour and evolution during the period of man's existence as a hunter and gatherer, and his early symbiotic relationship with other living forms, is largely restricted to the stone tools he abandoned, to the remains of the animals with which he was associated and to the few traces of man himself. In searching for major trends in human development, these are pitifully meagre supplies on which to feed our theories, and it has seemed preferable to present in this book some of the basic data concerning cultural developments by geographically limited areas, without necessarily attempting to provide connecting links or theories between different regions. A developing archaeology is not likely to be interested only in possible human migrations based on tool similarities. The use of similar cultural names for stone tool assemblages from widely different areas follows accepted practice and serves to distinguish the broad trends of industrial development during the Pleistocene, but only the persistent application of increasingly precise methods of absolute dating will eventually allow us to distinguish, for example, between culturally related and functionally related groups of early man (p. 67). For the present, we have attempted to provide a guide to further interest and reading, some illustrated examples of sites and industries, and a survey of some of the most important methods by which the material remains of early man may be dated and placed in their proper environmental and economic situations.

Note on the organization of the book: this book is broadly arranged on a geographical basis, and within the area chapters will be found a general survey of the evidence followed by brief descriptions of some important sites. The faunal/terminology recorded in the original site reports has been retained.

Part I
CHRONOLOGY,
ECOLOGY AND ECONOMY

1

Some Events of the Pleistocene

In the north temperate zone the geological division between the Pliocene and the Pleistocene periods is considered to be the point in time when warmth-preferring flora and fauna of the Pliocene period were partially replaced by cold-tolerant genera and species which mark the first stage in a climatic sequence which culminated, in northern latitudes, in the appearance of enormous ice sheets descending from the mountains of Scandinavia and other regions. These ice sheets traditionally served as the chronological basis for the Pleistocene (Charlesworth 1957).

In recent years the discovery of the $^{18}O/^{16}O$ method of palaeotemperature measurement, however, has altered the concept of glacial and interglacial periods originally established on the basis of these glacial morainic and outwash deposits (Emiliani 1955, 1966). The $^{18}O/^{16}O$ method rests upon the temperature-dependent isotopic fractionation of oxygen which is measurable in the secretion of calcium carbonate by marine organisms. The building of calcareous shells by organisms involves the incorporation of ^{18}O and ^{16}O in proportions dependent on the water temperature, and the shells of foraminifera living in the surface waters of the sea are most susceptible to changes in temperature. Foraminiferal layers have been obtained by taking deep sea cores in equatorial regions and have been combined to produce a palaeotemperature curve for much of the Pleistocene (fig. 1). To the upper layers of these

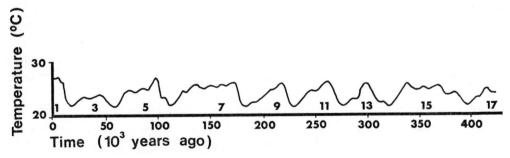

Fig. 1. Generalized temperature curve for the surface water of the Caribbean; with core stages 1–17. *Based on Emiliani 1966*

25

cores, the radiocarbon dating method (p. 35) has been applied, and the protactinium/ thorium method to earlier layers (Rosholt *et al.* 1961). This has given an indication of a time scale for the alternating cold and warm conditions of the Pleistocene period. The overall picture so given differs markedly from the traditional four great glacial advances of Günz, Mindel, Riss and Würm (p. 28). Instead there appears to have been a series of rapid alternations of glacial and interglacial, or interstadial, periods, few of which appear to have been of long duration. This evidence tends to be supported by such geological observations as the multiple weathering horizons in the loess of central Europe (p. 29), and the numerous variations in the climate of the Netherlands and elsewhere as deduced from pollen analysis (p. 39).

It has been suggested, however, that the changes recorded in the foraminifera are due to alterations in the composition of the sea caused by changes in the amount of water abstracted from the oceans and locked up in the glacial ice sheets, and that the movements of planktonic faunal provinces during the Upper Pleistocene were due to salinity rather than to temperature changes (Shackleton 1967); while the differences recorded may not then be directly related to temperature changes they are nevertheless good indicators of glacial and interglacial episodes, and the basic results of the method must be accepted. They indicate the incomplete and fragmented nature of Pleistocene climatic evidence derived solely from northern latitudes and point to the necessity of relating terrestrial to marine deposits by absolute dating methods (p. 35). Such dates as are available point to the fact that the glacial advances in northern latitudes only began on a large scale late in Pleistocene times.

The Glaciated Areas

The ice sheets of the northern regions at their maximum effectively covered about one-quarter of the world's land surface, compared with one-tenth coverage today. The ice in North American at one time concealed more than half of that continent and almost all of Canada. At the centre the ice sheet was over 3,000 metres in thickness. Its southern limit passed through New York. In Europe the ice sheet reached as far south as London, Berlin and Warsaw; in Russia it reached the Dniepr and the Don. In Scotland the ice rose some 900 metres above the lowlands (Charlesworth 1957).

Periodically there were ice recessions and a warmer climate. It is possible that at these times the Polar ice caps even ceased to exist although some authorities believe that Antarctica and Greenland became glaciated millions of years ago and have remained so ever since. During these Interglacials, which may be defined as a time when the ice sheets melted to about their present levels, and a warm climate was maintained long enough to allow certain changes in the vegetation to take place, the climate is believed to have been at least as warm as it is today. Mixed oak forests developed in north-west Europe and animals such as the hippopotamus reached as far north as Yorkshire. There were also minor warmer or temperate episodes called interstadials which occurred within the glacial periods. These were either too brief or too cold for mixed oak forests to develop in north temperate Europe.

These climatic changes left many kinds of evidence for their existence in the geological record. The term 'drift' is a general term for accumulations relating directly or indirectly to Pleistocene ice. In many areas advancing glaciers transported accumulations of debris called moraines. End or terminal moraines were deposited where the debris was laid down in front of the advancing ice. Beneath the ice there formed a bottom moraine or boulder clay (till), a fine-grained deposit which does not necessarily contain either boulders or clay (Zeuner 1959).

The initial stages of the Pleistocene, prior to widespread glacial activity, are thought to be recognizable in the discontinuous sequence of deposits known in East Anglia as The Crags. They consist of marine and estuarine deposits wherein marine gastropods are preserved. A basal deposit, the Coralline crag, has been contrasted with the overlying Red crag by three elements which are taken to indicate a geological separation between the end-Pliocene and beginning-Pleistocene. These three elements are: a geological unconformity separating the deposits, an influx of cold-preferring marine gastropods preserved in the Red crag, and the appearance of *Equus* and *Elephas* in the Red crag (p. 45). Of the quantities of marine gastropods in these and succeeding crags, many are extinct and cannot be employed for climatic purposes, but certain forms are extant and can be employed to show the change in climate towards cooler conditions (West 1968).

Crags	Percentages of marine gastropods (approx.)				
	northern forms	southern forms	extinct	unclassifiable	total species
Weybourne ⎫ Chillesford ⎬ Icenian Norwich ⎭	26	0	28	46	98
Red ⎧ Butley	21	2	40	37	163
⎨ Newbourne	12	7	53	28	226
⎩ Walton	16	11	48	25	352
Coralline	4	12	57	27	303

The cooler conditions during the deposition of the Weybourne crag are equated by some authorities with the first of the four major glacial advances of the Alpine region, the Günz. Unfortunately there is little evidence for direct correlation between the phases of the Alpine succession and those of the north European area or the North American area, and there is little doubt that the Alpine fourfold sequence disguises or omits a number of important climatic events.

The superimposed tills of East Anglia also give a succession of events which occurred within the area of ice formation, and give a relative chronology for a later part of the Pleistocene. The sequence may be summarized as follows, combining a number of exposures, at Cromer, Hoxne and Ipswich:

Character	Name	Climatic inference
glacial gravels	Gipping gravels	glaciation
lake muds and peats	Hoxne	interglacial
glacial till	Lowestoft till ⎫	
sands and gravels	Corton ⎬	glaciation
glacial till	Cromer till ⎭	
pebble series		
peat series	Cromer Forest Bed	interglacial (composite)

The moving ice also carried with it 'erratics', that is, fragments of rock detached from their parent source. They may be small or, as with the Madison Boulder in the United States, up to 10,000 tons in weight. The source of the erratics can sometimes be determined and this indicates the direction of flow of the ice. The study of the erratics in the tills of East Anglia showed that they came from two different directions and were the products of two different glacial episodes. The first episode, to which the Lowestoft and the Cromer tills belong, relates to ice moving eastwards across the area from the Southern Pennines. The second, the Gipping, relates to ice moving southwards.

Ice also moves in some ways like water and erratics tend to be orientated with their long axes lying in the direction of the flow of the ice. The study of stones in the tills also showed that they lay with a different preferred orientation in the different tills and that there was therefore more than one glacial episode.

The classic study of glaciations, however, is that of the Alpine succession where in 1909 four Pleistocene glaciations were distinguished. They were named, in chronological succession, after four Alpine streams, Günz, Mindel, Riss and Würm. This work was based on the gravel terraces and fans formed by the waters of the melting glaciers. Subsequently, on the same basis, earlier glacial phases were recognized and were called the Donau phases.

In northern Europe, there is little evidence of the Donau or Günz episodes, and the earliest Pleistocene glacial material, recognized in Denmark, Poland and Russia, is the Elster moraine which was deposited by an ice sheet moving in several directions from the mountains of the north. In north-west Germany, marine deposits with warmth-preferring molluscs rest upon boulder clays of the Elster glaciation, and mark the succeeding interglacial period, called the Holstein, on the basis of the evidence of a high sea level (p. 31).

The succeeding glacial period, the Saale, marks the first major ice movement into the Netherlands. The centre of dispersal of the ice was varied, and the evidence of the moraines suggest a twofold division of this glacial period, an earliest Saale (*sensu stricto*) and a later Warthe advance. In eastern Europe this glacial episode has been divided into both two and three (Poland) divisions.

The interglacial period following is called Eemian, and represents a phase of climate probably warmer than today's with a high flooding sea, the waters of which in northern Europe contained marine fauna found today off south-west Europe.

SOME EVENTS OF THE PLEISTOCENE

The final major climatic episode in the north was the Weichsel glaciation, which covered a less extensive area than the Saale or Elster. Some of the temporary halts in the retreat stages of the Weichsel ice sheet are represented by well-preserved terminal moraines in northern Germany and southern Scandinavia.

THE PERIGLACIAL AREAS

Outside the areas covered by the ice a number of periglacial phenomena have also been observed, and help to form a relative chronology of Pleistocene climatic events.

Loess is commonly a fine grained, brownish yellow or buff coloured deposit. The grain is rounded or sub-angular, in size 0·05–0·01 millimetres. Its origin is disputed, but periglacial loess is considered to be associated with dry glacial conditions. Its mineral content indicates a source in river floodplains during temporary periods of exposure, at intervals between seasonal floods. Contained snails, rodents and larger mammals indicate cold conditions.

Loess deposits, which are commonly from 30–100 metres in depth, are found over a great part of Europe, from France and Germany east to the Carpathians, Russia and Siberia. In North America loess covers many thousands of square miles and reaches as far south as the Gulf of Mexico. In South America east of the Andes there is a large area of loess west and south-west of Montevideo. Loess itself is not usually truly bedded and so fossil soils are generally thin except those formed during lengthy periods of warmer and perhaps wetter climates; such fossil soils indicate interglacial or interstadial phases. Most archaeological material occurs in or on fossil soils and not within the unweathered loess itself.

In Europe a number of superimposed depositions of loess have been recognized. In France an ancient loess contains Villafranchian (Lower Pleistocene) fauna, but most of the loessic deposits in west and central Europe belong either to an Older Loess complex or to a Younger Loess series. The Older Loess is characteristically dark yellow-brown in colour, weathered through its thickness by percolating waters, and contains a thick fossil soil at the top. This loess is generally considered to be of the Saale glacial period, with the Last Interglacial on top. A number of fossil soils occur in the Older Loess, generally two or three in west and central Europe, more in south and eastern Europe. The Younger Loess, overlying the thick weathering soil of Eemian age, is paler in colour, yellow-grey, and occurs stratigraphically upon all ground moraines except those of the Weichsel-Würm. In central Europe, in Czechoslovakia and Austria, the Younger Loess was formerly believed to be divided into three phases, separated by soil formations called Göttweig and Paudorf, but more recent work has suggested that the situation is less clearly distinguished and that the earlier part of the Würm was cold and rather damp and included several interstadials p. 42); the latest part of the Würm, following a short middle phase of intermittent milder and cooler conditions, was very cold and dry.

Other geological deposits in the periglacial zone considered to indicate cold climatic conditions are usually referred to under the general term cryoturbation. Frost effects are used in the chronological and climatic interpretation of stratigraphic successions.

Today 22% of the world's land surface is underlain by permafrost, an area which was vastly greater in glacial times. In permafrost conditions the ground is frozen up to 70 metres in depth, well beyond the reach of the summer melt. Consequently there is an impervious layer which prevents percolation and drainage, and the upper levels become saturated with water. Under seasonal alternation of freezing and thawing, sludge will form wherein movements of particles take place. Such movements have left behind observable patterns, such as 'festoons', the folding of layers and a sorting of large and small particles. On sloping ground 'solifluction' occurs and the sodden mass may slide to the foot of the slopes. An example is the 'Coombe rock' of Britain which is composed principally of material of chalk or limestone origin.

Terrestrial phenomena relating to cold climates have the advantage that they provide a time and climatic sequence in a particular locality, but it is commonly impossible to correlate with any confidence such successions with similar successions elsewhere. In view of the difficulties of long distance correlation it has become customary to name stages and sub-stages on a type site system, wherein a particular stage is named after a place where its relation with other stages is clearly demonstrated in the stratigraphy. Where correlations can clearly be made with other areas regional names have often been substituted. The result has been an intricate and sometimes confusing and confused nomenclature.

Pluvials

The recognition of a glacial succession in the northern hemisphere gave rise to speculation as to what climatic oscillations might have occurred during the Pleistocene in the southern hemisphere. Evidence for glaciation and hence for periglacial phenomena is rare as might be expected from the distribution of the land mass, and has been recorded in only a few areas such as Tasmania, the Australian Alps and South America.

In Saharan and southern Africa it was at one time thought that there was evidence for a succession of pluvial periods which were named in chronological order Kageran, Kamasian, Kanjeran and Gamblian sub-pluvials, including which were contemporary with the Alpine glacial succession. While, from a number of disciplines and from numerous localities, there is evidence for climatic oscillations wetter or drier than now (the depression of snowlines, phytogeographical distribution studies, the distribution of birds and butterflies, for example) it is not at present possible to correlate this evidence on a continental scale. Recent palaeobotanical work has indicated that pluvial and non-pluvial periods were not synchronous over all of sub-Saharan Africa, and that each region may have had its own local sequence of alternating climatic episodes, but there is some indication that temperature changes in Africa were synchronous with those of the Northern Hemisphere.

There is, however, evidence to show that there were wetter or cooler periods, which were contemporary with the Last Glaciation in the northern hemisphere, over large areas of Africa, and that two post-glacial pluvials occurred. Such evidence comes from Haua Fteah, from lignite deposits (20,000 ± 1,000 B.P.) in Algeria, from pollen in Kenya, from southern Tunisia, from the Hoggar, from the southern Sahara in the Lake Tchad area and from Angola. At Kalambo Falls in Zambia an analysis of pollen samples suggests climatic oscillations contemporary with warmer and wetter phases of the Last Glaciation; and a warmer period, contemporary with the Brørup Inter-stadial (c. 57,000 B.P.), was followed by a cooler phase interrupted by two milder oscillations. Evidence from Florisbad in South Africa, and from Kalambo Falls, indicates a warmer period, with a relatively low rainfall, c. 29,–27,000 B.P. At Florisbad, there followed a period of increased humidity, c. 26,–19,000 B.P. In the Sahara, temperate forest (*Alnus*, *Tilia*, *Pinus*, *Quercus* and *Salix*) was established in mountainous areas, and grassland in some present desertic regions, c. 20,000 B.P., according to pollen from Saoura. In Kenya, evidence from Cherangani suggests a phase of lowered temperature and humidity before 16,000 B.P., and the same site has yielded indications of a warmer period c. 11,500 B.P., contemporary with the Allerød of northern latitudes (van Zinderen Bakker 1967a). Evidence has also been put forward which suggests a 'pluvial' period in the Sahara in Neolithic times, but many of the 'Neolithic' deposits of the Sahara are under suspicion as being of a date no earlier than historical times.

WORLD-WIDE GEOLOGICAL PHENOMENA

The difficulties of correlating geological evidence for 'pluvials' with that for glacials has led to considerable problems in attempts to determine degrees of intercontinental industrial relationships or culture-contact. One of the possible avenues of approach to this problem is the study of geological phenomena which are world wide in their distribution and were not dependent on purely local factors such as proximity to glacial ice sheets. The alternations of sea level during the Pleistocene, and evidence from the deep sea cores, may allow such long-range correlations to be attempted

Sea Levels During the Pleistocene period the level of the seas fluctuated from one extreme to another, from a maximum of about 200 metres above present sea level, to a minimum of about 150 metres or more below today's level.

The traces of high sea levels are found mainly as raised beaches in many parts of the world. The heights of these beaches vary considerably, but they are all lower than those beaches assigned to the late Pliocene period, when sea levels were up to 250 metres above that of today. Although it may be that continental uplift has exaggerated these heights, which due to tectonic movement and erosional forces are not widely found, nevertheless, there is no doubt that the average sea level of the following Pleistocene was well below that of the Pliocene.

A second factor to be considered is that in certain limited areas, particularly in North Africa, raised beaches range from several hundred metres to only a few metres above the present level. This is thought to indicate a progressive Pleistocene elevation of the land unconnected with local instabilities or glacial phenomena. The explanation of this fact is perhaps more likely to be a continued expansion of the earth thereby increasing the potential capacity of the ocean basins, than isostatic uplift of the continents through the loss by erosion of an average 100 metres per million years. Another explanation is based upon evidence of submerged coral reefs in the Pacific Ocean, indicating a dip in the ocean floor.

In any case, it is a fact that throughout the Pleistocene there was an overall tendency towards a lowering of the sea level. Such a general lowering was not, however, uninterrupted because the fluctuations of the ice sheets caused quite remarkable variations in relatively short time ranges. The extent of these *glacio-eustatic fluctuations* has been partially determined by surviving ancient shore lines, by estimations of the water volume of existing ice sheets in the north and south, and by calculation of the water content of the Pleistocene glaciers.

Recent work in the Arctic and Antarctic regions has suggested that complete melting of these ice sheets would result in a rise of sea level of about 66 metres which would effectively cover a great area of the land masses of today. This is, however, not sufficient to account for the high sea levels of the early Pleistocene, or of the Pliocene, nor is there in fact any conclusive evidence that the present ice sheets were grossly smaller during the Pleistocene.

The estimates of Pleistocene glacier extent and volume are fraught with uncertainties, particularly for the earlier ice advances, although there seems to be some indication that the north European ice sheet was at times about 1,400 metres thick, the North American one even thicker. Although it might be possible to provide estimates of the volume of water caught up and held by the Pleistocene ice sheets, our ideas about the sinking of sea levels are widely variable. Submerged shorelines exist, but these are too divergent and cannot easily be correlated with any specific ice advance. In general terms, a sea level about 100 metres below that of today for the last ice advance is often proposed.

Geological deposits indicating high sea levels are particularly well preserved along west Mediterranean shores, where work by de Lamothe and Depéret remains basic to more recent examinations. The heights of Pleistocene raised beaches along the Mediterranean coast are as follows:

Approximate height above mean sea level	*Name*
c. 200 metres	Calabrian
90–100 „	Sicilian
55–60 „	Milazzian
28–30 „	Tyrrhenian
18–20 „	Monastirian I
6– 8 „	Monastirian II
3 „	Epimonastirian

The Calabrian deposits have been correlated with a 600′ beach in England which is associated with Red Crag materials, and with deposits in the Nile valley at *c.* 180 metres above sea level. These suggest that at or near the beginning of the Pleistocene, the sea level stood at *c.* 200 metres higher than that of today. Raised beach deposits from the Black Sea, along the Caucasus coastline, have not yielded confirmatory evidence of this level, but have indicated the presence in this region of sea levels at heights of 95–100 metres, 55–60 metres, 35–40 metres, 22–25 metres, 12 metres and at lower levels. This important work shows that the Mediterranean heights of 90–100 metres and 55–60 metres are probably accurate measurements of ancient sea levels. The difficulties in correlating these high sea levels with glacial and interglacial periods rest in the almost total lack of physical contact between beach deposits and morainic material. Nevertheless, it seems reasonable to correlate the 6–8 metre sea with the Eemian, as nowhere is this beach overlaid with deposits indicating interglacial conditions, and in many cases the succeeding deposits suggest that glacial conditions obtained subsequent to the beach formation. Thorium-uranium dates suggest *c.* 80,000 B.P. for the 6–8 metre sea. There is also some evidence that the 28–30 metre sea was contemporary with the Hoxnian interglacial, according to polleniferous deposits in England. The precise positioning of the other high seas, 100, 55–60 and 18–20 metres, remains uncertain.

Associated fauna in the Mediterranean region have occasionally been employed in attempting such correlations. The basis of such faunal studies are foraminifera which are sensitive to temperature changes. An early Pleistocene stage of this fauna is the *Calabrian*, with present-day north Atlantic foraminifera including *Anomalina baltica* and similarly disposed mollusca including *Cyprina islandica*. Isotopic temperature determinations indicate that oscillations occurred during this faunal stage, including episodes when the water temperature was much warmer than that of today, as well as periods slightly cooler than today.

The succeeding faunal stage, the *Emilian*, suggests a warm phase such as that obtaining at the present time in the Italian area. A later assemblage is the *Sicilian*, with a fauna including *Cyprina islandica* and indicating rather cool conditions. There follows the *Milazzian*, at first with a fauna of warm conditions, later with cold-preferring forms indicated.

The *Tyrrhenian* fauna is recognizable over a wide area of the Mediterranean coasts, and posseses a characteristic molluscan fauna with a number of species now inhabiting the warm waters off the west coast of Africa, including *Strombus bubonius*. The succeeding *Versilian* fauna, recovered from deposits below sea level, contains northern mollusca and foraminifera. The correlations of these faunal assemblages with climatic episodes are difficult, but there seems little doubt, if the present-day interpretation of the evidence is accepted, that the Versilian is of Würmian age. The Tyrrhenian fauna probably survived the Saale glacial series and may have been present during the Hoxnian and the Eemian. Beyond this it is profitless to conjecture, and it has recently been suggested that there was no great change of sea temperature during the Pleistocene in this region.

Other geological phenomena intimately associated with high and low sea levels are river terrace systems. By their nature, river valleys were always important areas for animal, including human, occupation, and much of the archaeological evidence for the earlier phases of human occupation in western Europe and southern Africa has been obtained from river gravels.

RIVER TERRACES

The formation of stream and river terraces in the Pleistocene has been the subject of numerous studies. Among the river systems often considered in such studies are the Vaal, the Zambezi, the Thames and the Somme.

In northern latitudes, two major and interacting agencies combined to produce the complex series of Pleistocene river terraces. The terms sometimes given to the terraces thus formed are eustatic and thalassostatic. If a river drains into a base level, whether it be a lake or the sea, any change in this (eustatic) base level will be transferred to the gradient of the river. If the level is raised, the river will lose much of its velocity and therefore its carrying capacity in the downstream area. The result of this is deposition of the gravels and sands that were being transported in the river. The reverse effect occurs if the base level is lowered, when the river gradient increases and erosion occurs at a nick point initially at the mouth of the river but which gradually works its way upstream. If this subsequently reaches upstream sufficiently to avoid being submerged by a succeeding high base level, erosion must continue through the interglacial period. In Pleistocene times, the alteration in base level of the ocean would theoretically have caused considerable and complex deposition and erosion in the lower reaches of rivers.

Although the gravels deposited by a river where it flowed into a high sea will be eroded during a drop in base level, such erosion will not be complete as the diminished river narrows and cuts down through part of the previous broad floodplain. The sides of the former floodplain will, theoretically, remain as a terrace on each side of the river. Because each succeeding rise in base level was lower than the previous one (p. 32) the subsequent gravel deposition in downstream regions is considered not to have attained the height of the previous gravels. Alternating phases of downcutting through the gravels, and deposition of gravels, resulted therefore in a series of steps, with the highest terrace representing the oldest period of deposition. However it is also true that a river, having cut down to a new low level, will subsequently and gradually fill this deep erosion channel with gravels and other deposits. Such gravels will lie altimetrically at a low level, and may become incorporated or buried by further aggradations. Terraces may therefore be composite, with a series of stratified or unstratified deposits of variant age.

In the middle and upper reaches of rivers, other climatic phenomena were responsible for erosion and deposition. In warm temperate periods of the Pleistocene the vegetation along the river banks and valley sides would serve to bind the soil, and inhibit the acquisition and deposition of gravels in the river; erosion of the river bed would be possible. During glacial phases, however, in periglacial regions, solifluction through the absence of binding vegetation would tend to clog river beds, while inadequate water supplies caused by retention of water in ice sheets would force the river to deposit its (thalassostatic) load. The terraces of upstream rivers in periglacial regions would, under these simplified conditions, represent cold conditions, in contrast to the temperate terrace formations in downstream areas. Clearly, the middle reaches of such rivers will be extremely complex in the interaction of these two elements.

In areas outside the compass of periglacial conditions, such as parts of sub-Saharan Africa, river terrace formation has been linked climatically with presumed alternating pluvial and interpluvial conditions (p. 30). In the lower reaches of rivers, eustatic terraces would form as in northern latitudes, but upstream gravel spreads would have different origins. In the Vaal and middle and upper Zambezi rivers, terrace series exist and must be explained as the results of cycles of deposition and erosion (Bond 1967). High veld plateau rivers, with flat gradients, are abundantly represented in southern Africa; the flat gradients and generally wide valleys result in alluviation, and often such deposits yield traces of man's activities in the area. In this type of situation, semi-arid climatic conditions with attendant mechanical weathering produce only a thin mantle of coarse material which will be transported by torrential streams into the rivers and carried downstream. Under wetter (pluvial) conditions, chemical weathering may extend to great depths, up to 15 metres, and will yield fine material such as clay or silt which may be carried into streams by torrent action. Although vegetation will hold some of this material, the quantity available may result in the choking of the stream and in fact the stream may lose its course and become a dambo, a grassy depressed area with no stream channel. Another type of river is the low veld trunk streamed, such as the Zambezi, which acts as a local base level. Terrace formation through aggradation and erosion phases may result during climatic fluctuations. The Vaal river is difficult to incorporate into any hypothetical scheme, because it is extremely long and its gradient varies from one to several feet per mile.

ABSOLUTE CHRONOLOGY

Attempts to establish an absolute chronology for the Pleistocene have been hindered by the difficulty in correlating regional sequences built on different lines of evidence. The climatic stages of the Würm are now relatively well established (p. 42) and precision obtained through radiocarbon dating. This method of dating is one of a group of radioactive decay methods which are beginning to revolutionize ideas about the chronology of the Pleistocene. The radioactive carbon 14 isotope is continuously formed in the upper atmosphere from atmospheric nitrogen by the action of neutrons produced by cosmic rays, and forms a constant proportion of atmospheric carbon dioxide which is taken up by all living things. At death the exchange of molecules ceases and the ^{14}C atoms decay at a rate which leads to their concentration being reduced to one half its initial value in about 5,600 years, to one quarter in 11,200 years and so on. By measuring the residual radioactivity, the time which has elapsed since the death of an organism can be measured. The practical range of ^{14}C dating is *c.* 60,000 years from the present day for most laboratories. Carbon is commonly found in archaeological sites in the form of charcoal from hearths, vegetable matter, bones, etc. The method therefore has a wide application (Brothwell and Higgs, 1969).

The gross nature of relative chronologies in the past has meant that archaeology has been particularly concerned with linear cultural successions. The more refined radiocarbon dating may make it possible to consider not only the linear succession but also the contemporaneity. Figure 2 shows a number of ^{14}C dates relating to sites in France and the range of time within which these dates probably fall. They suggest a considerable cultural overlap in time (p. 221). Figure 3 illustrates the time relationship as shown by ^{14}C dates of cultural groups in sub-Saharan Africa. While with certain

FRANCE–CARBON DATES

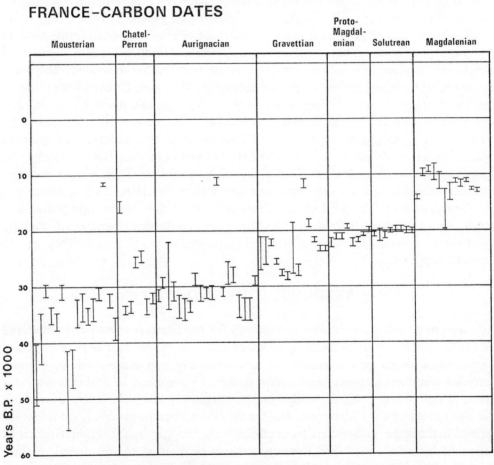

FIG. 2. Distribution in time of radiocarbon dates taken from sites in France, at three standard deviations

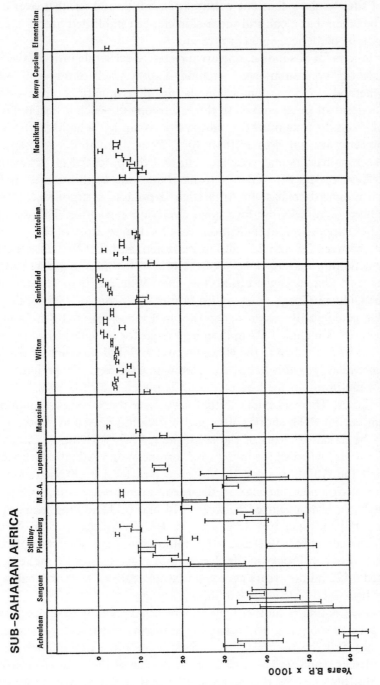

FIG. 3. Distribution in time of radiocarbon dates taken from sites in sub-Saharan Africa, at three standard deviations

'culture' groups there is sufficient evidence from the stratigraphy from a sufficient number of sites to show that one cultural phase followed another over a wide area, it cannot be taken that a cultural succession can be established over a wide area from the stratigraphy of an occasional or rare site.

Other methods for absolute dating are directed at earlier deposits of the Pleistocene, and include the potassium-argon method, fission track dating and the thorium-uranium method. In potassium-argon dating, determinations are based upon the radioactive decay of potassium 40 to the gas argon 40, which is held in the interstices of the rock from the time of its formation. Potassium has a half life of 1.3×10^9 years with an uncertainty not greater than 10%. Potassium occurs in many rocks and minerals such as basalts and volcanic tuff, and the potential of the method is considerable. Nevertheless it is unlikely to have the wide application to archaeological sites which radiocarbon has. In Antarctica, a potassium-argon date of 2·7 million years has been obtained from lava flows overlying glacial ice. This dating has been considered to support recent indications that the temperature of the oceans began to fall sharply between 2·3 and 2·7 million years ago, and that therefore the Pleistocene period by definition may have been of the order of 3 million years. Dates obtained for Pleistocene phases suggest that the later Villafranchian (Lower Pleistocene) deposits at Olduvai Gorge, East Africa, are of the order of 1·75 million years old, and similar geologically assigned deposits in France are *c*. 1·6 million years old. More recent dates include 0·27 million years ago for an interglacial period in Italy, considered to be equivalent to the Hoxnian, and 0·37 million years for terrace deposits in the Rhine valley, possibly to be correlated with a Günz glacial period.

The thorium-uranium method of dating is directed on the ^{230}Th/^{234}U content of marine molluscs. There is evidence that carbonate marine shells contain quantities of uranium but no ^{230}Th shortly after shell formation ceased at death, and that this event may be dated in terms of the subsequent ^{230}Th/^{234}U ratios. Recent dating of samples from geological stages in the Mediterranean and Atlantic Moroccan littorals suggest that the Anfatian stage of Morocco (sea level *c*. 30 metres) and the first appearance of *Strombus bubonius* in the Mediterranean are >0·2 million years old. A later high sea level occurred between 0·14 and 0·115 million years ago, and the Moroccan Ouljian stage (sea level *c*. 8 metres) with comparable Mediterranean deposits occurred between 0·09 and 0·075 million years ago. Recent application of this dating method to coral rocks in the West Indies suggests that a 6 metre sea level may have existed 0·122 million years ago, and that the sea was 13 metres below its present mean level between 0·103 and 0·08 million years ago.

Fission-track dating is another method which has recently developed. When heavy particles, such as spontaneously fissioning uranium atoms, traverse certain materials such as mica and the natural glasses, they leave trails of radiation damage. The number of background trails is a measure of the age of the material. Useful comparisons of dates obtained by this technique have been made with those obtained by radioactive decay methods.

2

Flora

PRESENT-DAY vegetational cover is commonly broadly classified into zones and such an approach is useful in considering the implications of Pleistocene climatic zones. At the present time, arctic regions contain both glaciated and unglaciated barren areas. Further south is herbaceous tundra with a nutritive leafy cover which includes the mountain avens (*Dryas spp.*), saxifrage, and gentian (*Gentiana spp.*), mosses including the reindeer moss (*Cladonia rangiferina*), grasses and sedges, the dwarf willows (*Salix spp.*) and the dwarf birch (*Betula nana*). Nearer to the equator is forest tundra with birch, spruce (*Picea*) and larch (*Larix*). The middle latitude woodlands consist of coniferous forests and deciduous forests. In Northern Europe and Asia coniferous forests have European spruce (*Picea excelsa*) and larches (*Larix decidua* and *L. siberica*), and, nearer to the temperate forest, Scots pine (*Pinus sylvestris*) and white fir (*Abies alba*). The North American boreal forests contain white and black spruce (*Picea glauca* and *P. mariana* and *Abies balsamea*). The European deciduous forests contain oaks (*Quercus spp.*), beech (*Fagus silvatica*), elm (*Ulmus campestris*), alder (*Alnus glutinosa*), hazel (*Corylus avellana*), lime (*Tilia cordata*), and hornbeam (*Carpinus betulus*). In North America there are oaks, maple (*Acer*) and hickory (*Carya*). The sub-tropical woodlands include oak (*Quercus ilex*) and the Aleppo pine (*Pinus halapensis*).

During the Pleistocene some plants became extinct and there were considerable shifts of vegetational zones due to climatic changes. In general, the changing and dynamic nature of vegetational cover has been established by the study of microscopic and macroscopic remains preserved in many different kinds of deposits such as bogs, tufas and lake sediments. An important contribution has been made by pollen analysis.

Pollen grains are liberated to fertilize the female parts of the plant. The grain is enclosed in an external layer, the exine, which is heavily resistant to many destructive forces. The method of transport of the pollen grain is important. Some plants are pollinated under water, some are self-pollinating and no pollen is exposed, some pollination is affected by animals, and with some, no pollen is released if the right animal is not present. Some plants are under-represented or not represented at all in the pollen rain. The most important group is composed of those which are wind-pollinated, and there is an annual pollen rain when huge quantities are wind-dispersed over wide areas. Various corrections based on field experiments are made in the analyses to allow for the different quantities of pollen which are given off by different plants, for the different distances which are covered by different kinds of pollen, and for a number of other variables. It has been said that 50–100 kilometres forms a natural limit of pollen dispersal. Further adjustments to the interpretation of pollen analytical diagrams may be expected in the near future in view of the studies of grain dispersion relevant to air pollution (Tauber 1967). Nevertheless, pollen analysis is a sufficiently refined technique to determine the broad aspects of large scale vegetational changes.

The climatic changes which have been so recognized during the Pleistocene can best be illustrated by the north-west European sequences, particularly those of Britain and Holland.

In Holland, the earliest recognized climatic phase has been named the Praetiglian. The *Praetiglian* is of a period before the deposition of the Tegelen Clay in the Netherlands. It is considered to be the equivalent of the Donau stages of the glacial succession, and in Britain of the Red Crag. The conifer *Tsuga*, which had previously been common, became less so. The fauna of the Praetiglian deposits include *Elephas* (*Archidiskodon*) *planifrons* and mastodon (*Anancus arverensis*). The *Tiglian* (Norwich Crag) is named after the Tegelen clay in Limburg (Netherlands). The flora includes *Azolla tegeliensis*, *Tsuga* (hemlock fir), *Najas intermedia*, *Pterocarya limburgensis*, *Trapa natans* (water chestnut) and *Corena intermedia*. The flora at this time in Holland contained 42% of exotic species, compared with 80% in the earlier period and 17% in the Hoxnian (Great) Interglacial. The water fern *Azolla* is not a good indicator of climate but it is of particular value because it changes its form and becomes extinct in Europe during the course of the Pleistocene. Many other species vanished from Europe during the Pleistocene including *Pterocarya*, *Sequoia*, *Laura canariensis* and *Trapa natans*.

The Tiglian fauna include the extinct forms of mice (*Miomys pliocaenicus* and *Mimomys savinii*), the rhinoceroses (*Dicerorhinus etruscus* and *D. merckii*), *Elephas* (*Archidiskodon*) *meridionalis*, *Trogontherium* (the giant beaver), *Equus robustus* (zebra) and a monkey *Macaca florentina*. At this time the Icenian sea covered much of the Netherlands (p. 33). The succeeding *Kedichem Series* of deposits contain the *Eburonian* (Glacial), the *Waalean* (Interglacial) and *Menapean* (Glacial) phases, and yield the earliest examples of *Microtus* (vole) and some of the early *Mimomys*. These three phases may be correlated with the oscillations of the Günz glaciation. The *Cromerian* (Cromer Forest Bed) deposits which follow the Kedichem have a traditional form of *Azolla*, between the earlier *Azolla tegeliensis* and *Azolla filiculoides*. *Trapa natans*, *Fagus sylvatica* and *Tsuga* still exist in Europe. The pollen spectrum differs from that of the later interglacials in that *Corylus* (hazel) has a low value and *Abies* (fir) is absent. The Cromerian may have lasted for 27–30,000 years. The glacial advance of the *Elster* ice (Lowestoft, Mindel) indicates a return to a cold flora and fauna.

During the following *Hoxnian* period (Holstein, Great Interglacial, Needian), the Holstein Sea invaded the Netherlands and *Azolla filiculoides* reached its present form. *Arvicola* (water vole) and *Microtus* are present. The Hoxnian may have lasted for 30–50,000 years. The succession of flora at the site of Hoxne (West 1956) shows a number of interglacial changes.

Stage I. The Late Glacial Stage

A late glacial phase with *Hippophae* (buckthorn) dominant, some *Pinus, Artemisia, Helianthemum* (rock rose) and *Plantago* (plantain). The only important tree is *Betula*.

Stage II. The Early Temperate Stage

Sub-stage IIa — a *Betula-Pinus* sub-stage. At first little pine, later more oak (*Quercus*) comes in.

Sub-stage IIb — the *Betula-Quercus-Pinus* sub-stage. There is no evidence for a *Pinus* stage, which indicates quick change, and *Quercus robur* is dominant. *Ulmus* begins to immigrate into the area. *Corylus* and *Hedera* (ivy) are in small quantities. Today *Hedera* will not tolerate an extremely cold season. Cool relicts, *Hippophae* and *Thalictrum*, are still present.

Sub-stage IIc — the *Alnus-Quercus-Betula-Tilia* sub-stage. *Alnus* and *Tilia* cf. *cordata* increase in the warmer conditions. *Hippophae* and *Thalictrum* (meadow rue) decline and disappear. *Azolla filiculoides* makes its first appearance.

Sub-stage IId — the *Alnus-Quercus-Ulmus-Tilia* sub-stage. The mixed oak forest remains dominant. *Corylus* is at its maximum, but the climate begins to revert.

Stage III. The Later Temperate Stage

There is a great increase of alder; aquatics and semi-aquatics also increase. The Mixed oak forest species decline in cooler and perhaps wetter conditions.

Stage IV. The Early Glacial Stage

Dwarf willows and beech indicate an arctic climate. The pollen spectrum indicates a park-tundra type of vegetation.

The succeeding glacial period, the *Saale* (Gipping, Riss) had at least two major stages. Full glacial conditions obtained.

In the *Eemian* (Last Interglacial) the *Corylus* peak occurs at the same time as the Mixed oak forest peak, whereas in the Hoxnian interglacial the *Corylus* peak is long after it. Only 9% of the species are exotic from today. This interglacial is characterized by a high hazel and hornbeam content. The end of the Last Interglacial occurred *c.* 70,000 B.P.

The *Last Glaciation* (Würm, Weichsel) covered only half the area of the previous glacials. It had a number of cold and temperate oscillations. The latter were either too short or too cold to permit the development of temperate deciduous forest. These oscillations include the *Amersfoort* (*Rodebaek*) interstadial; during this, *Betula nana* and Juniper were characteristic of the vegetation in Denmark (*c.* 64,000 B.P.). A second early temperate oscillation in early *Würmian* times was the *Brørup* (*Chelford*) interstadial during which forest conditions prevailed in north-west Europe with *Betula pubescens*, *Populus tremula* and later *Pinus sylvestris* and alder. In England, *Pinus* and *Betula* dominated at the site of Chelford in Cheshire (*c.* 58,000 B.P.).

Both the Amersfoort and the Brørup interstadials are included within the Early Würm phase of the last glaciation, which is marked in some areas by characteristic Younger Loess indicating cold and damp conditions. The succeeding period of loess deposition, formerly Main Würm, may mark a time of rather drier conditions, but with some short climatic oscillations (Paudorf complex, *c.* ?35,000–28,000 B.P.). From *c.* 28,000 B.P., full glacial conditions, both cold and dry, developed with an accompanying cold vegetational pattern in northern Europe (*c.* 28,000–16,000 B.P.).

The polleniferous deposits of Late Würmian times have been intensively studied. The sequence in northern Europe is as follows:

Zone Ia. *Oldest Dryas*, *c.* 16,000–13,000 B.P. Arctic flora.

Zone Ib. *Bølling Oscillation*, *c.* 13,500–12,500 B.P. A brief more temperate period.

Zone Ic. *Older Dryas*, *c.* 12,500–12,000 B.P. The vegetation was more alpine than arctic in northern Europe.

Zone II. *Allerød Oscillation*, *c.* 12,000–10,850 B.P. The tundra areas in north-west Europe changed to forest; there was a pine-dominated vegetation in southern France and southern Germany, with a birch-pine forest to the north.

Zone III. *Younger Dryas*, *c.* 10,800–10,300 B.P. A return to a colder climate with a decrease in tree pollen.

In Post-Glacial times, following the end of the Pleistocene, the sequence is:

Zone IV. *Preboreal*, *c.* 10,300–9,500 B.P. A return of trees and a forest tundra vegetation in north-west Europe.

Zone V. *Boreal*, *c.* 9,500–7,600 B.P. Warmer conditions with pine, hazel and oak immigrating into more northerly zones.

Zone VI. *Atlantic*, *c.* 7,500–5,000 B.P. Oak and elm forest.

Floral remains from areas other than north-west Europe have not been so fully studied. At the other climatic extreme, the Sahara has received some attention and Eurasiatic and Mediterranean species have been identified in the deposits of the Hoggar, for example, *Tilia*, *Alnus*, *Pinus halapensis*, *Cedrus atlanticus*, *Quercus ilex*. Their presence indicates possible existence of migration routes across the desert during the period of the Last Pluvial (p. 31). In Cyrenaica the Canary laurel (*Laurus canariensis*) has been identified. It does not now occur anywhere in the Mediterranean region but is confined to the Canary Islands, Madeira and the Azores. It is thought to indicate a warm climate more humid than that of the present day. In Tunisia there appears to have been both a cooler wetter period and a cooler drier period during the Last Glaciation.

During the Atlantic period, evidence suggests that in the Sahara there was also a period which was wetter than now, and which may be associated with a Neolithic pluvial phase as distinct from a continuing post-glacial drying of the area. In desert areas in Egypt tree stumps have been found which are of acacia, tamarisk and syca-more and there is similar evidence again from the Hoggar of conditions wetter than now.

South of the Sahara pollen studies have only just begun (van Zinderen Bakker 1967, 1967a). Ancient pollen-bearing deposits are rare and the necessary basic botanical studies have not as yet been completed. In Kenya, however, deposits show a pronounced change from a treeless vegetation to a *Hagenia-Juniperus* forest at 3,300 metres above the present sea level. This change has not so far been dated but it may mark the end of the last cold phase in the east African mountains. Again at Kalambo Falls at the southern end of Lake Tanganyika cooler conditions than now occurred from 40,000 B.P. to *c.* 12,000 B.P., a climatic phase which is inferred from the extension of montane plants to lower levels. The date also suggests that these cooler conditions were contemporary with a cold phase of the Last Glaciation in the Northern Hemisphere.

Early Agriculture

Towards the end of the Pleistocene it becomes evident from the archaeological record in the Near East that the production had developed of such food elements in the vegetation as could easily be stored. The selection of certain plants to the exclusion of less suitable plant competitors resulted ultimately in agriculture as we know it. The storage of seed over a season, a preliminary process necessary to agriculture, was known to the hunter-gatherers of the Stone Age, as were the techniques of reaping and grinding. Where and when sowing in order to reap first took place is not known. At this time rapid post-glacial climatic changes were taking place on a world-wide scale. Although in the Near East such changes were not climatically dramatic, nevertheless considerable areas previously marginal to this kind of economy became available for its extensive use and economies developed and spread over more — and perhaps less — favourable ecological areas. Such an extension may have been sufficiently great to have given rise to changes in the gene pool over a wide area and on a large enough scale to have given rise to changes in the form of the cultivated seeds. The fact that the domestication of plants and animals did take place in the Near East does not necessarily mean that it began there, nor should its presence there be taken as a measure of its antiquity. The Fertile Crescent and its foothills are likely to have been an area where many practices, which existed and had existed over a much wider area for many millennia, were gathered together on a sufficiently large scale to have caused changes in the structure of seeds and animals which are perceptible to us now in the archaeological record. This is the reverse, in fact, of the domestication hypothesis from an innovating nuclear centre. The origins of agriculture are in the food conservation and preservation practices of animals. In the Near East the seeds of emmer and einkorn wheats and two-rowed barley were selected for particular attention.

In the Americas the so-called incipient agriculture phase is more clearly shown in the archaeological record than it is in the Old World. The closer and closer man/plant relationship is in evidence over a long period. Peppers, avocado (*Persea americana*), squash (*Curcurbita*) and maize and a variety of other plants were selected. It is also of considerable interest to note that some plants, like *Setaria* in America, were probably at one time cultivated, but their cultivation was dropped in antiquity in the face of more successful and productive competitors, such as maize.

The development of agricultural practices meant that a much greater population could be maintained on a small area of suitable land when particular plants were grown to the exclusion of others. The greater population was also able to support itself while still living in one place. The mobile economies gave way to a sedentary way of life which permitted a major economic development, the creation and accumulation of durable wealth, wealth which lasted beyond the lifetime of the generation which created it.

3

Fauna

ALTHOUGH the precise age of the Plio-Pleistocene boundary is unknown, the border has been drawn at the time when the foraminiferal species *Hyalinea baltica* first appears in the marine section at Le Castella, Calabria, Italy. The Calabrian is commonly equated with a mammalian fauna called the Villafranchian. The Villafranchian, however, probably goes back to more than three million years ago and the earlier part may be the equivalent of the Lower Calabrian marine fauna of the Pliocene. The Villafranchian fauna include *Elephas meridionalis, Dicerorhinus etruscus, Equus stenonis* and *Trogontherium cuvieri* (Kurten 1968).

In all of the varied environments of the world, changes in animals and animal populations took place during the Pleistocene. As one author puts it, it may be a 'brief atypical and feverish episode in the long history of mammalian fauna'. The evolution and extinction of species, climatic change, the development and proliferation of a predatory species, man, and eventually the completion of man/animal symbiotic relationships in the late Palaeolithic, all played their part.

A traverse from north temperate Europe to South Africa gives an indication of some of the changes. In Europe, chronologically, the elephants are one of the most informative animals. From *Elephas (Archidiskodon) meridionalis* in Europe and *A. planifrons* in Asia, according to some authorities there developed the straight-tusked elephant, *E. palaeoloxodon antiquus*. Of *E. antiquus* there may have been three forms, early, typical and late, each of the last two probably associated with one of the last two interglacials. From the same source there also developed *Mammuthus trogontherii*, the early mammoth of the Mindel glaciation, which had an earlier ancestral intermediate form *E. meridionalis trogontherii*, and from which developed *E. mammuthus primigenius*, the mammoth with the curved tusks of the Last Glaciation (fig. 4).

The European Pleistocene Rhinocerotidae which are two horned are also informative. *Dicerorhinus megarhinus*, up to the early Villafranchian, and *D. etruscus* were early forms. Both appear in the Pliocene and early Pleistocene. By the time of the Elster glaciation *D. kirchbergensis (merckii)* (woodland) and *D. hemitoechus* (*R. leptorhinus*) (steppe) had appeared. *Coelodonta (Tichorhinus) antiquitatis*, the woolly

FIG. 4. Mammoths, Font de Gaume. *After Burkitt 1933*

rhinoceros, appeared in the colder periods from the Elster Glaciation onwards, and is thought to have been an invader from Asia (fig. 5).

Extinction of species is also in some cases a good chronological indicator. *Dama clactoniana*, a deer with palmate antlers, occurs frequently in Britain in Hoxnian deposits and rarely in later contexts. It was largely replaced by the fallow deer, *Dama dama*, in the Last Interglacial, although an Eemian sample occurs at Fontéchevade, and it possibly persists also under the name of *Cervus grimaldiensis*, Patte. *Trogontherium*, the giant beaver, also disappeared before the beginning of the Last Interglacial. The musk ox became extinct in temperate Europe and withdrew to colder latitudes at the end of the Last Glaciation, and the mammoth may have lived for

FIG. 5. Woolly rhinoceros, *D. tichorhinus*, Font de Gaume. *After Breuil 1952*

some time into the postglacial period in Siberia. *Megaceros*, the giant deer, and the cave bear also became extinct at the end of the last cold phase. The European bison now survives only in captivity and *Bos primigenius* was presumably hunted out and absorbed into the domestic herds in late historic times. The wolf (*Canis lupus*), although ancestral to the domestic dog, the wild goat (bezoar), ancestral to the domestic goat, still survive, as does *Sus scrofa* the wild pig. How much the extinction of species was due to human influence is debatable, but there can be little doubt that man was a contributory factor as a predator and as a competitor, in an already existing unstable situation.

In North Africa, an early Villafranchian fauna includes a mastodon, *Anancus osiris*, and *E. africanavus*, possibly derived from *E. planifrons*. There is also *Stylohip-*

parion libycum, Equus numidicus, Libytherium maurusium, Machairodus and a number of other animals including antelopes, gazelles, ovicaprines and a giant tortoise. A later Villafranchian fauna still contains some of the earlier elements such as *Stylohipparion* and *Libytherium*. There is a more evolved elephant, probably *E. recki*, and a hippopotamus similar to that of today. What has been called a Middle Pleistocene fauna still has survivals of earlier forms such as *Machairodus*, but others such as *Leptobos, Stylohipparion, Libytherium* and *Omochoerus* become extinct. Bear and *Bos primigenius* are probably Eurasiatic immigrants. There is a more evolved elephant, *E. atlanticus*, much like the present African form. An Upper Pleistocene fauna contains further Eurasiatic immigrants, *Sus scrofa, D. merckii* and a deer, *Megaceroides algericus*. *E. atlanticus* persists but latterly *D. merckii* becomes extinct. With increasing warmth and the competition of man in an increasingly isolated area the Eurasiatic forms and most of the African forms eventually became extinct in North Africa.

In South Africa, recent work has indicated that the Pleistocene fauna may be divided into four stages (Cooke 1967). The earliest of these, the Sterkfontein stage, contains forms such as *Parapapio whitei* and *P. jonesi, Palaeotomys gracilis, Procavia antiqua* and *P. transvaalensis* and *Australopithecus africanus* (p. 82). A second stage, Swartkrans, contains most of the forms above except *Australopithecus africanus*, and adds *Australopithecus (Paranthropus) robustus, Papio robinsoni, Megantereon eurynodon* and *Phacochoerus antiquus*. The third stage, called Vaal Cornelia, introduces many new elements; representative sites include the younger gravels of the Vaal, and Elandsfontein (p. 128). The fourth stage, Florisbad-Vlakkraal, consists basically of present-day fauna, with some archaic forms (p. 113).

Climate and Environment   As indicators of climate and aspects of environment, the mammals, because of their mobility, are difficult to interpret. They pass easily from one area to another, a few may linger on after an adverse climatic change, and many forms are tolerant of a number of different environments. It is therefore not uncommon to find animals which flourish in one environment in a faunal assemblage with animals usually associated with another environment. For example, *Bos primigenius* (wild cattle, fig. 6), which have been found commonly in deposits which indicate a woodland environment, are numerous in archaeological sites in desert steppe areas with a dry climate. In North Africa they are most commonly associated with the open country zebra, antelope and gazelle. At Romanelli in Italy the wild cattle have been found with *Equus hydruntinus*, the steppe ass. It is clear that the wild cattle could thrive in warm or cold conditions where there was pasture and water.

It is also true that it is necessary to infer from the habitats of present-day animals what may have been the environments of the same species in the past. This may not always be a reliable method and indeed there is some evidence to suggest that fallow deer changed their habits during the last forty thousand years. Also, the present-day distribution of animals is not as yet very well determined and for the extinct animals knowledge of their environments relies either on the form of certain skeletal structures or on inferences drawn from a number of different disciplines. Here again caution is

FIG. 6. Cattle, Teyjat. *After Breuil 1952*

needed as too narrow an interpretation can be grossly misleading. The territories of predators, including humans, as well as those of their prey, need to be studied before a reliable environmental interpretation can be made of most cave fauna.

However, there are differences between assemblages which are of value, and certain animals are so restricted by some factors that they give useful environmental information. During the earlier periods, species were not so sensitive to alternating warm and cold episodes as they were in the later Pleistocene. By Middle Pleistocene times, warm and cold forms were developing, for example, among the elephants.

In Europe a warm fauna of the Last Interglacial might contain *Palaeoloxodon antiquus* (the straight-tusked elephant), *Dicerorhinus merckii* (the woodland rhinoceros), *Hippopotamus amphibius major*, *Dama dama* (fallow deer), *Sus scrofa* (wild pig) and *Meles meles* (badger). The elephant, the deer, the pig and the badger indicate the presence of woodland and the nearness of water. A Last Glaciation cold fauna might contain *Elephas primigenius* (the mammoth), *Rangifer tarandus* (the reindeer), *Ovibos moschatus* (the musk ox), *Lepus timidus* (the variable hare), *Lemmus lemmus* (the lemming), *Alopex* (*Vulpes*) *lagopus* (the arctic fox) and *Microtus nivalis* (Alpine vole) as well as *Gulo gulo* (the wolverine or glutton).

48

The reindeer, one of the animals represented most commonly in Palaeolithic sites, is worth some individual attention. There are a number of species, *Rangifer tarandus fennicus* (fig. 7) in Europe and *Rangifer tarandus* (caribou) in North America, both of which are associated with coniferous forests, as well as *Rangifer tarandus arcticus*, the North American tundra reindeer. The forest forms have flattened antlers and these have been found for example at the site of the abri Pataud and La Rochette (Dordogne) and are depicted at the painted caves of Font de Gaume and Les Combaralles. Some of these flattened antlers have been found in loess deposits of Riss age. On the other hand the abundant remains in Middle and Upper Palaeolithic sites in the south-west of France are in some respects more like the rounded antlers of the North American *R. tarandus arcticus*, the tundra reindeer. It is therefore clear that the reindeer occupied a number of different environments and they had probably wider distribution than might be inferred from that of the present day. Associated with a cold fauna they reached the French-Italian Riviera and northern Spain during glaciations, but presumably found southern Spain, most of Italy and Greece too warm even in such

FIG. 7. Reindeer herd, Teyjat. *After Burkitt 1933*

glacial periods. Some idea of their limits may be gained from the fact that reindeer have been regularly introduced into Britain since 1820, not only into Scotland but as far south as the Midlands. These introductions until recently have met with little success, but reindeer remains are said to be common in post-glacial deposits of Scotland. Indeed they have been said to have survived in Scotland until the Middle Ages, perhaps encouraged by a climatic deterioration known as the Little Ice Age. While the reindeer may therefore indicate coniferous forest as well as tundra conditions, the wolverine, the lynx (*Lynx lynx*) and the elk (*Alces alces*) may indicate forested conditions such as obtain in Northern Canada today. With them may be found the red deer (*Cervus elaphus*, fig. 8), the brown bear (*Ursus arctos*) and the wild cat (*Felis sylvestris*), although the last group are present in a number of other environments.

Cold steppe or open country conditions may be indicated by *Equus hydruntinus* (the wild ass) of southern and eastern Europe, the Near East and possibly in glacial time of North Africa, by the bison, and by *Megaceros* (the giant Irish deer); *Bos primigenius* is also common in such environments. It is convenient here to make clear a difficulty in the literature with regard to the use of the term 'aurochs'. In Germany the bison was called the 'wisent' and *Bos primigenius* the 'aurochs'. The wild cattle became extinct but the bison (fig. 9) continued and in some of the older literature bison came to be referred to as 'aurochs'. The aurochs is also called the *Urus*.

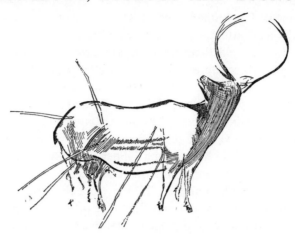

FIG. 8. Stag, La Peña de Candamo. *After Breuil 1952*

The Saiga antelope (*Saiga tatarica*) is also associated with cold open country as was the tarpan, the small wild horse, which migrated seasonally from north to south, and Przewalski's wild horse which lived in similar conditions in Eastern Europe. Cold conditions also are indicated where animals which live today at high altitudes, such as the wild goat, the ibex (*Capra ibex*), the chamois (*Rupicapra rupicapra*) and the Alpine marmot (*Marmota marmota*), spread to lower altitudes.

Some animals are closely tied to particular aspects of their environment, the elk to pine bark, the rhinoceros and cattle to within three days at the most of a water supply. Cattle are particularly useful indicators of climatic changes in marginally arid areas. Others are so opposed in their habits that a change of species indicates a change of climate. The well-known *dama gazella* graph at Mount Carmel shows alternating wet and dry climates by the relative percentages of the bones of fallow deer and gazelle. Studies of rodents indicate otherwise (Tchernov 1968). Of little help in indicating environmental differences are cave bear (*Ursus spelaeus*), spotted cave hyaena

FIG. 9. Bison, Le Portel. *After Breuil 1952*

50

(*Crocuta crocuta spelaea*), the cave lion (*Felis leo spelaeus*) and the red deer (*Cervus elaphus*) which in Europe appears to have been successful in such diverse environments as cold steppe and deciduous interglacial woodland and was equally at home with *Sus scrofa*, *Alces alces*, the roe deer *Capreolus capreolus*, *Rangifer tarandus arcticus*, *Equus hydruntinus*, bison, ibex, chamois, *Bos primigenius*, the musk ox, the badger, the beaver, the Alpine marmot, the lemming, the hippopotamus, *E. antiquus*, *Dama clactoniana*, *Dicerorhinus etruscus* and *E. meridionalis*.

Migration   Animal migrations in the Pleistocene are well established by the osteological record. They serve, for example, to indicate possible human migration routes as well as forming a chronology not only in a particular area but also on an intercontinental basis.

The similarity and close relationship of North American and European animals has long been observed and the sabre-toothed cats are a good example. It may be assumed that migration between America and Asia took place over the Bering Straits only at times when there was a land bridge, that is during a glaciation. All the Eurasian forms refer to the genus *Megantereon* and all the European Villafranchian forms refer to the evolving species *M. megantereon*, which survived in Asia and Africa until the middle Pleistocene. In Asia the last representative is known from the site of Choukoutien, perhaps of Elster or Hoxnian date. The *Smilodon* of America has a characteristic of the lower jaw which relates it to *Megantereon*. Other characteristics indicate that the migration took place at about the time of the last known *Megantereon*. It is suggested that the migration was of Elster date.

A further migrator across the Bering land bridge in Elster times was probably the black bear *Ursus americanus*. During the Riss glaciation the wolverine probably passed from Asia to North America. During the Last Glaciation *Bison bison* possibly passed from North America to Asia and it may be noted that the paintings in the Dordogne caves depict a bison which is more like the North American bison than the European.

Work such as this opens up tremendous possibilities for future research but at the present stage conclusions should be regarded with reserve. Recent events in Africa, for example, have shown that in the consideration of African fauna too much emphasis has probably been placed in the past upon migrations into Africa of Eurasiatic faunas, and that probably Africa was more of a centre of evolving species and dissemination than a receiving cul-de-sac. Contrary to the view that *Crocuta crocuta* (hyaena) evolved out of a Villafranchian species in India and spread to other parts of Asia and Africa, more recent evidence shows that it appears much earlier in Africa than it does in Europe and Asia. At any rate *Crocuta crocuta* occurs in Europe in deposits associated with the Mindel I glacial stage and not earlier, while in Africa it occurs throughout the Pleistocene. Although the Sahara seems to have been a formidable barrier between northern and southern Africa, it could have been crossed at the end of the Pliocene or at the beginning of the Pleistocene, during the Middle Pleistocene, and possibly during the Last Glaciation.

Certainly some Eurasiatic forms did pass into North Africa, the bear and deer for example. They are thought to have arrived there during the Riss Glaciation, but they did not succeed in crossing the Sahara. In the reverse direction the warthog (*Phacochoerus garrodae*) and the hartebeest (*Alcelaphus*) have been found in some of the Palestinian caves (p. 366). In fact the Mount Carmel caves, situated on the north-to-south migration routes, have a number of Eurasiatic and African forms represented in the deposits. The climatic changes of the Pleistocene not only opened up migration routes but also made available large new areas for colonization by forms adapted to a new environment, as well as closing areas to those which found the new environment unfavourable. A rising interglacial sea cut off continents and made faunal intercontinental migrations impossible or created islands where faunas adapted and evolved along different lines.

The hypothetical warming up of world climate about 11,000 years ago appears to have brought about a radical change in animal populations in areas which had previously been under the influence of the glacial cold. In Europe the vegetation during the cold period was of a rich Alpine type which supported great herds of game. One example from North America will serve to illustrate their size. One observer estimated a caribou herd in 1917 as consisting of over 25 million individuals, but herds of 100,000 were not uncommon in recent times. The warming climate slowly replaced the tundra by coniferous trees, and, by 8,000 B.P., an increasing deciduous forest. The reindeer were replaced by red and roe deer and fallow deer. The deer population was still considerable. The reindeer requires 40 acres of territory per individual, and the red deer requires about the same quantity of open country, but 100 acres are needed in heavily wooded conditions, and other open country animals like *Bos primigenius*, bison and horse probably decreased in numbers as the forest increased. Apart from the reduction in game consequent upon the deciduous forest, there was also the human influence upon environment caused by the development of the closer man/animal relationship called in its later stage domestication.

PALAEOLITHIC HUSBANDRY

The process of domestication is a change in the environment of those animals which were selected for a closer relationship. The criteria which are used to determine which animals are 'wild' and which 'domesticated', within a species, are a decrease in the size of the animal concerned and an increase in the percentage of young animals killed for consumption. However, the change in the killing pattern and the change in bone size are probably due to change in economic pressure rather than an expression of a closer man/animal relationship. There is no satisfactory line which can be drawn between a 'domestic' animal and its supposed wild prototype. Such changes in bone size and shape as are detectable in the archaeological record are no certain indication that the animals possessing them were in a closer man/animal relationship than those which did not happen to have them. A closer man/animal relationship entails the conservation of the herd, the preservation of its breeding members and the prevention of loss by natural agencies. It encourages the proliferation of a few animals at the expense of predators and competing species. Such a close association can be observed in Palaeolithic times as early as the Hamburgian culture of north Germany, and in Russia at Molodova, where in the deposits dated to *c.* 11,000 years ago there were 1,738 specimens of reindeer bones and only 65 of other animals, and in Natufian and pre-Natufian times with the gazelle. Such a high degree of specialization upon one animal is hardly likely to have occurred with a purely hunting community, and at Shanidar, only 800–900 miles away from Molodova but some 10 degrees of latitude further south, sheep had either developed as a domesticate from an ovicaprine ancestor or had already been domesticated from the wild sheep for some appreciable time. It is worthy of note that the earliest domestic dogs, that is, where certain morphological changes had taken place, are also known from north-west Europe and North America. It must be borne in mind that, while the neighbourhood of the Fertile Crescent clearly has the earliest known evidence for certain morphological changes having taken place, such as are known to have occurred in Hungary, for example, up to the invasion of the Tatars, the evidence at present clearly indicates that at least some of the techniques were known much earlier elsewhere, in more northerly areas, and for economic reasons were gathered together in the Fertile Crescent at this later time.

From this time onwards, the animals favoured by the post-glacial climate change occupied the areas from which the reindeer had retreated. With the encouragement of man and his expanding economies they spread throughout the world, except for a relatively few inhospitable areas with minimum human and animal populations. Animal habits were changed by human economies. Cattle, goats and sheep which normally live in restricted areas became, under pastoralism, long-distance migrants, flexible instruments of exploitation able with human guidance to utilize ill-distributed natural reserves. The process has continued to the present day with the recent attempt to domesticate such animals as the eland in Africa and the successful domestication of the musk ox in Alaska and the elk in Russia. Such animals are adapted to restricted ecological zones which have not so far been successfully colonized by the species originating from the temperate regions. The domestication of the musk ox was, however, a rapid process covering only a few seasons.

It must be said, however, that the classification of animals into two groups, 'wild' and 'domesticated', does not take into account that many animals now regarded as wild may be feral domesticates, their domestication having lapsed in antiquity by the substitution of economically more useful species. Close symbiotic relationships between man and animal may have occurred in the earliest times of man's history (Higgs and Jarman 1968).

4

Industries and Stone Technology

THE principal source of evidence for human behaviour in the Old Stone Age is in the stone tools and debris found on many sites, in lake muds and in river gravels and on the surface of eroded deposits. Although these stone tools make up the bulk of prehistoric material that has survived, and therefore assume a great importance to the prehistorian, there is no doubt that perishable material, such as wood, bone and antler, played a substantial part in prehistoric technology and industry.

The stone employed by Palaeolithic man to fashion his artefacts ranges from easily-worked flint and obsidian to the most intractable quartzites. Although in most cases early man chose the most suitable available rock for chipping into tools, in a few cases the rock does not seem to have been selected for its flaking suitability. In Europe, particularly in England and France, flint was readily available as a material eminently suitable for chipping into tools. Flint is a moderately pure siliceous rock and occurs as nodules, concretions and tabular layers in chalk. It is generally grey to dark grey in colour when fresh, and it has a porous white crust called cortex. Flint often weathers through greys and whites to shades of yellow and brown and this chemical alteration of the surface is called patina. Like flint, other substances such as obsidian and chalcedony also possess near perfect conchoidal fracture. Chert is a term often given to coarse-grained siliceous stones. Such rocks and minerals were only available in limited regions of the Old World, and in other areas more intractable rocks and minerals had to be employed. Quartz, a crystalline form of silica which occurs in granite-enclosed veins, is difficult to work because it breaks irregularly. Silcrete (a hardened sandstone), quartzite (recrystallized sandstone), and slate and indurated shale were often used for the manufacture of tools, as well as volcanic rocks such as basalt, rhyolite and phenolite lava. Most of these rocks are close- or medium-grained, and they would not flake as readily as flint. Igneous rocks such as diorite were also used on occasion, and even limestone.

All these rocks and minerals are relatively easy to chip or break into a number of pieces, and some if not all of these will have naturally sharp edges which could be employed for cutting. But to produce an implement of a preconceived shape, more

54

care must be taken to control the chipping or flaking. The rock itself can be flaked to form a *core tool*, or one of the flakes knocked off the core can then be fashioned into a *flake tool*. Such fashioning of the flake, subsequent to its detachment from the core, is termed *secondary flaking* or *retouch*. The combination of core tools and flake tools, and cores and flakes not retouched into tools, found on one occupation site, makes up an *industry*; it is now considered that the segregation of groups of industries into core-tool and flake-tool traditions is no longer valid, because many industries used both cores and flakes as implements.

Flakes were struck off cores by the use of a hammer or a punch. The hammer might be of stone or a softer material such as bone or wood. The methods by which flakes were detached are many and varied. The core could be held in the hand, or against the knee, or laid on another support. Each blow with the hammer would be delivered onto the edge of a flattened area, the *striking platform* (fig. 82, 8), at an oblique angle. The type of flake detached depends upon the exact position of the blow and its angle to the striking platform. The use of a stone hammer sets up shock waves which often curtail the lengthening crack of the detaching flake because the vibration snaps off the flake before it has completed its run. A damping of the surface by the hand, or by other means, will assist in the production of longer flakes because this will absorb some of the shatter effects. The use of a soft hammer will also act in this way, and this *soft hammer technique* is sometimes taken to mark one of the principal technological developments in the early Palaeolithic times. However, it is sometimes difficult to distinguish the difference between a flake struck from a core by a rounded stone hammer and that struck off by a bone or wooden hammer.

Another way by which flakes can be knocked from a core is by the *anvil technique*, sometimes called 'block on block'. In this, the core itself is struck against a fixed anvil, a large stone, and the flake knocked off the core is distinguishable from those detached by ordinary hammerstones in the high angle between the platform and the flake scar (fig. 76, 6; 170, 6).

A method less commonly used was the *bipolar technique*. In this the core was placed upon another rock and struck with the hammer. The result is the detachment of a flake that often has a bulb of percussion at the lower end, due to the rebound blow from the underlying rock, as well as the bulb of percussion produced by the hammer-stone (fig. 45, 2; 168, 1).

One of the major technological advances in the Old Stone Age is believed to have been the development of the *punch technique* for the detachment of flakes. In this, the point of a punch of softer material such as wood or bone was placed on the striking platform of a core and a force applied by hammerstone or by some other method to the other end of the punch. The soft punch absorbed some of the shock of the blow, while at the same time concentrating the force at a particular and suitable point. The flake detached from the core was prolonged by this method, and often had parallel sides. Such long flakes are called *blades*. They are sometimes defined as having a length at least twice the width, with more or less parallel sides, although the defining features are a diffused bulb, a minute platform and sometimes shatter scars at the platform end (fig. 86, 24).

Our information about the exact methods used by Palaeolithic man is very incomplete, and the great variety of techniques employed by primitive people of recent times shows that there are many ways of producing virtually the same effect. These involve indirect percussion as outlined above, but applied in various ways, as well as the application of pressure upon the point on the core. In this latter method, the core would be held immovable and a bone or wooden shaft placed on it at a suitable point. A thrust upon the shaft would split off a flake, and no true percussion was involved. Only material such as flint, chert or obsidian would consistently yield blades by the punch technique, other rocks being too coarse-grained to allow such a method to succeed.

Flakes that have been detached by direct percussion (by hammer or by anvil), or by indirect percussion (by punch) or by pressure are often called *primary flakes*, and need not have thereafter been used as tools. Some were detached during the production of a core tool, for instance, and only those flakes of suitable shape might be selected for further trimming into flake tools. This trimming, as stated, is called *secondary flaking* or *retouch*, and this could be carried out by direct percussion, with a hammer of stone or softer material, by indirect percussion, with a stone or wooden or bone implement, or again by pressure flaking. In the first case, direct percussion, the flake or core would be retouched with a light hammer, perhaps weighing 2–3 oz. in contrast to the 3 lb. hammer used in the primary and preliminary flaking, the secondary flakes splitting from the edge of the flint flake or core. A large and rather rough core tool might require 20 or 30 such flakes to be removed, taking only a few minutes to produce, while a smaller and finer flake tool with delicate retouch would involve more care and preparation. For such secondary flaking, a small soft hammer might be useful, or pressure applied to the edge of the flake to remove small flat flakes which in the case of flint would be rarely over half an inch in length. To retouch a flake or core by the removal of larger flakes might require the use of indirect percussion.

The suitable flattened area of the core upon which the blow is struck is called the *striking platform* (fig. 82, 8). When such a force is applied directly to a slab of flint, a conchoidal fracture theoretically will appear although the mass of the rock will most often absorb the blow and prevent completion of the fracture. The conchoidal character of this is evident from the shape of the solid core, which has its apex at the point of impact. When however such a blow is applied obliquely and near the edge of the flint, the fracture will be complete and a flake will be detched bearing half a cone, or *cone of percussion*, at the point of impact, which leads directly into a less well-defined continuation of the cone sides called the positive *bulb of percussion* (fig. 76, 5; 76, 6 double). Below this, and concentric about the point of impact, are ripples or *percussion rings* (fig. 18, 2). The core from which a flake was detached will naturally have a *negative cone* or *bulb*, and *rings*, which combined form the *flake scar* (fig. 81).

From the positive bulb (of the flake) there may have been detached unintentionally a small chip of flint, leaving a *bulbar scar*, the chip loosened by a particularly sharp impact of the hammer. The bulb may also have shatter cracks on the bulb or below it which lead from the impact point (fig. 18, 2; 72, 7; 171, 2–3). The flake's complete bulb and ringed surface form the *primary flake surface* or *bulbar surface* (fig. 18, 2).

The cone and bulb of percussion varies in its form dependent upon the type of force applied to the core, by hard or soft hammer, by punch, by pressure. Generally a stone-struck flake will have a smaller and more distinct cone due to the unyielding nature of the hammerstone's point of impact while the cone on a flake struck by a soft hammer is flatter and wider as the area of impact was greater. The cone and bulb on a punch-struck flake or blade are very much smaller, and often the bulb is barely distinguishable on the primary flake surface.

In general, the flake scar on a stone-struck core is deeper and more concave than that on a core struck with a soft hammer or punch. In the last case the numerous closely placed and prominent ripples on the flake scar, and the thinness of the flake itself, are perhaps sufficient guide to distinguish this indirect percussion from direct percussion, but it is often difficult to distinguish indirect percussion from pressure flaking. The two methods are both in fact a form of indirect pressure, although the punch's impact is more abrupt. Considerable confusion seems to have arisen over the use of pressure as a flaking agent, and it can hardly be employed as marking a technological development of sufficient magnitude to serve archaeological typology.

It must not be forgotten that not all flakes exhibiting cones and bulbs of percussion are thereby of human manufacture. Natural agencies for flaking by percussion and pressure are many and varied, and include storm beaches and river beds, soliflucted deposits and rock falls. In addition, such natural actions are also capable of applying 'secondary retouch' to previously fractured flints and stone (fig. 71). In general, an absence of logical application of this trimming is apparent, but this is not always the case and perfectly logical 'implements' can be found in impossibly early geological contexts, or in modern beach and river gravels. Only by association with other traces of human activity can such flaking be accepted as certainly of human agency.

In contrast to the sometimes difficult situation in distinguishing between human and natural flaking of the above form, the second way by which flint or stone is naturally fractured was never consistently or successfully employed by man. This is thermal fracture, in which a rapid alteration in temperature causes an expansion or contraction of the surface of the stone that is not matched in the interior. Thermally-fractured stones are common in desert regions where day and night temperatures are widely separated. In cold regions the freezing of water absorbed by the surface of the rock wall will cause fracture through expansion. Such thermally-fractured stones are often recognizable by a concavity on the surface which has a complete series of rings or ripples concentric about a point near its centre. A small nipple or hollow may be present at the centre. The fragment of stone that has split away is circular or slightly domed, and is the product of a 'potlid' fracture. Occasionally thermal action causes previously weakened flint to break along straight lines, into prisms, and no rings or bulbs are present. This is called a 'starch' fracture. Flints and stones splintered by fire are often found on prehistoric sites, but there is no evidence that man ever used this method to fracture rock, because there is no way of controlling the fracture as there is by percussion of one form or another.

Flakes that have been detched by percussion may vary not only in their cones and bulbs of percussion, but also by the manner in which the flake finally broke away from the parent core. Where the junction of flake and core has been smooth and even, i.e., where the end of the flake was extremely thin and sharp, the technique is called *free-flaking* or *feather-edge flaking* (fig. 49, 11 primary flake; fig. 92, 5 retouch). Where the fracture has led more directly into the body of the core, and where considerable shock has been induced by the blow, the flake will snap off abruptly, leaving an angular junction with the core. Such a technique is called *step flaking* or *resolved flaking* (fig. 115, 4–6). Step flaking results, generally, in rather short flakes, and was therefore employed mainly in secondary flaking or retouch, particularly for sharpening or re-sharpening of tools. In certain industries, it was an important technique. Sometimes the developing fracture in a core will curl over and leave the core with an angular but not broken edge where the flake detached. This is called a *hinge fracture* and is distinguishable from a step fracture by its smooth surface.

All unbroken mechanically-struck flakes will exhibit certain of the above features, the cone and bulb of percussion, incomplete concentric ripples or rings on the primary flake surface, and part of the striking platform. As the rings of the bulbar surface are concentric about the point of impact of the hammer or punch, it will be possible to estimate the length of the flake if, as is often the case, the flake is broken and we are left with only the lower part. Near and at the bottom of the flake, however, these rings may be distorted and tend to follow the edge of the flake, so that caution is required in this method. Flakes that have subsequently been struck along their edges will possess small negative scars where minute fragments have been detached. In this, of course, they might theoretically be called cores, but in practice a useful general rule is that the presence of a primary flake surface is diagnostic of a flake, no matter how many smaller negative scars are evident.

The question of priority can be carried back to the original breaking up of a block of flint, but for practical purposes the above rule is sufficient. The secondary work, or retouch, of a flake is generally but not inevitably carried out using the primary flake surface as a striking platform, so that the small trimming flakes or chips are detached from underneath this platform, the negative scars therefore being left on the other side of the flake, the back or *dorsal* surface. The bulbar surface is occasionally called *ventral*. In the case of natural retouching of a flake, through river or wave action, or pressure in landslips, the retouching will most often take place indiscriminately from both dorsal and ventral surfaces, but, again, under certain circumstances this retouch will be from one side only.

From the general features of flakes and cores, we turn now to the different forms produced by man in his stone technology. The block of stone, when first selected, will be roughly fashioned into a suitable shape for handling by breaking it with the anvil technique or by percussion with a stone hammer. A number of waste flakes will be detached in this work. For the production of flakes suitable for retouching into tools a striking platform may have to be prepared. This was done by detaching a number of often parallel flakes along an edge of the core to produce a satisfactory surface upon which the final detachment blow could be struck or the punch placed in the final detachment of the flake required. Such a striking platform is called a *prepared platform*, or a *faceted platform* (fig. 20, 3; 82, 1–4; 84, 1). Of course if a suitable surface (*plain platform*) (fig. 20, 2; 82, 5) was already present on the core, there would be no need for a prepared platform.

The core on which such platforms may have been prepared also possessed certain distinguishable features. In the case of single flaking without any preparation of a platform the only prerequisite is of a suitable core intersection of two surfaces at an angle of about 90° or less. If this angle is appreciably greater than 90° it will not generally be possible to detach a flake partly because of the massiveness of the core and its absorption of the blow. Experiment is the best demonstration of this. If however a suitable angle exists a blow will detach a flake from the core leaving a flake scar on the core that can be used itself as a striking platform for further detachment until the angle of intersection becomes too great for further success. With care, flakes could be detached consecutively from suitably opposed surfaces until the core itself was made into a tool such as an axe, or until suitable flakes were made for subsequent trimming into tools.

Apart from the above cores, certain other forms of core involving rather more preparation and attention were produced at certain times in the history of stone technology. Of these, three mark important changes in this technology. All were used primarily for the production of suitable flakes, and not themselves as core tools. The first is the *tortoise-core* or *prepared core* (fig. 81; 53, 8). In this a core was prepared by the careful flaking of one of the surfaces of the core to produce a rounded and dome-like face. At one end of this, a striking platform was prepared if necessary, and the core was then ready for its final flaking. The blow, delivered at a carefully chosen point on the platform (sometimes at the top of a humped platform called 'en chapeau de gendarme'), detached a flake from the domed surface, a flake which was of broader and more regular proportions than was possible with an unprepared core. Such flakes would require little secondary flaking as their edges would have been preformed on the core.

Opposed to this elaborate preparation of the core is the *disc core*, which in its final form is a flaking method not at all similar to the tortoise-core technique. A rather flat core or large flake, each presenting a suitable flattened striking platform, was flaked around its edge, detaching short and rather broad flakes. The resultant core assumed a circular or disc shape (fig. 53, 6) and once the initial surface had been exhausted, the flake scars could be employed as striking platforms for the removal of flakes from the original flattened surface. If necessary, these striking platforms would be prepared by the detachment of small flakes as outlined above. The flakes from a disc core and those from a tortoise-core will generally be distinguishable by the number of truncated flake scars on their dorsal surfaces. In the former, perhaps 2, 3 or 4 scars will be visible, representing the traces of flakes previously removed from the core, but the flake from a tortoise-core will show 7–10 scars, sometimes up to 15 or more, which represent the preparation of the core prior to the flake's removal. The basic difference in function of the tortoise-core and the disc core lies in the fact that the latter is designed for the continuous production of flakes (it is sometimes called *continuation core*) of generally small size up to 3″ long, while the former was shaped for the detachment of one flake only, a flake often 6″ or more in length.

For the production of blades, a different flaking was needed, and a different core (the *blade core*) resulted. The punch technique using percussion or pressure must have been employed for this, and the cores after the removal of blades assume characteristic shapes with parallel flake scars descending from platforms often prepared only by the removal of a single flake to present a smooth surface upon which the punch would be set (fig. 105, 4, 10). The use of two or more platforms, directly opposed, at either end of the core, or at right angles to one another, is common. Such cores generally assume certain classifiable shapes, such as pyramidal or biconical, when they have been worked to such a degree that blades of suitable length could no longer be removed.

All of the flakes or blades removed from the above cores are primary flakes, and subsequent to removal they might or might not require secondary trimming or retouch. Naturally sharp or otherwise suitable edges would of course have been used without retouch, but blunting through usage would also necessitate retouching. Two main types of secondary working occurred, which we may call sharpening retouch and blunting retouch. For the former, the blows or pressure would be applied at an oblique angle to the edge of the bulbar face, so that the small flakes would be detached from the dorsal surface in such a way as to leave as thin an edge as possible. Force applied in the same plane as the bulbar face would merely shatter the edge. The flakes removed by this sharpening retouch might be prolonged to run up onto the dorsal surface by judicious damping of the blow (fig. 92, 15), but step flaking would result through blows absorbed less by the hand or hammer. The tools produced by such sharpening retouch would include knives, scrapers, points and cutting edges of larger core tools such as handaxes. Blunting retouch (fig. 65, 4), to prevent the cutting or splitting of a handle or finger by a sharp edge, would be carried out by crushing the naturally sharp edge of a flake or blade against an anvil.

In recent years the functional aspect of Palaeolithic artefacts has been examined through microscopic study of utilization marks on the working edges of stone and other tools. This has shown that, in certain cases, a purely morphological classification of objects is misleading because the names given presuppose a function, e.g. scraper, point, graver. Even in those cases where the traces of wear are consonant with typological names, it has been demonstrated that the method of using such tools may differ from that generally expected by shape alone (Semenov 1964).

The material examined microscopically was mainly of Russian Upper Palaeolithic date, and little work has so far been published on west European, African or Far Eastern origin. It is doubtful if the majority of Lower Palaeolithic stone tools can be examined successfully because many of these are derived and their edges obscured through rolling.

There are a number of tools which are universally recognized by their names and we have included here a brief description of some of these. Their appearance is not in doubt, their manner of fashioning is in little doubt, and although their precise function must be for the moment in considerable doubt, we can perhaps suggest certain broad groups of functional artefacts. It is important however to remember that a great number of perfectly usable tools at all periods of the Palaeolithic will not have conformed to a specific tool form recognizable by ourselves; there will have been freshly struck sharp flakes and cores at once functional without further work, perhaps discarded immediately after use, and leaving little sign, apart from utilization traces visible by microscopic examination, that early man had fashioned or used them. The development of technology however will have gradually produced more standardized forms of implements and these can be grouped as an aid in correlating industries from adjacent regions. Such artefacts are recognizable as tools by their standardized form, because they have been made to a set and regular pattern. This pattern or tradition is one of the bases upon which the recognition of man-made artefacts rests. Stray finds of implements in a recognized pattern can therefore be accepted as of human manufacture, and of certain typological groups. For these recognizable tools a second criterion of proof of human manufacture does not need to be fulfilled. This second rule is based on association, that an object is not acceptable as being humanly-made unless it has been found in a primary *in situ* position with other traces of man's activity. For known types of tool, which required elaborate flaking, the association is hardly necessary, but for more primitive productions that do not conform to a set pattern or are of such an unspecialized form that no set pattern exists, the association is absolutely vital. Stray finds of these objects are unacceptable, because they will be within the range of formation by natural agencies; such finds in river gravels or storm beaches are probably self-evidently unacceptable, but discovery on eroded surfaces less so. Nevertheless, only association for these primitive tool forms can provide proof of their human relationship. The best example of this is Olduvai Gorge, where, upon the silty margins of former lakes, unaccompanied by spreads of river gravel, lie flaked rocks foreign to the immediate locality associated with the bones of animals and of man himself. By themselves, the fractured rocks would be hardly recognizable as tools or the waste from their manufacture. In more developed industries, a number of standardized tool shapes will be present, but these will only make up a small proportion of the total objects found, the majority of which will be waste flakes and discarded cores, flakes utilized as tools without further retouch, or retouched only slightly, cores utilized and partially trimmed to produce a functional working edge.

Rather than list by descriptive name the varying tool types, we have attempted here to group the standardized forms by their function. This method is open to some doubt because work on the functional aspect of artefacts is only in its infancy, but already the results published seem to us to warrant careful attention. Both the functions we list, and the variety of implements included therein, are general and not necessarily to be accepted as valid for all artefacts of certain type.

The functional aspect of stone artefacts has been divided into six, (1) for scraping or shaving skins and wood, (2) for piercing skins and hide, (3) for cutting and ripping meat and skins, (4) for grooving and engraving bone, antler and stone, (5) for projectile heads or barbs, (6) for use as multipurpose tools. We begin with the last-named.

The earliest and most primitive recognized tool at present is the *Oldowan chopper* (fig. 13, 1–4). This is often called a pebble tool because many of the tools are made on water-worn pebbles, but a number were formed from blocks or flakes of chert, quartz and quartzite. The chopper varies from 2″ to 8″ in normal length and its chopping edge is formed by the removal of flakes at one end, flakes being detached from both faces, or around the end of a pebble if this was used. The intersections of the flake scars form a very sharp and uneven edge; the tool was probably used for cutting, pounding and digging. It must not be forgotten that flakes and pebbles showing even less primary flaking occur at Olduvai and elsewhere, but the Oldowan chopper is the first recognizable standardized tool. Variations and improvements in the chopper have been noted from stratified sites (p. 101).

An improvement in technical skill, and thereby in the functional ability of the tool, resulted in the production of the ubiquitous *handaxe* or *coup-de-poing*. These are generally called core tools, but many of them were made on large flakes. In any case, however, the method of flaking over much if not all of both faces removed most of the original surfaces. The basic handaxe form is a pear shape with one end rather pointed and the other rounded (fig. 17, 2; 21, 1). Often the rounded base or butt has the original surface remaining as this provided a suitable grip for the hand. There is little evidence that these axes were hafted in any way, and most were in fact handaxes. Very great variation exists in handaxes. The coarser and cruder forms have irregular edges and diamond or triangular cross-sections (fig. 15; 74, 1). This was probably caused by the failure of the flaking technique to prolong the flake scars so as to thin down the centre part of each side of the flint or stone. The use of a stone hammer would probably account for the shortness of the flake scars. These axes, struck with a stone hammer, and of thick section, are often called Chellean or Abbevillian axes, but at the present time they are better considered only as a typological form in the Acheulean tradition. The appearance of the soft hammer, of bone or wood, resulted in the production of axes thinner in section and with edges more regular. The use of the soft hammer allowed the prolongation of the trimming flakes so that those from the two main edges overlapped at the centre of the tool. The cross-section then is thin and evenly curved, often of lenticular shape. The outline of the axe was more regular, and in side view the axe had a straight or evenly curved cutting edge (fig. 16, 2; 69, 3). A feature of certain axes of Acheulean tradition is a reverse S-twisted cutting edge (fig. 20, 1). A number of specialized forms of Acheulean axe are known. The main type remained pear-shaped, but ovates (fig. 16, 2; 74, 3), lanceolates (with elongated straight-sided point, fig. 79, 1), ficrons (elongated but with slight concave-sided points, fig. 78, 1) and cordiforms (small and heart-shaped, fig. 79, 5) occur. There are a number of minor forms, as well, but these are perhaps better explained numerically rather than by their somewhat involved names (Roe 1964).

A tool-form generally associated with African handaxe industries is the *cleaver*. This is characteristically made on a large flake, retouched at butt and sides, leaving an intersection of two primary surfaces to form a wide cutting edge (fig. 16, 1; 20, 4).

Both cleavers and handaxes must have been multi-purpose tools. It has been demonstrated that they are particularly effective as skinning knives and meat choppers. Axes could also have been used as digging implements, for grubs or for pits, and would serve as well to despatch trapped game as to cut off branches for windbreaks.

In parts of India and further east, early industries contain *choppers* and *chopping-tools*. The choppers are in reality unifacially trimmed cleavers, made upon pebbles or rock slabs. They are rectangular, rounded or triangular in outline, with cutting edges steeply inclined to the original surface (fig. 164, 4). Chopping-tools are bifacially worked, with flakes removed from both dorsal and ventral surfaces to form a sharp rather irregular intersection (fig. 167; 168, 3).

Allied more to the handaxe is the *pick*, found in parts of tropical Africa. This is a heavy pointed tool distinguished from the axe by its massive cross-section which is roughly circular or oblong (fig. 26, 1, 3; 170, 4, 5).

Less certain as a multipurpose tool is the *Levallois* flake (fig. 69, 4, 5). The method by which this is produced has already been described. The Levallois flake is generally large, from 3″ to 6″ in length, and often broad in relation to this. The flake is thin and, on the dorsal surface, the distal ends of the flake scars from the prepared cores are preserved. Part of the faceted or plain platform can be seen above the bulb of percussion on the ventral surface. It required little retouch after detachment from the core, because of the prefabrication of its shape on the core (fig. 81). Such flakes were probably employed in much the same way as thin handaxes, as knives or scrapers or whittlers. Study of wear traces on fresh specimens should reveal much information.

Tools for cutting and ripping include axes, cleavers and Levallois flakes, but specialized forms occur in later times. The meat knife, for cutting fibres and tendons, was often made on a long blade which might be trimmed to provide a hand hold at one end; the other end might be blunted to avoid cutting the skin. It is probable that the 'Aurignacian blades' with flat sharpening retouch on one edge or both, retouch that extends up onto the dorsal surface, were used for skinning and dividing (fig. 87, 1–7). Traces of wear would be expected on both dorsal and ventral faces. At least some *shouldered points* have been shown to be cutting and ripping knives. Shouldered points have retouched tangs and are trimmed to a point. Some may have been used as projectile heads (fig. 139, 4, 5). *Backed blades* are another form generally considered to be knives, for more delicate cutting (fig. 65, 1–5; 89, 1–4). Most backed blades are straight-backed, with blunting retouch down all or part of one edge, the other edge remaining naturally sharp. In some the backing may have provided a comfortable surface for the finger during use. The retouch around the base of some curved backed blades (fig. 86, 3), perhaps for a further supporting position, suggests that the tip of the tool may also have been important functionally.

Another form of knife, for whittling or as a type of scraper-cutter, is the *notched* or *strangled blade*. Generally long, the blade has one notch or opposed notches formed by retouch on its long sides (fig. 87, 2).

Tools for piercing and drilling are less varied. The *awl* is a form common to many industries. A true awl has a working end formed by careful and minute retouch, leaving a sharp projection (fig. 87, 9). Other awls are on long thin blades with backing on both edges up to the tip (fig. 106, 21). Any flint with a satisfactory point will serve as an awl, and there is some evidence that shouldered points were thus employed. The use of skins for clothing would probably necessitate the employment of awls as an aid in providing fastening attachments.

Scraping tools were also necessary in the preparation of skins and hides. There are several major forms of scraper, and functional studies have suggested the manner in which these were used. The *side scraper* (fig. 79, 2; 115, 1) is a tool made on a rather broad flake, the essential feature being the provision by retouch of a convex sharp edge, generally an edge next to the bulb but sometimes opposed to the bulb, that is, at the base of the flake. Many variations in form are claimed for this implement. The convex surface is essential so that the edges of the tool will not cut the skin. It has been demonstrated that some side scrapers were pushed both forwards and backwards over the surface of the skin, striations from this work being left on both dorsal and ventral surfaces leading from the retouch edge. Often this edge has been carefully step-flaked. Of different function must be the variety of flake scraper with a straight retouched edge (fig. 115, 2, 6). The '*Kasouga flake*' of southern Africa, with flat scale-like flaking along one convex edge, would serve as a scraping tool or as a knife. *End scrapers* are self-descriptive. They occur mainly on blades, and the retouch is limited to the end where a sharply convex cutting edge is formed (fig. 40, 12; 91, 1). In some cases the retouch takes the form of a series of blade-like scars converging onto the dorsal surface, and this is called *fluted retouch* (fig. 89, 30). Some of these end scrapers were held with the ventral side facing the user, and the scraping motion was towards the user. Traces of wear then would only occur on the dorsal face. Blunt end scrapers were perhaps employed to soften the skins after more rigorous cleaning away of fat and fibres by knives or by sharper-end scrapers. The *duck-billed scraper* is a form of end scraper on a broad flake with wide convex retouched end (fig. 34, 11).

The less common *keeled scrapers*, *nosed scrapers*, and *core scrapers*, were probably used in similar manner to the above. The keeled scraper is generally a thick broad flake which has fine convergent retouch rising to a keel-like angle on the dorsal face (fig. 121, 9; 157, 13). The nosed scraper is often similar but retouch has produced a projecting nose between two notches, and generally the fine fluting retouch is not as evident (fig. 87, 21, 23). The core scraper is a worked-out core, with scraper edge produced by the intersection of a large flake surface with a series of small scars (fig. 105, 10).

The *round scrapers* are another form perhaps employed for finer work, or, in some cases, as small whittling knives (fig. 38, 9; 93, 27). The retouch extends almost or all around the flake, and the term sometimes applied to these, thumbnail scrapers, provides a rough approximation of their size.

The notched blades noted previously might also be included here as a form suitable for scraping away excess material on a spear shaft or bone artefact, in spokeshave fashion. Another scraping or shaving implement is the *push-plane*, a characteristic African form, made on a large flake with high back and with retouch extending around part of the circular edge (fig. 46, 5).

The simplest *projectile* is an object hurled at game or an adversary, and the first recognizable projectile is the *missile stone* (fig. 170, 2). Where flaked, these are roughly spherical and often 5″ to 6″ in diameter but later ones are smaller and more perfectly formed. It has been suggested that a trio of these could have formed a bolas. Sometimes natural diabase spheroids were collected and used.

Other projectiles were parts of composite tools, forming only the sharpened point of spears and arrows. Many points were made on flakes with secondary step retouch along two converging edges (fig. 29). Probably of comparable use are a variety of *tanged points*. The *Aterian* point has a tang which was formed by the removal of a series of flakes from two edges leaving a triangular-sectioned projection between. Duplication from the other surface of the flake resulted in a diamond-shaped cross-section to the tang (fig. 55). Other types of tanged point commonly occur, including slender forms with differing treatment of the shoulders (fig. 89, 12; 124, 4) and some with retouch extending over both dorsal and ventral surfaces (fig. 50, 8; 97, 1–2).

Shouldered points are also varied in their form. The basic type has sufficient retouch at the butt to remove part of the blade or flake, leaving a constricted, although asymmetrical, projection. Often the tip of the implement was flaked. Some shouldered points were made on rather broad blades or flakes (fig. 124, 8; 139, 4) but others were more slender (fig. 131) and sometimes had pressure or punched flaking scars over part or all of the dorsal surface.

A different form of projectile is the *leaf-shaped point* (fig. 32, 20; 92, 7; 116). These points generally range in size from 2″ to 8″ and are often bifacially-worked, thin in section, sometimes with one end more pointed than the other. The bifacial flat retouch may extend from both edges and remove all of the dorsal and ventral surfaces. Leaf-shaped points with bifacial flaking have been recognized in many areas of the Old World; recent study of certain of these groups has indicated that pressure-flaking or skilful punch-percussion could have been employed for the flat flaking.

Microlithic forms are often considered to have been the heads or barbs of arrows or the sharp lining of an arrowshaft. In some cases they have been discovered with traces of their adhesive fastening, or in such positions that their employment on arrowshafts is not in doubt. The microlithic forms used in this way range from small *obliquely-retouched* flakes (fig. 106, 1–6) to geometric forms. Of the latter, the *triangle* (fig. 106, 7–12), *crescent* (fig. 158, 2) and *trapeze* (fig. 106, 14–15) are most character-istic. These were formed either by simple flaking of a snapped blade, or by the micro-burin technique. In this, the blade was notched by retouch (fig. 106, 17) until a carefully directed blow or simple breaking of the blade resulted in the separation of the triangle or trapeze shape from the discarded end or ends of the blade, called the micro-burin (fig. 98, 7, 9; 106, 16) which is not a small burin and not a tool in itself. The triangles and trapezes could have served as tips or barbs of arrowheads, or as composite cutting implements.

The *tranchet arrowhead* is also characteristic of certain Stone Age groups. This artefact consists of a snapped blade with retouched convergent edges and parallel naturally sharp edges (fig. 52, 10–12). These, as in certain Mesolithic contexts with trapezes, were mounted so that the impact edge was wide.

Engraving and grooving tools, for the shaping of bone, antler and wooden objects, and for their decoration, generally are grouped under the name *burin* or *graver*. A burin is a flake or blade which has had one or more narrow flakes removed along the length of the edge (fig. 87, 8). This differs from ordinary retouch which is normally delivered into the ventral side of the edge so that the flake scar runs at a right angle to the line of the edge. The burin flake scar or *facet* as it is often called runs along the edge, removing the intersection of the dorsal and ventral surfaces. The blow itself is struck along the length of the flake in most cases. The flake that is removed is called the burin *spall* and will carry a small area of both dorsal and ventral surfaces; it will be triangular in cross-section if it was the first burin spall removed, but a second spall removed in the re-sharpening of the tool will generally be trapezoidal in cross-section, the convergent surfaces being the dorsal and ventral faces, the roughly parallel sur-faces being the first and second burin blows.

The working edge of the burin is the intersection of the flake and the burin facet where it truncates the flake's edge. At this point the angle of intersection will be of the order of 90° or less, and the actual point itself will be strengthened because it does not lie on the original thin edge of the flake but nearer the centre where the flake is thicker. The working edge will then be capable of transferring considerable pres-sure to the work, whether it be bone or antler or stone, without breaking, although resharpening by the removal of a second spall might be necessary. Although it has generally been assumed that all flakes with such facets are burins and used for engraving, recent study of a few isolated specimens has demonstrated that in these cases the burin facet was in fact used to blunt the edge and the working surface of the tool was elsewhere on the edge. Tools with naturally sharp edges may therefore have been used as knives or scrapers, and the burin facet served the same purpose as blunting retouch. The importance of these regrettably few observations can hardly be over-emphasized for the typological studies of relevant industries and their functional significance.

The 'burin' edge can be produced in a number of ways, and these provide a method by which burins have been classified. The simplest form is the *single-blow burin*, the working edge formed by the intersection of a burin facet and a natural or snapped off flat surface (fig. 86, 11). Where such a surface is not available, the intersection of two burin facets, one on each side of the working edge, forms a common type called the *ordinary* or *bec de flûte* burin (fig. 86, 14; 93, 31). Resharpening of an edge, or the original provision of more than one facet on one or both edges, are variants of the basic ordinary burin, and have been called double or multiple-faceted burins, sometimes *polyhedric* burins, but in the latter case the burin scars on one edge are generally inclined to form a convex faceted surface, which would form a gouge-like implement (fig. 89, 37; 92, 26).

All of the above types, except the single blow, are formed by the intersection of burin facets. The second major type of burin is formed by the junction of a burin facet and a retouched edge, and this is called the *angle burin* (fig. 86, 15; 93, 16). All angle burins have had ordinary retouch applied along part of one edge, and a burin facet on the other. The angle formed by the intersection of the retouch and burin face may be acute or right-angled, and the retouched edge may be straight, concave or convex. The convex angle burin is called a 'parrot-beak' burin (fig. 93, 29). Most of these angle burins have had the burin facet formed along the length of the flake or blade, the retouch applied across one end. Where the positions are reversed, the result is a *transverse burin*, the burin facet being transverse to the length of the flake (fig. 65, 10–13).

Interpretation Procedures of nomenclature as in other disciplines have not so far been adopted in archaeology and the terms are as a rule used loosely without precise definition. Wherever a collection of artefacts is found in a deposit and there is no evidence that they were brought there by natural agencies it is assumed that that place was a site occupied by human beings.

A collection of artefacts from a single site, believed to be of the same age, is called an industry. In order to arrange data in an orderly form for further study, a taxonomic device is to group similar industries within a circumscribed geographical area into archaeological 'cultures'. Similarities and dissimilarities are determined by the consideration of attributes (traits) of artefacts or of collections. As all attributes cannot in practice be used, few or many may be selected as probably having some significance. The archaeological term 'culture' is not to be equated with the term 'culture' as it is used generally today, or as it is used by other disciplines. Some authorities have in fact suggested, in view of the several meanings and interpretations of the word, that the use of the term culture should be discontinued in the study of prehistoric man.

A model or hypothesis in common use in archaeology, however, is the assumption that the taxonomic cluster called a culture represents an expression of the material wealth, ideas and technology of a single people such as the Natufians, Gravettians and the like. And because some known (historical) tribes are associated with distinctive assemblages, it is agreed to assume that distinctive assemblages in prehistory represent tribes.

At least partly complementary to this culture/tribe/people hypothesis, wherein culture is '*sui generis*', is the environmental approach which is in common use. Here the hypothesis exists that human behaviour is enacted selectively and at free will against an unrelated or little-related background of environment, by which, however, it may be to some extent modified. By this approach culture clusters are used to form a model of the past which is related to the historical framework as we know it. The development of numerical analysis of data offers considerable scope for refinements in this field (Clarke 1968), and may form a basis for alternative hypotheses concerning the reasons for artefactual clusters. It must be remembered, however, in the statistical treatment of archaeological assemblages, that a palaeolithic site is commonly only one of a number of sites occupied by the same hunting band, and the assemblage from a particular site is not a 'random' sample, wherein each component is known to have an equal chance of being selected, but an unsystematic or grab sample of the total tool equipment of the band. Nor is the type site from which the culture is named necessarily a cultural norm.

Another view is that all archaeology is environmental and that human behaviour is a factor related to other dynamic factors in the biotope. Such an approach, the study of the natural forces in archaeology, would accept that the varied data from an archaeological site are in a relationship at a point of time, which is in itself of value. But in an inter-disciplinary approach to archaeological sites as it is at present conducted, the hypotheses of the different disciplines are unrelated or only marginally related to each other and to the relationship of the various forms of data available within the sites. In consequence, their separate conclusions are often only of peripheral interest to each other and indeed not uncommonly represent considerable labours and a vast literature with little reward. Archaeology may well develop the study of the relationships of the various dynamic factors represented within the sites, 'physiodynamics', with concepts of its own, using the approach of the humanities and the techniques of the natural sciences but not necessarily with their concepts. Such an attempt may provide a remedy for a situation wherein 'none of our archaeological models, inherited or recently devised, seems capable of providing a wholly convincing picture of prehistory' (Piggott 1959).

It has also been said that a case can be made that 'man is essentially a predator whose natural instinct is to kill', and 'a primate with instincts demanding the maintenance and defence of territories' (Ardrey 1961). Studies along these lines, the relation of animal to human behaviour, have been largely outside the archaeological field. Further, as man is a primate, the assumption has usually been made that primate behaviour studies are most likely to yield valuable results. However, man, with his extensive range of adaptability, has probably behaved in the manner of animals other than primates, where his food supply has been akin to those of non-primates. Considerations of this kind lead on to the study of territories and their exploitation, a matter relevant to the distribution of archaeological sites (Jewell 1966, Wynne-Edwards 1962). This work requires area research rather than the excavation of single sites and so far only a few areas have been studied this way.

Another current model is based on the economies practised by prehistoric peoples. Economy as the means by which the human group exploits its environment is attractive in that it forms the direct links between man and the natural resources. Human groups may be divided into hunters (plate I), hunter-gatherers, pastoralists or agriculturalists, and it is possible to consider their way of life and the consequences of it. Such a model is of value when considering the transitional phase from hunter-gathering to agricultural economies, a transition which is in evidence from biological data, but which is not clearly shown by the artefacts. This approach has not been developed to any great extent and the blanket term hunters, hunter-gatherers and agriculturalists have not been refined. They cover an economic complexity which is little understood (Nash 1966). Some recent advances in Switzerland and Denmark and in the study of Maori sites in New Zealand, however, are promising for the future of economic prehistory.

At this point, however, it is of some consequence to distinguish between 'a people' as defined by the degree to which artefactual assemblages share a common influence, a tradition, in fact, which may last for many millennia and exist over a vast area, and the human groups which exploit an area and are bonded together in social and economic groups.

The Palaeoeconomic approach is concerned with exploitation of territory and is therefore closely linked with some forms of ethology, demography, social anthropology and sociology, to which fields it offers perspective in time. It may use ecological data but its concern is basically with territories and economic units and their integration rather than ecological zones. Clearly, a human group which forms an economic unit to exploit the whole of an area commonly cuts across ecological boundaries, particularly those which are economically complementary. Such economic units require a regrouping of artefactual assemblages. It is a commonplace of archaeological sites that there is evidence that human groups exploited more than one environment. Some preliminary studies have been made, such as those in the Tehuacán valley in America (MacNeish 1964), in Epirus in Greece (Higgs et al. 1967) and in Highland Peru (Lynch 1967).

The basis of study of the assemblages of stone tools and animal bones of the Epirus sites lies in the fact that hunting or gathering bands largely practise *mobile* economies which, as with pastoral economies, cross the boundaries of economically complementary ecological zones. In consequence any one particular site in a particular environment is only one of a number of sites occupied by one band in perhaps a

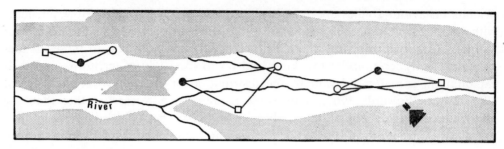

● **Wet-season camps**

□ **Fall camps**

○ **Dry-season camps**

Mountains

FIG. 10. Distribution of hunter-gatherer camps in the Tehuacán valley, Mexico. *After MacNeish 1964*

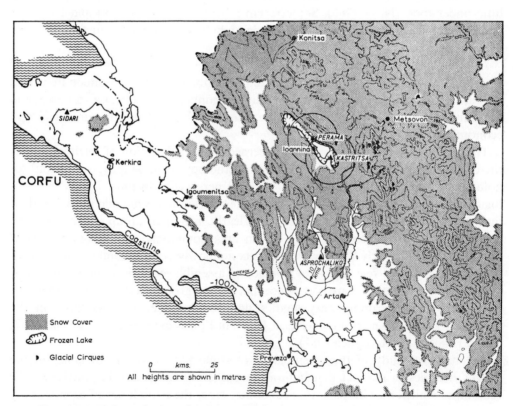

FIG. 11*a*. Epirus during the Last Glaciation — a reconstruction of winter conditions. *From Higgs* et al. *1967*

number of different environments. Bands are usually mobile in order to avoid the limitations placed upon them by minimal quantity of necessities for survival which will be available at particular seasons in a particular environment. A sedentary band would be basically limited by 'the amount of the least available necessity' in the lean season, and not by the total available resources. However, a band will prefer to move, if it can, once the most favoured supplies have been used up. A preference or ceiling may intervene before a scarcity arises. Averages do not exist in practising hunting bands, and each band will seek to find an 'optimum' situation or a number of such situations according to seasonal supplies, the existence of complementary ecological zones and other factors. A cave situated in the *centre* of a hunting territory which provides a supply of food and other material may be regarded as an 'optimum' site, from which supplies may be obtained with a minimum amount of 'output' of labour per unit of 'intake' of supplies.

The sites in Epirus have been divided into three groups. The first group is at the foot of the Pindhos range and parallel to it, at Perama, Kastritsa and Konitsa (fig. 11). The main game animals eaten by the hunting groups in Advanced Palaeolithic times were deer, a form of equid and wild sheep or goats. Usually such animals move away from higher ground in the face of heavy snowfall. Fig. 11a shows an estimate of the coverage with deep snow of this area during the Last Glaciation. It also shows how inadequate were the available hunting territories of the Kastritsa cave (p. 321) during the winter season, and how Asprochaliko (p. 321) would have been in an optimum situation in winter with a cave adjacent to a relatively snow-free area and the winter territories of the game animals. The first group of sites would have been in an optimum situation only in the summer season, with a cave adjacent to a plentiful supply of game (fig. 11b). The second group of sites contains the coastal sites at Barda, near Sidari, and Asprochaliko, which are 'optimum situation' sites for winter occupation. It follows that the circumstances which would have been most favourable to human survival would have been a migratory movement of the hunting bands from the coast to the inland areas to which the game would have migrated in order to exploit the summer flush of upland grass. Fig. 11c illustrates how the present-day Zagori Sarakatsani pastoralists migrate annually and meet a similar need to exploit the similar uneven seasonal distribution of resources by an economic unit which crosses over boundaries between economically complementary ecological zones. Thus, this aspect of the behaviour of hunting and pastoral mobile economies is determined in each case by that basal distribution of resources.

Between the inland group of sites and the coastal group there are a number of open sites. These are regarded as 'kill' sites after the American fashion, or as temporary transit halts (fig. 12) between the cave or 'home base' sites, or camps of occasional forays into territories not continually exploited. It is suggested, therefore, that the Palaeolithic sites should be divided into two main groups, (*a*) home bases, that is those sites which are continually but not continuously occupied over a long period, and (*b*) temporary sites, those which are occupied briefly and whose function is different

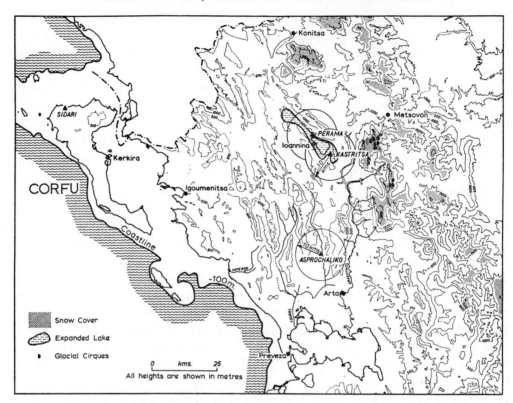

FIG. 11*b*. Epirus during the Last Glaciation — a reconstruction of summer conditions. *From Higgs* et al. *1967*

in that they may be (1) 'kill sites', after the manner of the American kill sites, or (2) 'transit sites', where a brief halt has been made between home bases and also occasional brief hunting camps outside the continuously exploited areas.

It is unlikely, by their nature, that the different functions carried out at these different types of site will have led to assemblages precisely similar in their tool types or in the relative quantities of tools. Seasonal activities may be reflected in the artefacts, for example, in only one of the group of sites. Deer skins are at their best in autumn and their preparation may be shown only in autumn-occupied home bases. To take an example from north temperate Europe, the Maglemose, a band fishing at their winter site, would have their assemblages heavily weighted with fishing gear and tools related to that environment, whereas they would probably not need such artefacts when hunting deer on their summer upland pastures. It is suggested that the differences between assemblages, both in type and relative quantities of the artefacts used, may be due to the seasonal exploitations of different environments, and that it is thus theoretically possible that the two different 'cultural' groups of assemblages may have been made by the same band. It is therefore thought to be of value to group

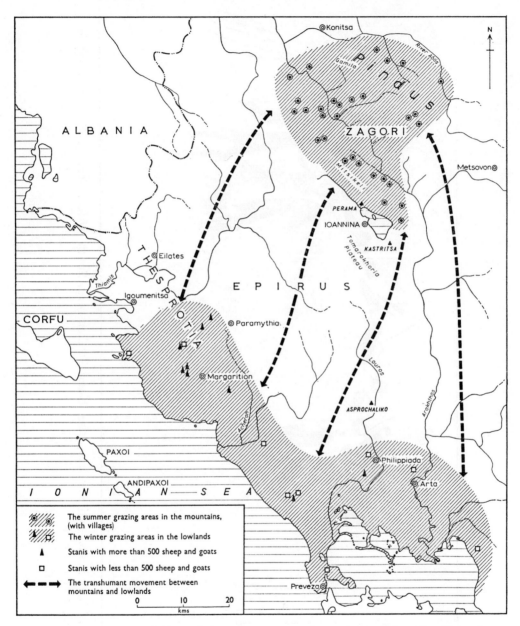

FIG. 11c. Routes followed by the present-day pastoralists, the Zagori Sarakatsani tribe. *From Higgs* et al. *1967*

FIG. 12. A hunter-gatherer camp site. Natal Drakensberg, South Africa. Scale ½. *From a tracing by Patricia Vinnicombe*

the assemblages into economic units, rather than into cultural units where, according to the customary hypothesis of equating 'culture' with human groups, a human group might well appear to be isolated in an area in which it could not possibly survive over a winter season. The economic group is formed on the hypothesis that on a prehistoric time-scale territories would tend to be aligned to the best advantage, and that those groups which did so would tend to survive. As the most advantageous territorial alignment would have been highland and lowland across the economically complementary ecological zones, the inland sites are grouped together with the coastal sites as an economic entity, an entity which exploited the area at that time.

Developments such as these in archaeology are promising. It appears unlikely that typology and the natural sciences will hold their dominating positions for long. It may well be expected, particularly in view of the impact of more and more refined chronologies, that ethology and economics will have more important influences in the future than they have at present.

Part II
AFRICA

5

Early Industries in Sub-Saharan Africa

THE history of stone tool manufacture in Africa south of the Sahara is bound up with the controversial 'pebble-tool cultures', because it is assemblages of flaked pebbles and other stones that have been believed to provide the earliest evidence for industrial activity in this area. Such assemblages have also been considered to lie behind the development of stone tool manufacture in other parts of the Old World, as they provide typologically ancestral material to the easily recognizable handaxe and flake industries of later Middle Pleistocene times. The problem of these 'pebble industries' is therefore of more than tropical African importance (Clark 1962).

In 1919 E. J. Wayland recovered a number of small flat pebbles of quartz and quartzite from the terrace gravels of the Kafu River valley in Uganda; the pebbles had been flaked at one end, and he believed that these were man-made tools. Other discoveries were made in subsequent years in Uganda, and the name Kafuan was given to the assemblages in 1927. In 1932 work at Olduvai Gorge resulted in the discovery of fractured pebbles in the lake muds and silts of Bed I. As these pebbles were, in general, flaked upon both main surfaces, they were believed to represent a stage of industry developed out of the simpler, unifacially-flaked, Kafuan. The bifacially-flaked pebbles from Olduvai Gorge were named Oldowan (fig. 13), and they were considered to represent a stage ancestral to the earliest handaxes at Olduvai Gorge, in Bed II. The fact that these flaked objects were found in lake sediments, and were associated with the bones of animals, must account for the almost universal acceptance of the Oldowan assemblages as evidence of human activity.

Many other finds of 'pebble tools' were made in south, central and north Africa in the following years, but in the last decade it has become apparent that a considerable proportion of 'Kafuan' assemblages may consist only of naturally-fractured rocks. The apparent divergence of opinion about the natural agencies responsible for flaking pebbles remains unresolved, but prehistorians are agreed that most Kafuan sites require further investigation before they are reinstated as showing any human element, and that only sites where natural flaking agencies are excluded, by virtue of specific geological circumstances, can be accepted as demonstrating the presence of man.

79

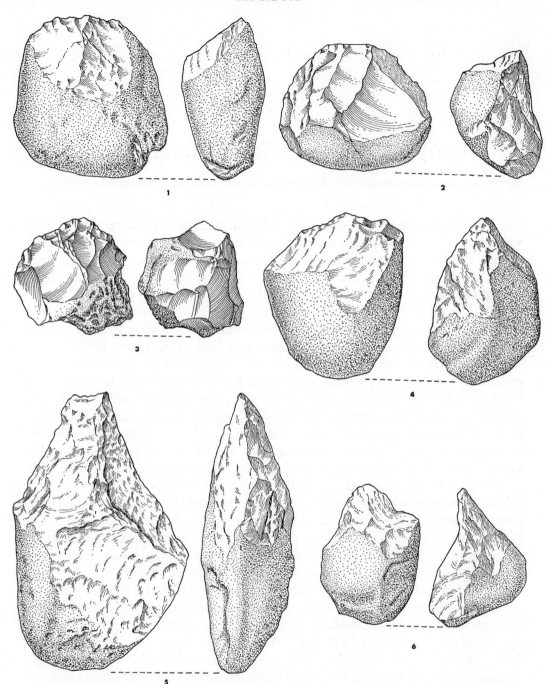

FIG. 13. Oldowan ½; Olduvai Gorge, Tanzania; 1–4 Bed I, 5–6 Bed I–II junction; 1–2, 4–6 lava; 3 chert. *After Leakey 1951*

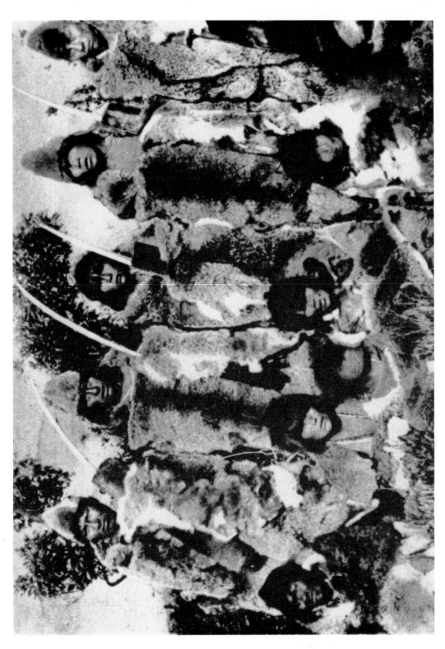

PL. I. Ona Indians of Tierra del Fuego who lived in conditions approximating those of Europe during the Last Glaciation. From 'Las Onas' by Carlos R. Gallarado by courtesy of the Director, Libreria Nacional del Colegio Buenos Ayres, and taken from *Uttermost Part of the Earth* by E. Lucas Bridges, Hodder and Stoughton, London, 1951

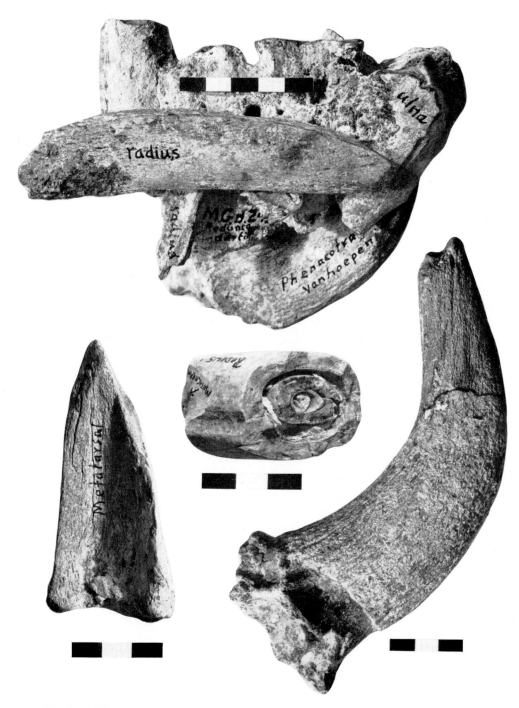

PL. II. Makapansgat, The Transvaal. Osteodontokeratic material. (Scales in centimetres.) Photographs by courtesy of Mr. A. R. Hughes and Professor P. V. Tobias, Department of Anatomy, University of the Witwatersrand, Johannesburg

Few such sites are in fact known at the present time. In North Africa, Aïn Hanech seems to qualify (p. 181), as does Ubeidiyeh in south-western Asia (p. 357). For sub-Saharan Africa, Olduvai Gorge presents indisputable evidence of a pre-handaxe tradition (p. 98), and other sites have been reported from east, central and south Africa. The tools in question consist of pebble choppers worked on both faces to form a sharp cutting edge (fig. 13). This irregular edge may lie at one end or along the side of the pebble. Large flakes were also retouched to produce a working edge suitable for cutting or scraping. Although some of these bear only traces of flaking on one face, all are now grouped under the term Oldowan, in view of the controversial nature of the evidence from 'Kafuan' sites. The tools have been classified into the following groups: choppers, protobifaces, polyhedrons, discoids, spheroids, scrapers, anvils, hammerstones and utilized flakes (M. D. Leakey 1967).

At the present time, Oldowan industries tend only to be accepted as such if they occur in association with animal remains, or in positions where flaking by natural means is excluded. This attitude allows only a very small proportion, how small we do not know, of sites to be acknowledged, and there seems little reason to assume only a limited distribution of this early manifestation of human activities. The recognition of pebble tools in north Africa, and in south-west Asia, probably too in Europe, must indicate the widespread nature of this tradition. We therefore believe that a large number of workshop and living sites must be incorporated in river gravels in east, south and central sub-Saharan Africa, and that further comparative work on *natural* flaking processes will eventually allow recognition of these artificially-flaked stones.

Recent work in Angola has demonstrated the presence of artefacts in the Oldowan tradition in contexts where some limited natural flaking might have taken place, but the artefacts are sufficiently developed in their typological characteristics to allow their recognition as manufactured tools. Associated with pebble and core choppers are small flake implements as at Olduvai. The larger tools were made on quartz and quartzite, the flake tools on chert. They are found in the 80–100 metre beach conglomerates of western Angola, from Luanda southwards to Baía Farta, and are believed to date to Middle Pleistocene times. At Baia Farta, unrolled Acheulean industries overlie the rolled Oldowan in the conglomerate (p. 103).

The evidence we have at the present time suggests that the Oldowan industries developed in sub-Saharan Africa during a remote period in the Pleistocene, dated by fauna to the Villafranchian, by the pluvial theory to the Kageran, and by absolute methods to between 2 and 1 million years ago. Oldowan-like tools continued to be made as integral parts of many later industries, as well as presumably playing an important role in the gradual evolution of the succeeding industrial tradition, the handaxe or Acheulean tradition.

Our information about the makers of the Oldowan industries is limited to one area in sub-Saharan Africa, Olduvai Gorge, and here the evidence suggests that it is likely that *Homo habilis* was the principal agency involved in this lithic industry

(Tobias 1965). In Bed I at Olduvai there are at least three levels which indicate the association of *Homo habilis* and stone tools. On one of these levels, *Australopithecus boisei* was also present, whether as a victim or collaborator is not certain. The numerous finds of *Homo habilis* at Olduvai have provided a quite remarkably complete picture of this early man. He stood about 4 feet tall, and had feet rather like those of modern man with a big toe in line with the other toes, and a transverse and longitudinal arch system. Although his hands are less aligned towards those of modern man than his feet, in that they were not capable of the 'precision grip', with opposed thumb and forefinger, nevertheless the finger tips were broad and stout with flat nails. The jaw of the *Homo habilis* was large and the teeth again closer to those of modern man than are Australopithecine teeth. The brain capacity of *Homo habilis* was nearly 700 c.c. The finds at Olduvai are estimated to cover a time range of one million years on the basis of potassium-argon dates, but those remains in Bed II are said to be distinct from those of Bed I in certain characteristics.

In addition to *Australopithecus boisei* from Olduvai Gorge, remains of Australopithecines have been recovered from other sites in east Africa, and from a number of sites in the Transvaal. No certain trace has been found outside sub-Saharan Africa. The first Australopithecine to be recognized was a skull recovered in 1924 from a cave deposit at Taung in the Transvaal. It was called *Australopithecus*, or the Southern Ape, and seemed to exhibit both simian and human features. In the succeeding 25 years, many more such remains were recovered from stalagmitic limestone deposits in the Transvaal, and a number of different generic names were given to them, *Plesianthropus*, *Paranthropus*, and *Australopithecus*. Recently, these fossil remains have been grouped into two genera, *Paranthropus* and *Australopithecus*. Because it has been suggested that the range of differences between these is not sufficiently great to warrant such a generic separation, we prefer to follow the view that groups all of these Transvaal finds under one genus, *Australopithecus*, with two species represented, *A. africanus*, and *A. robustus (Paranthropus)*.

The division of the southern *Australopithecus* into two species, *A. africanus* and *A. robustus*, is based upon many divergent features. *Australopithecus africanus* was a smaller creature, standing about 4 feet high and weighing 60–70 lb. The face was rather narrow with an arched forehead, and the canine and incisor teeth were large. *Australopithecus robustus*, in contrast, stood over 5 feet high, and weighed 130–150 lb. The face was relatively wide with little trace of a forehead, but there was a pronounced sagittal crest and supra-orbital ridge. The incisor and canine teeth were small, but the molar and premolar teeth were large. Because of the differences in dentition, it was formerly believed that *A. robustus* was mainly dependent on plants, a vegetarian diet, and the wear on the teeth suggested that this included the more gritty roots and bulbs. *A. africanus* may have been omnivorous and perhaps had a major dependence upon meat of one form or another. This dietary hypothesis has now been discarded.

The finds from east Africa, including those called *Zinjanthropus boisei* and *Meganthropus africanus*, have also been incorporated within the genus *Australo-*

pithecus; the latter is of *A. africanus* type, the former *A. boisei*. A current view is that ancestral forms to these species probably existed in sub-Saharan Africa during late Pliocene or early Pleistocene times; these are believed to have given rise to *A. boisei, A. africanus* and *Homo habilis* by the mid-Villafranchian. *A. robustus* appeared in middle Pleistocene times as a descendant of *A. boisei*; neither *A. boisei* nor *A. africanus* survived into the middle Pleistocene, but *Homo habilis* is considered to have survived to give rise to another species, *Homo erectus*. Such is the hypothesis founded upon recent studies of the materials from the Olduvai Gorge (Tobias 1967). Controversy has developed over the status of *H. habilis*, and another view is that possibly the differences between *H. habilis* and *A. africanus* have been over-emphasized, and that possibly these are single species from different geographical populations.

On both stratigraphical and faunal grounds, it appears that Kromdraai (The Transvaal) and a find in upper Bed II at the Olduvai Gorge represent the youngest deposits yielding Australopithecine remains; these are of the middle Pleistocene. Recent studies on the fauna from Olduvai Bed I indicate a Late Villafranchian age for *A. boisei* and *Homo habilis* remains (Leakey 1965). At the moment it is not possible to correlate the other South African Australopithecine sites with Olduvai Bed I, but opinions have been expressed that Taung and Sterkfontein Type Site antedate Bed I. All three sites seem to be of the late Villafranchian, and, as such, they indicate the presence of both *Australopithecus africanus* and *A. boisei* at this time. Recent finds in east Africa suggest an even earlier age for Australopithecines in this area. The other Transvaal sites, Makapansgat, Sterkfontein Extension Site, and Swartkrans, may be placed on faunal and geological grounds intermediate between the upper and lower limits, that is, near or at the boundary between the Lower and Middle Pleistocene. At the moment, there is no evidence that *A. africanus* survived in this form into Middle Pleistocene times. In recent years remains of Australopithecines have been reported from Koro Toro, Chad, and from the Omo valley, Ethiopia; details of the fauna associated with this material are not yet available, and the precise taxonomic position of the fossils remains to be established (Chavaillon 1967).

The first report of Australopithecine industrial activities was made in 1955 by Dart, who claimed that at Makapansgat he could recognize deliberate selection and fracture of bone, tooth and horn fragments (p. 103). Dart's Osteodontokeratic culture was elaborated in a series of publications, from which a number of significant facts emerge. Analysis of thousands of bones from the Makapansgat site shows evidence of selection of specific bones, and parts of bones; as an example, the ratio of proximal to distal pieces of humeri is 1 : 10, and that of femora to humeri is 1 : 5. At Makapansgat, and at Taung and Sterkfontein, 80% of baboon skulls had been battered by a blunt instrument. Examination of fragments of bone reveals traces of wear along certain edges (plate II). Occasionally, smaller bones and horn-cores have been found rammed into broken larger bones (plate II). It has been claimed that many of the long bones were broken by a twisting action. This apart, there appears to be suitable evidence that some agency of selection was at work at Makapansgat, and that the Osteodontokeratic industry has a valid existence (Tobias 1967a). Comparable material has not been recovered from Taung or Sterkfontein, but it may be that local circumstances have prevented their accumulation or recovery. At Swartkrans, faunal remains are not abundant, and this was originally taken to support the theory that *Australopithecus robustus* was primarily a vegetarian, and that perhaps he himself was the victim of a contemporary, *Telanthropus* (*?Homo erectus*), at this site.

The problem of an Australopithecine contribution to the manufacture of *stone* tools is less conclusive. At Makapansgat, fractured pebbles were reported in association with an Australopithecine bone near the top of the deposit, and undoubted stone tools were found with similar remains in the Sterkfontein Extension site. Olduvai Gorge, too, has yielded evidence for the contemporaneity of Australopithecines and stone tools. However, Robinson pointed out in 1962 that nowhere have Australopithecine remains and stone tools been found without some evidence for the presence of a more advanced hominid. At Olduvai Bed I, at least three levels yielding Oldowan tools have also revealed the remains of *Homo habilis*, with an associated Australopithecine at only one of these sites. At Taung, Makapansgat and Sterkfontein Type Site, *Australopithecus africanus* is present, but no stone tools have been found other than the disputed stones at Makapansgat. At Swartkrans, *Australopithecus robustus* is said to be associated with stone tools, but also with *Homo erectus* (*Telanthropus*). The Sterkfontein Extension Site, with indisputable stone artefacts (fig. 18), has yielded Australopicine teeth as well as teeth believed to be outside the range of variation for *Australopithecus*, and within that for *Homo habilis* (p. 102). No stone tools have been found with the other Australopithecine sites in south and east Africa.

A conclusion to be drawn from these facts is that it is likely that *Australopithecus* practised a form of industrial activity through selection and breakage of bone, tooth and horn fragments, but that he did not extend his range to the making of stone tools. The contemporary presence of advanced hominids at a number of sites suggests that *Australopithecus* may have been the victim of these industrially more advanced hominids.

Apart from one or two sites in south Africa, there is not much evidence to suggest that industries based upon the Osteodontokeratic principle continued to be made to the exclusion of stone as a primary source. At the site of Kalkbank in The Transvaal, implements of bone, in all respects comparable to those of the Osteodontokeratic industry, were produced by men apparently contemporary with the Pietersburg culture, but this site is an isolated example of an industry dominated by bone as the primary source of raw material. Nevertheless, it must be remembered that organic materials such as bone, horn and wood must have been commonly employed as ancillary sources to stone; the absence of suitable preservative conditions in many areas forces us into accepting stone artefacts as the dominant distinguishing element of industries.

Because of these conditions, we divide our material into groups, industries, based upon commonly-occurring stone tool types or assemblages of types. The Olduwan industry is the first of these that can be recognized, but it is unlikely that all those industries containing stone tools comparable to those at Olduvai Gorge are related to the Oldowan industry of east Africa. It is necessary to demonstrate the connection rather than to assume it.

The chronologically and typologically succeeding stone industries of sub-Saharan Africa are generally grouped together under the term Chelles-Acheul or Acheulean culture.

The terminology followed here involves the use of the term Acheulean in place of Chelles-Acheul, and instead of Earlier Stone Age. Recent publications have tended to avoid the necessity of distinguishing the supposed differences between Chellean and Acheulean handaxe industries. In sub-Saharan Africa, the Acheulean culture represents the first tradition that can be demonstrated to have a wide distribution both in space and time. Serious problems, however, exist both geographically and chronologically; mammalian fossils suitable for long-range correlations are very inadequately represented in many regions, and archaeological reconnaissance varies considerably over the enormous territories involved. Relative and absolute dating of these industries depends upon associated fauna and flora, and upon the suitability of other materials for ageing by geophysical methods. In all these respects, our knowledge of Acheulean man is inadequate.

As might be expected, the distribution of typologically earlier handaxe industries seems to be more restricted than is that of more developed handaxe traditions (fig. 19). In general terms, however, handaxe industries which might typologically be classified as in Early Acheulean traditions occur in the southern Cape, in the Vaal, Zambezi and Kasai River basins, and in eastern Africa at Olduvai and Olorgesailie, in the Victoria basin and in parts of the Western Rift valley (Clark 1967). There must be many contemporary sites in these regions, and in more northerly areas, which are not yet recognized or revealed through erosion of Middle Pleistocene deposits. Important sites for Early Acheulean industries include those at Olduvai Gorge (fig. 14–17, p. 98) and the Sterkfontein Extension Site (fig. 18, p. 102). There is some rather inconclusive evidence that industries typologically of this character were produced as far to the west as Angola, and to the north-west in Ghana (Davies 1964; p. 168). There is little evidence of coastal settlement at this time, but our state of knowledge is imperfect.

The developed Acheulean industries are much more widespread in sub-Saharan Africa, particularly in southern regions (fig. 19). Two elements must be involved here, the relatively later dating and hence greater chance of preservation, and the fact that such industries occur in riverine deposits which are particularly amenable for exposure through increased erosion following the end of a pronounced climatic episode of, generally, wetter conditions. Acheulean industries tend to be concentrated in areas of present-day grass or park savannah in eastern and southern Africa. All of these sites are located near water supplies, including a large number in certain local

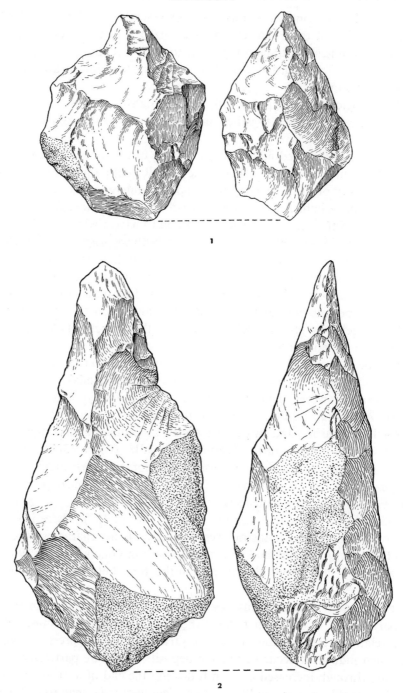

FIG. 14. Acheulean $\frac{1}{2}$; Olduvai Gorge, Tanzania; 1–2 probably Bed II; lava. *After Leakey 1951*

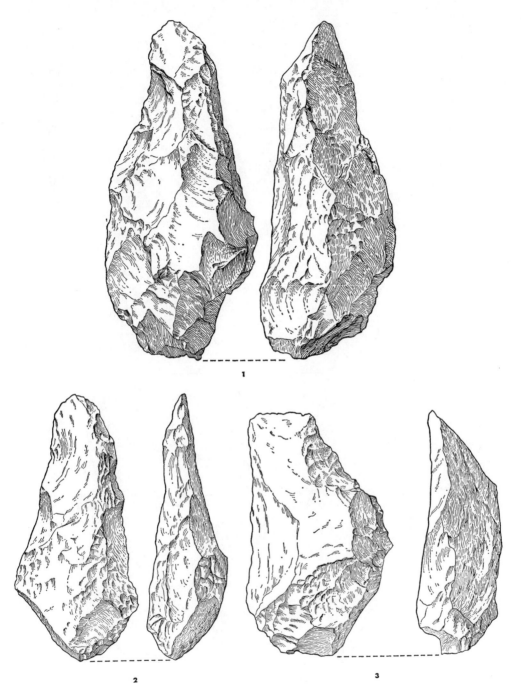

FIG. 15. Acheulean $\frac{1}{2}$; Olduvai Gorge, Tanzania; 1–3 Bed II; lava. *After Leakey 1951*

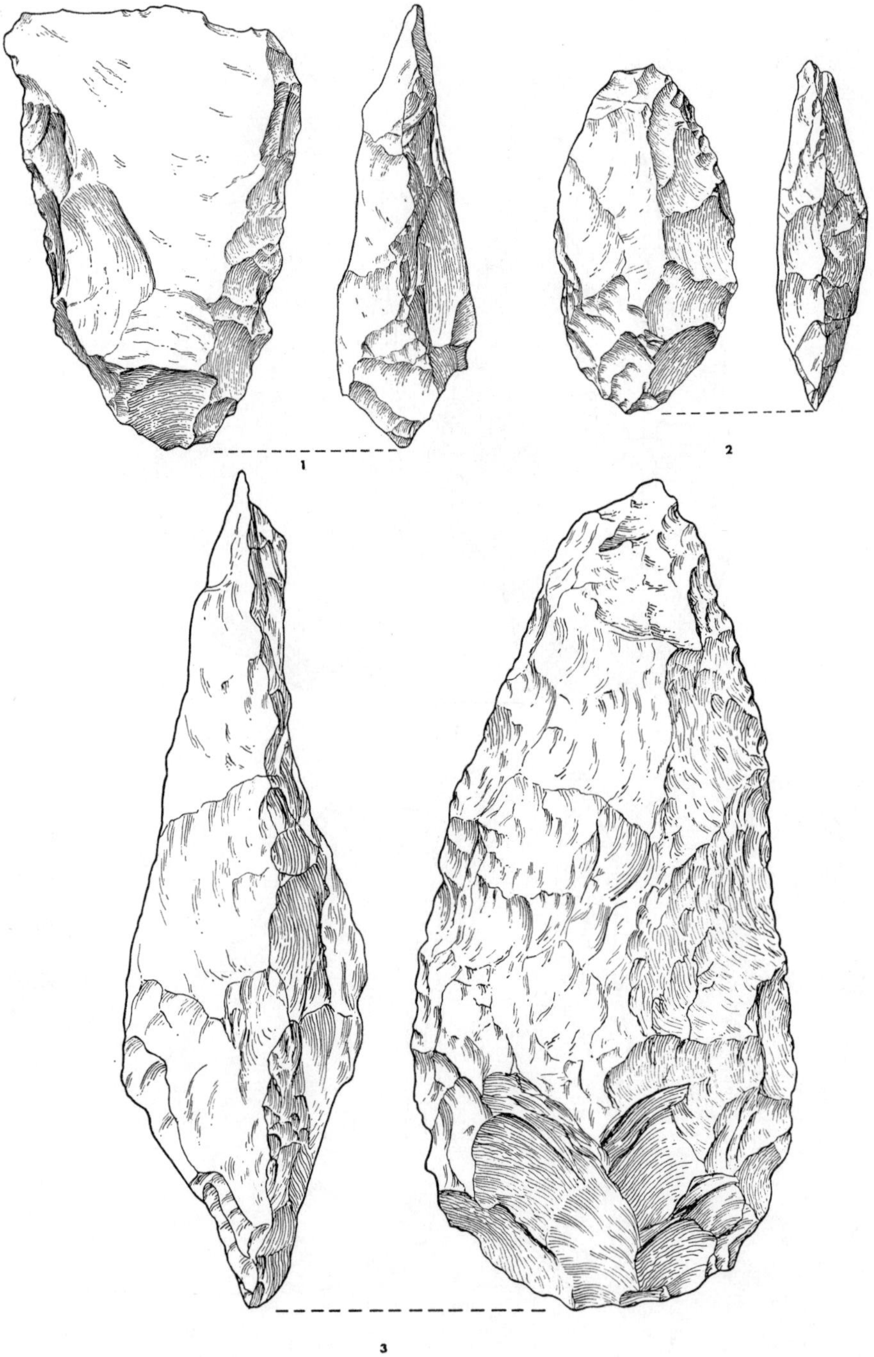

FIG. 16. Acheulean ½; Olduvai Gorge, Tanzania; 1–2 Bed IV, 3 Bed II; lava. *After Leakey 1951*

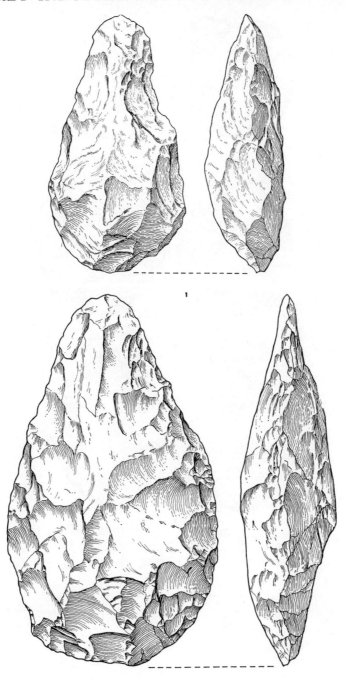

FIG. 17. Acheulean ½; Olduvai Gorge, Tanzania; 1–2 Bed IV; 1 lava, 2 quartz. *After Leakey 1951*

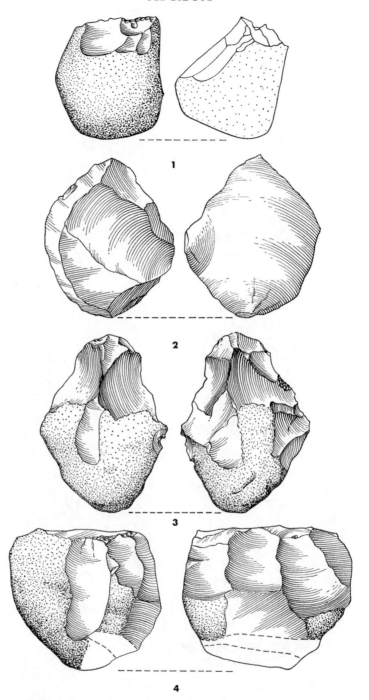

FIG. 18. Acheulean ½; Sterkfontein Extension, Transvaal. *After Mason 1962*

FIG. 19. Distribution of Oldowan △, Early Acheulean ○ and Late Acheulean ● in Africa. *After Clark 1967, overlays 12 and 13*

typographical situations where an increased rainfall would have been desirable. Few traces of Acheulean man have been found in arid regions, or in heavily forested areas. It is interesting to speculate upon the reasons for a spread of handaxe makers into the dry areas of the Horn and the Kalahari, as well as certain parts of the Sahara. Such occupations can only have been possible through an increase in rainfall of the order of 50% above that of today. Limited occupation of present forested country may indicate a reversal of conditions, a period when rainfall was perhaps only 75% of present-day rainfall in these regions.

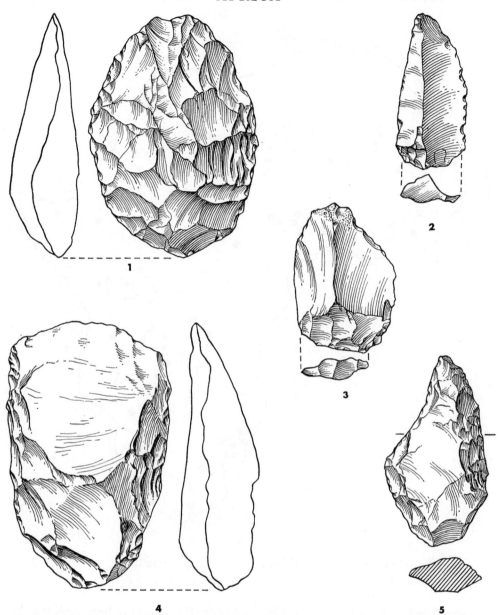

FIG. 20. Acheulean ½; Baía Farta, Angola. *After Clark 1966*

The absence of abundant cave or shelter sites in sub-Saharan Africa with associated Acheulean industries, allied with the general rarity of preserved floral and faunal remains, means that the dating of this phase of human activity must be dependent upon climatic interpretations of riverine deposits, whether erosional or depositional. Acheulean man does not seem to have been particularly attracted by coastal areas, and therefore the vital correlating link with marine levels is lacking. One of the few coastal sites occupied by Acheulean man is at Baía Farta in south-west Angola (fig. 20–21, p. 103). In general, many of the river systems of sub-Saharan Africa contain Acheulean material in their low terrace gravels, often covered by thick deposits of silts and sands which themselves contain the Fauresmith facies of the Acheulean in their upper part. Redistributed Kalahari Sands in Angola, Congo and

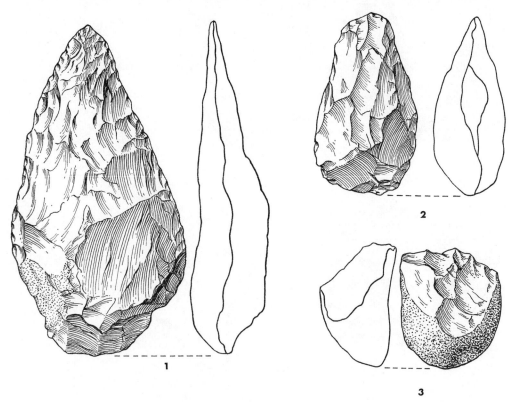

FIG. 21. Acheulean ½; Baía Farta, Angola. *After Clark 1966*

parts of Zambia and Rhodesia generally overlie Acheulean industries, with Sangoan-Lower Lupemban material contained within the sands.

One of the classic areas for the development of Acheulean traditions is the Vaal River system, where a series of Younger Gravels, sands and silts has been believed to contain a remarkably complete sequence of industries, from early Acheulean through to final Fauresmith (Clark 1959). In fact, the Vaal sequence is not at present capable of being employed to date its cultural material in terms of precise climatic fluctuations. The Zambezi gravels are also prolific in developed Acheulean industrial material. Natural hunting sites, such as gullies or gaps in ranges of hills, have often yielded evidence of hill and camp sites. One of these is the Wonderboom site where Acheulean man must have often camped during hunting expeditions (fig. 22–23, p. 104).

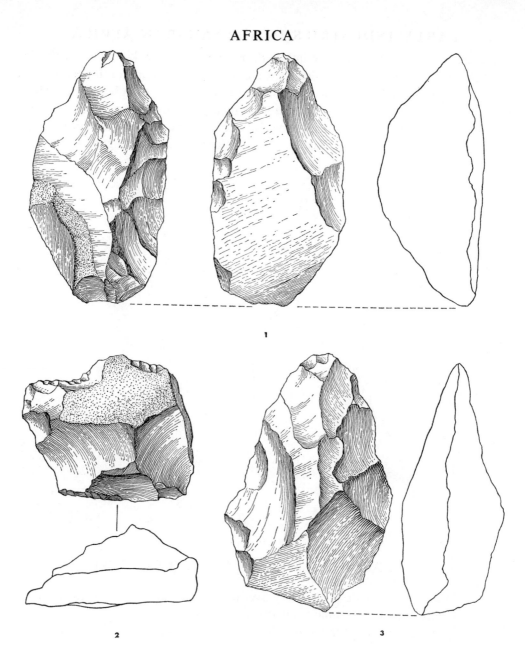

FIG. 22. Acheulean ½; Wonderboom, Transvaal. *After Mason 1962*

Of greater value to the prehistorians are assemblages recovered from undisturbed open stations, because these provide a fuller picture of the industrial specializations of early groups (Howell and Clark 1964). Such sites as those at Olduvai Gorge and Olorgesailie have yielded undisturbed material. At Olorgesailie, successive camps were probably sited on a peninsula jutting into the old lake of Olorgesailie, a lake which was reliant upon increased rainfall for its existence. The industrial material preserved

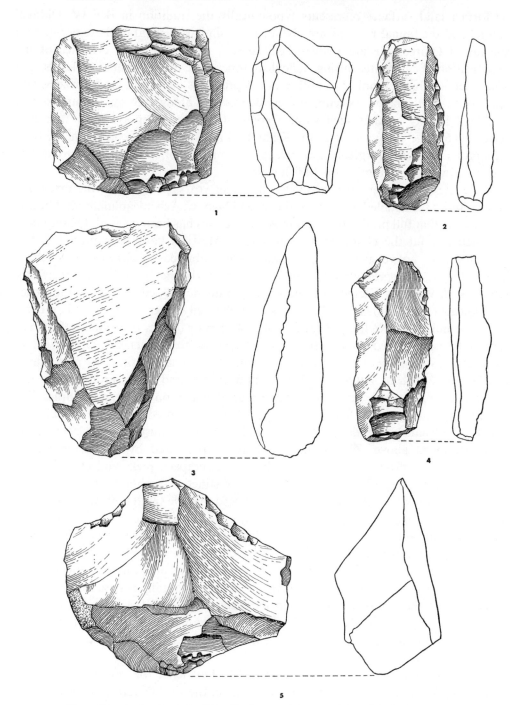

FIG. 23. Acheulean $\frac{1}{2}$; Wonderboom, Transvaal. *After Mason 1962*

on former land surfaces represents typologically the tradition in Bed IV, Olduvai Gorge, and the faunal remains are also broadly similar. Several of these occupation spreads at Olorgesailie are undisturbed, thereby providing some evidence of the organization of camp sites during Acheulean times. One of the occupation levels, in a sandy deposit, has a number of hollows or depressions in the old land surfaces, and much of the lithic material occurs in these depressions along with small rounded lava boulders. It may be that such stones represent flooring supports for windbreaks (Isaac 1966). The stone setting at the Kalambo Falls site is more conclusive (p. 105). At another level at Olorgesailie, an irregular semicircle of rounded lava stones has been interpreted as a simple form of fish weir.

These sites, and others also excavated in recent years, provide, for the first time, opportunities for detailed analysis of the assemblages of Acheulean material, but it is unfortunate that full publication of almost all the sites has been delayed. Quantitative statements about the characteristics of a few industries have been provided, but illustrations are not yet available. However, it seems abundantly clear that the Acheulean industry, as represented by collections from riverine gravels, is imperfectly represented. Work by Kleindienst and others on the developed Acheulean industries has indicated that handaxes and cleavers may play only a very minor role in a complete assemblage (Howell and Clark 1964). The major classes of stone artefacts are shaped tools, modified tools, utilized tools and waste. In general, three distinct Acheulean assemblages may be distinguished. One is characterized by many large cutting tools, such as handaxes, cleavers and knives, and waste products are not abundantly represented. Such industries occur at Kalambo Falls and Olorgesailie. Another assemblage has a few large cutting tools, and is predominantly a small tool industry with much attendant waste. Examples of such industries also occur at the sites mentioned above. The third assemblage, represented by an occupation at Isimila, consists of heavy-duty tools such as core-scrapers, picks and choppers. At the moment the significance of these three distinct assemblages has not been adequately assessed, although it has been suggested that the small tools were primarily implements for the working of wooden objects such as have been found at the Kalambo Falls site (p. 105). Also to be distinguished are seasonal and functional differences in industries, and differences in assemblages found on camp, kill or workshop sites. Quite basic variations may well represent only differing functions of the same groups of people, and it is evident that our grouping is based upon only a proportion of the equipment possessed by these people. At the moment, only the Acheulean occupation at the Kalambo Falls has been preserved sufficiently to allow us to appreciate the importance that wood, bark and other vegetable remains must have played in the economy.

The occupation site at Isimila has also revealed evidence for industrial activities, some carried out on the site and others away from the site. Differing concentrations of rubble with artefacts suggest that, on the one hand, small tools were produced on the site from imported raw material, and, on the other hand, large tools were gener-

Pl. III. Haua Fteah, Libya. Photo by courtesy of Dr. Charles McBurney

PL. IV. Swanscombe, England. Lower Middle Gravels and Upper Middle Gravels (mainly sands) with tags marking the horizon (at base of Upper Middle Gravels) from which the cranial bones were recovered. Photo: Director of Geological Survey. Rep. by permission of Controller of H.M. Stationery Office

ally made elsewhere; there is very little debris on these occupation surfaces which would result from the preliminary shaping of large blocks into cores for the production of large flakes suitable for these large tools. Supporting evidence has come from the discovery of a workshop or factory site where trimming flakes from blocks, and flake roughouts, are abundantly represented, but where there are very few finished tools.

Two major problems about these and other open sites still remain unsolved. The first is that we have little idea about the length of time that these sites were occupied, whether it was seasonal or irregular, whether it was over a time span of hundreds of years or merely a short period of perhaps only a month or so. The local climatic conditions that buried such occupation surfaces are also imperfectly understood. The second problem is that of subsistence, and here we are dependent upon varying conditions of preservation. At Isimila, little evidence of animal remains was found associated with artefactual material. The site at Olorgesailie allowed better preservation of fauna. On one land surface, horse, giraffe and antelopes seem to have been popular; other land surfaces yielded elephant and antelope, or baboon, horse, hippo and fish, or warthog, hippo and tortoise. Few other Acheulean sites have yielded such information; Olduvai Gorge is perhaps potentially the most important area in this connection, as animal bones are well preserved. In all cases, however, it is important to distinguish between those remains of animals killed or scavenged by humans, and remains left by carnivorous animals.

The evidence for the makers of handaxe industries is regrettably imperfect, and there are in fact only three finds of fossil human remains in sub-Saharan Africa that may plausibly be associated with the handaxe traditions. The earliest of these is the skull from Olduvai Gorge (Hominid 9), recovered from a deposit near the top of Bed II and broadly contemporary with an early Acheulean industry found some 100 metres away. The find consists of a calvarium lacking its face and basal part of the vault. The brow ridges are very prominent and the frontal region is flattened. This skull has been classed as *Homo erectus*. The mandibular remains from Swartkrans in the Transvaal have also been described as *Homo erectus*, although they are not associated with handaxe material.

Another find of fossil material which may be connected with the handaxe traditions is the Kanjera remains. At least four individuals are represented among the many cranial and post-cranial fragments. It is significant that, of these, three indicate the absence of a supra-orbital torus, and the fourth individual had only a moderate degree of brow-ridge development. The deposits in which a few fragments of these people were found are believed to be contemporary with Bed IV at the Olduvai Gorge although the evidence is imperfect (Tobias 1968).

At the Cave of Hearths, Makapansgat, a final Acheulean industry, contemporary with the Fauresmith tradition of South Africa (p. 108), was associated with a human mandible of robust form.

The distribution of industries in the Acheulean tradition is widespread in sub-

Saharan Africa, and although without doubt many regional and temporal facies may be demonstrated to exist after future research, for the moment all these industries incorporating handaxes and cleavers, sometimes in very small quantities, are grouped under the all-embracing term Acheulean. At the present time, evidence suggests that this traditional way of fashioning stone tools in sub-Saharan Africa was practised without interruption from early in the Middle Pleistocene to a period contemporary with the final major glacial advance in northern latitudes. Radiocarbon dates (Deacon 1966) from the Kalambo Falls site suggest Acheulean occupation between 60,000 and 50,000 years ago and dates in South Africa are younger still (fig. 3). By this time, or shortly thereafter, the overall industrial continuum was in the process of fragmentation into regional traditions, designed and adapted to meet changing environmental conditions. These may conveniently be discussed under five broad and partly overlapping geographical groups. In studying these traditions, the tendency has been to apply wholesale cultural names to assemblages from widely separated regions, although quantitative studies have already begun to indicate the wide divergences present within individual 'cultural' assemblages. The appellation of cultural terms to much of this material on the basis of one or two types may be a convenient method of describing the character of the industries, but should not be taken as indicating a linked community participating in traditional methods of subsistence.

OLDUVAI GORGE
(Hay 1967, Leakey 1951, Leakey 1965, M. D. Leakey 1967, Tobias 1967, 1967b)

Olduvai Gorge is a canyon or erosion gorge cut through the Pleistocene deposits of the Serengeti Plain at its south-east corner in Tanzania. The gorge consists of two branches, a Main Gorge running overall from west to east and served by water from a small lake, El'Garja, and a Side Gorge running south-west to north-east and serving as a drainage for the slopes of Mt. Lemagrut. The combined gorge runs eastwards to its end at the Balbal depression to the north-west of Ngorongoro.

The deposits, of fluviable, lacustrine and windblown origin with a series of volcanic tuffs, rest on a lava base. At the present time the deposits are divided into four Pleistocene beds, but recent work has indicated that it may be necessary to revise this division. During the Pleistocene, the succession of deposits was laid down in a shallow basin, some thirty miles by ten miles in maximum dimensions, near Ngorongoro and other volcanoes of the Rift valley. Subsequently, these deposits were exposed by a rapid erosion caused by the rejuvenation of a river flowing into the Balbal depression to the east. The maximum exposed thickness of the Pleistocene deposits is over 100 metres, and has recently been divided into two sequences, the earlier represented by the lowest Bed (I) and part of Bed II, generally without tectonic faulting, and the later represented by the upper part of Bed II, Beds III and IV. Bed

I consists of trachyte pyroclastic deposits and basalt flows up to over 120' in thickness, with a lower limit of about 40'. These volcanic fine-grained rocks and tuffs and conglomerates are especially well-represented on the eastern part of the Gorge, and they interfinger with the tuffaceous clays of a shallow lake on the west. The succeeding Bed, II, is marked primarily by the establishment of a saline lake, and the deposits consist of greenish clays and some tuffs, with indication of periodic flooding which extended the margin of the lake some 2 or 3 miles east of the normal edge. The lake basin was very gently shelving so that even minor fluctuations in water level would expose or cover quite considerable areas of land. Upon these exposed deposits early man made his temporary camps, and the relatively rapid flooding of the lake-side areas has covered and preserved the traces of these occupations. The lower lacustrine and fluviatile deposits of Bed II are said to be conformable with those of Bed I, and are overlaid by aeolian sands and weathered clays which indicate a drying period in this region.

The fauna recovered from Beds I and lower II has been published in considerable detail, although certain elements still remain to be examined more fully. In general, the assemblage from Bed I is believed now to be of Villafranchian age, probably of the late Villafranchian. The assemblage as a whole seems to be younger than that from Kanam and Kaiso, but older than the Omo fauna. Small mammals, birds and reptiles are well represented, particularly on the earlier camp sites, but larger mammals such as elephant, pig, antelope and carnivores, too, are also present in Bed I. Some of these are proboscideans, *Deinotherium* present throughout Bed I, *Elephas* cf. *africanus* in lower and early *Elephas recki* in upper Bed I. Bovids and giraffids, rodents, carnivores and primates are present, and various forms of pig (*Ectopotamochoerus* sp., *Promesochoerus* sp., *Notochoerus* sp., *Potamochoerus* sp., and *Tapinochoerus* sp.). In the upper part of Bed I the presence of gazelle, antelope and horse indicates a drier environment than that of the earlier deposits where damp-preferring creatures are common. The fauna of the lower part of Bed II is comparable in its general content to Bed I, and is probably of the end of the Villafranchian period.

The second sequence of deposits at Olduvai begins with torrent gravels succeeded by fluviatile and lacustrine deposits which partially interfinger with one another in the upper part of Bed II. Faulting late in the history of this sequence resulted in the establishment of a broad playa lake, the deposits of which are Beds III and IV. These deposits are separable from each other in the eastern area of the Gorge, where Bed III consists of reddish volcanic conglomerates and sandstones rather like smaller deposits in upper Bed II and in lower Bed IV. Geological considerations may indicate that the red bed, Bed III, was deposited under drier conditions. Bed IV is made up of waterlaid clays and marls, with some lenses of gravel and tuffs. Probably much of the lake's area was seasonally dry at this time, and the upper part of IV is of windblown tuffs representing accumulation during an arid period. Other faulting occurred at this time, and erosion of the gorge began.

The fauna of the second sequence apparently is appreciably different from that of

Bed I, and includes, in upper II, wet and swamp-preferring animals such as *Hippo* (*gorgops*). Also present are pigs (*Afrochoerus nicoli*, *Mesochoerus olduvaiensis*, *Potamochoerus majus*), giant sheep (*Pelorovis oldowayensis*), equids (*Equus oldowayensis*, *Stylohipparion albertense*) and carnivores, primates and rhinoceroses.

The sequence of climatic change proposed by Leakey and others then would begin with a wet phase of Beds I and lower II, dry in mid II, where erosion and therefore non-accumulation of deposits may be indicated, then a flooding episode in upper II, followed by the drier Bed III before the lake reasserted itself in Bed IV. The overall Pleistocene climate may in fact have been somewhat comparable to conditions of today in east Africa, but it is uncertain if the fluctuations represented at Olduvai represent widespread (climatic) change or local (topographical) conditions. Although it is unlikely that tropical Africa would have experienced *no* climatic alterations while in the northern latitudes the glaciations were undergoing expansion and contraction on a major scale, the *nature* of such climatic change in tropical regions, whether or not it took the form of correlating pluvials and interpluvials, is not easily recognizable, and it may be that erosion and desiccation were the main agencies. The deposits at Olduvai are complex, and it may be that their division into four Pleistocene Beds, as proposed by Leakey in his 1951 publication, is oversimplifying the problem. It seems evident that many of the conclusions reached in this early publication are now untenable, due it must be added to Leakey's own subsequent work. These include a complete reassessment of the fauna, the recognition of a major geological, faunal and cultural break within Bed II, and the realization that the developmental sequence of industrial traditions is far more complex and involved than the simple one proposed in 1951. As the excavations have not yet been reported in detail, critical evaluation of the interpretation of the relationships between sites in the gorge is not yet possible.

The dating of the deposits at Olduvai has been given fresh impetus by the potassium-argon method, which has yielded dates of the order of 1·9 to 1·6 million years from three volcanic horizons in Bed I. A date of 0·5 million years for upper Bed II may not be stratigraphically reliable. A fission track date of *c.* 2 million years has been obtained from the ignimbrite in Bed I.

The hominid remains from the sites in the Gorge are remarkably abundant. Over one dozen finds have been made since 1955, some associated with industrial material. Perhaps the best known is the skull of *Australopithecus* (*Zinjanthropus*) *boisei* found in 1959 at Site FLK I about 22 feet below the top of Bed I, and associated with stone tools and a fauna including small amphibia, rodents, reptiles and fish. A second form, called *Homo habilis*, was discovered in 1960 at FLK NNI, and there have been subsequent finds. The original *H. habilis* remains came from a deposit about 14″ below that of *Australopithecus boisei*, some 300 yards away from FLK I, and were associated with stone tools, a bone tool, and a fauna of tortoises, catfish and aquatic birds. Other remains of *Homo habilis* have been more recently discovered at FLK I, the same site and level where *Australopithecus boisei* was found, and at MK I which is a site near the base of Bed I. At a site contemporaneous with MK I, called DK I, a semicircle of loosely-piled lava blocks may represent a shelter occupied by *Homo habilis*.

The hominids from Bed II are also relatively abundant, and include finds originally classified as *H. habilis* from the lower part of Bed II. In the upper part of Bed II, subsequent to the major break, at LLK II, Leakey found a calvarium in 1960 which seems to fall within the *Homo erectus* group. A contemporary deposit some 100 yards away yielded a handaxe industry and animal remains. In addition, a molar tooth of certain Australopithecine status was recovered from the upper part of Bed II.

The cultural material from Olduvai was described in Leakey's 1951 book, where, under a simplified scheme, two main groups of material were postulated. The first of these, the Oldowan culture, was represented in Bed I, and the other, the Chelles-Acheul culture, in Beds II to IV. Since this time, however, more detailed work on the early industries has indicated that the major cultural change occurs at the break in sequence in Bed II (M. D. Leakey 1967). The cultural material from the first sequence of deposits, Bed I and lower Bed II, is said now to represent one tradition in which the principal diagnostic tool is made on blocks or pebbles (fig. 13). These have been flaked to produce irregular but sharp flake-scar intersections, and probably were employed mainly as choppers. Many of these tools bear signs of utilization. Flakes may have been used as cutting or scraping tools. The material of these implements is lava and quartz, both of which were available quite near the camping sites either as extrusions or as river-transported material. Also present on the occupation floors are unretouched and unutilized stones, which must however have been carried by man to the sites. These are sometimes called 'manuports'. Many of the implements have been classified under such names as choppers, scrapers, discoids, spheroids, polyhedrons and burins, but some forms tend to merge into one another, particularly as the raw material is limited in its potential degree of flaking precision. Certain of the choppers from Beds I and lower II, for instance, are now considered as proto-handaxes, with flaking along both sides and pointed end, and with a thick butt.

The industrial material from the middle and upper Bed II contains equipment of Oldowan character, coarse handaxes of 'Chellean type', a term now to be discarded from African terminology, as well as some axes that have a cutting edge all the way around and that would normally be called Acheulean (fig. 14–15); these have more extensive secondary trimming than the typologically earlier forms. Three types of industry have been recognized, a developed Oldowan, an Acheulean, and a combination of the two; it is now considered that the Acheulean industries were intrusive, and had not developed *in situ* from the Oldowan. The handaxe industries of Beds II, III and IV show the presence of Acheulean traditions in East Africa from early Middle Pleistocene times until a time probably in the late Pleistocene. Cleavers appear for the first time in the Acheulean of Bed II, and by Bed IV times the handaxes, pointed, ovate or lanceolate, are very finely flaked from quartzite or lava flakes (fig. 16–17), and the cleavers are more symmetrical in cross-section (fig. 16, 1). Certain variations in these industries must represent either the alternating presence of different groups or seasonal and functional differences. In the uppermost levels of Bed IV, the industry is highly evolved, and there are certain standardized forms of flake tools as well as axes and cleavers.

STERKFONTEIN
(Robinson and Mason 1962)

The Sterkfontein Valley lies about 20 miles north-west of Johannesburg in the southern part of The Transvaal. Within the valley there are at least three important Pleistocene sites wherein hominid material has been found. Of these sites, Sterkfontein, Kromdraai and Swartkrans, only the first-named has yielded undisputed evidence of Pleistocene activity in the form of stone artefacts. Like the other sites in The Transvaal, Sterkfontein lies in a formation of dolomitic limestone. Within the Dolomite series are a large number of caverns, and the enlargement of these by percolatory water and by collapse along bedding planes generally results in the cavern and its filling becoming exposed to the surface. The original Sterkfontein site consists of an exposure of cave-brecciated sediments some 175′ in length and as much as 45′ in width. The north-western part of this fissure exposure is called the Type Site, and it is from here that a majority of hominid material has been recovered. The Extension Site lies farther west and overlaps with the Type Site deposits. The stratigraphy is as follows: The Type Site deposits consists mainly of a reddish Lower Breccia, from the upper levels of which has been recovered almost all the Australopithecine remains and an extensive fauna. Overlying the Lower Breccia to the west is the red-brown Middle Breccia and this breccia extends into the Extension Site. From this deposit at the Extension Site has come the stone industry and a few traces of remains, mainly teeth, originally said to be of Australopithecine character. Recent work at Sterkfontein has indicated that the breccias were separated in time by an unconformity. Work by Brain suggests that the climate was not uniform during the time when these breccias were being deposited, but the problem of absolute dating, and even relative dating with other sites, is still open to discussion.

The fauna from the Type Site includes *Parapapio jonesi*, *P. broomi* and *P. whitei*, *Canis mesomelas pappis*, *Crocuta brevirostris*, *Procavia antiqua*, *Gazella wellsi*, and insectivores and rodents. *Equus* is reported only from the Extension Site.

The artefacts recovered from the Extension Site, and not in association with the bulk of Australopithecine remains, form an industry that may be said to indicate that the tradition of handaxe-making was present in the Sterkfontein Valley at this time. One complete axe (fig. 18, 3), and part of another, were found along with choppers, flakes and a spheroid (fig. 18, 1, 2, 4). The tools and flakes are made on diabase, quartzite and chert. Of the 286 stone objects reported, 59 are tools, 39 are cores and the others include flakes and natural pebbles, all, however, brought into the site by some carrier, whether Australopithecine or not.

MAKAPANSGAT

One bone artefact is reported from this middle breccia. It is made on a split bone with a sharp point, and there are two polished surfaces on the tapering sides.

MAKAPANSGAT
(Dart 1957, Mason 1965, Tobias 1965, Tobias 1967a)

The Makapansgat Limeworks Dump lies on the south side of the Makapan valley in The Transvaal. The site consists of a large cavern in the dolomitic limestone filled with consolidated breccia which is exposed to the surface by the erosion and dissolution of much of the cave roof. There are two main breccias represented in these deposits, and it is from the lower part of the basal breccia (Lower Phase I) that the major finds have come. A number of Australopithecine remains were found with a fauna which includes *Simapithecus darti*, *Parapapio jonesi*, *P. broomi* and *P. whitei*, *Crocuta* cf. *brevirostris*, *Hyaena makapani*, *Equus helmei* and many antelope, gazelle, giraffe and pig. This assemblage is in general considered appropriate to an early stage of the Australopithecine sites, perhaps roughly contemporary with Sterkfontein, of the upper Villafranchian.

Among the vast accumulation of animal remains, Dart and others have recognized a number of bone, tooth and horn fragments which they believe to have been utilized as tools and weapons (plate II). Over 100,000 pieces of bone have been recovered from this site, and appear to reveal consistent patterns of breakage. Tooth-marks of hyaena, leopard and porcupine are represented only on a small proportion of these broken bones, which incidentally must themselves form a small fraction of the unexcavated deposits in the cave. The ratio of humeri to femora is 5 : 1, and that of proximal to distal humeral pieces is 1 : 10, and these ratios must indicate some agency of selection. Differential wear on certain edges or ends of bones, and a broad similarity of piece-shapes, allowing the distinction of general classes of bone, have prompted Dart to recognize these as daggers, scoops, ripping tools, etc. There is little doubt that some agency was at work here, and the presence of *Australopithecus* suggests that it was responsible for this activity. Recently it has been claimed that certain stalactitic fragments, and dolomite and chert pieces, were used as tools or slightly modified to make tools. A few shale and quartzite fragments must have been transported into the cave from outside, but bear no signs of utilization.

BAÍA FARTA
(Clark 1966)

The prehistoric site of Baía Farta lies in the south-west of Angola, in an area of present-day desert to semi-desert conditions, Palaeobotanical studies indicate that in late Pleistocene times temperatures in central Africa were lowered on average by 4°

or 5° Centigrade, and that rainfall increased. Such conditions would have made south-western Angola a more favourable region for settlement, and must account for the abundance of evidence for man's presence in the Moçâmedes desert and at Baía Farta. The occupation at Baía Farta consists of a workshop site resting upon the conglomerate of a marine platform approximately 100 metres above present sea level, covered by red argillaceous sands. Most of the stone tools recovered are on quartz, with some on chert and quartzite. All of this material was readily available in the form of pebbles or cobbles in the 100 metre conglomerates. The industry (fig. 20–21) is in a late Acheulean tradition, with ovate (fig. 20, 1) or lanceolate handaxes (fig. 21, 1) shaped by the cylinder-hammer technique, associated with some coarser sub-triangular specimens. Cleavers, made on large flakes and with U-shaped butts (fig. 20, 4), and pebble choppers (fig. 21, 3), also occur. Most of the flakes are irregular with plain platforms, and seem to have been struck off by some form of anvil technique. Bifacial retouch on flake edges, opposite to the bulb, formed knives, and there are some unifacially-retouched tools classed as scrapers. This Acheulean industry represents one of the relatively few examples of early settlement on the western sea coasts of Angola. Other finds have been made in association with a 25–35 m. beach. The evidence surviving suggests that it was only favourable climatic and environmental conditions that would have persuaded Acheulean man to extend his occupation into this region. It has been suggested that the coastal areas of Angola supported an environment comparable to that of highveld grasslands, an environment eminently suitable for Acheulean exploitation. The increasing evidence for coastal settlement in this region contrasts strangely with the relative lack of Acheulean occupation of the eastern coasts of tropical Africa.

WONDERBOOM
(Mason 1962)

The stone-using hunters of Sterkfontein represent the earliest known occupation of The Transvaal, at a time which may be well back in the Middle Pleistocene. Although there is abundant evidence for the continued existence of handaxe makers in The Transvaal, it is only the later stages of this tradition that have survived undisturbed the extensive erosion and re-sorting of materials in later Pleistocene times. Typologically earlier industries are reported from Klipplaatdrif, and the Riverview Estates collections in The Transvaal, but only the later and final episodes of the Acheulean tradition are represented in stratified and undisturbed deposits.

At Wonderboom a very large quantity of artefacts was recovered from the floor of a shallow valley, representing occupation near a low ridge on the southern side of the valley where raw materials were available as weathered quartzites. The occupation here occurred over an area some 76 m. by 9 m., and most of the artefacts appear to have suffered little or no transport by natural agencies. The 3 metres of occupation deposit cannot be dated other than by typological means, and must represent inter-mittent settlement near a natural gap in the barrier hills of the Magaliesberg range. The hills rise to over 350 m. above the plateau, and formed a barrier between the Vaal River valley and the bushveld to the north. The Wonderboompoort is one of six gaps in these hills over a length of 130 km. (80 miles).

The excavation of the occupation deposit at Wonderboom revealed no strati-graphical division between the artefacts which occurred throughout the 3 metres of deposit. Handaxes were very rare, as were cleavers (fig. 23, 3), and a majority of the tools consisted of irregular flakes, some with blunting retouch or uneven retouch (fig. 23, 2, 4), and heavier choppers made on thick natural slabs (fig. 22, 2; 23, 1, 5). Typologically it has been shown that this industry is similar in its overall proportions to that from Bed 3 of the Cave of Hearths.

KALAMBO FALLS
(Howell and Clark 1964)

The prehistoric site of Kalambo Falls lies at the south-eastern end of Lake Tangan-yika, where the Kalambo River drains westwards through a short (500') deep gorge and falls over 700' into the Rift escarpment. Above the falls is an area some 2 miles square which is surrounded by low (600') hills of quartzite; the basin contained by these hills was occupied for short periods during late Pleistocene times. One of the reasons for this must have been the plentiful supply of quartzite and chert for the manufacture of tools, as both the gorge and other exposures of these materials are available. Archaeological investigation in the Kalambo basin has been carried out intermittently since 1953 by J. D. Clark.

This work has shown that the level of water in the Kalambo basin fluctuated on several occasions from early in the upper Pleistocene, perhaps due to the temporary blocking of the drainage gorge with gravel and stone from the valley sides. Subsequently the gorge would be partially cleared by torrential conditions of rainfall or other events. During periods when the gorge was blocked, the Kalambo river would pond, and high water conditions would develop, perhaps swampy at the edges and with open water nearer the centre of the valley. During conditions of adequate drainage, the river would cut down into the lake-deposited sediments.

These sediments cover a wide area of the basin, particularly to the north and west, and range from fine-grained deposits in the north-western part of the basin, to coarse-grained and boulder deposits in the eastern part, where the river enters the basin. It is estimated that these sediments, or 'Lake Beds', may extend to some 30' below the present level of the Kalambo River, and they occur in the other direction up to 79' above the river level, particularly to the north where a cliff has been formed by these deposits. In the central part of the basin most of the sediments have been removed by erosion.

The sequence of deposits in the Lake Beds exhibits at least 4 important phases of erosion, represented by disconformities within the sand and gravel sediments. These disconformities represent breaks in time between some of the major industrial traditions at Kalambo, between the Acheulean and the Sangoan, between the early and later 'Middle Stone Age', and within the Magosian and later industries. Cultural materials have been recovered from approximately 2′ below present low-water level up to near the top of the 70′ high deposits lying above the river level. At the moment we do not know if the industrial remains extend any deeper within the unexplored sediments that extend well below the present water level.

The industrial sequence at the Kalambo Falls site may be summarized as follows: at the base of the known deposits is a series of fine and coarse sands, clays and gravels within which have been found a number of sand or fine gravel surfaces with occupation debris. These represent short-lived settlements by Acheulean man during times when the water level in the basin was low; the occupation floors are thin and are adjacent to former watercourses. Such sands and gravels with settlement debris are separated from each other in a stratified sequence by lenses of peat-filled clays with quantities of carbonized wood, from tree trunks to twigs and leaves. Seed pods, seed stems and fruits have also been preserved by the waterlogging conditions. This material has allowed full use of palaeobotanical studies, and conclusions bearing on environmental and climatic conditions have been produced. During the occupation of the area by Acheulean man, the climate was, in general, cooler and wetter than that of today; the earliest of the known deposits indicate temperatures similar to those of the present time, but cooler conditions gradually developed. The immediate environment of the site must initially have been moist forest bordered by savannah trees, with less dense woodland cover, and increased grasses, near the end of Acheulean times.

The vegetation in general has been compared to that at present offered in the region at altitudes of 4,000′ to 5,000′; the Kalambo Falls site lies between 3,200′ and 3,500′. The preservation qualities of the site have also allowed radiocarbon determinations to be made, and one of the Acheulean occupation floors, near the middle of this series, has been dated by this method to 57,300 ± 300 B.P.

The upper two Acheulean floors have yielded extensive collections of artefacts, but the lower industries are less abundantly represented. Most of the equipment is in fresh condition, although there is apparently some dulling of fine edges on the stone tools in the lower levels where water action has been prolonged. The importance of the Acheulean occupations at Kalambo lies in the fact that they are to all intents and purposes intact and undisturbed. We might therefore expect to distinguish areas within each occupation where specialized activities were carried out. Concentrations of handaxes and cleavers occur, without accompanying large flakes and cores, and this must indicate that these implements were made elsewhere and transported to the camping site. Abundantly represented, however, are small flakes produced during the final shaping of the large tools, or from repeated resharpening of these tools. Smaller implements, made on chert flakes, were produced on the spot and are associated with cores and waste. These small tools include a few points, many scrapers and other less regularly shaped artefacts with rather steep retouch.

Some large boulders are also present on certain of the Acheulean occupation floors and must have been deliberately transported to the site. Some were used as anvils, other smaller ones might have acted as hammerstones and pounders. Most of this stone material was locally available to the campers, but a few rolled quartzite pebbles may only have been available for collection some miles to the west.

Of considerable interest is the discovery made by the excavators of an arc of stones which seems to represent the surviving traces of a windbreak or primitive shelter. The area enclosed by the arc is over 2 metres in overall length from one end of the stone line to the other, and the depth of the curve is about 1 metre. Inside this setting the floor was virtually clear of tools and waste.

Another important discovery made on these Acheulean occupation levels at Kalambo is a range of equipment made from organic matter, preserved by water-logging. Fire was employed to shape and to harden wooden digging sticks, club-like implements and other forms. One of the clubs has a slender shaft and widened short head. Logs of wood were burnt, and at least one hearth has been found. Presumably fire was used not only to help in the shaping of wooden tools but also for warmth, possibly for cooking meat, and for protection from animals.

Two of the later Acheulean occupation floors at Kalambo also yielded traces of oval-shaped shallow depressions, measuring about 100 cm. by 60 cm. and 6 cm. deep in the central area. These were filled with compressed grass stems and plants, which probably represent carbonised bedding materials.

Above the Acheulean industries at this site is a long series of sand and gravel deposits, interrupted by erosional disconformities, and containing a number of industries of Sangoan, Lupemban, Magosian and Later Stone Age character. These are not yet published in detail, but undoubtedly will provide remarkably detailed information about the sequence of industrial traditions in this area. A number of radiocarbon dates have been obtained from associated material with these industries, which indicate Sangoan occupation c. 40,000 B.P., later Lupemban from 30–27,000 B.P., and developed Magosian c. 9,500 B.P.

6

South Africa

An industry in south Africa developed from the final Acheulean tradition is the Fauresmith (Clark 1959). This industry might better be grouped with Acheulean traditions. In southern Africa the Fauresmith is generally found in open country, particularly on high plateau regions, where the dominant raw material available was indurated shale. This stone was well suited for the production of the characteristic small pointed handaxes (fig. 24, 1) although cleavers continued to be made on diabase stones (fig. 24, 2). Other tools commonly found on Fauresmith sites include flake scrapers, often rather broad with retouch along one side, long blades and chisel flakes. The handaxes may be almond-shaped or pointed, but wider forms also occur. Many of the tools have step-retouch, and it has been suggested that this method is in contrast to the cylinder-hammer scale-method of developed Acheulean industries. The cores used for the production of large or small flakes were prepared by shaping the core in discoid fashion.

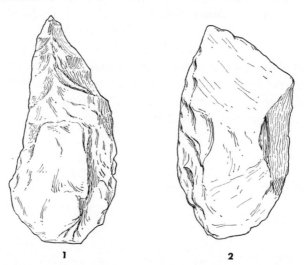

1   2

FIG. 24. Fauresmith (Late Acheulean) ¾; Elandsfontein, South Africa; 1 handaxe; 2 cleaver. *After Singer and Crawford 1958*

Regional differences in the Fauresmith industries of south Africa tend to be based upon varying raw materials. In parts of the northern Transvaal, quartz and quartzites were apparently used, and the tools are therefore somewhat coarser in appearance. In the southern Transvaal, diabase and quartzite were employed as well as shale. At the site of Saldanha in the Cape, a Fauresmith-related industry (fig. 24) was on silcrete, quartzite, porphyry and sandstone (p. 128). This site provides reasonably conclusive evidence that the makers of at least some Fauresmith industries were of *Homo sapiens rhodesiensis* type, occasionally termed African Neanderthaloid. The remains consist of a calvaria and a fragment of a mandible. The cranium has a low vault and large brows, and is probably the earliest of at least four large-browed forms from sub-Saharan Africa. The others are crania from Florisbad, Broken Hill and Lake Eyasi.

Fauresmith industries are abundant in the republic of South Africa, and Basuto-land, with some extensions into south-west Africa and Bechuanaland; there is some trace in Natal (fig. 25).

In south Africa a divergent development from the Acheulean resulted in the gradual emergence of an industrial tradition called the Sangoan (Clark 1950). The Sangoan is basically a central African culture of wooded regions, but it is unlikely that it was in the equatorial forests of the Congo Basin that this first distinct stage towards occupation of a closed landscape was developed. Although the Sangoan seems to have been developed as a response to the need to cope with wooded areas, recent climatic dating has suggested that it developed only at a time when conditions had recently become cooler and wetter. If such dating is correct, the traditional view that the Sangoan developed due to increasing aridity, forcing man to press into more wooded country, is incorrect, and we might look for alternative explanations for the emergence of this industry. It is unlikely that Sangoan man ever penetrated into dense equatorial forest; wooded savannah regions were the focal areas. It is probable that changes in environmental conditions at the onset of the Gamblian pluvial were slight, and we might even think of population pressures at this remote time. The distribution of Sangoan industries is wide, with a central area in the expanses between the Zambezi and Lake Victoria, including parts of the Katanga (fig. 25). It remains to be revealed whether or not the Sangoan industries of south Africa represent borrowings from the north, or a local parallel development through comparable economic or environmental circumstances.

In south Africa, the Sangoan industry has a limited distribution, with particular concentrations north of the Limpopo River and in Natal. A number of regional variants have been distinguished, called the Zambezi, Bembezi, Luangwa and Tugela facies. The characteristic Sangoan artefacts of central Africa, crude heavy picks (fig. 26, 1), heavy handaxes (fig. 27, 1, 3), choppers on pebbles, and large circular high-backed implements called push planes (fig. 26, 3) are present in the south African groups but in varying quantities. The Zambezi variant of the upper Zambezi valley has less-developed forms of pick but the handaxes were flaked into pointed shapes. The Luangwa variant (p. 129) in the middle Zambezi valley and the Luangwa

FIG. 25. Distribution of Sangoan ●, Fauresmith ○, Acheuleo-Leval-loisian ■ and Levallois-Mousterian ▲ industries in Africa. *After Clark 1967, overlays 14 and 15*

basin is characterized by the use of quartzite cobbles, and the heavy equipment of pick, handaxe and push plane is generally flaked on one face only (fig. 26–27). In western Rhodesia and northern Botswana the Bembezi variant may have been developed to cope with a more open landscape than were the Zambezi and Luangwa facies. Handaxes are generally heavy, but finer examples occur. Picks are rarely found, but small flake blades and scrapers made on silicified sandstone are abundant.

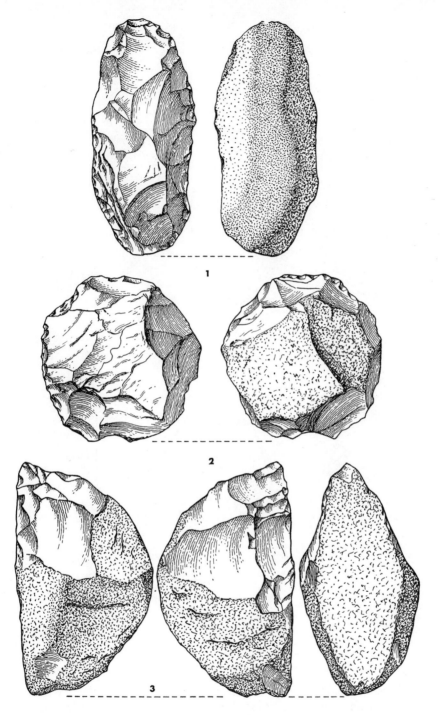

FIG. 26. Sangoan $\frac{1}{2}$; 1–2 Chikunka, Isoka, Luangwa valley, Zambia; 3 Mpangala, Luangwa valley; 1 pick, 2 disc core, 3 high-backed pick or push-plane. *After Clark 1950*

111

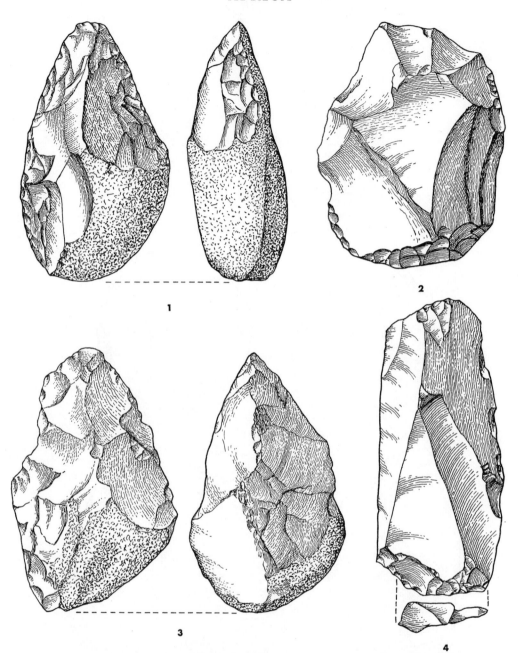

FIG. 27. Sangoan $\frac{1}{2}$; 1 Zimbo river, Luangwa valley, Zambia; 2 Kavengulo river, Luangwa valley, Zambia; 3 Chikunka, Luangwa valley, Zambia; 4 Mpangala, Luangwa valley, Zambia; 1 unifacial axe, 2 flake scraper, 3 handaxe, 4 flake-blade. *After Clark 1950*

In southern Mozambique, the Sangoan industry occurs on quartzite cobbles, with flake handaxes, picks and choppers, and flake tools as the characteristic forms. The Natal Sangoan is a coastal variant, and picks and handaxes form the bulk of heavy equipment; flake blades and scrapers are also common.

The succeeding industrial traditions in south Africa are varied in detail, but most exhibit a common basis in their general approach to artefact production. In Rhodesia and Botswana the proto-Stillbay industry had developed by *c.* 35,000 years ago (fig. 3), at a time of drier conditions following the wetter period of Sangoan occupation. The proto-Stillbay industry of Rhodesia includes unifacially-worked points and scrapers, some rather large handaxes or choppers, and a few thick bifacially-retouched points. In general terms this is often considered as an unspecialized industry, and it was just such an assemblage that was associated with *Homo sapiens rhodesiensis* in the cave at Broken Hill. This fossil has recently been studied, and it is not considered to represent a late, specialized variant of an ancestral stock of modern African types. The remains consist of a skull, a maxilla and fragments of cranial and post-cranial bone. The cranium is heavily built with very massive brow ridges, a flat vault and receding forehead. The post-cranial bones have few features distinct from the range of variation in modern man. The limb bones appear to belong to a tall individual. These remains, and those from Eyasi, Saldanha and Florisbad, are believed to represent a late specialization of a basic *Homo sapiens* stock which itself had developed from a pithecanthropine stock.

Typologically the proto-Stillbay, such as was found in the Bambata Cave of Rhodesia (fig. 28, 6–10; p. 130) has links with the Stillbay industry, also represented at Bambata (fig. 28, 1–5; fig. 29). The Stillbay contains bifacial and unifacial leaf-shaped points with thinned butts, and triangular points as well (fig. 29). Crescents (fig. 28, 2), scrapers (fig. 28, 3) and burin-like tools (fig. 28, 5) also occur.

In The Transvaal, the Pietersburg tradition is contemporary with the Stillbay industries to the north and south (Mason 1962). Pietersburg material occurs in caves and shelters, or is exposed in dongas of the northern Transvaal. It appears to be effectively restricted in distribution to The Transvaal, but in general it has much in common with the Stillbay traditions of Rhodesia. Quartzite flakes and blades, including some produced by a prepared core technique, mark the early stage of the Pietersburg, but in the later stages felsite, shale, silcrete or chert was preferred as raw material. The Pietersburg occupation in the Olieboompoort represents the middle phase of this tradition (fig. 30–31, p. 131) in which there occurs sub-triangular flakes with peripheral flaking on the dorsal surfaces and with thinned butts (fig. 30, 1–2). The late Pietersburg material is smaller in general, and blades appear (fig. 30, 6–7).

Industries related to the Pietersburg occur in the Orange Free State and in the Natal highlands (Clark 1959). At Florisbad, a fragmentary skull was probably associated with one of these related industries which is called the Hagenstadt variant. The Florisbad skull consists of part of the face and vault; the cranium is large, the face only moderately prognathic, and there is little evidence of a protruding supra-orbital

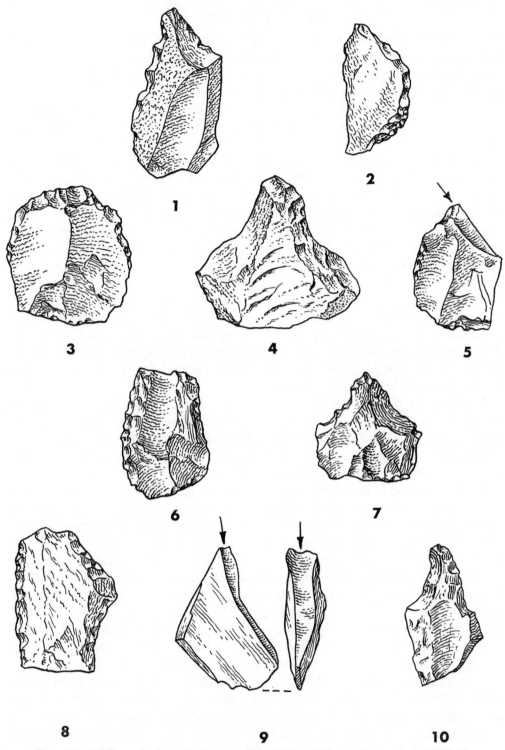

FIG. 28. Stillbay ¾; Bambata cave, Rhodesia; 1–5 upper cave earth (Stillbay); 6–10 lower cave earth (proto-Stillbay); Quartz. *After Jones 1949*

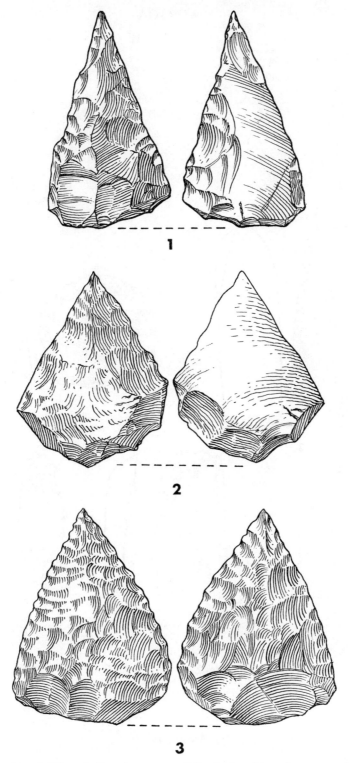

FIG. 29. Stillbay ⅓; Bambata cave, Rhodesia. *After Armstrong 1931*

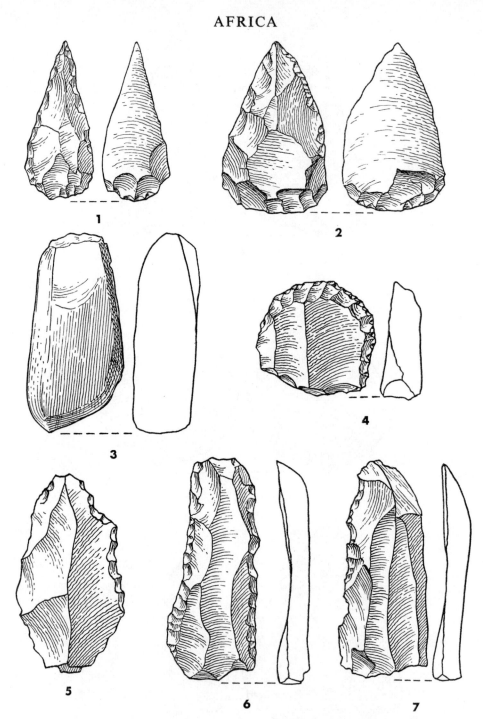

FIG. 30. Pietersburg $\frac{1}{1}$; Olieboompoort, Transvaal; 3 haematite. *After Mason 1962*

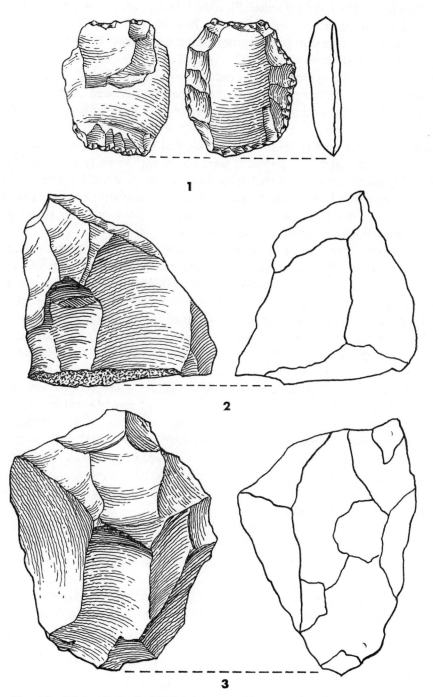

FIG. 31. Pietersburg $\frac{1}{1}$; Olieboompoort, Transvaal. *After Mason 1962*

torus. Recent studies have included Florisbad in the group of Upper Pleistocene men called *Homo sapiens rhodesiensis*. Near Bloemfontein the Mazelspoort variant is found, with characteristic long slender triangular flakes. In part of Griqualand West the Alexandersfontein variant is also related to the Pietersburg tradition.

In the western Cape, typical Stillbay industries have been found, made on silcrete, and containing bifacial leaf-shaped points, scrapers and backed blades. To the east, the Mossel Bay variant is characterized by a triangular flake with prepared platform and little retouch.

A series of radiocarbon dates for the Stillbay and Pietersburg industries, and their variants, indicates that these traditions were under way as early as 35–40,000 years ago, possibly much earlier, and that their final phases may not have appeared until 10,000 years ago. The Hagenstadt variant at Florisbad is believed to date to *c.* 35,000 B.C., and the late Pietersburg at the Cave of Hearths, Transvaal, has rather unsatisfactory radiocarbon dates of *c.* 13,000 and 9,600 B.C.

A development from the Stillbay, and possibly from the Pietersburg, industries near the end of the Pleistocene resulted in the emergence of a series of industrial traditions which are generally classed as Magosian (Clark 1959). There is little evidence that the term Magosian is a proper cultural designation, but it serves as a general term to indicate the appearance of a blade technology, and in some areas, microlithic forms. Backed blades and lunates are widespread, but there are many temporal and regional variants. One of these variants, in coastal areas of the Cape, is called the Howieson's Poort Variant, and occurs at Fish Hoek in several caves (fig. 32; p. 132). In the high plateau regions of the south, a different variant has been recognized, and the Rose Cottage Cave at Ladybrand provides three stages of this Magosian facies. Earliest are prepared-platform blades and flakes, sometimes retouched into scrapers or points, and microlithic blades. The Middle stage is characterized by a dominance of blades with some end and side scrapers. The latest stage has unifacially-retouched points. Wilton industries overlie the Magosian at this site. These Magosian industries have been termed the Modderpoort variant, a tradition distributed in the Basutoland (Lesotho) highlands.

The final industrial traditions of the Stone Age in south Africa are represented by the Wilton and the Smithfield industries (Clark 1959; Inskeep 1967). The Wilton industries occur in the Cape with other centres in Natal, the Free State, parts of the Kalahari and South West Africa. A number of regional variants have been recognized. The eastern Cape Wilton was recognized in a rock shelter near Grahamstown; the industry is microlithic, with small lunates and thumbnail scrapers, end-scrapers, awls, small blade cores and bone points. Many Wilton cave sites are known in this region, often with associated burials. The upper Wilton levels in some of these sites have pottery as well as lithic and bone equipment. The Melkhoutboom cave in the Zuurberg mountains yielded a deep deposit of Wilton material, with associated layers of grass bedding and wooden pegs stuck into crevices of the walls; the pegs probably served to hang equipment or skins for drying. Wooden artefacts, bone tools and

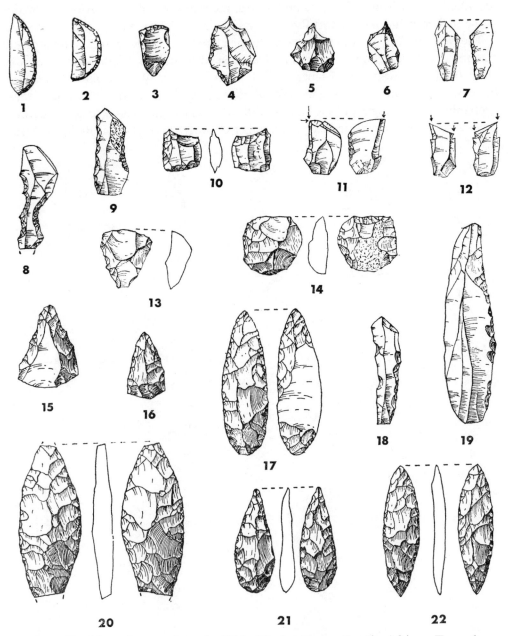

FIG. 32. Magosian variant ½; Fish Hoek, Cape, South Africa; Tunnel Cave except 14, 18, 19 Skildergat Kop; Silcrete, except 3, quartz; 5 quartzite. *From Malan 1955*

pottery were recovered from the upper levels at this site. The bedding has been identified as consisting of grasses and leaves, reeds and wood chips. Animal remains in the shelter included crab, tortoise, porcupine, lizard, dassie, aardvark and antelope.

The western Cape Wilton industry is characterized by double crescents, lunates and thumbnail scrapers, and is commonly found in open station middens or sand dune sites. In the Free State and parts of The Transvaal, the Wilton industry includes lunates, thumbnail scrapers and bifacial tanged or shouldered arrowheads; these probably have an origin in Magosian traditions. Pottery and glass artefacts are some-times associated with this industry. A number of other variants occur in South Africa

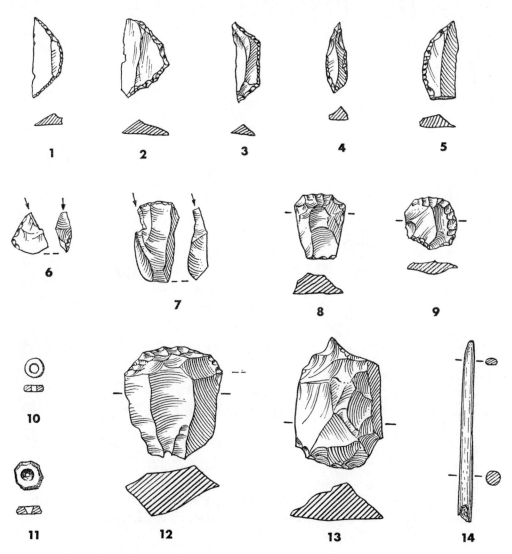

FIG. 33. Wilton $\frac{1}{1}$; Bambata cave, Rhodesia. *After Armstrong 1931*

and Rhodesia; in Matabeleland the painted cave of Bambata serves as a typical Wilton site (fig. 33, p. 130). At Amadzimba in the same area, an important assemblage of bone tools was associated with a Wilton industry. Arrow and spear points, needles and bodkins, tubes of bird bones, and discs of ivory and bone were recovered.

The contemporary Smithfield tradition is more restricted in distribution in South Africa (Clark 1967). It rarely occurs north of The Transvaal, and its central area is in the basins of the Vaal and Upper Orange rivers. Variants occur in Natal and north and eastern Cape. The industry has been divided on the basis of a few stratified sites into several phases. Characteristic forms of earlier Smithfield industries are large circular and end-scrapers and a concave-convex knife or scraper. Flakes with divergent sides leading to a curved retouch edge are called duck-bill scrapers (fig. 34, 11). Grindstones, perforated stones and drills also occur. At the Umgazana cave in Pondoland an industry of this general character was recovered, with pottery in its upper layers, and with associated wooden pegs and bone link shafts, awls, needles and spatulas. Bedding deposits included banana leaves. Later Smithfield industries have quantities of duck-bill scrapers with notched or hollow scrapers, perforated and ground stone tools (fig. 34). Other late Smithfield industries have more microlithic forms, and thumbnail scrapers of Wilton character. There are various coastal versions of the late Smithfield tradition (Clark 1959).

A recent programme of rock shelter excavation in the middle reaches of the Orange River has been designed to establish a sequence for the Smithfield industries of the region (Sampson 1967; Sampson, G. and M. 1967). The shelters include Riversmead, Zaayfontein, Glen Elliot and Zeekoegat. The industries recognized in the deposits of these stratified shelters have been provisionally correlated with phases of the classic Smithfield, and provide clear indication that the traditional grouping should be critically examined. Six industrial phases have been identified from the Riversmead group of sites; the tool types represented include end-scrapers, side scrapers, small round scrapers, outils écaillés (thick flakes with a curved edge formed by a negative scar on one surface), backed points and blades, crescents, bone points, bored and ground stone tools, pottery and glass beads. Radiocarbon dates suggest that phase 3 of this local sequence existed c. 2,500 B.P., and phase 5, with pottery, existed c. 700 B.P. Phase 6 material includes glass beads and is considered to be contemporary with European domination in the area, perhaps c. 200 B.P.

Another relatively late date for a Smithfield industry is c. 900 B.P. from Olieboom-poort (fig. 34; p. 131); these dates demonstrate that stone industries of this general character were being practised for centuries after iron-working had been established in parts of sub-Saharan Africa, c. 1,100 B.P.

Smithfield industries in south Africa often occur in decorated shelters, but there is little stratigraphical evidence that proves contemporaneity of this occupation and some of the art. The rock art of southern Africa, taken as a whole, is remarkable both for its distribution and its quantity (Willcox 1956, 1963; P. Vinnicombe, pers. comm.). The art appears in a tremendous arc from South West Africa down to the

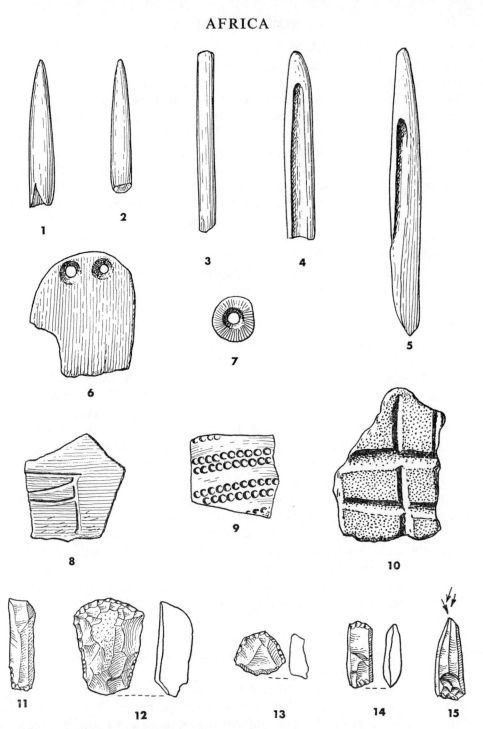

FIG. 34. Smithfield; Olieboompoort, Transvaal; 1–5 bone $\frac{5}{3}$; 6–9 shell $\frac{5}{3}$; 10–15 stone $\frac{1}{1}$. *After Mason 1962*

Cape and up again northwards through The Transvaal and into Rhodesia, Zambia and Tanzania. Several thousand sites are known from this territory, compared with 100 from late glacial France and Spain (p. 251), and fewer from early post-glacial Spain (p. 261). The African distribution is also notable because of the divergent areas of paintings and engravings. Engravings tend to be concentrated in the central part of

FIG. 35. Paintings in dark and bright red at Etheldale in the Matatiela district of East Griqualand, South Africa. Human figures, some wearing masks. The figures are superimposed on older, fainter paintings. Scale $\frac{2}{7}$. *From a tracing by Patricia Vinnicombe*

south Africa, in the middle reaches of the Orange river, the lower Vaal and Harts river basins. Painted sites lie in broad belts nearer the coasts. In south-west Africa, paintings in rock shelters and engravings on exposed rocks occur in the same areas. The distribution of the art of southern Africa as a whole tends to coincide with the spread of industrial traditions of Smithfield and Wilton character.

Almost all the paintings are naturalistic (fig. 12; fig. 35; fig. 37), except for a geometric and curvilinear group associated with certain industries in Zambia (p. 136). Although the painted art appears on the walls of rock shelters there is little evidence of dating by the deposition of occupation debris over the art. A few such sites are known in Zambia. Most of the animals represented in the art are modern species, and include cattle and fat-tailed sheep which show that certain sites were not decorated before the arrival of Europeans (1652). The humans represented in the art also indicate relatively recent groups; in addition to forms which have been subjectively interpreted as Bushmen, Bantu or Hottentots, a few Europeans occur. Some of the humans are of small stature and carry bows and arrows. Others have ornaments on arms and legs, and carry shields and spears.

The equipment and activities shown in the art are remarkable in their variety, and have led to a general division of the paintings into an early period, represented by

Fig. 36. Pecked engravings at Twyfelfontein, South West Africa. Ostriches with antelope spoor and what is possibly a nest of eggs. Scale ¼. *From a photograph by P. L. Carter*

124

FIG. 37a. Paintings in dark red and white. Poacher's shelter, Ndidima valley, Natal Drakensberg, South Africa. Bushmen hunters. Scale ⅔. *From a tracing by Patricia Vinnicombe*

FIG. 37b. Bichrome buck from Sebaaini's cave, Natal Drakensberg, South Africa. Scale ⅔. *From a tracing by Patricia Vinnicombe*

FIG. 37c. Tracking. From Sebaaini's Cave, Natal Drakensberg, South Africa. Scale $\frac{2}{3}$. *From a tracing by Patricia Vinnicombe*

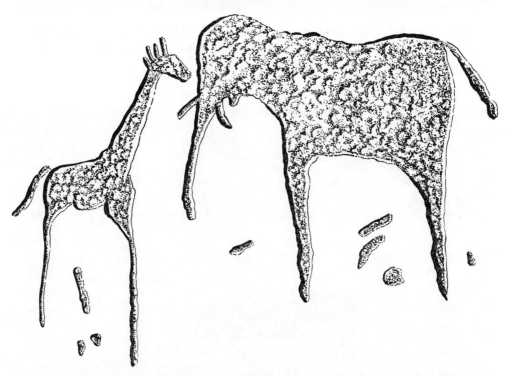

FIG. 38a. Pecked engravings at Twyfelfontein, South West Africa. Scale $\frac{1}{5}$. *From a photograph by P. L. Carter*

peaceful simple naturalistic scenes, and a late period with scenes of conflict, with presumed Bantu and other non-Bushmen groups present. The art suggests that the hunters occasionally wore fringed karosses with skin caps, although many figures were naked; body decoration including white paint was common. There is no evidence to support claims that some figures are of Mediterranean origin.

Engravings were done with sharp burin-like edges, or by pecking (fig. 36; fig. 38). Paintings involved the use of iron oxides and haematite for reds, browns and yellows. Manganese and charcoal produced black paint, and kaolin or bird droppings were sources of white.

The early engravings of the central region of south Africa are often fine-line figures of animals, but geometric designs also occur. Animals represented include rhinoceros,

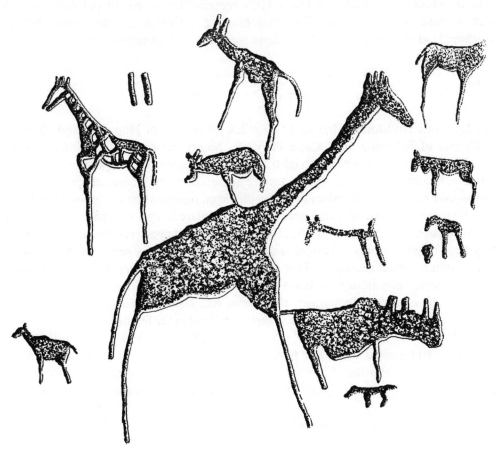

FIG. 38b. Portion of a large panel of engraved animals at Twyfelfontein, South West Africa. The large central giraffe is in the fully pecked silhouette technique, while the smaller one (upper left) is patterned with the rectangular markings typical of this animal. Scale $\frac{1}{6}$. *From a photograph by P. L. Carter*

buffalo and eland, as well as smaller numbers of elephant, hippo, wildebeeste and ostrich. Often these animals were drawn in groups. The geometric designs include zigzags, ladders, chevrons and the like, and these and the fine-line animals are generally found beneath pecked engravings wherever superpositions occur. The pecked figures represent animals as well as some humans.

The paintings are more widely distributed in southern Africa, but a great concentration has been recorded in the Drakensberg region. These have been divided into pre-Bantu and post-Bantu, with a dividing date in the early seventeenth century. Art in the western regions includes groups in the Brandberg area as well as 'stylistically decadent' groups, marking areas into which the Bushmen artists were driven in recent times.

In Rhodesia, the granite Matopos Hills are another source of painted sites. In Matabeleland simple scenes of normal hunting activities are dominant, but in Mashonaland more complicated events are recorded, including ceremonies.

ELANDSFONTEIN (SALDANHA)
(Singer & Crawford 1958)

The farm of Elandsfontein lies some 10 miles south-west of Hopefield and 15 miles south-east of Saldanha Bay, Cape Province, South Africa. Surface finds in 1951 revealed evidence of three industrial traditions, represented by approximately 1,000 stone tools, and over 3,500 fossils including human remains. There are approximately four square miles of fossiliferous sands on the farm, representing a dried-out hard-pan on which surface materials had gradually accumulated. Various erosion gullies cut across the site, and the floor was eventually covered and preserved by sands. The area may have originally been a coastal swamp separated from the sea by ridges of sand. The abundant faunal remains include giant pig (*Mesochoerus lategani*), hippopotamus (*Hippopotamus amphibius*), baboon (*Papio ursinus*), buffalo (*Homoioceras* sp.), elephant (cf. *Loxodonta atlantica*), rhinoceros (cf. *Diceros bicornis* and cf. *Ceratotherium simum*), the primate (cf. *Simopithecus* sp.) and other forms.

The site also yielded over two dozen fragments of a human skull, generally called Saldanha or Hopefield man. The remains have recently been included in the *Homo sapiens rhodesiensis* group. Fluorine and uranium analyses indicate the contemporaneity of the skull with the fauna cited above, and in view of this a late Pleistocene date is suggested.

The stone tools are of three traditions, of handaxe, Stillbay and Late Stone Age affinities. The handaxes are made on silcrete, quartzite, felspar porphyry or sandstone; the Stillbay implements are of silcrete with some quartzite, while the Late Stone Age tools show a greater variety of materials, gritstone, silcrete and quartzite, felspar porphyry and sandstone.

The handaxe industry (fig. 24) contains a number of small axes, many under 4" in length. Pointed forms, cordiforms and ovates occur, and many are made on flakes.

Cleavers are rare, and there are a number of flake scrapers and battered spheroids. The industry as a whole has been classified as an atypical Fauresmith, although our knowledge of the regional, industrial and temporal variations of the Fauresmith is still imperfect. The pointed axes, and small rather rough cleavers, are characteristic of Fauresmith traditions, but the range of smaller flake tools at Elandsfontein is much more limited than in some Fauresmith industries, in which points, long flakes, and chisels occur, with faceted platform flakes.

The Middle Stone Age material is in typical Stillbay tradition, and the Later Stone Age forms include pottery. The major question at this site concerns the contemporaneity of the human remains with the industries, and recent work has suggested that it is probably the Fauresmith group that was associated with Saldanha man. At other fossiliferous sites in tropical Africa, modern assemblages of fauna, or assemblages with few extinct types, have been associated with developed Middle Stone Age industries, and the Elandsfontein faunal assemblage does not appear to belong to this recent or modern phase, but rather to Cooke's Vaal-Cornelia stage. It has been suggested that the Elandsfontein fauna may be, in general terms, contemporary with Olduvai Bed IV, and of probable early Upper Pleistocene age. The contemporaneity of Saldanha man with this fauna is shown by fluorine and uranium analyses, and there is therefore a strong probability that the remains, the fauna and the Fauresmith-related industry are contemporary.

LUANGWA VALLEY
(Clark 1950)

The Luangwa River is a tributary of the Zambezi, and flows south and south-west through eastern Zambia. On both sides of the river, throughout its length, industries of Sangoan character have been found; these form a specialized Luangwa variant of the Sangoan tradition (fig. 26–27). The stone tools overlie an extensive gravel deposit composed of quartz and quartzite pebbles which occurs at heights from 60 m. to 9 m. above the river. The tools, made on this locally-available material, include rather crude picks (fig. 26, 1), handaxes (fig. 27, 1, 3) and unifacially-flaked push-planes (fig. 26, 3). Other variants occur in Zambia and Rhodesia, the Zambezi variant characterized by heavy picks, push-planes, and finely-pointed handaxes, the Bembezi variant in western Rhodesia by a preponderance of flake-blades and few picks. Some of these variations are due to differing raw material, but environmental conditions may also be responsible for different basic tool-types.

The Luangwa Sangoan picks are either high-backed with a sub-triangular section or flatter with a more rounded plano-convex section. Handaxes are thick, with irregular edges and unflaked butts. Less common than these are elongated picks, large flake scrapers (fig. 27, 2) and discoid cores (fig. 26, 2). Some utilized flakes have prepared striking platforms.

AFRICA

BAMBATA, RHODESIA
(Jones 1940, Armstrong 1931)

Bambata is a granite hill in the north-west of the Matopo range of hills, rising in smooth slopes to a height of approximately 1,000 feet above the valley base. The cave opens from a small platform on the south side of the hill, about 300 feet below its top, and is quite small, 26 feet in depth and about 38 feet wide. On the wall of the cave is a frieze of paintings. The site was found by Neville Jones in 1918, and his small excavations were followed by a larger amount of work by A. L. Armstrong in 1929. Subsequently, Jones returned to the site in 1938–9 and excavated a small area of the cave. His results have been generally accepted, although they contradicted those of Armstrong.

At the top of the cave deposits is a two- to four-foot layer of ash with Late Stone Age material. Below is the Upper Cave Earth, some $9\frac{1}{2}$ feet deep, and distinguished by its dark colour from the light-brown or yellow Lower Cave Earth which extended for about 6 feet to the rockbottom of the cave. The distinct change in colour of the soil has been taken to indicate a disconformity and possible climatic break between the Lower and Upper Cave Earth at this site.

The industry of the Lower Cave Earth is an unspecialized proto-Stillbay. Tools are made on flakes of rather irregular shape, and the retouch is often steep. Faceted platform flakes are common, but many plain platforms also occur. Scrapers are often notched and saw-like (fig. 28, 8) and pointed flakes are rather small (fig. 28, 7, 10). Chunky flakes with longitudinal retouch have been described as burins (fig. 28, 9). A number of heavy chopping-tools, originally called handaxes by Armstrong, complete the assemblage of the Lower Cave Earth.

The industrial material from the Upper Cave Earth shows the development of the proto-Stillbay industry into a highly specialized tradition, with fine triangular and leaf-shaped points made in quartzite and felsite by unifacial or bifacial flaking (fig. 29). Recent technological studies have indicated that such retouch need not indicate pressure-flaking, but could have been produced by careful percussion methods. Other tools of this Stillbay industry include large crescentic flakes (fig. 28, 2), various forms of convex or concave scrapers (fig. 28, 3–4), serrated flakes (fig. 28, 1) and simple burin-like tools (fig. 28, 5).

The industry from the top of the cave deposits is of Late Stone Age Wilton character, with microlithic forms, scrapers, burins, points and grindstones, bone awls (fig. 33, 14), pestles and ostrich egg-shell beads (fig. 33, 10–11). The microliths include triangles, crescents, obliquely-retouched bladelets and trapezoidal forms, all tending to be made on rather broad flake-blades (fig. 33, 1–5); small awls, short end-scrapers and irregular round scrapers occur (fig. 33, 8–9) as well as larger flakes with retouched edges (fig. 33, 12–13), some lames écaillées, and small burins (fig. 33, 6–7). Small nodules of haematite and red ochre were found. There is no evidence that this industry is to be associated with the wall-paintings, although recent work has indicated that the makers of some of the industries of the Wilton complex were in all probability artists.

OLIEBOOMPOORT
(Mason 1962)

The Pietersburg industry from Olieboompoort has been described as belonging the sands of the Kalahari Desert. A section was recently excavated by R. Mason, who was able to show the existence of a stratified deposit which yielded artefacts in the Acheulean, Pietersburg and Smithfield traditions. The excavated deposits in the sandstone shelter were approximately 2 metres in depth. Bed 1 contains stone rubble and some traces of Acheulean activity. It is overlaid by Bed 2, between 2 and 3 feet in thickness, which has less heavy rock rubble; the Pietersburg industry here is associated with a radiocarbon date of $> 33,000$ B.P. Above is Bed 3 with a late Smithfield industry, dated here to 870 ± 150 B.P. Iron Age occupation is attested from the uppermost level.

The Pietersburg industry from Olieboompoort, has been described as belonging to the middle phase of the tripartite Pietersburg culture in The Transvaal. The overall resemblance between Pietersburg and Stillbay has been noted previously. The characteristic industrial type of the Olieboompoort assemblage is a triangular-shaped flake with rounded base, flaked peripherally on the dorsal surface and at the bulbar end on the ventral surface (fig. 30, 1–2). The reduction of the butt thickness in this way would facilitate hafting. Also present are flake scrapers and flake-blades with edge retouch (fig. 30, 4–7). A circular dished grindstone and haematite and ochre pencils (fig. 30, 3) were recovered. The worked-out cores are pyramidal or quadrilateral in shape (fig. 31, 2, 3).

Overlying the Pietersburg deposit is a Smithfield industry of some 400 specimens, dated to 870 ± 150 B.P., one of the most recent Stone Age dates from southern Africa. Characteristic stone tools of the Smithfield at Olieboompoort include a duck-bill scraper (fig. 34, 11), small 'button' scrapers (fig. 34, 12), narrow burins (fig. 34, 14) and retouched blades. Bone and wooden points, ranging from 2 cm. to 3 cm. in length, and shafts of the same materials occur (fig. 34, 1–5). Grooved stones of sandstone (fig. 34, 10) probably represent a process used in the production of arrowheads and shafts. Bone spatulae, ground or shaved to shape, probably represent hide-working activities. Ostrich egg-shell beads with hour-glass perforation and pendant fragments were found (fig. 34, 6–9). A few pieces of specular haematite are the only colouring materials found in this industry, in contrast to the haematite and ochre pencils of the Pietersburg industry. It is possible that the rather abstract paintings on the wall of the Olieboompoort shelter represent the activities of the Smithfield people, but this is not at all certain.

AFRICA

FISH HOEK, CAPE PROVINCE
(Malan 1955)

The Fish Hoek valley cuts across the Cape Peninsula from False Bay to the Atlantic at Kommetjie. A central ridge of sandstone known as Skildergat Kop divides the valley longitudinally. Near the top of Skildergat Kop is the Tunnel Cave, about 40 feet long and open at both ends although access is only possible from the north-east. The occupation deposits are thin, as rain and wind have scoured through the tunnel. Within the deposits an industry on silcrete, with some quartzite and quartz, was discovered in the 1940's (fig. 32). The industry is based on blade production, with prepared cores, and characteristic tools include unifacial or bifacial points which may be triangular or leaf-shaped (fig. 32, 17, 20–22); some of these are completely worked over by a flaking technique generally described as pressure. The leaf-shaped points range from 9 to 2 cm. in length. Small backed blades, side and notched scrapers, small round scrapers and 'Kasouga' flakes are also important. There are a few burins, some red ochre and haematite.

The industry represents one of the variants of the Magosian tradition, and has been called the Howieson's Poort variant.

7

East Africa

INDUSTRIAL traditions developing out of the Acheulean in east Africa have been linked with those emerging in south Africa, called the Fauresmith and the Sangoan. Although there may be valid reasons for distinguishing a widespread Sangoan tradition in sub-Saharan Africa, the Fauresmith industries of east and south Africa are separated geographically by wide expanses of territory, and no certain contact has been demonstrated. Common to both areas is the development from the preceding Acheulean, and this resulted in a common interest in certain tool forms. The Fauresmith of east Africa is, in general, restricted to high-level areas in Kenya and in Ethiopia (Cole 1963). The Kenya variety was originally called Nanyukian, after an area where artefacts were exposed through erosion at 7–8,000 feet above sea level. Such high-level regions may only have been favourable for settlement during climatic periods warmer than the present time; it is possible that occupation at these heights was designed to allow access to permanent water supplies at a time when lowland sources were drying up, but it may also be that these industries represent Acheulean activities at a different economic level.

The Sangoan industries of east Africa, like those of the south in Rhodesia, Natal and elsewhere, probably represent isolated yet parallel developments in areas where climatic and environmental conditions prompted such a reaction to a more forested environment (Clark 1964). The type site for the Sangoan is in the hills above Sango Bay in Uganda, on the western shore of Lake Victoria, and Sangoan sites in general tend to be restricted to the western parts of the east African area (fig. 25). In the Kagera valley in Uganda, a classic site at Nsongezi has provided a sequence of industries from claimed 'pebble tools' through Acheulean and Sangoan assemblages into a Lupemban form. The precise stratigraphical positions and climatic dating of these industries is at present under review. The site at Astrida, in Rwanda, indicates the presence of a strong Sangoan tradition in the western areas of east Africa, in areas to the west of Lake Victoria and Lake Tanganyika (p. 140).

In the Orichinga valley of Uganda, Lupemban assemblages suggest that this area belonged to the central province of the Congo and Angola during late Pleistocene times. Parts of western Kenya, also, have early Lupemban as well as Lupembo-

Tshitolian industries in the Nyanza area of Lake Victoria. At Astrida, in Rwanda, the Sangoan industry was succeeded in time by a Lupembo-Tshitolian tradition (p. 140). At the Kalambo Falls, a late Lapemban industry is dated c. 30–27,000 years ago (p. 105).

Industries succeeding the Fauresmith and Sangoan in east Africa belong to the Stillbay tradition. Most of the important stratified sites which have yielded Stillbay material are in Zambia and Rhodesia (p. 130; Clark 1950, Cole 1963). In the upper Zambezi valley, a proto-Stillbay phase has been recognized, the industries occurring on the eroded slopes of Kalahari Sands overlying Sangoan material. The developed Stillbay industries of east Africa, characterized by bifacially-worked points of sub-triangular or leaf shapes, are comparable to those of Zambia, Rhodesia and farther south. Some east African Stillbay industries, however, appear to contain backed blades, lunates and burins, and may represent contact with other groups in Kenya. Radiocarbon dates suggest that the Stillbay tradition had appeared by c. 40,000 years ago, and may have existed until as late as 10,000 years ago. More dates are required before this lower limit is established. An industry originally called 'Developed Levalloisian', which may be broadly contemporary with certain of the Stillbay traditions, was recovered from Eyasi in Tanzania, associated with skull fragments. The pronounced brow-ridge and other features of the skull indicate its position in the *Homo sapiens rhodesiensis* group.

The Stillbay industries of east and south Africa are believed to lie behind an industry called Magosian. The Magosian occurs as far north as the Horn and extends through eastern Africa southwards to the Orange Free State and Lesotho. The industry is considered to be characterized by microlithic forms and Stillbay-derived triangular and leaf-shaped bifacial points. End scrapers, burins and small blade cores also occur.

The type site is Magosi in Uganda, which typologically has always been considered to represent a late stage of the Magosian industries. Recent work indicates that this is a mixed industry (fig. 39, p. 140). In western Kenya, the Magosian is well represented; it is stratigraphically later than the Lupembo-Tshitolian at Muguruk. At the Kalambo Falls a Magosian industry has been dated to c. 9,500 years ago, but earlier and later dates are known from other sites in east Africa. At the Apis Rock shelter in northern Tanzania, the Magosian was stratified between a Stillbay and a Wilton industry. Pottery was associated with the Magosian at this site. At Nyarunazi in Burundi, industries in a Magosian tradition were stratified below a microlithic assemblage (p. 139).

Another development from industries in the Stillbay tradition is represented in the Kenya Rift valley and northern Tanzania by the Kenya Capsian industries (Leakey 1931). The early phases of this tradition contain large backed blades, burins and end scrapers, but only the late phases are widely represented in the Kenya Rift. The type site for this upper Kenya Capsian is Gamble's Cave II in western Kenya (p. 141). Although originally this cave was believed to contain industries of early Gamblian pluvial age, it now seems evident that most of the deposits at Gamble's Cave II are

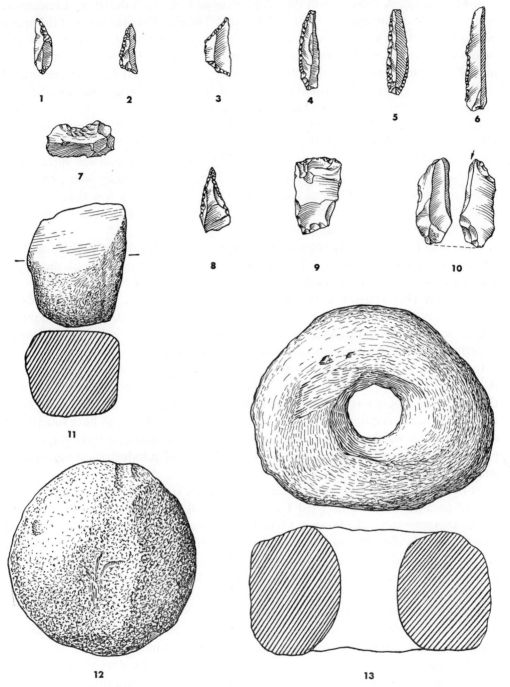

Fig. 39. Magosian; Magosi, Uganda; 1–12, $\frac{3}{4}$; 13, $\frac{1}{2}$. *After Clark 1957*

post-Pleistocene. A radiocarbon date for a Kenya Capsian industry at Elmenteita, however, indicates an age of 10,560 ± 1,650 B.P. The characteristic tools of the upper Kenya Capsian are backed blades, burins, end scrapers and lunates, almost all made on obsidian (fig. 40, 6–15). The lunates were probably hafted into wooden shafts. The quantity of ochre, and decorative objects such as ostrich eggshell discs and perforated shells, suggest considerable attention was paid to personal ornamentation. Several potsherds were discovered in the lowest occupation deposit.

The inhumed burials in the upper levels of the Kenya Capsian deposits at Gamble's Cave were tightly flexed, with the knees drawn up to the chin. The bodies had been decorated with red ochre and were protected by the cave wall and the stones. The individuals are of *Homo sapiens* type, and had long narrow skulls with prominent chins; they resemble the Olduvai I specimen which was buried before the deposition of Bed V, and which was probably contemporary with upper Kenya Capsian industries in the same stratigraphical position.

Layer 6 in Gamble's Cave represents the type site for a local Kenya Rift tradition called the Elmenteitan (fig. 40, 1–5), which probably developed out of the upper Kenya Capsian. Common to both are lunates, end scrapers and bone awls. Burins are rare and the characteristic tool is a long obsidian blade with unretouched edges. Pottery is abundant, including some vessels with pointed bases; decoration is rare. A similar industry from Bromhead's Site in the same area was contemporary with disturbed inhumations generally comparable to those in Gamble's Cave.

In Zambia a regional industry was developed in the wooded savannah areas (Clark 1950a). The type site is the Nachikufu caves which lie in a quartzite ridge in the Muchinga mountains (p. 143). The industry is microlithic in character although there is also heavier equipment including perforated stones which may have functioned as digging-stick weights (fig. 41). The industry here is divided into three stages, and pottery was recovered with the latest level. The Nachikufan industries are associated with a geometric rock art.

At the Chifubwa shelter, engraved and painted art is entirely schematic and consists of parallel lines and inverted Us with a central line (Clark 1958, 1959); these motifs are remarkably like those in French and Spanish caves interpreted as male and female symbols (fig. 102, 4). Painted sites in Zambia, southern Tanzania and the eastern Katanga also have strong geometric elements, although there is some evidence that naturalistic art was an earlier tradition here. The designs include circles, ladders, crescents and gridirons, but only the earlier stages of this art are considered to be a part of the Nachikufan tradition.

North of the Limpopo River an industry known as the Wilton developed from the Magosian and allied traditions and appears to extend in time from relatively early in post-Pleistocene times down to an uncertain date perhaps in the second millennium A.D. In the south-western part of Zambia sites such as the Mumbwa Caves have yielded industries on quartz dominated by microlithic forms.

The Wilton settlement at Gwisho in Zambia has yielded quantities of wooden

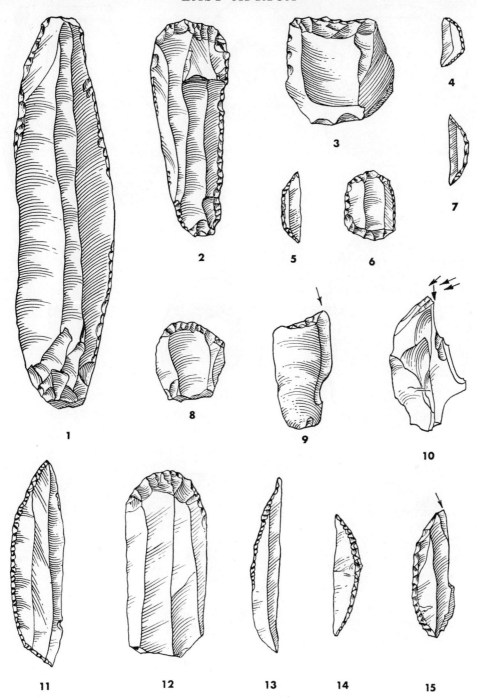

FIG. 40. Gamble's Cave II, Kenya $\frac{1}{1}$; 1–5 Elmenteitan; 6–15 Upper Kenya Capsian; Obsidian. *After Leakey 1931*

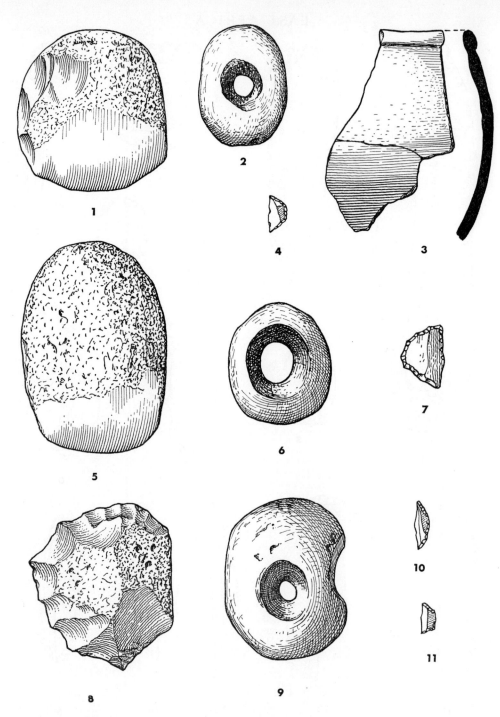

Fig. 41. Nachikufu, Zambia ¾; 1–4 level C Nachikufan III; 5–7 level D Nachikufan II; 8–11 level E Nachikufan I; 1, 5 diorite; 2, 9 schist; 3 pottery; 4, 7, 8, 10, 11 quartz; 6 soapstone. *After Clark 1950a*

artefacts including arrowheads and link-shafts, digging sticks and a variety of pointed objects. Radiocarbon dates from the site range from *c.* 2000 B.C. to *c.* 1700 B.C. A number of burials were found at the site, some in extended positions and others contracted. Fragments of a windbreak were also exposed, composed of grasses and sticks. The food supply of these people consisted of antelope and some larger animals such as elephant and hippo, fish, particularly catfish, and plants. In the upper Zambezi basin, comparable industries are associated with polished axes, bored stones or pottery.

In Kenya and northern Tanzania, Wilton industries occur with thumbnail scrapers, lunates, burins and lames écaillées, and pottery. The small scrapers were probably used for woodworking, and larger forms for cleaning of hides. Shell mounds along the shores of Lake Victoria and other lakes represent camp sites of other groups who seem to have relied almost entirely upon shellfish; stone tools are rare. In Uganda, the Nsongezi rock shelter yielded Wilton material including microlithic lunates and borers or points, coarse pottery and iron objects; industries basically of the same character are known from the recently explored area of Burundi.

NYARUNAZI, BURUNDI
(Nenquin 1967)

Nyarunazi is a hill in the territory of Muhinga, Burundi. Surface collections of prehistoric material were made sporadically until excavations were carried out in 1960 on the right bank of the river Kavuluga. The excavations, directed by J. Nenquin, extended to a depth of 4·6 metres. Nine separate levels were distinguished, consisting of layers of reddish-brown earth, clays and gravels. Level 1, of brown earth, contained an industry on quartz or quartzite, with a small proportion of flint. The dominant artefacts are lunates and tranchet-like segmented blades; side scrapers and points also occur, as well as blade cores. Typologically this industry may be compared with the Wilton of Zambia, although some differences may be discerned. Level 2, of reddish-brown earth, yielded a small industry containing a few lunates and segmented blades with a larger quantity of side scrapers, and two bifacially-worked artefacts. Level 3, of earth and clay, was sterile. Level 4, of grey, loose clay, contained a scraper and blade industry without lunates; bifacially-worked tools include a core axe. This small assemblage is considered to represent a Magosian tradition. Level 5, of clay with gravel, yielded a few implements including flake scrapers and heavier forms. Level 6 consisted of river pebbles, overlying the clay and gravel of disintegrated bedrock (Level 7 and below). The implements from Level 6 are on pebbles of quartzite, with some quartz. Characteristic forms in this industry include small handaxes and a cleaver, small core tools resembling those from the Camafufo sands of Angola. Pebble or thick flake points, choppers and flake knives also occur, as well as quantities of side scrapers and other edge-worked flakes. This industry is considered to be in a late Acheulean tradition. Very large quantities of handaxes, choppers, picks and core-axes have been recovered from the surface along the Kavuluga river, and these, as well as numerous flakes, were probably eroded from deposits comparable to Level 6 of the excavations.

ASTRIDA, RWANDA
(Nenquin 1967)

The prehistoric site of Astrida lies on the right bank of the river Rwabuye in Rwanda. Excavations were carried out in 1960, and yielded a stratified deposit of clays and gravels extending to a depth of approximately 2·5 metres. Level 9 in this sequence consisted of fluviatile gravels from which quantities of fresh and slightly rolled Sangoan artefacts were obtained. Handaxes, choppers and picks, biconvex-sectioned core-axes and hammerstones form the bulk of the heavy equipment; flake scrapers and points are also well represented. This industry has been compared to the Sangoan of Uganda. Its geological position in torrent gravels appears to be similar to that of the Sangoan at the Kalambo Falls.

Above this deposit is Level 8, of smaller gravel and sand, which contained a Lupembo-Tshitolian industry. Characteristic forms include lunates, backed and truncated blades, pointed flakes and bifacial points; these points recall those in the industry from Mbalambala (p. 164). Core-axes and pebble and flake scrapers are also well represented. This industry is considered contemporary with the Magosian assemblages of the same region, sharing flake-points and core-elements.

MAGOSI
(Clark 1957)

The relatively early excavation and publication of this small site in northern Uganda has led to the use of its name as indicative of a very widely distributed group of industries linked in a common tradition of microlithic character. It now seems likely that the name Magosian should be discarded as a cultural term in tropical Africa, and the type site described here may be taken as an illustration of the difficulties in assuming a cultural tradition from a single site with uncertain stratigraphical homogeneity (G. Cole, pers. comm.).

The site of Magosi lies in north-eastern Uganda some 5 miles to the west of the Rift escarpment. It is in fact a rock cistern, formed by decomposition of the gneissose granite and subsequently altered by human activity. The cistern was about 11 feet deep under an overhanging cliff-face, but shallower at its outer edge, and was approximately 10 feet wide. The filling of reddish brick-earth, deposited in the cistern as water-laid sediments, probably originated as aeolian clay. The cistern would have served as a proved, although not infallible, source of water, as it collected wash from the granite cliff, and its outer edge, steeply sloping yet with an irregular surface, would provide access to the varying levels of the water supply. This outer slope was covered by a layer of rock rubble, brought in through mechanical means, and incorporating within it a prolific stone industry. The remainder of the silted-up cistern was sterile of artefacts. The site was excavated in 1926 by E. J. Wayland, who arbitrarily divided the section into 2 foot layers, which yielded six groups of industrial material totalling over 4,500 stone tools and waste made on chalcedony with some chert and quartz, and a few pieces of lava and obsidian from the volcanic regions to the east. A few differences in frequencies were observed for certain types over the entire 11' of deposit, with a tendency towards the production of more small blades rather than flakes, and smaller tools, in the higher levels; this fact is apparently due to the mixing of an upper microlithic industry with a lower unrecognized flake industry.

Microlithic forms are the most common artefacts (fig. 39, 1–6). Most of these have blunting retouch directed from the bulbar face, although a few have been flaked from both edges. Straight and curved backed bladelets are common, and obliquely truncated, lunate and triangular and trapezoidal forms also occur. A number of microlithic blades with nibbling retouch and utilization 'retouch' are also known. Other small artefacts include saws, small burins (fig. 39, 10) and small unifacial or bifacial points. Double-edge retouch awls are well represented, as well as some forms called drills with facial retouch. The waste flakes and blades from this lithic industry are generally small with plain platforms.

Larger tools consist of scrapers, chisels and other heavier equipment. Rubbing and pestle stones were found (fig. 39, 11), along with two quartz missile stones (fig. 39, 12) and two bored stones (fig. 39, 13). The scrapers consist of hollow (fig. 39, 7), round, flake and core scrapers; the chisels are on bipolar or unipolar cores or flakes (fig. 39, 8). Worked-out punch-cores were also found.

The Magosi industry, in a recent reassessment, has been shown to represent a quite atypical and probably mixed microlithic industry, with some Late Stone Age features such as bored stones, and some Middle Stone Age forms such as points and missile stones. The later elements are better represented, and certain of the microlithic forms indicate an affinity with southern Somaliland industries termed Magosio-Doian.

GAMBLE'S CAVE II
(Leakey 1931)

Gamble's caves lie in a hillside to the east of the River Enderit, in western Kenya, approximately midway between Mt. Kenya and Lake Victoria. The hill is tuffaceous with sandy deposits, and a terrace with caves was cut by the waters of Lake Nakuru during a period of high water level. At present the lake is about 510 feet below the

141

caves, and 12 miles away. Two caves were examined by L. S. B. Leakey, and Gamble's Cave II was found to yield the evidence for climatic and cultural series.

The total depth of deposit was 28 feet. At the base, resting on the rock floor, were pumiceous sands and gravel (layer 15) with freshwater shells (*Corbicula africana* and *Melanoides tuberculata*) and rolled implements. This beach, representing a strandline 510′ above the present level of Lake Nakuru, yet within the Nakuru and Naivasha water basins, has been accepted by most authorities as representing a climatic event in Late Pleistocene times involving a large and deep body of water. Similar exposures of beach have been found at other locations in the Naivasha and Nakuru basins, and it is not disputed that this must infer a pluvial period with a climate wetter and probably cooler. A strandline nearly 200′ higher than this one may represent an early part of this pluvial although its exact number of phases is still uncertain. Resting upon the beach deposit in the cave was a thick accumulation of ash, dust, bone and obsidian (layer 14); it is uncertain if this deposit lies conformably on the beach or not. Some small freshwater shells occur near the base of layer 14, and there are fish remains throughout. This occupation was succeeded by a sterile deposit of rock debris (13), followed by a further occupation accumulation with burials (12). Above is a thin sterile deposit (11) underlying a group of hearths and rockfall with some traces of industrial material (10) which again is sealed by sterile rock debris (9). Layers 14–9 are taken to represent a period during the retreat of the lake waters down to an unknown level, climatically correlated with the later stages of the Gamblian pluvial or the initial stage of the succeeding dry phase, the 'first post-pluvial dry phase', which is represented at Gamble's Cave II by an aeolian deposit of reddish sand (8), probably indicating a drying climate. Above this is a deposit of sterile rock debris (7) underlying a grey-black and brown horizon with ash, hearths, bone and rock rubble incorporating occupation industrial material (6). These deposits, and the succeeding rock debris (5), are considered to represent the 'Makalian post-pluvial wet phase', and to correlate, by industrial material, with a strandline 375′ above the present Lake Nakuru. The strandline in this basin is a suitable indicator of wetter climatic conditions. Aeolian deposits of reddish sands (4) above probably represent a 'second post-pluvial dry phase', and are succeeded by rock debris (3) and modern occupation levels (1–2). Possibly layer 3 represents renewed wet conditions, called the 'Nakuran post-pluvial wet phase', and elsewhere indicated by a beach 145–185′ above the present Lake Nakuru.

The industries from Gamble's Cave II represent two traditions; upper Kenya Capsian (layers 14 and 12), and Elmenteitan (6). The lowest occupation, in layer 14, was divided by Leakey into two arbitrary divisions, and some degree of industrial development was seen in the upper part of this. The implements are made on obsidian, and the technique employed involved the production of long slender blades. Characteristic tools of the upper Kenya Capsian include curved-backed blades (fig. 40, 11, 14), smaller forms of crescentic shape called lunates (fig. 40, 7), end scrapers (fig. 40, 12) and short scrapers (fig. 40, 6, 8), and many types of burin (fig. 40, 9, 10). Worked-out blade cores, a few hammer-stones, some bone awls and red ochre were also found, as well as many beads of eggshell and molluscan shell pendants. At least two pieces of pottery were found in indisputable association with this industry, one decorated with basketry impressions. The industry of layer 12 is in the same tradition, and yielded some pottery sherds comparable to a coarse sherd from layer 14. A number of flexed inhumation burials with red ochre were recovered.

An industry of layer 10 is very sparsely represented, consisting of a few flakes with faceted platforms and no consistent retouch. The attribution of this industry to the Stillbay tradition seems unjustified.

Layer 6 at Gamble's Cave yielded an Elmenteitan industry. Characteristic are symmetrical lunates (fig. 40, 4–5), end scrapers (fig. 40, 2) and long blades with un-retouched sharp edges (fig. 40, 1). Burins are rare, but lames écaillées are characteristic. Potsherds are common, representing a range of wares from small bowls to large jars.

NACHIKUFU CAVES
(Clark 1950a)

The Nachikufu caves lie west of the Luangwa river in Zambia, and form the type site for the Nachikufu culture of this region. The site consists of small rock shelters and a cave lying at the northern end of a bluff. Paintings occur on the walls of one of the shelters and the cave. The cave is approximately 30 metres wide and 24 metres in length. The excavations, carried out by J. D. Clark in 1948, revealed a series of deposits extending in places to over 4 metres in depth, and sealed by a Bantu occupation level. At the base, resting upon bedrock in places, and upon a stony yellow sandy deposit in others, was a compact black cave earth containing an industry called Nachikufu I. This industry consists of non-geometric microliths made on small quartz blades struck from bipolar cores, double-backed microliths, lunates and trapezes (fig. 41, 10–11), micro-drills and bone points. Grindstones, pestle-stones and fragments of haematite pencils indicate some preoccupation with body-colouring or wall-painting. Large scrapers on nodules (fig. 41, 8), and other retouched heavy equipment, were also found. Bored stones were numerous, and of varying sizes (fig. 41, 9); they probably served as digging-stick weights, for arrowshaft straightening, for bark rope manufacture, and for throwing clubs.

Overlying this black earth deposit was a thick layer of reddish-brown cave earth containing a Nachikufu II industry. Microlithic blades are less common, being replaced by larger trapezes, triangles and crescents (fig. 41, 7). Bored stones (fig. 41, 6), hollow scrapers, awls and bone arrowheads are comparable to those in the level below. Polished stone axes and adzes appear, apparently for the first time, in this second Nachikufu industry (fig. 41, 5). These are generally sub-rectangular or sub-triangular in shape, and often have only the working-edge ground. Their asymmetrical shape in side view suggests that many were used as adzes.

The third Nachikufu industry is incorporated in a stony black or grey earth near the top of the deposits, and is overlaid by the Bantu occupation level. The industry is characterized by pottery (fig. 41, 3) and microliths of lunate form (fig. 41, 4). Other tool types are broadly similar to the preceding Nachikufu tradition (fig. 41, 1–2). The pottery consists of thin-walled baggy pots and bowls, with plain rolled rims.

The cave at Nachikufu was decorated with semi-naturalistic art, some of which appears only 2·5 cm. above the present floor-level; this has suggested that the painting may have been done during Nachikufu times when the floor was lower. At Solwezi, a small rock shelter above the Chifubwa stream also bears painted engravings of a schematic stylized nature. The lower part of these was covered by 2 metres of sterile sand mostly washed into the shelter. Beneath this sand was a Nachikufu I red earth occupation deposit. Charcoal fragments from the lowest 30 cm. of sand and top part of the Nachikufu deposit yielded a date of 6,310 ± 250 B.P. The art on the wall of the shelter extends down to within 45–60 cm. of the occupation, but inscribed lines were also found on a rock only 2·5 cm. above the occupation. The art itself is schematic, consisting of vertical lines, inverted U's and shallow cup-marks, with other less common motifs. The evidence of the Chifubwa shelter suggests that it is likely that the art was produced by Nachikufu I people, prior to the steady and uninterrupted accumulation of sands during a period of abandonment. The radiocarbon date may apply not to the occupation but to fossil charcoal washed into the shelter.

8

The Horn of Africa

(Clark 1954)

THE earliest recognizable industries of the Horn of Africa (Somalia and Ethiopia) and of the Sudan are of a developed Acheulean character. Although there is little stratified evidence of these industries in Somalia, surface collections of Acheulean material in the north probably represent ancestral groups to the first well-established industrial tradition in the area, the Acheuleo-Levalloisian. Farther west, near the confluence of the Blue and White Niles in the Sudan, the site of Khor Abu Anga, where quantities of artefacts were found, is generally considered to represent one of the most northerly extensions of the Sangoan tradition rather than a pure Acheulean industry. Acheulean sites, however, lie along the Sudan Nile from Wadi Afu on the White Nile northwards to the Egyptian borders, and at sites on the Atbara. The occupations are probably to be connected with those of the middle and lower Nile in Egypt (p. 194).

The Acheuleo-Levalloisian industries of Somalia occur in the north-western plateau region with a few extensions to the south and west. At Hargeisa, erosion has revealed deposits of the local Older Tug Gravels containing series of industrial material on quartzite. The artefacts include handaxes of ovate and single-pointed forms, cleavers, and tools made on both faceted and plain platform flakes. Discoid and large round prepared cores were used.

Stratigraphically later than the Acheuleo-Levalloisian tradition in Somalia is the Levalloisian which occurs in both the Lower and Upper Tug Gravels over wide areas, from the Kenya border northwards to the tip of the Horn and into French Somaliland (fig. 48). The earlier stages of the Levalloisian industries contain prepared cores and flakes with plain or faceted platforms; the industry as a whole is unspecialized, many flakes containing steep and rather irregular retouch, which appears on core-scrapers and choppers as well. The later industries are also rather unspecialized, but prepared cores produced smaller flakes some of which contain unifacial or part-bifacial retouch. In the Sudan, comparable Levalloisian industries have been recovered both from Nile gravels at Tangasi and farther to the west. It has been suggested that

145

climatic conditions must have been more favourable than those of the present to allow such westerly occupation.

The succeeding industry in Somalia and the eastern Sudan is in the Stillbay tradition, which is well represented over much of the plateau area of the north-west as well as along the eastern coast and the upper Webbi Shibeli. At a site near Hargeisa, typologically early Stillbay material occurs in a red sandy alluvium overlying the Younger Tug Gravel, with later material incorporated in the upper levels of this deposit. The industries consist of unifacial and bifacial points, flake scrapers and backed flakes, with prepared cores and other material. The Stillbay industry of this region appears to show an ancestry in the earlier Levalloisian traditions (fig. 42). The human jaw from the Porc Epic cave in Ethiopia may represent one of the makers of Stillbay artefacts in this region (p. 149). The jaw is large and robust, and has been compared with the Kanam mandible in suggesting the persistence of archaic features of the jaw into the Upper Pleistocene of Africa. The skull from Singa on the Blue Nile, apparently with an industry utilizing prepared cores, may represent a neanderthaloid rather than a Bushmanoid form.

The cave at Porc Epic in the Danakil Rift area of the north-west provides a stratified sequence from Stillbay to Magosian, and there is little doubt of the derivation of the Magosian tradition from the Stillbay (p. 118). The Magosian of the Horn is found in southern Somalia and in the north-western areas of Ethiopia.

Industries have also been recovered from the Horn which indicate a gradual development of a local tradition called the Doian from the Magosian industries; the transitional phases have been called Magosio-Doian. At Jesomma, the assemblage is basically Magosian but there are some hollow-based points as well as leaf-shaped points, both types with bifacial working. This industrial phase has been compared with the late Magosian industry from the type site of Magosi. At the Gure Warbei shelter, a transitional industry of this general character occurred between Magosian and Doian levels (fig. 43; p. 149).

In the northern areas of the Horn, in former British Somaliland, industries stratigraphically overlying Stillbay deposits have been called Hargeisan. This is a blade and burin industry, with backed blades, end scrapers, simple forms of burins, as well as Magosian forms such as unifacial subtriangular points.

To the south, in Somalia and eastern Ethiopia, the Doian industries represent another local development. At Gure Warbei, this industry was stratified above Magosian and Magosio-Doian deposits (p. 149). Characteristic artefacts of the Doian include unifacial leaf points and backed blades; bifacially-worked points occur in later Doian industries. Flake scrapers, round scrapers and burins are also found, and potsherds are associated with this industry. Variant Doian industries have been recognized in the Horn, including a coastal variant. The Wilton industries of the Horn represent a final episode of Stone Age activity. This tradition is distributed mainly on the northern plateau and along the coast, but other facies occur in central and eastern Ethiopia. The industry is microlithic in character, with crescents, backed

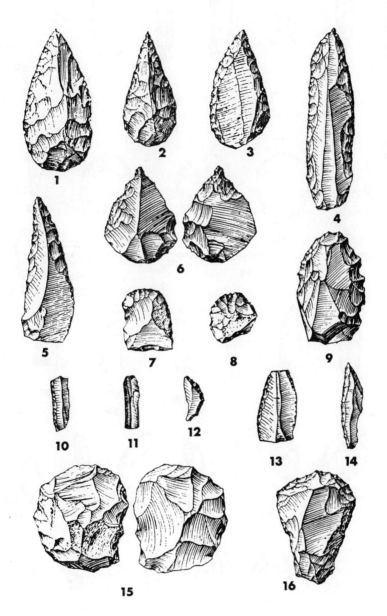

FIG. 42. Porc Epic, Somalia ¾; Stillbay. *From Müller-Karpe 1966*

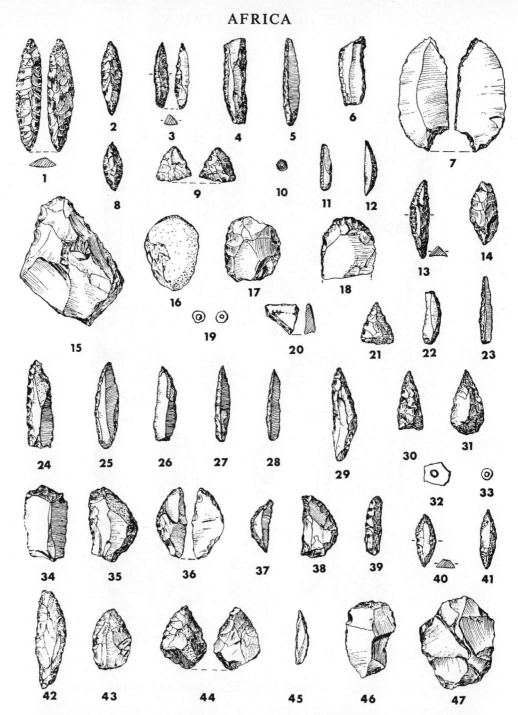

FIG. 43. Gure Warbei, Somalia ½; 1–12 layer B1 (Doian); 13–23 layer B2 (Doian); 24–41 layer C (Magosio-Doian); 42–47 layer D (Magosian). *From Clark 1954*

blades and thumbnail scrapers; burins, end scrapers, utilized blades and cores, as well as plain pottery, make up the remainder of the industry.

PORC EPIC, ETHIOPIA
(Clark 1954)

The Porc Epic Cave lies near Dire Dawa in the Danakil Rift area of Ethiopia. The deposits in the shelter were 1·70 metres thick, consisting of fine ash and earth lacking visible stratification. The industrial material found in this deposit was on obsidian and chert, with some quartz and other rocks. The industry from the lowest levels contains unifacial and a few bifacial points, scrapers and flakes with prepared platforms; typologically this assemblage has been called a final Stillbay (fig. 42). Above, in the middle and upper levels, is a Magosian industry with small unifacial and bifacial points, round and side scrapers, retouched and denticulated blades, backed blades and rare burins and microliths; the microliths include geometric forms. The commonest implement is the unifacial point, often with some retouch on the bulbar face. Discoidal cores and faceted platform flakes indicate the method of flake production. It is uncertain whether or not coarse potsherds found in these deposits represent contemporaneous pottery-making during the Magosian occupation.

A human jaw was recovered by H. Breuil from a lime deposit on the rock floor; its provenance is not certain, but it is possibly to be attributed to the final Stillbay industry in the lowest levels.

GURE WARBEI, SOMALIA
(Clark 1954)

The Gure Warbei shelter is situated at the foot of Bur Eibe in southern Somalia, and was excavated in 1944. Below recent deposits with pottery was a layer (B) of grey earth containing industrial material of Doian character. Layer C, of grey calcareous earth, yielded material of a Magosio-Doian transitional nature, and was preceded by a Magosian industry contained in a gritty, reddish brown earth (D). The sequence of deposits has been interpreted as indicating a drier period in C separating wetter periods in B and D, and these latter have been called the Nakuran and Makalian phases, respectively.

The Magosian industry of layer D consists mainly of waste flakes and blades, with discoid cores (fig. 43, 42–47). Artefacts include subtriangular unifacial and bifacial points and flake scrapers, and several backed bladelets. The transitional industry of layer C (fig. 43, 24–42) is characterized by small leaf-shaped points with unifacial retouch, hollow-based points and quantities of microliths, mostly curved backed blades. Larger backed blades and end scrapers occur, but burins are poorly made.

Ostrich eggshell beads and haematite represent decorative materials. The blade cores are of single- or multiple-platform types, but there are also small prepared discoid cores. In layer B, the Doian industry (fig. 43, 1–23) is characterized by leaf-shaped points with retouch on one or both faces, backed blades and microliths with straight or curved backs, side and end scrapers and quantities of utilized blades and flakes; also present are asymmetric triangles with bifacial retouch. The retouch in some of the bifacially-worked points is alternate, to form a wavy edge. Associated with the Doian stone industry here at Gure Warbei are sherds from thin brown ware with plain rims and little decoration, and thicker reddish wares. Ostrich eggshell beads and pieces of haematite are present.

The industrial sequence in the Gure Warbei shelter is important in that it demonstrates the gradual development of the Doian tradition from a Magosian source. The basic differences between these two industries in this region are the increase in proportions of blades to flakes, with an attendant decrease in the discoidal core technique, and the development of leaf-shaped bifacially-worked points from sub-triangular and other forms.

9

West Africa

(Clark 1963 1966)

THE earliest evidence of man in the Congo and Angola is represented by material of Oldowan character; typologically this is followed by the appearance of Acheulean traditions in the Congo zone which includes north-eastern Angola, in the uppermost Zambezi basin, and in coastal and south-western Angola. In the last-named area, the developed Acheulean at Baía Farta and elsewhere is believed to be contemporary with a high sea level of the order of 25–35 metres (figs. 20–21; p. 103).

In south-western Angola, and in the upper Zambezi basin, there are a few traces of a succeeding Sangoan industry, including an assemblage associated with a 9 metre beach at Punta das Vacas, Benguela. In north-eastern Angola, however, there is abundant evidence of an industrial tradition called Sangoan/Lower Lupemban which occurs unrolled in the lower part of the Redistributed Sands II in northern Lunda. The details of stratigraphy, and description of the artefacts, is provided in the report on Musolexi and other sites in north-eastern Angola (p. 162). The divergent nature of certain of these contemporary industries suggests the presence of workshop or mining facies as well as more typical assemblages on settlement sites.

These industries do not appear to belong, typologically, to the full Sangoan tradition, but contain certain artefacts which indicate a late stage of development towards the Lupemban tradition. Picks (fig. 44), core scrapers, heavy handaxes or choppers (fig. 47, 4), and polyhedral stones are characteristic of these assemblages, but there are also long core-axes (fig. 46, 4) and a few, rare, bifacially-worked long points (figs. 45, 3: 47, 1–2). In the Katanga, such refined products are not so common, and the typical Sangoan industry consists primarily of coarse heavy picks, heavy handaxes, pebble choppers and the high-backed push planes. Utilized flakes and nodules are common. Sites at Brazzaville seem to indicate a stratigraphical separation between the Sangoan and a later Sangoan-related and Lupemban industry.

Climatic dating of the Sangoan industries in sub-Saharan Africa indicate that the preceding Acheulean persisted until the beginning of the Gamblian pluvial. Chemical analyses of deposits at a number of sites has demonstrated that strata with Sangoan

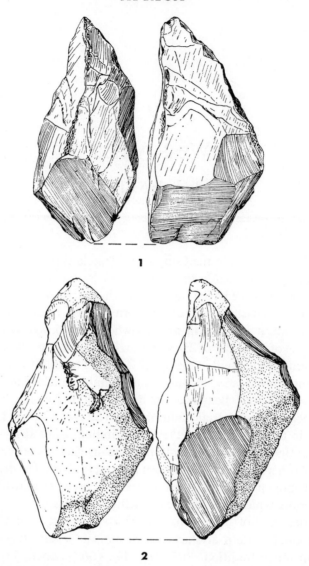

FIG. 44. Sangoan/Lower Lupemban $\frac{1}{2}$; 1 Camafufo, Angola; 2 Musolexi, Angola; 1–2 picks. *From Clark 1963*

artefacts were deposited during a climate wetter than that of today. Pollen analysis at the Kalambo Falls indicates a colder and wetter climate during the pre-Sangoan final Acheulean occupation. In north-eastern Angola, pollen analysis shows that the climate was beoming drier near the end of Sangoan occupation, with a radiocarbon age of 36,000 ± 2,500 B.C. It has been said that the Sangoan industries developed from Acheulean traditions at a time when climatic conditions had become colder and wetter than at the present day, and that these industries continued to develop through

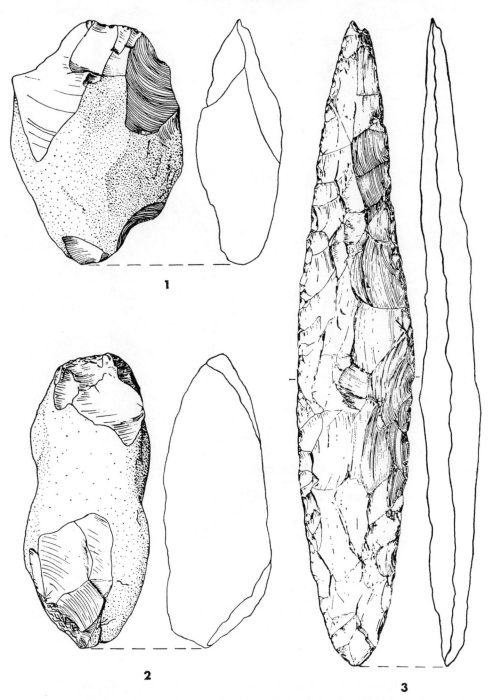

FIG. 45. Sangoan/Lower Lupemban ½; 1 Catongula, Angola; 2–3 Musolexi, Angola; 1–2 core-choppers. 3 point. *From Clark 1963*

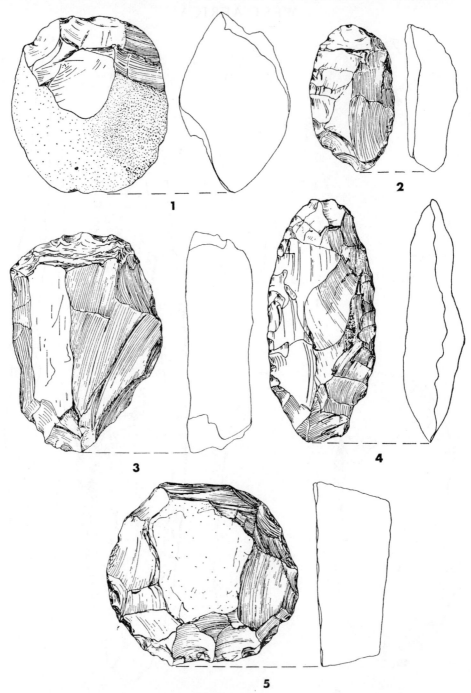

Fig. 46. Sangoan/Lower Lupemban $\frac{1}{2}$; 1, 3, 4 Catongula, Angola; 2 Camafufo, Angola; 5 Musolexi, Angola; 1 double-ended chopper, 2 double-edged scraper, 3 double-end scraper, 4 core-axe, 5 push-plane. *From Clark 1963*

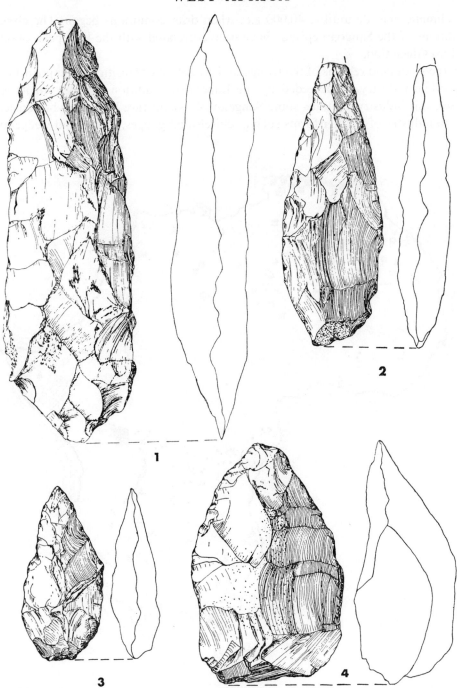

FIG. 47. Sangoan/Lower Lupemban ½; 1 Muazanza, Angola; 2–4 Catongula, Angola; 1–2 points, 3 pointed axe, 4 handaxe-chopper. *From Clark
1963*

this climatic episode until *c.* 40,000 B.C. when drier conditions began. The climatic conditions of the Sangoan episode have been correlated with the European onset of the Last Glaciation.

In the woodland regions of the Congo and Angola the transitional Sangoan/Lower Lupemban industry is succeeded by the Lupemban tradition (fig. 48). In its early phases, this industry contains some Sangoan picks and rare handaxes, but basically it is an industry of smaller forms such as chisels and gouges, planes and wedge-axes,

FIG. 48. Distribution of Lupemban ●, Aterian ■, Epi-Levalloisian □, Stillbay-Pietersburg ▲, Levallois ◊, and 'Mousteroid' ▽, industries in Africa. *After Clark 1967, overlays 16, 17 and 18*

and scrapers. The distinctive tool, however, is the bifacially-worked lanceolate point which represents some of the finest flaking technique, probably controlled percussion, yet known from sub-Saharan Africa. Developed Lupemban industries contain quantities of backed and utilized blades, and the leaf points sometimes have serrated edges. Tanged points also occur. In north-eastern Angola, the developed Lupemban industries are abundant, occurring in the upper levels of the Redistributed Sands II at Musolexi and other sites (p. 162), on the land surface under Redistributed Sands II and, in rolled condition, in the gravels of the 3–4 metre terraces of the rivers in this area. At Mufo, a late industry of Lupemban character has been dated to *c*. 12,000 years old. Both workshop and living sites are known from this important area, and a majority of sites occur in the 3–4 metre terrace gravels, indicating an intensified occupation of the valley floors at this time. Climatically this episode appears to have been a wet phase, succeeded by the deposition of Redistributed Sands III, during a dry period and beginning perhaps *c*. 9,000 B.C.

The succeeding industries in north-eastern Angola are called Lupembo-Tshitolian, and they occur on top of the 3–4 metre terrace gravels of the river valleys, and under Redistributed Sands IV, as well as on the upper slopes of the valley sides in the upper levels of Redistributed Sands III. At Mufo, a radiocarbon date of *c*. 9,200 B.C. is associated with an industry of Lupembo-Tshitolian character (p. 167). The tradition is well represented in north-eastern Angola at sites such as Mbalambala near Dundo (p. 164), and also occurs to the west near the Congo estuary. In south-western Angola an industry at Palmeirinhas, associated with upper sands over a marine platform at 20 metres above sea level, appears as a coastal variant, with discoidal prepared cores and blade cores, and continues as a variant industry into Tshitolian times. The Lupembo-Tshitolian itself is characterized by some heavy elements (fig. 51) including the core-axe, which may have long parallel or convergent sides, or may be shorter and broader (fig. 50, 1–6). Bifacial lanceolate points and tanged points occur (fig. 50, 7–9, 11–13), and there are flake scrapers and a few backed flakes (fig. 49, 4). Flake tranchets are also present (fig. 49, 6–7).

The final cultural episode in the region is represented by the development of the Tshitolian industries which again are particularly evident in north-eastern Angola. In Lunda the Tshitolian occurs in deposits overlying Redistributed Sands III, itself covered by Redistributed Sands IV, and also in valley bottoms covered by the same sands. Dates at Calunda 3 suggest an age for an early phase of the Tshitolian of *c*. 11,000 B.C. The Lower Tshitolian is represented by the site of Cauma (fig. 52; p. 166). The material used for the production of artefacts is grès polymorphe, and many of the finished tools are tranchets on flakes or blades (fig. 52, 10–12, 16, 19). There are some axe-choppers, and core-axes are well represented (fig. 52, 1–4, 14). The latter are highly evolved, and of varying types, particularly in the latest phases of the Tshitolian of north-eastern Angola. In the Kasai and Lower Congo, the Tshitolian industries of the river valleys are similar to those of north-eastern Angola, but in upland areas the tranchet, the dominant object elsewhere, is less important. The presence of Lupembo-

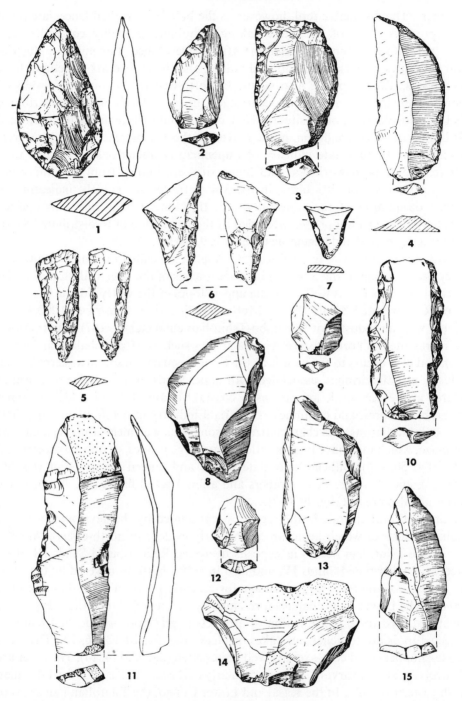

FIG. 49. Lupembo/Tshitolian ½; Mbalambala, Angola. *From Clark 1963*

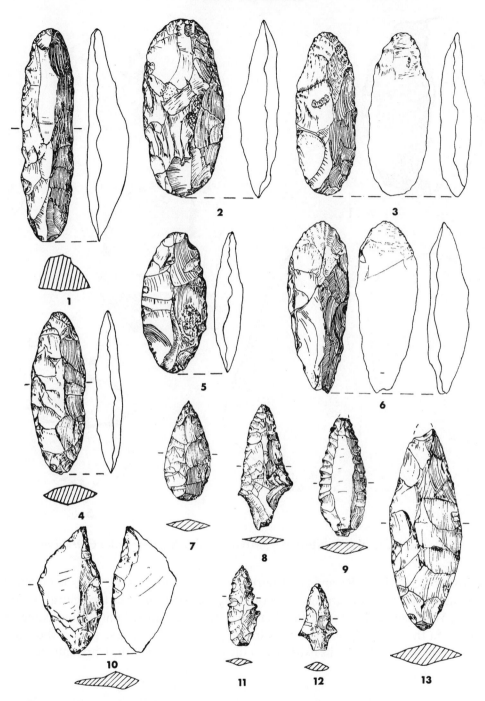

FIG. 50. Lupembo/Tshitolian $\frac{1}{2}$; 1–7, 9–11, 13 Mbalambala, Angola; 8, 12 Caimbunji, Angola. *From Clark 1963*

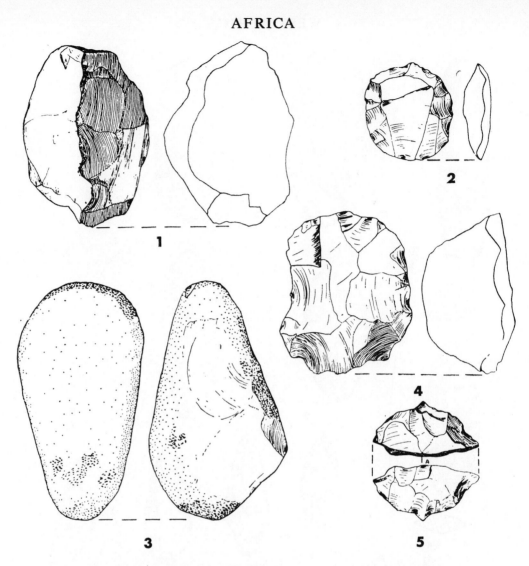

FIG. 51. Lupembo/Tshitolian $\frac{1}{2}$; Mbalambala, Angola. *From Clark 1963*

Tshitolian industries in Rwanda and Burundi (p. 140) indicates the widespread nature of industries directed towards a mode of existence common over the central African region. With the final phase of the Tshitolian the prehistoric hunting and gathering cultures in the Congo basin pass into Iron Age times. The latest radiocarbon date for the Tshitolian indicates its existence in the first centuries of the Christian era.

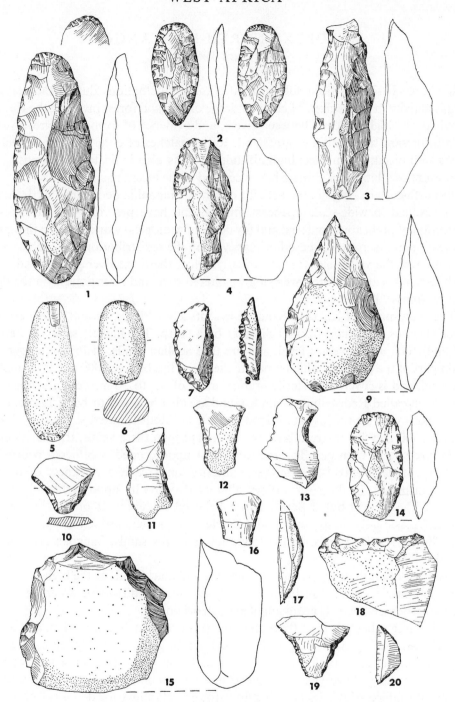

FIG. 52. Tshitolian $\frac{1}{2}$; Cauma, Angola. *From Clark 1963*

MUSOLEXI, NORTH-EAST ANGOLA
(Clark 1963)

The Congo basin has been subjected to climatic fluctuations during the period of man's activity in this region. There is evidence of lowland forest invading the Kalahari Sands of the high plateaux between rivers, and evidence of former evergreen vegetation in present savannah and grassland. Relict patches of cold-preferring species in areas well distant from their high altitude habitats also indicate that extensive and important oscillations of climate have occurred in the recent past.

In north-eastern Angola, the activities of the Companhia de Diamantes de Angola have resulted in wide-scale opencast mining, and have provided opportunities for collection of prehistoric material and for detailed geological work. The stratigraphical succession in this region is based primarily upon the redistribution of Kalahari Sands which cover the valley sides; altimetrically below these are river gravels and sands, with ferricretes and laterites overlying weathered rock and river gravels on the flanks and bottoms of the valleys.

The main spread of Kalahari Sands represents a late Pliocene event. They rest upon three surfaces, separated from each other by a scarp. The highest sands lie between 900 and 1000 m. above sea level, and are true aeolian sands, yellow in colour. The main part of the plateaux which separate the rivers lies between 800 and 900 m. above sea level, and is covered by sterile orange sands of up to 30 m. depth. These sands have been called Redistributed Sands I, and are also believed to be of Pliocene age. The sands overlying the lowest of three surfaces are Redistributed Sands II, and occur between 700 and 800 metres above sea level. Through these sands, tributaries of the main rivers have been cut. The red sands rest upon eroded, weathered bedrock or upon Pleistocene gravels, ferricrete or laterite, and reach a thickness of over 30 metres in places. In the river valleys, thinner deposits lie upon earlier Pleistocene gravels. The Redistributed Sands II are believed to represent one major climatic phase. Occasionally these sands seal Acheulean implements which rest upon eluvial and alluvial sterile gravels. In the lower levels of the sands, Sangoan artefacts are found.

Analyses of all these sands indicate that the Kalahari Sands at the highest level are of aeolian origin, the Redistributed Sands I were subjected to some water action, and the Redistributed Sands II are again of aeolian origin.

In the river valleys, at least three terrace levels occur, at 20 m., 10–4 m. and 3–4 m. above the river. The 20 metre gravels of the Luembe valley probably represent a deep aggradation during a period of gullying and filling in an erosion sequence; these gravels are said to have yielded abraded quartzite pebbles of human origin. Stratigraphically later are laterites affecting fluviatile gravels above the deposits forming the 10 m. terrace, representing a single phase of deep leaching. The 10 m. gravels, with extensions down to 4 metres, must indicate aggradation under semi-arid climatic conditions; they are unsorted and consist of pebbles and cobbles of quartz, quartzite, agate and chalcedony, with derived ferricretes and blocks of grès polymorphe. In the gravels occur rolled assemblages of pebble choppers, flakes and cores.

A second laterite deposit lies disconformably against Laterite I, and is separated in places by hillwash gravels. At Mufo it seals a late Acheulean industry, and may indicate a seasonally moist subsoil during a time when chemical weathering was active. Redistributed Sands II cover the valley sides and extend down into the valley bottoms, overlying ferruginized gravels. The sands occurring below 70 m. above the river are less than 10 m. thick; no visible indication of colour change occurs, and there is little sign of temporary surfaces. The lowest 5 m. of sands contain Sangoan-type artefacts, and similar tools occur on the surface of the underlying gravels. Working floors in situ are rare, and the tools are generally scattered sporadically throughout the sand levels. Some Lower Lupemban lanceheads and core-axes occur in the lowest levels of the sands, and it is not possible to separate these stratigraphically from Sangoan forms. It may be that these forms represent one tradition with specialized activities. The middle and upper levels of the sands contain Upper Lupemban implements on small workshop floors, and, near the top of the sands, Lupembo-Tshitolian artefacts have been found.

Contemporary with the deposition of these sands was the formation of the 3–4 m. terrace, the gravels and sands of which lie in a buried channel exposed by present river action. The gravels contain Upper Lupemban artefacts, and a radiocarbon age of 14,503 ± 560 B.P. has been determined for the upper part of the gravel formation. A temporary land surface on the gravels, with indication of Lupembo-Tshitolian activity, has been dated to 11,189 ± 490 B.P. The succeeding deposits include Redistributed Sands III and IV on the valley sides, and alluvium and resorted gravel and sands in the valley bottoms, contemporary in general with Tshitolian industries.

Collections of Sangoan and Lower Lupemban artefacts from the base and lower levels of the Redistributed Sands II have been made at a number of mining sites in north-eastern Angola, particularly the mines at Musolexi, Camafufo and Catongula. The major feature of these industries is the rough nature of the stone technique, with little evidence of the use of a cylinder-hammer. Most of the tools are on pebbles or thick flakes of quartz, quartzite or grès polymorphe. Edge battering and the use of anvil and bipolar technique (fig. 45, 2) are predominant. Handaxes are rare (fig. 47, 3), but handaxe-choppers with pointed or rounded working-ends are common (fig. 47, 4); the remainder of the tool was roughly prepared or left untouched. End- and edge-used picks (fig. 44) occur, with flat ventral surfaces and varying sections. Core-choppers on pebbles, and core-scrapers on thick flat flakes or rock fragments, are common (figs. 45, 1–2; 46, 1–3), but the finer core-axes (fig. 46, 4), of elongated ovate or limande shape, and with biconvex section, are rare. Lanceolate points, bifacially-worked, represent the most evolved artefact in these assemblages (figs. 45, 3; 47, 1–2). Most of the flakes show no preparation of the core or the striking platform;

they are broad and large, and indicate in every respect their derivation from the core by way of a stone hammer, or by the anvil technique.

The artefacts from the three sites, Musolexi, Camafufo and Catongula, are not homogeneous, and it may be that the first two named above represent a workshop or mining facies, located near the quartz outcrops, in which the finer finished products are absent or present only as roughouts.

The dates of these industries depends upon the interpretation of the geological deposits in north-eastern Angola, allied to a few radiocarbon determinations. Basically, three major climatic episodes are indicated, the earliest phase during which lowland evergreen forest was allowed to populate the Sands of the 800–900 m. plateau surface and the plateau surface at 700–800 m. The Kalahari Sands of the 900–1000 m. plateau are believed to have been free of this forest because of adequate drainage. The evidence then suggests a period when the forest retreated from the 700–800 m. surfaces into the valleys where local conditions allowed areas of forest to survive. At the same time, the Redistributed Sands II began to form through mainly aeolian action. The Sangoan/Lower Lupemban industries date from early in this climatic phase. There followed a wetter phase, with a generally lowered temperature and intensified seasonal dry phases which prevented the forest from extending back onto the plateaux. The Redistributed Sands II continued to build up over the 700–800 m. surface and valley sides. The 3–4 m. terrace with Lower Lupemban artefacts correlates with this phase. The Redistributed Sands II may indicate the dry phase succeeding the Gambian period at about 9000 B.C. Polleniferous remains of later date are probably of the succeeding Makalian warm and wet phase.

MBALAMBALA
(Clark 1963)

The river Luachimo flows to the east of the town of Dundo in north-eastern Angola. Tributary streams, the Gasolina, the Camuseu and the Capama, flow northwards and eastwards to join the Luachimo, separating a number of ridges which fringe out from the plateau. The deeply weathered granite and gneiss rock of these ridges is partially covered by eluvial gravel overlaid by several metres of orange clay sand, although most of this superficial deposit has been eroded away on two of the ridges, the Mbalambala and Caimbunji ridges.

Over much of these two ridges, where erosion has removed the sand, extensive scatters of worked stone tools occur. There is little depth to these workshop and living floors but they are found over considerable areas on the tops of the ridges, rarely on the slopes or valley bottoms. In the valleys, moist rain forest relics are preserved, while on the ridges a savannah vegetation, called mbalambala, occurs, consisting of a thin grass cover with some trees and bushes. Mbalambala vegetation is associated with dry, stony ground at high altitudes above water. It is believed that this vegetation is similar to that occurring in Lupembo-Tshitolian times in this region, that is, disconnected rain forest in the valleys and dry scrub and grass on the ridges. The assemblages of stone tools found on the Mbalambala and Caimbunji ridges indicate a considerable and concentrated occupation. The richest localities on these ridges are around large granite boulders which must have afforded some protection to the inhabitants.

Although most of the collections of tools made in these areas are surface finds and therefore selective, one area measuring 20 by 10 metres near the centre of the Mbalambala site was exhaustively searched, and this assemblage is believed to represent all or most of the elements of the industrial activity carried out in the immediate area in Lupembo-Tshitolian times.

The industry contains a small number of handaxe-choppers and picks, as well as heavy core-choppers, but the dominant form of heavy equipment is the core-axe (fig. 50, 1–6). This occurs in varying forms, some with long parallel or converging sides, others shorter and broader. In side view the working ends are generally asymmetrical, which may mean use as an adze rather than an axe. The ends themselves may be chisel-shaped or gouge-shaped. Bifacially-worked long points also occur (fig. 50, 9, 13); most are of lanceolate form but some tanged points have also been found (fig. 50, 8, 12). The butts of all these points have been reduced and rounded. Present in small quantities are tranchets made on flakes with retouch on both faces (fig. 49, 6–7). Flake scrapers of varying forms are present (fig. 49, 2, 3, 10), with a very few crescentic or backed flakes (fig. 49, 4). Most of the flakes have plain striking platforms, but a number show intentional faceting of the platform (fig. 49, 10–12, 15). The cores may be single- or double-platformed, and a few biconical and discoid cores occur as well (fig. 51).

Almost all of the artefacts from this and other sites were made of grès polymorphe, either chalcedonic or quartzitic in character. This material was obtained from erratic blocks in the area. The absence of unworked raw material on the sites suggests that the raw material was carried up to the top of the ridges from workshop and mining sites on the valley slopes.

The industry at Mbalambala belongs to a stage of lithic activity called Lupembo-Tshitolian, in which the preceding heavy core-tool element is still dominant, but in which the flake tradition is of increasing importance, foreshadowing the developed Tshitolian culture. The core-axes and bifacial points show a finer degree of finish than previously occurred, involving skilful use of the punch technique.

Lupembo-Tshitolian material has been recovered from old land surfaces on the gravels of the 4 metre terrace of rivers in north-east Angola. These gravels contain Upper Lupemban artefacts, with an associated radiocarbon date of 14,503 $\pm$ 560 B.P. The gravels are considered to be in part contemporary with the deposition of Redistributed Sands II (see Musolexi), and to represent the late stages of the Gamblian pluvial period with its attendant lower temperatures and intensified seasonal dry phases. Redistributed Sands III overlying the old land surface may correlate with the post-Gamblian dry phase. A radiocarbon date of 11,189 ± 490 B.P. for a Lupembo-Tshitolian industry at Mufo, recovered from a land surface on gravels of the 3–4 m. terrace, and covered by sands, fits well with this sequence.

CAUMA
(Clark 1963)

Near the right bank of the river Chiumbe, there are a number of workshop sites of the Tshitolian culture which lie near large outcropped granite boulders in the present river bed. White sands cover these floors nearer the sides of the Chiumbe valley. Breuil recovered a number of stone objects near the bank of the river at Cauma in 1950, and subsequently J. D. Clark excavated in the same area. The site lies on the edge of the Middle Pleistocene 10 metre terrace where the 3–4 m. terrace banks against it. The mining activities at Cauma enabled large areas of exposed gravels to be examined, from which workshop and living floors could be recovered. A sample area of 48 sq. metres was excavated.

The section at Cauma shows a deeply weathered bedrock altered to a clay with angular or rounded quartz fragments. On this surface lies a dense resorted gravel of the 10 metre terrace set in a sandy clay. A few Lupemban artefacts occur in the upper part of this gravel, the surface of which is undulating, forming low hummocks. Upon this surface, and partially dug in, is an industry of Tshitolian tradition, traces of which also occur in the base of the overlying clay and surface soil. The industry recoverd from Cauma is fresh and unrolled, and was made on grès polymorphe in its chalcedonic or silcrete facies. Some quartz and quartzite were also used. The raw material occurs as rolled boulders and cobbles in the gravels of the site, and outcrops of grès polymorphe were also available some 20 km. to the west of Cauma.

The distribution of Tshitolian tools and waste on the workshop floor at Cauma shows a concentration of artefacts, such as might have been produced by a single individual over a short period of time. Most of the waste occurs in the depressions in the gravel surface, and it is likely that this resulted from a grubbing-about for suitable raw material in the gravels. Some of the larger depressed areas might have served as living areas protected by windbreaks, but no trace of postholes or stakeholes were found.

The industry itself contains a large proportion of waste material, as well as numbers of unfinished artefacts. The bulk of finished tools are tranchets which are between 1·5 and 8 cm. in length, and were made on both flakes and blades (fig. 52, 10–12, 16, 19). Varying types are known, some with single edge truncation opposed to the snapped edge, others with double edge truncation, either parallel-sided or trapeziform; the latter merge into sub-triangular specimens. Other tools consist of a few handaxe-choppers (fig. 52, 9) and numerous core-axes of unifacial (fig. 52, 3–4, 14) or bifacial form (fig. 52, 1, 2). Side and end scrapers on flakes occur (fig. 52, 18),

166

as well as notched types (fig. 52, 13). Backed blades and microlithic forms are rare (fig. 52, 17, 20). Elongated quartz and quartzite pebbles were employed as hammerstones (fig. 52, 5–6), and grès polymorphe grindstones are also present. The workshop waste, 94% of all pieces recovered, consists of irregular flakes, most with plain platforms, a small number of blades, and cores, most without prepared platforms; a few blade-cores and high-backed disc cores are known.

The Tshitolian culture is known from a large number of sites in the Congo basin. Their dating is established geologically by their occurrence in some areas in a pebbly hillwash overlying Redistributed Sands III and sealed by orange-red Redistributed Sands IV. In valley bottoms, the industries occur on gravels in the stream beds, and are again covered by Redistributed Sands IV. Radiocarbon dating at Calunda 3 indicates an age for the Lower Tshitolian of 12,970 ± 250 B.P., from the lower levels of these Sands. At Mufo, a land surface on the gravels of the 3–4 metre terrace, overlaid by Redistributed Sands, and associated with a Lupembo-Tshitolian or Lower Tshitolian industry, has been dated to 11,189 ± 490 B.P.

10

The Gulf of Guinea

(Davies 1964)

IN West Africa, north of the Gulf of Guinea, research has been carried out only in restricted areas, and although a number of industries have been recognized, our knowledge of the sequence of industrial development is limited. There is some evidence for the existence of Oldowan-like material on the 24 metre terrace at Yapei in northern Ghana, and rolled typologically Early Acheulean handaxes have also been recognized, particularly at Angeta Bridge in the Dayi valley of eastern Ghana. More developed Acheulean industries are widespread in the region, extending into parts of the Sahara where they occur as far east as Bilma, between Lake Chad and the Djado plateau in eastern Niger, and Tibesti in northern Chad. Comparable material is recorded from central and western Saharan areas, and must indicate occupation during periods of favourable climatic conditions, when rainfall was considerably higher than that of today. Along the Gulf, Acheulean material is reported from Nigeria westwards through Dahomey and Togo, Ghana, Upper Volta and the Ivory Coast to the Republic of Guinea. It has been suggested that the makers of both the Acheulean and the succeeding Saharan industries penetrated into West Africa from the Niger valley, along the quartzite range of the Atacora mountains.

In Togo and eastern Ghana, an Acheulean/Sangoan tradition was dominant, and it is succeeded typologically by a full Sangoan industry which occurs in southern Ghana, in northern Dahomey and Togo. In Ghana it has been found at Asokrochona on a 9–13 metre beach. Pebbles were extensively employed to produce Sangoan picks and coarse handaxes, choppers and stone balls. Flake scrapers of various sorts are also well represented.

In parts of the region, the next phase of industrial activity is represented by industries of Lupemban character. In southern Ghana, stray finds are numerous, but there is little evidence of stratified sites. Traces of the Lupemban have been noted in Nigeria, Togo and as far west as Bamako in French Guinea. The sites on the Niger have been called Kalinian, an industrial tradition that may have been separate from the Sangoan-Lupemban series in West Africa. Basically, however, the material equipment of these industries is comparable, although the Kalinian is characterized by narrow tools such as chisel-like cleavers and gouges. Material of this form is also reported from Dakar, Senegal, and is believed to represent occupation during a wetter period than the present, when a more wooded environment had developed. The industry from Cap Manuel, Dakar, consists of large picks, bifacial axes with parallel sides, long triangular-sectioned picks, scrapers and chisels.

In the savannah of northern Ghana and Togoland, there is evidence for an industrial tradition called 'Guinea Aterian' succeeding the Lupemban. From the stratified site at New Todzi, a representative industry on quartz and other pebbles contains tanged scrapers and some points as well as picks, chisels and push-planes, unifacial points and a few lunates. Blades, including backed blades, awls and a few burins occur. The tanged element in this industry is not highly developed, the tang being made by a single or double notch; the relationship with the Aterian of the north remains to be demonstrated (p. 173); recent work has suggested that no true Aterian industries existed south of 15° North (Hugot 1967).

In Ghana, other industries on quartz and quartzite are stratified above Sangoan forms, and may represent a local facies of the Sangoan-Lupemban traditions, with heavy gouges, and picks and choppers; some 'Guinea Aterian' elements are also reported. Other industries are represented from stratified sites near Dakar, consisting of flakes with little retouch; it is not possible to distinguish any contributory elements to these industries.

Succeeding the flake industries of the Guinea coastlands are microlithic traditions called Mesolithic. The industries occur widely upon geological unconformities, considered to represent a period of dry conditions. Small quartz pebbles were regularly employed, and the artefacts include lunates, tranchets, backed bladelets, end and notched scrapers, awls and small picks, with a few burins and pointed flakes. The site at Okudaw in southern Ghana is believed to represent a stage of this tradition antecedent to that at Bosumpra Cave in Ghana where pottery, hoes and polished axes were associated. Industries of the same appearance are reported from Upper Volta and Guinea, and from Nigeria.

11

North-west Africa

THE Pleistocene deposits in Morocco have been extensively studied for many years
(Biberson 1961), and the succession at present proposed represents one of the most
detailed sequences advanced for any area in the Old World. The terminology is
complex, and involves marine phases and climatic phase-names which together are
considered to provide a complete periodization of the Middle and Upper Pleistocene.
The marine phases are represented by raised beaches at heights from 100 metres to 8
metres above the present sea level. These are interpreted as representing interglacial
or interstadial periods, separated by colder climatic episodes, all of which have been
given local names. Industrial material is associated at many sites with these deposits,
and may therefore be dated in terms of the local sequence. Inter-regional correlations
are less certain. The combined sequence has been presented as follows (Biberson
1961, 1967):

Marine phase	Climatic phase	Industries
	Soltanian	
Ouljian		Aterian
	Presoltanian	Mousterian
Harounian		Acheulean VIII
	Tensiftian	,, VII
		,, VI
		,, V
		,, IV
Anfatian		,, III
		,, II
	Amirian	,, I
Maarifian		Pebble-culture IV
	Saletian	,, III
Messaoudian		(Tardiguetian) II
	Moulouyen	,, I

On the basis of associated fauna, some attempts have been made to relate this
sequence to those of other areas. The Villafranchian fauna of north Africa includes
Machairodus, Equus numidicus, Ceratotherium (rhinoceros), *Bos* and the early

170

elephant *Archidiskodon africanavus* and *Elephas reckii*. This assemblage is considered by some authorities to have extended over a period of Villafranchian time which may be correlated with the northern Günz glaciation and its preceding phases, a warmer period and an earlier colder period. In the Moroccan sequence this fauna has been divided into an early and a later stage; in the latter, *Bos* and *Equus* are more common.

During the Moulouyen climatic phase, it is believed that conditions were wet and erosion of deposits with Villafranchian fauna occurred. The pebbles and clays of this Moulouyen phase, which appear to show signs of solifluction, have yielded pebble tools flaked in one direction only. Pebble tools have been discovered in succeeding geological deposits, the Messaoudian marine transgression (100–110 m.) deposits with warm molluscs, and the sands and clays of the wet and cool Saletian phase, in which a late Villafranchian fauna has been recognized. During Saletian times, both Moulouyen and Messaoudian deposits were eroded. The correlation proposed for these three episodes is that the Saletian is the equivalent of the Günz glaciation.

The industrial material of these climatic and marine phases consists of pebble tools. Those in the Messaoudian deposits are rolled and typologically are considered to represent early stages in the development of pebble tools, flaked in one direction (chopper tools, fig. 53, la; p. 79). The Saletian tools appear more evolved, in that they are flaked in two opposed directions (chopping tools, fig. 53, 1b; p. 62) or in multi-directions. This technique, involving the progressive removal of cortex, may be said to lead on to the production of polyhedric balls of the type known at Aïn Hanech in Algeria (p. 181). The fauna of Aïn Hanech has Villafranchian elements including *Anancus* and *Stylohipparion*. Of some interest is the typological similarity between the Moroccan pebble tools, flaked in opposed directions, and the Oldowan flaked pebbles of east Africa.

The second Pleistocene marine transgression, the Maarifian (60–70 m.), eroded Saletian deposits and laid down pebbles and sands associated with pebble tools and primitive handaxes; this industrial material has been classified as the final stage of the pebble tool succession (fig. 53, 2) leading on to an apparent indigenous development of handaxe industries. Fig. 54 illustrates examples of pebble tools from Tardiquet-er-Rahla in Morocco (1, 2), from Aïn Hanech in Algeria (3, 4; p. 181), from Portugal (5; p. 204) and from France (6, 7; p. 205).

The marine regression from the Maarifian stage allowed the formation of the great Dune (Layer H) at Sidi Abderrahman (p. 181) and there are a number of geological phenomena which indicate a colder pluvial period, the Amirian. By this time the Acheulean handaxe assemblages had begun and the prepared core technique is in evidence (fig. 53, 4, 5). This phase is believed to be contemporary with the Alpine Mindel glaciation. It may also be contemporary with the hominid remains of *Atlanthropus mauretanicus* at Ternifine, Algeria, which were associated with handaxes and a fauna containing *Phacochoeroides* (wart-hog), *Cynocephalus* (ape) and *Machairodus* (sabre-toothed tiger).

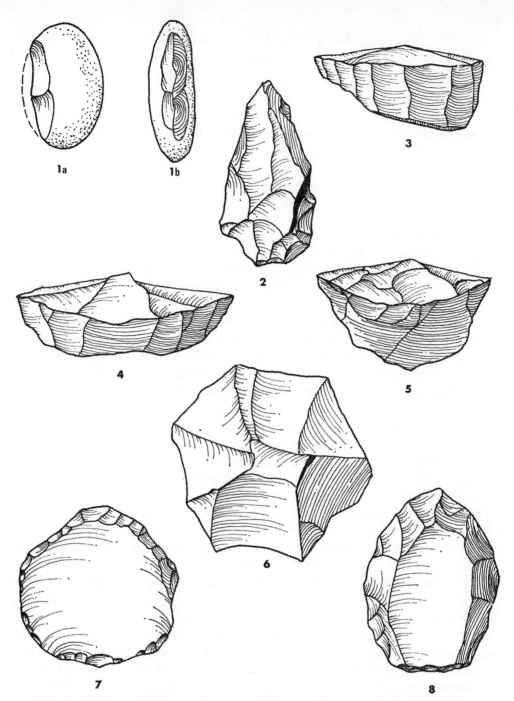

FIG. 53. Chopper-chopping tools and Early Acheulean forms. Schematically drawn, North Africa. 1a chopper tool; 1b chopping tool; 2 transitional handaxe form; 3 Middle Acheulean core, stage IV; 4, 5 Acheulean circular cores, stage V; 6 Evolved Acheulean pyramidal core; 7 Evolved Acheulean tortoise core, Stage VII; 8 Evolved Acheulean core, stage VIII. *After Biberson 1961*

The third marine transgression in Morocco reached 30 m. O.D. and is called the Anfatian. Isotopic dating has given a reading of > 200,000 years old for this stage. Anfatian deposits are believed to be contemporary with handaxe occupation in this area, although a number of the evolved handaxe industries are associated with cooler deposits of the succeeding Tensiftian pluvial and erosional phase. The Tensiftian may be correlated with the Alpine Riss. The Sidi Abderrahman pithecanthropine, probably a descendant of *Atlanthropus*, is associated with these deposits and the contemporary industries are evolved Acheulean in type (fig. 53, 6–8; p. 181). A further marine transgression, the Harounian, has been noted at 18–20 m. O.D. and this is followed by two cool phases known as the Presoltanian and the Soltanian. Between them there was a minor transgression, the Ouljian (5–8 m.), dated to between 75,000 and 90,000 years ago. These phases appear to be associated with the end of the Last Interglacial and the Last Glacial, or with the Riss and Würm glaciations and the Last Interglacial. The Presoltanian is associated with Levalloiso-Mousterian industries which developed into the Aterian. Finally, the Ibero-Maurusian (Oranian) industries are dated *circa* 11,000 years B.P. at the site of Taforalt (p. 175).

The Moroccan sequence is important in that geographically it provides a link between the sub-Saharan and the European succession, with regard to both skeletal material and the industrial, faunal and climatic successions.

Succeeding the handaxe industries of north Africa are the Levalloiso-Mousterian industries similar to those of the Levant (p. 358). The Levalloiso-Mousterian tradition continues until it is ultimately replaced by an Advanced Palaeolithic technological complex. Commonly, however, in the Atlas region, in Tripolitania, in Cyrenaica in the Wadi Bu Mras south-east of Sirte, at Dakhla, on the southern borders of the Sahara and eastwards to Kharga, Aterian points have been found in caves, shelters and open sites.

The Aterian point is recognized by the method of working the tang (fig. 55). Some of them are used as points, a number are retouched as end- or side-scrapers, some have been used as burins and others as awls. There is a considerable variation in size from 13·5 centimetres in length to 2 centimetres. In fact the tang was applied to many forms of Mousterian tools at this time (Tixier 1961).

The type site of the Aterian type industry is Bir el Ater in southern Tunisia but the artefacts from this site have not been fully reported or studied.

Broadly speaking it may be said that the Levalloiso-Mousterian technological complex continued to develop with time and was associated particularly in the later stages in this area with Aterian points.

The Aterian point has been taken as a cultural indicator, a type-fossil which identifies industries as Aterian. These industries include Middle Palaeolithic material and have been divided into three different phases, an early phase with a few Aterian points, a 'typical' phase, and a late phase with tanged bifacially worked pieces. Radiocarbon dates for Aterian material in Morocco have indicated an age > 30,000 B.P. for an early phase, and > 27,000 B.P. for a later phase, but some authorities

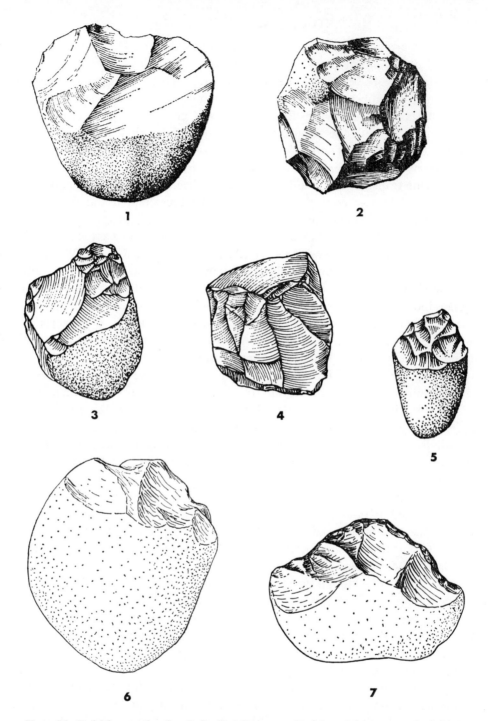

FIG. 54. Pebble tools $\frac{1}{2}$; 1–2 Tardiguet-er-Rahla, Morocco; 3–4 Aïn Hanech, Algeria; 5 Magoito, Portugal; 6–7 Mondavezan, Haute-Garonne, France. *From Coles 1968*

174

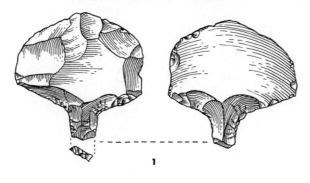

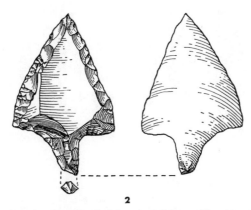

FIG. 55. Aterian Points $\frac{1}{1}$; North Africa. *After Tixier 1961*

believe that Aterian continued in some areas of the Sahara almost down to Neolithic times.

The Middle Palaeolithic industries in the Maghreb are succeeded by industries of Oranian type which overlie the industries with Aterian points in the caves of the coastal areas (fig. 59). There are also a few known inland sites. The Oranian is sometimes called Ibero-Maurusian, a name which arose from a belief that these north African industries had a close relationship with, what has now been shown to be, much later industries of the Iberian peninsula.

The type site of the Oranian is the cave of La Mouilla in the province of Oran (fig. 59). The site of Taforalt (fig. 59), 50 kilometres to the north-west of Oujda, has given a radiocarbon date of 12,070 ± 400 B.P. for an Oranian level.

The Oranian industries are essentially blade industries with a high proportion of small backed blades (fig. 56, 9–11). There are geometric microliths (fig. 56, 6–7, 12–13), end scrapers (fig. 56, 2, 5), and truncated blades. The trapeze (fig. 58, 1), common in the later Capsian, is, except for a few dubious specimens, absent. There are some bone points (fig. 56, 8), but very little in the way of art. The associated physical type is *Homo sapiens*.

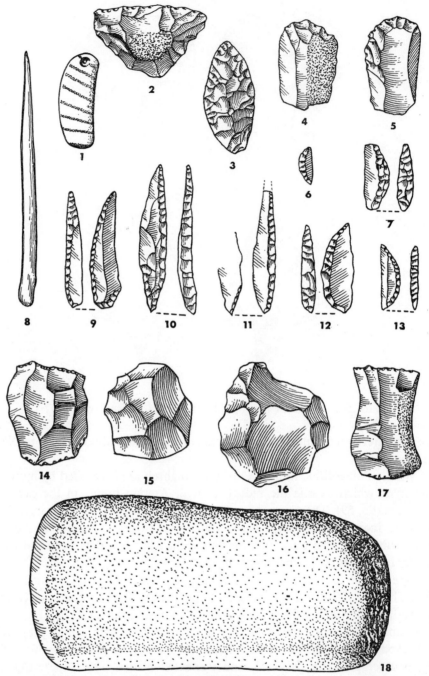

FIG. 56. Oranian $\frac{1}{1}$; North Africa; 1 stone pendant; 2, 4, 5, scrapers; 3 bifacial; 6, 7, 12, 13 crescents; 8 bone point; 9–11 backed blades; 14–17 cores; 18 grindstone. *After Roche 1964*

	No. of occurrences in 33 sites	Addax	Sus scrofa	Cervus barbarus	Cervus algericus	Erinaceus algirus	Mungos ichneumon	Rhinoceros simus	Connochoetes taurinus	Gazella dorcas	Gazella Cuvieri	Canis anthus	Vulpes atlantica	Lepus kabylicus	Ovis sp.	Ovis tragelaphus	Bubalis boselaphus	Equus mauritanicus	Bos
Addax	2																		
Sus scrofa w	3	0																	
Cervus barbarus w	2	1	1																
Cervus algericus w	4	2	0	1															
Erinaceus algirus w	4	1	1	1	1														
Mungos ichneumon	4	0	0	0	0	3													
Rhinoceros simus o	5	2	0	0	2	2	1												
Connochoetes taurinus o	6	1	0	1	1	1	0	2											
Gazella dorcas o	5	0	3	1	0	2	2	1	0										
Gazella Cuvieri o	6	0	2	1	1	2	2	0	1	2									
Canis anthus	9	0	2	1	1	2	2	1	2	3	3								
Vulpes atlantica	9	0	2	1	1	2	2	1	2	5	4	6							
Lepus kabylicus o	10	0	2	0	0	2	3	2	2	3	4	3	4						
Ovis sp. o	5	0	2	0	0	1	2	1	2	0	0	2	2	3					
Ovis tragelaphus o	15	0	3	1	1	2	3	3	4	5	5	7	7	8	4				
Bubalis boselaphus o	24	2	3	2	3	4	4	4	4	4	3	5	6	10	4	12			
Equus mauritanicus o	23	2	2	2	3	4	3	4	6	5	3	8	9	9	4	14	19		
Bos	26	2	3	2	4	4	4	4	5	5	5	7	8	9	4	13	17	19	

w — woodland
o — open land

FIG. 57. The association on a presence or absence basis of animals from Capsian and Oranian sites. *After Vaufrey 1936*

The fauna associated with the Oranian industries includes gnu and hartebeeste and a form of equid. There are also bear and deer. The flora at Taforalt includes *Pinus halapensis* (Aleppo pine), *Quercus ilex* and Juniper. The climatic indications, together, are that the area was essentially dry as it is now, and that temperature changes have not been severe enough to cause a change in the flora and fauna of this area from Oranian times until the present day. Nevertheless the Maghreb is geographically isolated by deserts to the east and south and a seaboard to the north and west, and may have been so at an early date, if the climate at the time of the Last Glaciation was dry and cold. The entry of new species into the area would have been

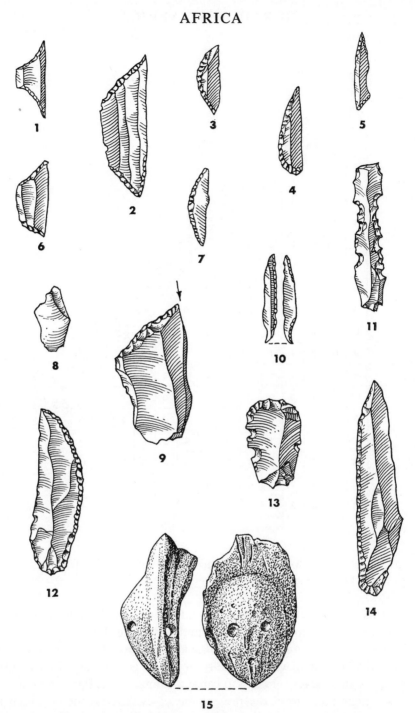

FIG. 58. Capsian ⅔. North Africa; 1 trapeze; 2–7, 10 microliths; 8 micro-burin; 9 burin; 12, 14 broad backed blades; 13 scraper; 15 carved face in limestone. *After McBurney 1960*

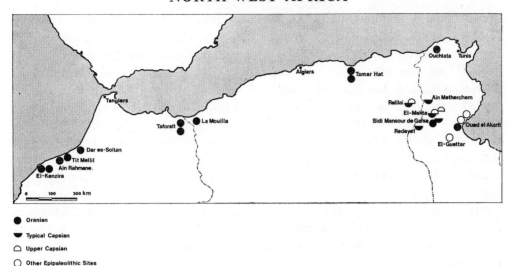

FIG. 59. Distribution of Capsian and Oranian Industries. *After Tixier 1963*

difficult, and a better indication of climatic change may be in the extinction of the bear and the deer rather than in the absence of species new to the area. The extinction of the bear and the deer may have been due in part to a slowly drying climate since Oranian times, as well as to the proliferation of the competitive species *Homo sapiens*.

The later Oranian industries are believed to be contemporary with the appearance of the Capsian tradition, and both industries may in fact be culturally related. The type site of the Capsian is El Mekta near Gafsa (Capsa) in southern Tunisia. The Capsian sites are commonly associated with shell middens and are geographically situated inland and adjacent to the great salt lakes (fig. 59). The closely grouped distribution of the sites and the similar technology employed suggest the possibility of the presence of a human group rather than a diffuse cultural entity over many different groups. It does appear to show a close industrial relationship to a particular biotope but the occupations may be only seasonal in character. If this is so, then the human groups which made these industries must have been elsewhere at a different season. There is no evidence for contemporary industries elsewhere except those of the later Oranian type. The possibility then arises that the late Oranian industries were made by the same human groups. This would be in accord with the present-day movements of pastoralists, who move from the coast to the desert in the rainy season when food and water become available for their animals. Game in dry Capsian times would have tended to move in the same way. An outlier, of Capsian type, has been observed in Cyrenaica at Haua Fteah. There is, however, no evidence for the Capsian in the desert areas between Gafsa and Cyrenaica. At El Mekta there are three super-imposed layers in a shell midden which have yielded, for an evolved type of Capsian, a radiocarbon date of 8,400 ± 450 B.P.

The Capsian is commonly said to divide into an early or Typical Capsian and an

Upper Capsian. Although the Late Oranian may have overlapped in time the Typical Capsian, at the present it appears that some Oranian industries are appreciably older than the Early Capsian. The climate, as deduced from the plant remains in the middens, was dry. There is evidence for a sub-desertic mountain type flora. Phoenician juniper has been observed and in the Upper Capsian there is Aleppo pine at least in certain areas. This has been taken to indicate a return to wetter conditions, presumably the onset of the hypothetical Neolithic pluvial. The eating of molluscs, a characteristic of the Capsian as shown in the shell middens, may well have been as much for their liquid content as for their nutritional value. Snail haemolymph is well known as a source of liquid of use for survival in the desert. The consumption of molluscs has also been observed with the Oranian industries and also in probably contemporary deposits in Italy; shell middens, however, have been observed in many parts of the world from north-west temperate Europe to Australia. They may indicate no more than a seasonal visit by peoples exploiting a variety of different environments within their territory.

Fig. 57 shows the association of animals on a presence or absence basis from 33 Oranian and Capsian sites (Vaufrey 1936). The close association of cattle with open country animals and the rarity of woodland creatures is evident. The mammalian faunal assemblages most commonly contain quagga (*Equus mauretanicus*), hartebeeste (*Alcelaphus* sp.), *Bos primigenius*, *Ovis tragelaphus* (Barbary sheep) and hare or rabbit. Gazelle, desertic and woodland forms are rare. The fauna is one of open country. The hartebeeste with its known preference for salt water is the animal most commonly present in these sites.

The lithic industry contains a number of large curved backed blades (fig. 58, 12), similar in type to those of the much earlier Chatelperronian of Europe. At one time the fact that they were associated with microliths was not recognized and for some time it was believed that the Capsian industries were of Pleistocene date. The microliths include backed blades (fig. 58, 14), crescents (fig. 58, 3, 7) and trapezes (fig. 58, 1, 2, 6). There are burins (fig. 58, 9) and end scrapers (fig. 58, 13), and the microburin technique was used (fig. 58, 8). Among other artefacts are carved limestone faces (fig. 58, 15) and various carved and engraved limestone pieces, grindstones and egg-shell beads. There are rare bone points or awls, and grooved stones which might have been used to make the awls. In the middens are great quantities of stones which have been heated and presumably used for cooking.

The origin of both the Oranian and the Capsian industries is obscure (Tixier, 1963). A people, 'the Oranians', with their equipment could have entered north Africa from perhaps western Europe, from the eastern Mediterranean or through Italy by way of Sicily at a time when the sea level was lower than now. A Capsian origin is even more uncertain in the almost complete absence of evidence of any kind from any point of compass. A hypothesis could be put forward that from elsewhere the Oranians entered and developed a complementary *desert* tool equipment, the Capsian, which superseded the Oranian technology as the post-glacial drying of the area developed.

NORTH-WEST AFRICA

The people who practised the Capsian technology appear to have accepted new ideas, new technologies and possibly a new economy, for the subsequent 'Neolithic' industries are so similar that it has been proposed that they should be called the Neolithic of Capsian tradition. Here is an instance where there may have been a major change in the economy and the way of life of the human groups without there being any great change in the artefacts made by them.

AÏN HANECH

The site of Aïn Hanech lies near St. Arnaud in Algeria. Although there is still some uncertainty about the contemporaneity of part of the industrial material to be noted below, there is no doubt that this site marks one of the earliest known traces of human occupation in north-west Africa. The fauna from the open site includes *Anancus osiris, Elephas* cf. *meridionalis, E. planifrons, Rhinoceros* cf. *simus, Stylohipparion libycum, Libytherium maurusium* as well as other forms. In general, while we may not necessarily accept that this assemblage is Pliocene or even Villafranchian in its affinities, it nevertheless seems to represent an early stage in the vertebrate evolution of the Pleistocene. The assemblage seems earlier than that recovered from Palikao (Ternifine) in Oran, where an incompletely developed handaxe industry, analogous to that from the lower beach deposits at Sidi Abderrahman, is believed to be of early Middle Pleistocene age. Hence the Aïn Hanech finds represent, at latest, occupation of this area of Africa by the early Middle Pleistocene. The stone objects associated with the fauna are polygonal nodules of limestone flaked over much of their surface, perhaps worked out cores (fig. 54, 3–4). Some flakes were associated, and, not certainly, handaxes.

SIDI ABDERRAHMAN

The site of Sidi Abderrahman is a quarry cut into the hillside on the Atlantic coast of north Africa, 4 miles south-west of Casablanca. The excavation of the quarry has revealed a section some 20 metres high and extending over 1 kilometre. The dating of the stratified deposits and their contained industrial material depends upon the relative heights of Pleistocene sea levels.

In this area, generally, the Pleistocene high sea levels have been recorded over considerable distances and by their horizontal undistorted character these have been recognized as at the absolute heights of Pleistocene seas. Correlations with the well-preserved raised beaches along the east coast of North America have aided this interpretation, and the generally accepted conclusion is that beaches at 7–9 metres above present sea level, and others at 15–25 metres, belong to the last interglacial period, while the next highest beaches, at about 30 metres, through isolated marine and estuarine formations, are often believed to be of the Hoxnian interglacial.

The interpretation of the deposits at the Sidi Abderrahman quarry depends upon this latter correlation. The sequence may be summarized as follows: resting upon an eroded bedrock is a shingle beach deposit (M) which today lies at approximately 19 metres above sea level. Just above this beach's high-water mark is an occupation site (L) which yielded a handaxe industry and a fauna including hippopotamus and rhinoceros. Over this beach and its associated settlement material is a freshwater and terrestrial series itself covered subsequently by a marine deposit (J). Some slight traces of industrial activity were found with the non-marine formations, and there is evidence of a period of erosion before the marine sands and other material of layer J covered this occupied area. In the region this marine deposit has been recognized at heights up to 55–60 metres above the present sea level, where it has been identified by a characteristic and rich molluscan fauna. Overlying this deposit at Sidi Abderrahman is a thick dune (H) which here reaches up to a height of 34 metres and which provides the source of quarried material. The consolidated nature of the dune indicates a considerable period of exposure, and in this area must signify a sea level lower than that of today.

Eroded in this dune is a scarp and several small sea caves, formed by a sea level of 28–30 metres, which laid down extensive deposits of beach shingle (G) at this level. The shingle forms a series of deposits with intercalated sandy loams, and within this series there is evidence of occupation of the scarp and caves, in the form of numerous handaxes of various forms, pear-shaped, oval and cordiform, as well as cleavers originally struck off as flakes from enormous discoid cores. The overlying terrestrial cave-filling also provides evidence of Pleistocene occupation in developed handaxe industries without cleavers. One of these stratified industries has also yielded a human mandible, of the *Atlanthropus* type.

Above this level in the caves a further industry has been identified, with highly developed handaxes of oval or cordiform shape, some with 'twisted' section, associated with a fully evolved tortoise-core tradition.

The Sidi Abderrahman finds provide unequivocal evidence of human occupation of the north-west African Atlantic seaboard at an early time, possibly prior to the main phase of the Hoxnian interglacial, and also evidence of the developmental stages of the handaxe industries of this interglacial and later ages.

12

Libya

In Tripolitania other variants of the North African industrial succession have been observed. South of Tripoli at Gasr ed Dauun, near Tarhuna, a small Mousterian assemblage has been found (fig. 60). Small Mousterian industries have been found in Italy (The Pontinian), at Jabrud in Palestine and in Yugoslavia. If a relationship does exist between them, it has not yet been established. The Tripolitanian material is in a calcareous crust, a geological phenomenon which is common in North Africa but as yet has not been accurately dated. In the same neighbourhood there is also present a Middle Palaeolithic type of industry with leaf bifacials.

Between Sirte and Buerat there are also over twenty sites in a red dune which runs parallel to the coast and which is now being eroded away. Typologically the industries are considered to be of late Mesolithic date and include a characteristic artefact, the roundbased point (fig. 61, 32), and many winged and tanged arrowhead (fig. 61). The sites in this area are essentially associated with the coast.

HAUA FTEAH
(McBurney 1967)

The cave of Haua Fteah (plate III) is in Cyrenaica at the foot of the Gebel Akhdar and is approximately at the same latitude as Mount Carmel (fig. 62). It is some seven kilometres east of Apollonia and overlooks the sea. Geographically it is situated half way between the Levant and the Maghreb.

A study of the species represented in the faunal remains, of palaeotemperatures determined from sea shells, of sedimentation rates, and the relevant radiocarbon dates, shows that during the cave occupation there were climatic fluctuations which have been interpreted as drier and/or warmer periods, and wetter and/or colder periods. Fig. 63 (reading from left to right) shows the relative percentages of different animals represented in the deposits plotted against a time scale. It will be seen that high bovine content and relatively low *Ammotragus* content were contemporary with high sea temperature readings and that low bovine content and high *Ammotragus* content were contemporary with low sea temperatures. These fluctuations were

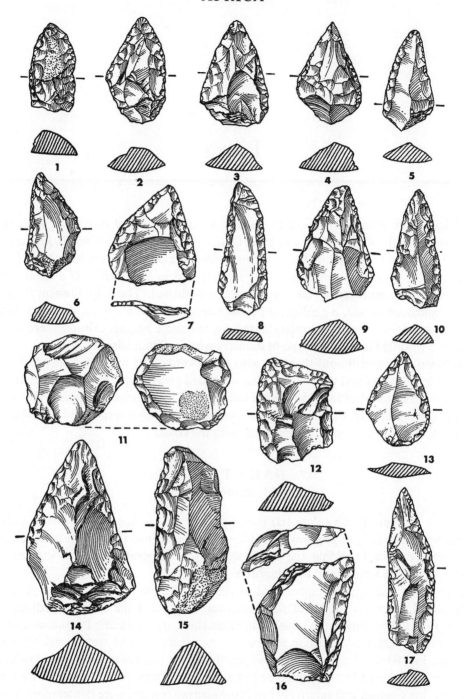

FIG. 60. Mousterian, small variant $\frac{1}{1}$; Gasr ed Dauun, Tripolitania; Points, sidescrapers and other artefacts

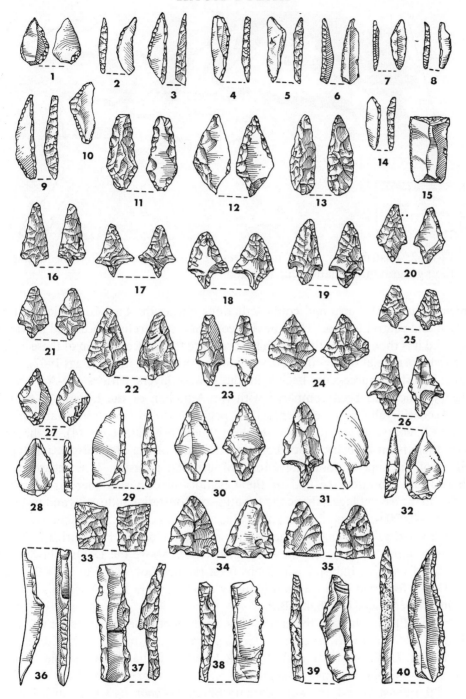

FIG. 61. Sirtican $\frac{1}{1}$; Sirte, Tripolitania; Backed blades, winged and tanged points; 26, 30 Sirtican points; and other artefacts

185

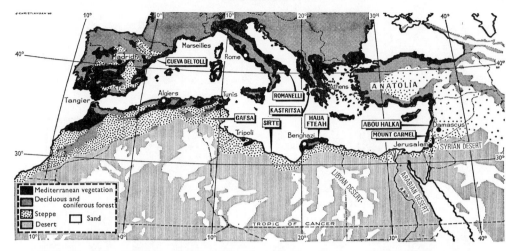

FIG. 62. Distribution of the main sites in the Eastern Mediterranean and their geographical relationship to Haua Fteah

contemporary with warm and cold oscillations during the Last Glaciation in north western and central Europe. High bovine contents seem to have occurred in warmer times and it is thought that this may have been due to a concentration of these around the coastal perennial springs in the dry seasons of the drier period (Higgs 1967).

The industrial succession begins in the lowest layers with a pre-Aurignacian industry which has been compared with the Amudian of the Levant. It contains (fig. 64) considerable blade elements (1, 7), pebble choppers (5), triangular miniature bifaces (2), coarse bifaces (6), proto-burins (8), and prismatic cores (4). In the layers above there is an industry which contains elements of the pre-Aurignacian type as well as of the superimposed Levalloiso-Mousterian industry. It is regarded as a hybrid form. Towards the end of the Levalloiso-Mousterian there is a trace of Aterian in the assemblage. Above the Levalloiso-Mousterian industries and beginning c. 35,000–40,000 years ago there is an Advanced Palaeolithic type of assemblage called the Dabban (fig. 65), which contains end scrapers (15, 16, 17), burins (6–9, 18), transverse burins (10–13), and backed blades (1–5). Above the Dabban layers there is a type of Oranian industry which has been radiocarbon dated to c. 14,000 years ago. This is followed by a Capsian industry c. 9,000 years B.P. After this there are Neolithic layers dated to c. 8,400 B.P.

The Neolithic levels have the earliest known evidence for the domestic animals in Africa. Fig. 66 is a length/breadth scatter diagram of the astragali of the *Caprini* from the Oranian, Libyco-Capsian and Neolithic layers at Haua Fteah and the Neolithic sites of Nea Nicomedeia and Saliagos in Greece. In the area throughout the greater part of the Pleistocene there were Barbary Sheep, *Ammotragus sp.*, which have the characteristics of a well pronounced sexual dimorphism, the males being exceptionally large. The diagram shows how the larger specimens tend to be associated with

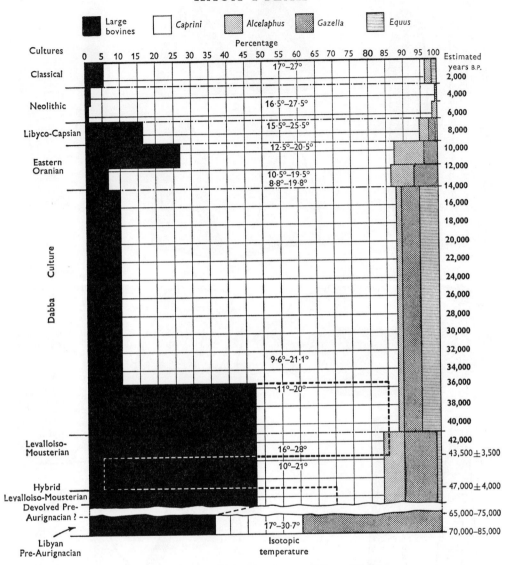

FIG. 63. Faunal Fluctuations at Haua Fteah

the Libyco-Capsian and Oranian layers as might be expected with hunting economies in this area. The Neolithic group is clearly smaller although among the specimens are no doubt some specimens from Barbary Sheep females. As there is no gradation of *Caprini* bone size from Oranian to Neolithic layers there is no evidence that domestication took place at this site but the domestic animals appeared there already beyond the early stages of domestication. It raises the question of whether or not the dates of the Neolithic in Egypt are perhaps somewhat too late in time and that there may have been a much earlier development of the domestic animals in that continent. On the

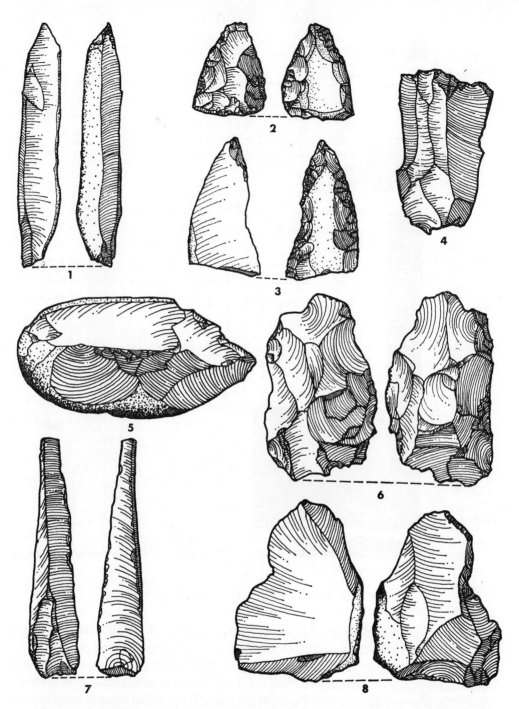

Fig. 64. Pre-Aurignacian $\frac{3}{5}$; Haua Fteah, Cyrenaica; 5 Pebble chopper; 2 triangular miniature biface; 6 coarse biface; 8 proto-burins; 4 prismatic core; 1, 7 blades; 3 point. *After McBurney 1967*

188

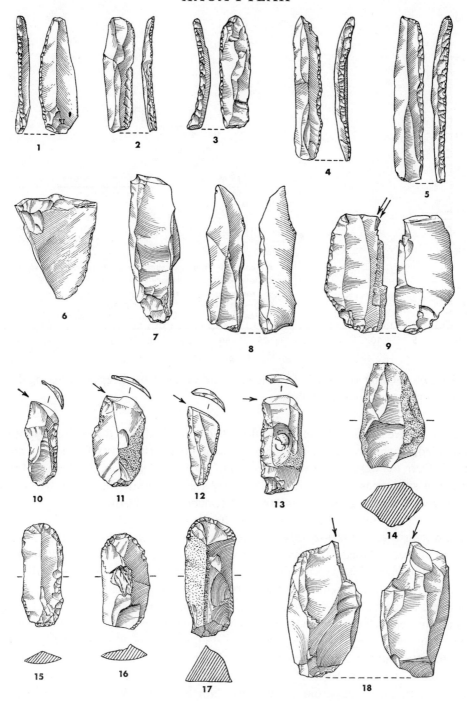

FIG. 65. Dabban $\frac{5}{6}$; ed Dabba, Cyrenaica; 1–5 backed blades; 14 core; 15–17 end scrapers; 10–13 transverse burins; 6–9, 18 burins. *After McBurney 1967*

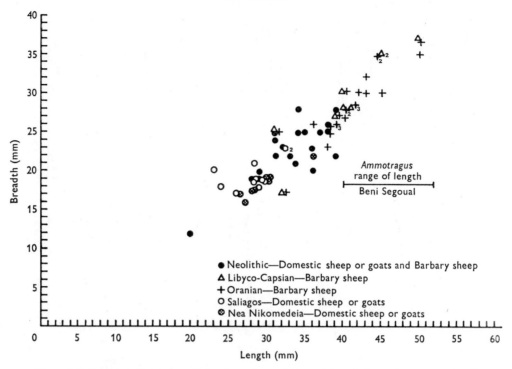

FIG. 66. Scatter diagram of the length and breadth of sheep/goat astragali from Haua Fteah and Greece

present evidence the dispersion of the domestic animals, if the dispersion hypothesis is accepted, appears to have been by sheep or goat pastoralists from the east, or possibly from the west, rather than a spread of cattle herders from the Aegean, for the few cattle specimens in the Neolithic layers are all within the size range of *Bos primigenius*. The sample is too small for firm conclusions to be drawn.

By the excavation of the Haua Fteah the known area of the Capsian and the Oranian industries is considerably enlarged, and their relationship to other Mediterranean cultures clarified. The occurrence of the Dabban, an Advanced Palaeolithic industry, as early as this in Cyrenaica, an industry intrusive in the area and earlier than the Advanced Palaeolithic of north western Europe, suggests, again if the dispersion hypothesis is accepted, an early dispersion from a more easterly source. The fact that for many millennia there was no further spread to the west in North Africa of Advanced Palaeolithic technology until the Oranian, *c.* 18,000 B.P., would suggest the presence of an adverse component or components in the environment which prevented it from taking place. Obvious possible adverse components are a resistant and at least equally successful occupation of western North Africa by groups practising a Mousterian technology, or perhaps the presence of a desert barrier between Cyrenaica and the Maghreb which the makers of Advanced Palaeolithic tools were unable to overcome. Other adverse components might be that the people practising the Advanced Palaeolithic technology, or the technology itself, were in some way unsuitable for the occupation of warmer areas. Indeed, so far there is little evidence for penetration of Advanced Palaeolithic peoples into the hinterland, except for some recent discoveries on the Nile, prior to the occurrence of the Oranian assemblages, and they appear to be concentrated in the coastal area. The desert itself may have been a

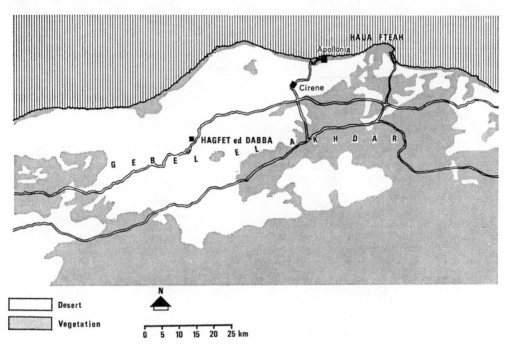

Fig. 67. Present-day environment of Haua Fteah and Hagfet ed Dabba

deterrent rather than a barrier to human migrations. Coastal deserts in the Mediterranean would not have been difficult to cross under the climatic influence of the Last Glaciation in winter time at least, the season 'when any place is a camping place' and the limiting factor of the least available necessity, water, is removed. In fact as Haua Fteah has sea to the north, and deserts to the east, west and south, the Advanced Palaeolithic cultures in the absence of boats must have already crossed one area which is at present desert.

A case can be made out for the unsuitability of Advanced Palaeolithic cultures to warmer climates. In the Levant, they may be earlier in the hinterland (Shanidar) than on the warmer coast sheltered by the Lebanon (Ksar Akil), and in Europe their entry and spread was earlier in the north (Hungary c. 40,000, France c. 34,000) than in Greece c. 30,000 B.P. (p. 227 and p. 315). Its subsequent late entry into some areas may have been simply a matter of population, in that eventually many could overcome an adverse component in the environment whereas a few were unable to do

191

so, or a further technological adaptation to environment, or the removal of the adverse component by some other factor or factors in the biotope. At any rate the quick spread of Advanced Palaeolithic industries, reminiscent of the explosive expansion of animal populations when limitations upon their development are removed, was apparently not matched by a similar rapid dispersion into the warmer areas.

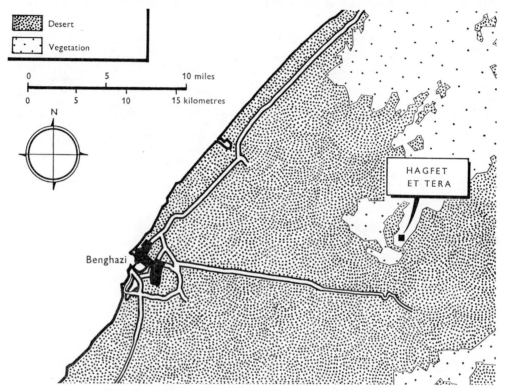

FIG. 68. Present-day environment of Hagfet et Tera

The presence of an industry of the Amudian type at the Haua Fteah enlarges the known area of distribution of industries which are possibly ancestral to the Advanced Palaeolithic industries of Europe (p. 358).

The Palaeoeconomy At Haua Fteah the inhabitants were exploiting the shore, the Gebel Akhdar limestone mountains and at least in drier times an economically complementary hinterland with an abundance of animal food and therefore of animal life in the wet season. Haua Fteah was probably a seasonal camp occupied during the dry season and one of a number of home bases. The more inland cave of Dabba (fig. 67) was yet another where the open country equids and gazelles were exploited in the wetter winter season. This form of territorial exploitation of the area suggests a similarity with the present-day exploitation of the area and similar resources by the Bedouin, who are also dependent upon animal food supplies, and whose movements north to west are based on the rainy season. Fig. 67 illustrates the present-day environment of the sites ed Dabba and Haua Fteah. There are similarities and dis-similarities in the artefactual assemblages from the two sites. Haua Fteah, a coastal site with perennial water supplies is in a different environment from that of the more desertic ed Dabba. It is therefore theoretically possible that the two caves may have been occupied by the same human groups and that some of the artefactual differences between the two sites reflect economic differences related to the environment while the similarities reflect in part a traditional element. A similar economic exploitation of coast and hinterland is shown in the comparison of Haua Fteah Oranian levels with those of the cave of et Tera. At Haua Fteah the group making the Oranian artefacts were exploiting cattle and the Barbary sheep probably in the drier summer season whereas at the more open hinterland site of et Tera (fig. 68) they were mainly hunting gazelle (61 %) in the wet season. It would seem unlikely that mobile economies would have for long accepted the restriction of a single ecological zone, or even have been able to do so in the face of more successful groups who had not. A north to south territorial alignment seems to have been inevitable.

Alternating drier and/or warmer, and wetter and/or colder climatic episodes are indicated by the fauna. From evidence at Haua Fteah, there would appear to be a warmer and/or drier postglacial period beginning about 11,000 years ago. Prior to that a colder and/or wetter period lasted from *c*. 30,000 to *c*. 11,000 B.P. From *c*. 40,000 to *c*. 30,000 B.P. there was a warmer and/or drier period, and from *c*. 53,000 to 40,000 B.P. there was a cooler and/or wetter period, prior to which it was again warmer and/or drier. Colder and warmer episodes are also indicated by sea temperatures determined from marine shells, and from a granulometic analysis of the cave sediments.

The interdisciplinary approach to the problems associated with the Haua Fteah illustrates well how fragile evidence from a single discipline can be corroborated by equally fragile evidence from other disciplines to provide convincing evidence for conclusions which it might not otherwise be possible to make.

13

Egypt

NORTH-EASTERN Africa represents one of the most crucial areas for our understanding of the early movements of mankind. The archaeological sequences of regions to the west, south and east are well established, and the demonstration of relationships between these areas may only be indicated by tracing comparable material in dated contexts in north-eastern Africa. In this region, two general areas have been subjected to extensive examination and provide potential but unrealized sources of evidence for inter-regional correlations. These are the Nile terraces and the Kharga oasis.

In the Pliocene, high sea levels in the Mediterranean flooded into the Nile valley and produced a gulf extending as far south as Kom Ombo in Upper Egypt. The silts and sands deposited by the rivers and streams in this gulf were subsequently eroded in early Pleistocene times during phases of lower sea levels, and further sands and gravels were laid down as terraces during the Middle and Upper Pleistocene.

A series of high-level gravels, at heights extending down to *c*. 50 metres above the modern flood plain, indicates the complex nature of the geological processes involved in the early history of the Nile, processes which without doubt were of different natures in the lower and upper reaches of the river. In the lower Nile, changes in sea level would result in downcutting or aggradation, but in the upper Nile, the major factor was probably alternating volumes of water in relation to the sediment in transport.

No trace of human industries has been reported from river gravels above 30 metres. In both the upper and lower Nile, deposits at *c*. 27 metres above the modern flood plain have yielded quantities of handaxes, cores and flake tools; in upper Egypt and Nubia, there is evidence of working floors preserved in situ, and the artefacts include both primitive and developed forms of Acheulean character. In lower Egypt, differential weathering indicates that the primitive specimens may be derived from earlier deposits.

The succeeding terrace in Upper Egypt and Nubia is at 15 metres, and contains more developed Acheulean material, smaller and thinner handaxes with straighter edges. Below this terrace is a 8–9 metre deposit with evolved handaxes and flakes with wide faceted platforms; the industry may be termed Acheuleo-Levalloisian (fig. 69).

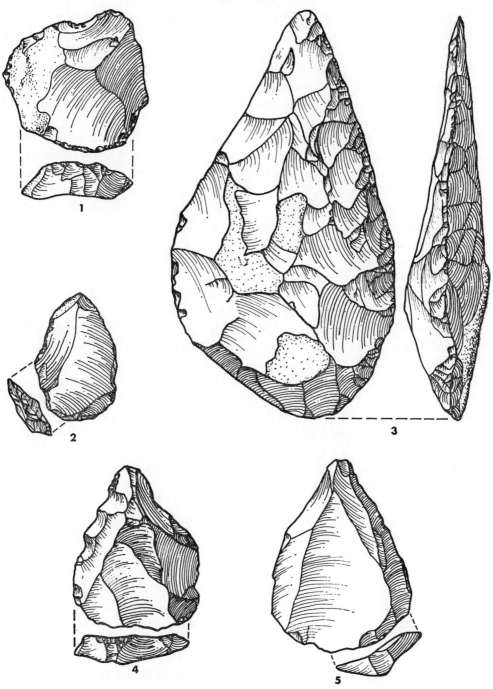

FIG. 69. Acheuleo-Levalloisian and Upper Levalloisian $\frac{2}{3}$; Refûf Pass, Kharga, Egypt; 1–3 Acheuleo-Levalloisian; 4, 5 Upper Levalloisian. *After Caton-Thompson and Gardner 1952*

195

Below, at 3–4 metres, are gravels containing Levalloisian cores, flakes and flake-blades without associated handaxes of Acheulean character. Neither the 8–9 metre nor the 3–4 metre terraces of the upper Nile are recognizable north of Samalut, *c.* 400 kilometres from the Mediterranean. In the lower Nile, however, another terrace at 8 metres is well-marked and contains industrial material comparable in its general character to that of the 3–4 metres terrace farther south. The probable geological correlation between these terraces is undemonstrated.

Geological evidence suggests that a major climatic change occurred subsequent to the deposition of the terrace gravels; the coarse gravels of these terraces, indicating a large and fast-moving river, are succeeded by silts which must signify a reduction in volume of the water, and which by their character indicate their source not in lateral valleys and the Red Sea Hills but in the Ethiopian plateau. The tributary rivers and streams north of the Wadi Halfa ceased to play any part in the sources of the Nile volume at this period.

The silts rise in Nubia to *c.* 30 metres above the present river level, but fall to a level below that of the modern flood plain at the bend to the north of Luxor in middle Egypt. If these silts represent a river gradient, they must indicate a sea level well below that of today, and in all probability that of the Last Glaciation.

At Kom Ombo in Upper Egypt, coarse gravels equivalent to the 3–4 metre terrace are covered by silts up to 20 metres in thickness. During temporary dry periods near the end of this period of silt accumulation, occupations took place on exposed silts in the drying swamp and marsh. The artefactual material includes smaller forms of core and flake, with increased flake-blades and greater use of secondary flaking. Successive industries accentuated this diminution of tool-size, but the prepared core technique continued. These industries have been called Sebilian, and have been considered to represent a purely local tradition, independent of the true blade industries of adjacent areas. The later stages of the Sebilian material contain micro-lithic forms, and are associated with aurochs, buffalo and shell middens. Suggested dates for the Sebilian industries range from *c.* 16,000 to 11,000 B.P.

Recent work in the Kom Ombo area has confirmed early suggestions that other industries were being produced on the plain. At least five different assemblages have been recovered, in addition to the Sebilian (fig. 70, 12–15). One of these, the Menchian (fig. 70, 16, 17) is of Aurignacian character with retouched long blades and high-backed scrapers. Others, found near Gebel Silsila, consist of the Silsilian (fig. 70, 3–5), an early microlithic industry with backed bladelets, geometric microliths, micro-burins, burins and pebble cores, and the Sebekian (fig. 70, 1, 2), stratigraphi-cally later, with narrow bladelets with nibbled retouch, burins, scrapers, awls and notched blades. The Sebekian is associated with antelope, gazelle, and hippopotamus. Radiocarbon dates indicate the Sebekian was in production before 14,000 B.P.

At Khor el-Sil, on the same plain, two other industries have been recognized. One utilized prepared cores with faceted platforms, in Sebilian fashion, but no backed bladelets or geometric forms occur; burins, scrapers and other retouched flakes are

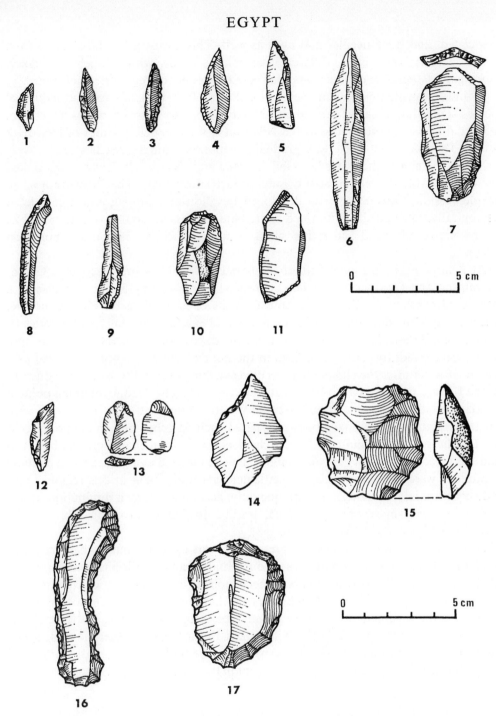

FIG. 70. Kom Ombo, Egypt; 1–2 Sebekian; 3–5 Silsilian; 6–8 Khor el-Sil II; 9–11 Khor el-Sil IV; 12–15 Sebilian; 16–17 Menchian. *After Smith 1966a*

associated, and bone needles and awls as well. This industry has been dated to *c*. 18,000 B.P. At other sites, different assemblages occur, with retouched bladelets lacking the association of either prepared core techniques or geometric microliths.

In lower Egypt, the Fayum Depression has yielded evidence for the industrial phases succeeding those of the 8 metre Nile terrace. The depression is some 80 km. wide and lies sufficiently close to the Nile that it was flooded at times of high river levels. The lake as it then was gradually deposited shingle beaches successively occupied by man as the water level fell. Terrace gravels along the river which linked the Nile and the depression also contain industrial material. The 34 metre level in the depression is associated with developed Levalloisian material, and is correlated geologically, as culturally, with the 8 metre Nile gravels. Beach deposits at 28 and 22 metres are of advanced and rather small Levalloisian character (Caton-Thompson 1946).

At Kharga oasis, in Egypt, further industrial material has been recovered Caton-Thompson and Gardner 1952). The depression, some 150 by 30 km., represents a wind-eroded basin containing tufaceous deposits of probable early Pleistocene age. Drainage systems developed from the north and east escarpments, and a series of climatic oscillations has been inferred from the deposition of gravels and tufas, and from further wadi formations. Springs in the floor of the depression continued as a source of water after the climate had become essentially that of today. The industries of the Kharga oasis appear to begin with a developed Acheulean, containing pointed handaxes and flakes, the latter essentially with plain platforms but some with prepared platforms. Animal bones associated include zebra and antelope or wild cattle. The succeeding industry is of Acheuleo-Levalloisian character, and both this and the preceding industry is considered to have flourished at a period when climatic conditions were more favourable to settlement and movement in this region. Later industries are in a Levalloisian technique only, accompanied by a diminution in size and an increase in secondary retouch, leading to industries comparable to the Levalloiso-Mousterian of Palestine (p. 358).

One of the final traditions in the depression appears to be of Aterian character, with miniature discoid and prepared cores, points and scrapers with fine retouch, flake-blades and bifacially-worked points; tanged points, in characteristic Aterian style, also occur. The presence of such industries at Kharga may indicate an eastern movement of people; similar material occurs in Tibesti and Wanyanga. Little trace has been discovered farther east in the Nile valley. From the south there is evidence of penetration of Lupemban traditions, apparent in the Sudan at Khor Abu Anga and possibly contributing to the leaf point element in the eastern Aterian.

Part III
EUROPE

14

Western Europe

ONE of the basic chronological frameworks for the European Pleistocene is based upon the evidence for glacial advances and retreats in the Alps and in northern Europe. These stratigraphical sequences in Europe tend, however, to be geographically limited and to represent only a part of the Pleistocene. Although in the Alps the Günz glacial advance was apparently preceded by a number of cold episodes of uncertain duration and severity, there is little evidence of related phases in the north, and it is only through interglacial polleniferous deposits that correlations for Pleistocene events are made possible. Here too, the record is incomplete, and the earliest climatic episodes of the Pleistocene are not recognizable. One area, however, has provided evidence for these early events, as well as providing ammunition to those who look for the earliest traces of man's activity in western Europe.

The climatic evidence for the earlier Pleistocene in East Anglia has already been indicated (p. 27), and it is within the Crags of East Anglia that evidence for the contemporary presence of man has been claimed by a number of prehistorians (summary in Coles 1968). The evidence consists of the eoliths, pre-Crag flints and Cromerian flints of many authors. Geologically, these flints have been recovered from the basal deposits of the Red Crag, from within the Red Crag, and from the base of the Norwich Crag. Others were found in deposits believed to be contemporary with the Cromer Forest Bed. In some cases, the flints are rolled, in others they are fresh. Flakes, cores and handaxe shapes with bifacial flaking occur, and often an isolated specimen appears so skilfully and deliberately fashioned that many authorities accept it as of human manufacture.

Some prehistorians accepted the Crag and immediately post-Crag eoliths as of human manufacture, because they did not believe that natural agencies could produce such finely-flaked specimens. Opposing this is the view that the stone beds at the base of the Crag sands are the result of slow submarine erosion of the chalk in this region, and that these exposed flint beds were subjected to the crushing action of icebergs, grounding near the shores of the Crag sea. Such an explanation would account for the local concentrations of fractured flints at Cromer and other areas, but does not so clearly explain away the position of flaked flints below and above a sand-with-gravel deposit *within* the Red Crag at Foxhall; these flints (fig. 71, 1–3) with an apparently associated human jaw, may represent local disturbance superimposing Crag sands on a recent land surface. Nevertheless, the Foxhall flints, and an enormous bifacially-flaked flint believed to be from the base of the Norwich Crag at Thorpe in Norfolk (fig. 71, 4) represent evidence that, at the moment, cannot be satisfactorily explained as of purely natural origin. Our present state of knowledge about the chronology of early industries elsewhere in the Old World suggests that it is unlikely that the East Anglian Crag assemblages are of human manufacture.

The earliest undoubted evidence for the presence of man in western Europe is provided by the mandible from the Mauer Sands near Heidelberg (Howell 1966). The mandible is large and robust although the teeth are small; the chin is receding. The affinities of this jaw are uncertain, and it has been classified as *Homo erectus*, *Homo sapiens* and *Homo sp.* The associated fauna is of the Cromerian interglacial period. Although attempts to associate the jaw with a lithic industry have not

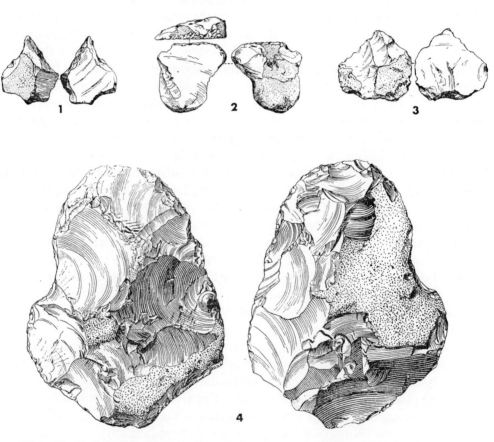

FIG. 71. Eoliths $\frac{1}{2}$; 1–3 Foxhall, Suffolk, England; 4 Whitlingham, Norfolk, England. *After Coles 1968*

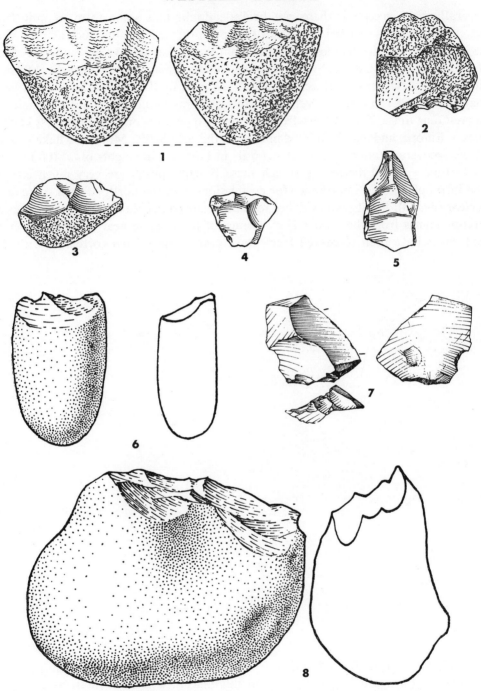

FIG. 72. 1–5 Vertesszöllös, Hungary ½; 6–8 Vallonnet, France ½. *After Coles 1968, and de Lumley* et al. *1963*

generally been accepted, there can be little doubt that some form of industrial activity was being practised in western Europe during this period. Such activity may be represented by the pebbles and flakes from the Vallonnet cave in southern France (fig. 72, 6–8; p. 264), dated by fauna to the Villafranchian, and by geological formations to a colder period succeeding a high sea level of 108 metres. Such a sea level may be of the Cromerian interglacial, although some authorities place this high sea in pre-Günz times. The industry from Vallonnet represents one of the earliest known sites in Europe, and may be related in time to the pebble (fig. 54, 5) and flake assemblages recovered from raised beach deposits in Portugal, at heights of ± 100 metres, as well as ± 55–60 metres. Although these beach deposits are very much eroded and incomplete, their importance for correlations with the north African succession is clear (fig. 73). Additional evidence for unspecialized pebble and flake industries in Europe comes from the Upper High terrace of the Somme near Montières, where flint flakes have been recovered from gravels which have been correlated with the

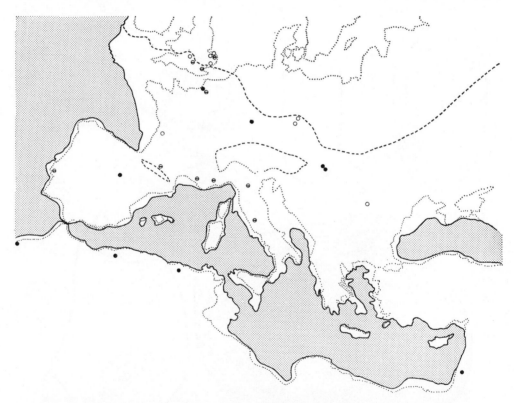

FIG. 73. Distribution of finds purporting to demonstrate the presence of man in Europe before the Hoxnian interglacial. ● finds certain; ⊖ finds probable; ○ finds improbable (England) or lacking dating evidence (Continent). Outline map drawn to show extent of Elster-Mindel ice advances and possible contemporary low sea-level. *After Coles 1968*

Eburonian phase of the Günz glaciation (p. 40), and from high terrace gravels of the Garonne, where quartz and quartzite objects have been recovered (fig. 54, 6–7). 'Pebble tools' have been recovered from pre-Mindel deposits of the Rhône and at Achenheim, but a possible natural origin cannot be ruled out. The existence of industrial traditions based upon pebble and flake elements continued through the early Middle Pleistocene in Europe. The site at Vertesszöllös in Hungary represents the earliest known evidence for the presence of man in central Europe (p. 303). There are also reports of pebble tools and flake tools from terraces on the Olf river in Rumania. The occupation at Vertesszöllös extended over a long period, during the Mindel interstadial and late Mindel. Flaked pebbles and small retouched flakes of quartzite, flint and chert form the industries (fig. 72, 1–5). Fire is attested by traces of hearths, but this may not be the earliest evidence of fire in Europe; heat-crazed flints from the Somme, and hearths from the Escale cave in southern France, may indicate that fire was controlled by man as early as the beginning of Middle Pleistocene times. In Italy, there is slight evidence of occupation in the late Mindel period near Rome, where a few flakes have been recovered from beneath the earliest tuffs of the Sabatino volcanoes. The volcanic activity apparently began during Mindel times.

This tradition of an unspecialized flake and pebble industry may lie behind the emergence of two other industries in Middle Pleistocene times. One of these is represented by the assemblages of flake tools and cores from Swanscombe and Clacton-on-Sea (fig. 76; p. 269; Breuil 1932). These are of Hoxnian date, although there is some evidence that this 'Clactonian' industry was being manufactured in Mindel times; flake tools which resemble these industries have also been recognized in western Europe in deposits of Rissian age, but culturally no connection has been demonstrated. A second west European industry which has been related to the early pebble and flake industry is the 'Abbevillian', an industry based upon flakes and heavy coarse chopping tools and handaxes (fig. 74, 1–2). This industry has been recorded from certain exposures in the valley of the Somme, where it is dated by a fauna of Cromerian affinities to, probably, the Mindel interstadial (p. 265). It is not at all certain that this restricted industry played any significant part in the appearance of the widespread west European handaxe tradition (Oakley 1964).

At this stage, it is convenient to treat the European sequence of industries on a regional basis; for this, western Europe is taken to consist of the classic area of Palaeolithic studies, north and south France, Spain, southern Britain and parts of the Low Countries. In the early stages of the western sequence we must refer to the river terraces of the Somme (p. 265), which combine to present a remarkably complete picture of the industrial traditions present in the west from the late Mindel through Hoxnian and into Rissian times and beyond. It is likely that the scheme of dating proposed for many of the deposits of these terraces is based upon an over-simplified version of the major Pleistocene events, but in terms of an internal relative stratigraphical sequence, the Somme terraces continue to be vital to our

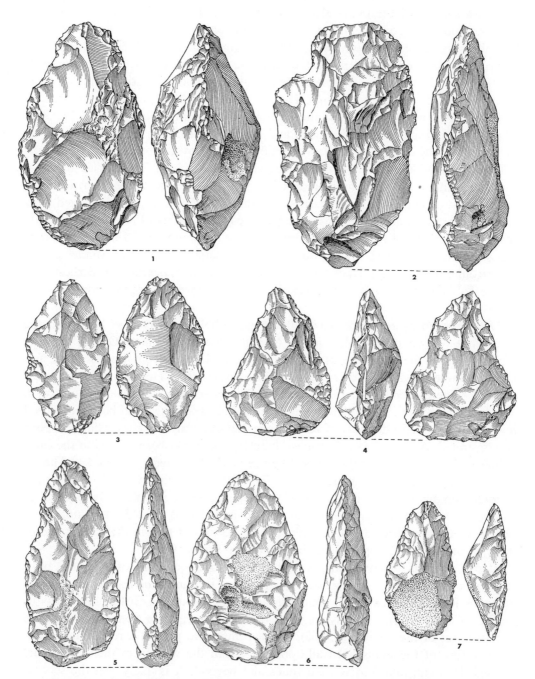

FIG. 74. Acheulean $\frac{1}{2}$; Caversham Channel gravels, England. *After Treacher, Arkell and Oakley 1948*

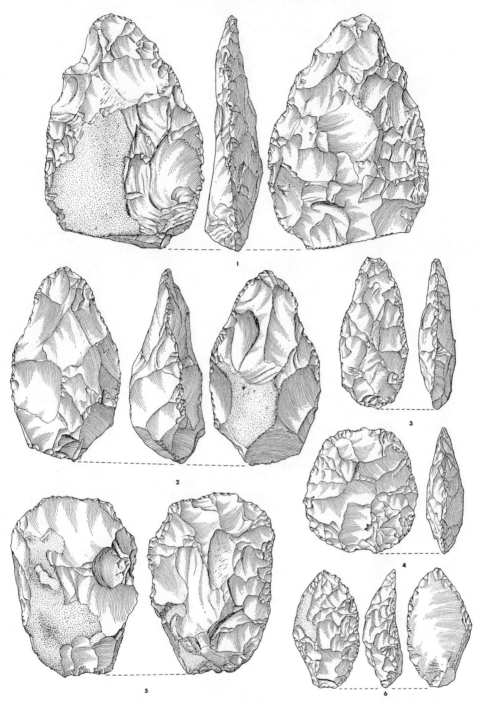

FIG. 75. Acheulean $\frac{1}{2}$; Caversham Channel gravels, England. *After Treacher, Arkell and Oakley 1948*

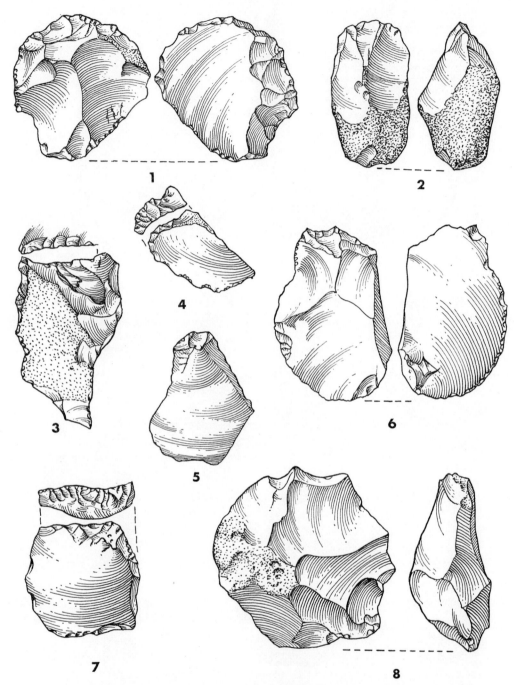

FIG. 76. 'Clactonian' $\frac{2}{3}$; Clacton-on-Sea, England. *After Oakley and Leakey 1937*

understanding of industrial developments in this part of western Europe (fig. 77, schematic diagram of 1933).

Using the Somme gravel exposures, Breuil classified the Acheulean handaxe industries into seven stages. These now tend to be combined into only three divisions, Early, Middle and Late, but it remains to be demonstrated whether or not even such a tripartite sequence is valid. Too many imponderables exist at the present time for us to accept any division based upon pure typology. It has for long been known that handaxe industries in Europe tend to be distributed in the west, in northern and western France, southern England, Spain and along coastal southern France into

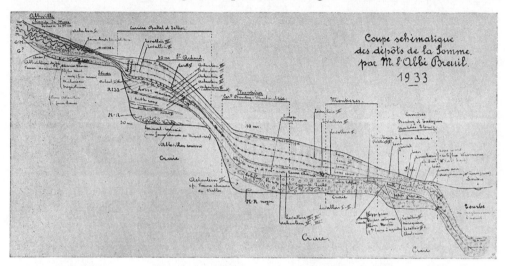

FIG. 77. Schematic diagram of the terrace deposits of the Somme River, based on early work by H. Breuil 1933 presented as an example of the complexities of river terrace systems. *After the original in the University Museum of Archaeology and Ethnology, Cambridge, England*

central and northern Italy (p. 311). Few finds are recorded outside these areas, for example the handaxes from Greece (p. 311).

These industries, although typified by the presence of bifacially-flaked handaxes, have a high percentage of flake tools, flakes perhaps deliberately obtained from cores, or flakes occasioned by the production of the handaxe. Cleavers are not at all common in west European handaxe industries, but they have been recorded from a number of sites along the Atlantic coasts. Handaxes have a variety of shapes and sizes, and must represent a whole series of activities by Palaeolithic man (Roe 1964). The handaxes, and flake tools, from the Somme River valley 30 metre terrace (fig. 78–80, p. 266) are of the Hoxnian interglacial, and have been compared with the industry from the Middle Gravels at Swanscombe (Plate IV; p. 269). In fact the correlation between the Acheulean of Swanscombe and that of the Somme 30 metre terrace lies not only in the typology of the artefacts but also in the specifically continental fauna at Swans-

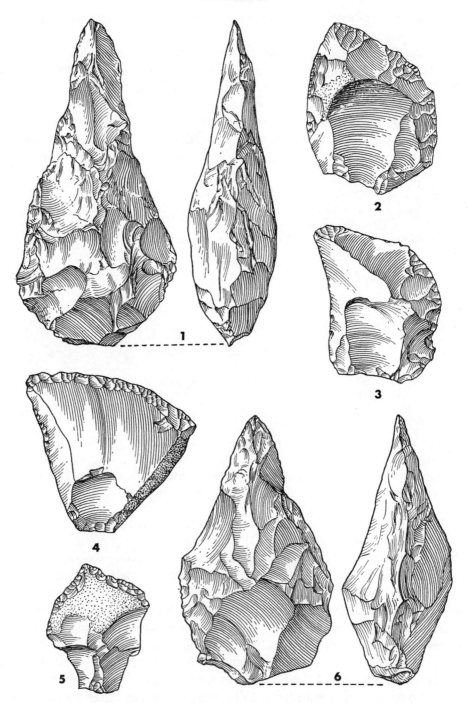

FIG. 78. Acheulean ⅔; L'atelier Commont. *After Bordes and Fitte 1953*

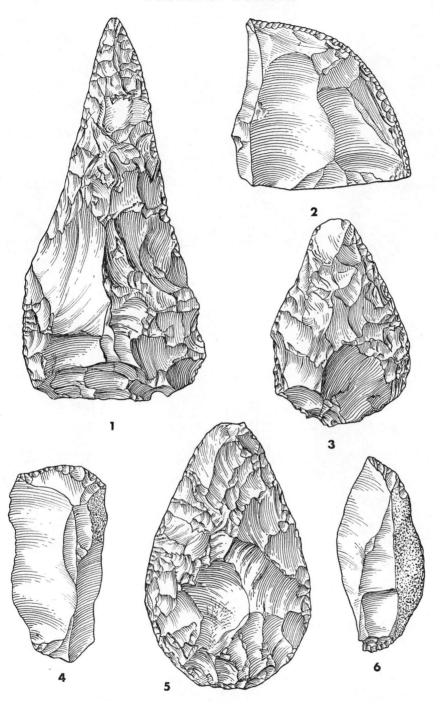

FIG. 79. Acheulean ⅔; L'atelier Commont. *After Bordes and Fitte 1953*

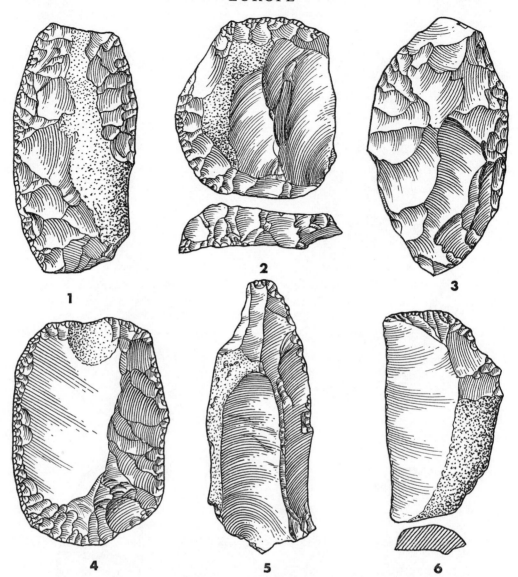

FIG. 80. Acheulean ⅔; L'atelier Commont. *After Bordes and Fitte 1953*

combe, which has suggested that some form of land-bridge between England and the Continent emerged subsequent to the deposition of the Lower Gravels at Swanscombe.

Of earlier date is the occupation at Torralba in central Spain (Butzer 1964; Howell 1966). A number of occupation levels in the sands, gravels and marls of this high-level site (over 1,100 metres above sea level) have yielded industrial material in the Acheulean tradition, with axes, cleavers and many flake tools made on quartzite, flint and limestone. Bone, ivory and wooden objects have also been recovered. Climatically, the occupation seems to have taken place during a series of minor oscillations, a generally cold moist period with an intervening temperate interval, which is believed to be of late Mindel times. Large mammals, elephant, horse, deer, and aurochs were hunted by the Acheulean handaxe makers of Torralba. Earlier still are the Winter Hill gravels of the Middle Thames near Henley which appear stratigraphically to precede the Lowestoftian boulder clays, and are therefore earlier than the Mindel 2 Glaciation; typologically the industry from these and related gravels at Caversham (fig. 74–75; p. 269), are not appreciably more archaic than assemblages of Hoxnian date, but this does not seem to be a valid basis for dating the Winter Hill gravels any later than the Mindel interstadial.

During Hoxnian times there developed in western Europe a method of flake production known as the prepared core technique (p. 59), and it can be demonstrated that this development occurred first within Acheulean industries, not only in western Europe but also in Africa, in the north-west, north-east and in other parts. Although in each of these regions the developed technique is of somewhat different character, the basic idea being practised is uniform and has led to the common use of the term Levalloisian to describe the groups participating in this tradition. Such a term should be used in the technological sense only, and without cultural connotations.

In western Europe, handaxe industries with elements of the prepared core technique were being made in Hoxnian times, but only in certain areas. Traces of this development occur in the Boyn Hill terrace of the Thames River (p. 269), in the contemporary 30 metre terrace of the Somme, and at Slindon in Sussex where it was in association with a raised beach of the order of 100′ above that of the present day (p. 32). Industries using the Levalloisian method are characterized by the pre-forming of the tool on the core before it is detached from the core (fig. 81). The

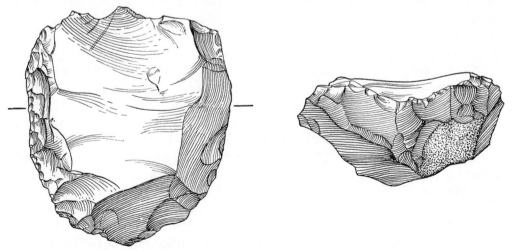

FIG. 81. Levalloisian core $\frac{1}{2}$; Northfleet, Kent, England

technique is expensive in terms of flint but in certain industries the resultant flake-tools may be long and narrow, or shorter and broad, each with extremely sharp and even edges unaltered by retouch. Again, however, such industries of Levalloisian character tend to vary over limited regions, and it is not possible to say if such divergent natures are due to differences of tradition, or raw material, or function, or chronology.

The Levalloisian industries of western Europe tend to be restricted to low-lying areas, and are particularly concentrated in northern France, Belgium and south-eastern England (McBurney 1950). The technique (fig. 81) was adopted by some handaxe groups in Rissian times, as at Baker's Hole in Kent, although other axe-making groups did not use the method at all. In Eemian times, the fashion of preparing flake-tools on the core became more popular in this restricted area, and in some industries the production of the bifacial handaxe ceased, being entirely replaced by thinner flake-tools which may be of equivalent size to handaxes. In the Somme Valley, Levalloisian industries with handaxes had a long history before the last Glaciation commenced. Levalloisian material without handaxes occurs in the earlier deposits of Younger Loess on the 30 metre terrace. On the basis of the stratified industries in the Somme gravels, the Levalloisian industries are divided into seven stages, but it is difficult to employ this typology elsewhere.

Flake industries of a different character from the Levalloisian were being manu-factured contemporaneously in western Europe from before the Eem interglacial, and these traditions gradually supplanted the Levalloisian until total replacement occurred during the Last Glaciation (Bordes 1961a). Two sites in the west, Fontéchevade and La Micoque, demonstrate the complex nature of the development of flake industries during the Upper Pleistocene, although current views suggest that these sites do not necessarily represent an indigenous source of the more standardized Mousterian industries in this area. At Fontéchevade, the industry from layer E appears to be of Eemian age, although perhaps late in this interglacial or, according to what defini-tions are adopted, of early Last Glaciation date. The flints consist of plain and faceted platform flakes, notched flakes, discoid cores and choppers (fig. 82–83; p. 270). A prepared core element is clearly present, although its Levalloisian nature is not particularly marked. The association of this industry with the remains of *Homo sapiens* has been compared with the Acheulean-associated remains at Swanscombe, and these two finds formed the 'Praesapiens' group of Vallois. At La Micoque, the sequence of flake industries, forming the basis of the ill-defined Tayacian group, seems to demonstrate only the presence of an unstandardized flake tradition probably during the Riss glaciation, but with, in layer H, the appearance of a discoid core technique superficially of Mousterian character (p. 271; Bourgon 1957). Both Fontéchevade and La Micoque have diminished importance now that it can be seen that by Eemian times a fully developed Mousterian tradition was in existence both in western and central Europe. Some evidence of an earlier date for the Mousterian industries exists along the Atlantic coast, and in Italy, at the Torre in Pietra, where a

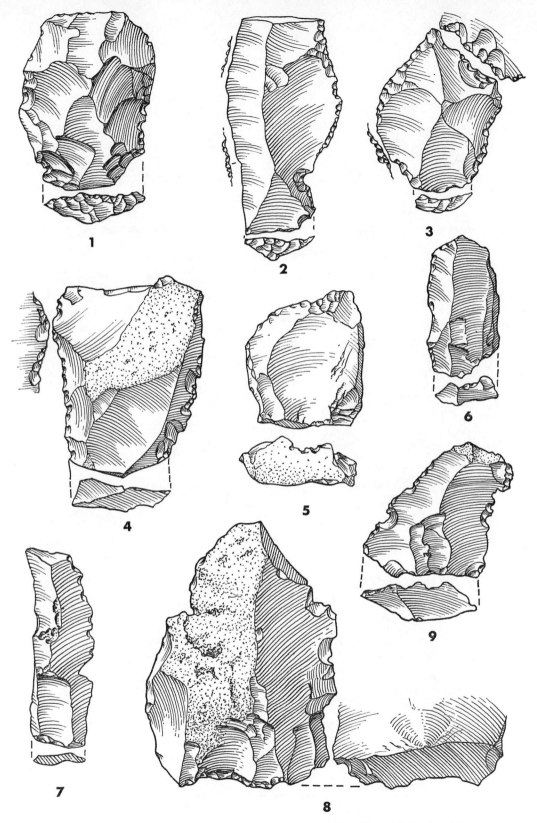

FIG. 82. Fontéchevade, France ⅔; Level E. *After Henri-Martin 1957*

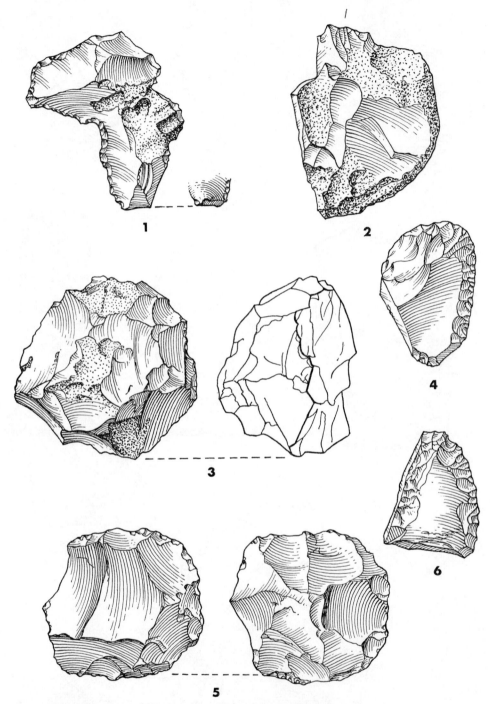

FIG. 83. Fontéchevade, France ⅔; Level E. *After Henri-Martin 1957*

flake industry has been recovered from deposits with cool climatic indicators and which have been eroded by a sea of the order of 18 metres.

During the Eem, it appears that industrial traditions involving the production of tools by retouching flakes struck from prepared cores were widespread over much of southern and western Europe (McBurney 1950). In the west, small cordiform axes (fig. 84, 4) were a part of the equipment, and at Castillo in Spain and other sites such industries also contained cleavers. The source of both these types is thought by some authorities to have been north-west Africa (p. 182). A majority of these flake industries in the west, however, lack axes and cleavers, and typologically have been taken to indicate a degree of general uniformity in tradition from western France and Spain along the Mediterranean coasts to Italy.

The Mousterian industries from western France have been studied collectively on several occasions, and differing interpretations have been placed upon the typological variations (Bordes 1961, Bourgon 1957, Mellars 1965). Recently it has been suggested that four major industrial groups existed in the region. The *typical Mousterian* contains quantities of flake scrapers and pointed forms, and is represented by the industry from the lowest levels of Le Moustier (p. 272). At this site the associated fauna indicates a temperate to cool phase. The typical Mousterian group is considered to have been developed from industries such as that from La Micoque, level 4 (p. 271). The *Charentian*, or Quina-Ferrassie Mousterian, is characterised by industries with a large variety of scrapers, most with convex retouched edges and including some bifacial implements (fig. 85). Most of the flakes have plain platforms unlike those of the typical Mousterian, where preparation of the platform is common (fig. 84, 1).

Another variant group is the *denticulate Mousterian*. This industry as a whole is poor in technique, with quantities of irregularly-shaped flakes with notched retouch. The *Mousterian of Acheulean tradition* consists of a flake industry in which scrapers (fig. 84, 2, 3, 5) and points feature, but with the addition of triangular and cordiform handaxes (fig. 84, 4). Retouch on these axes is bifacial, and the same technique was applied to some flakes. Additionally, there are flake-blades, retouched into awls, burins and backed knives. This industry has sometimes been considered to lie behind the emergence of the Chatelperron industries of the Upper Palaeolithic. Radiocarbon dates suggest that the Mousterian industries were generally contemporary with at least some of these flake and blade traditions (fig. 2).

More precise knowledge of the Mousterian industries and climatic dating has been obtained by the excavations at Combe Grenal (Bordes and Prat 1965). Above Rissian and Eemian deposits occur a large number of occupations dated by fauna, pollen and cryoturbation traces to the early episodes of the Würm glaciation. Levels with red deer, roe deer, bear and elk are associated with cryoturbation deposits indicating a cool but wet phase in early Würm. Succeeding deposits contain red deer and birds, followed by reindeer dominance to a peak during Mousterian occupation. The occupation continued during a period of milder conditions, when horse, then a bovid,

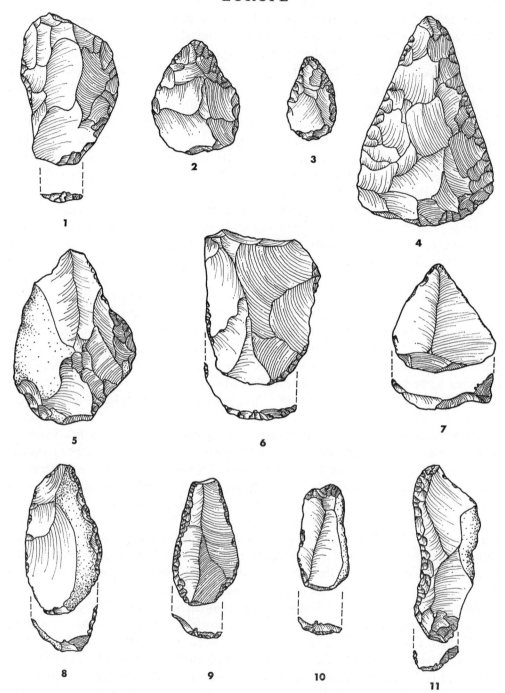

FIG. 84. Mousterian $\frac{2}{3}$; Le Moustier. 1 level B, 2–5 G, 6–8 H, 9–11 J. *After Bourgon 1957*

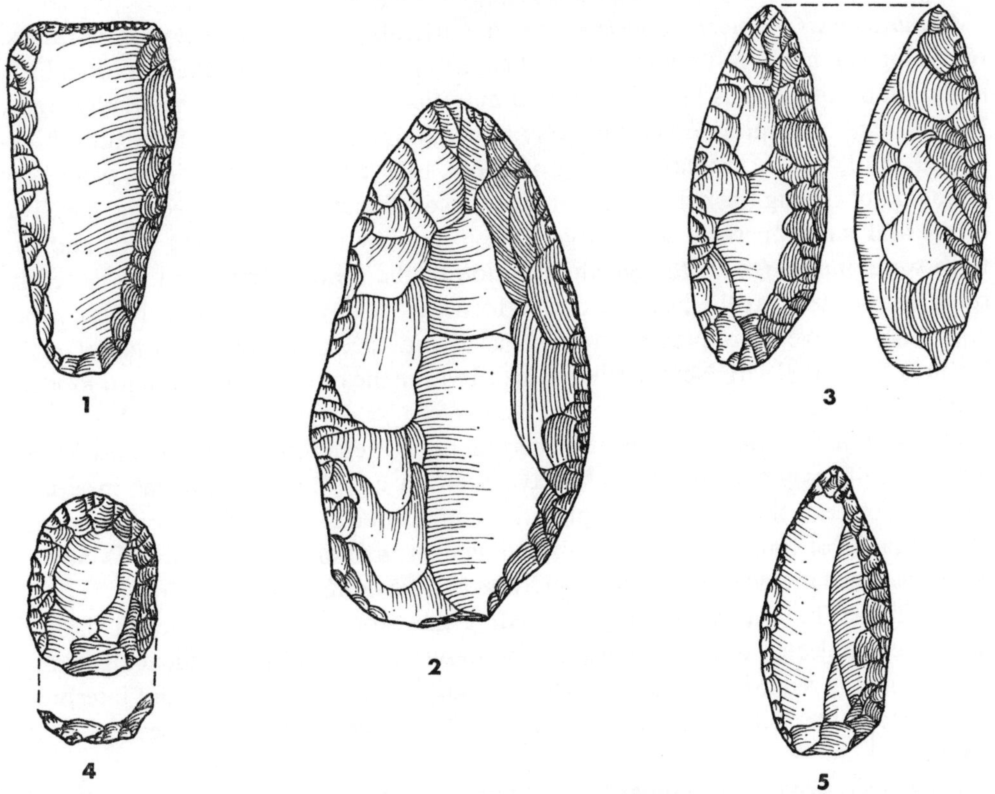

FIG. 85. Mousterian $\frac{2}{3}$; La Ferrassie C. *After Bourgon 1957*

then red deer, were the dominant forms hunted by Mousterian man. Near the top of the deposits, reindeer return and the industries contain cordiform handaxes.

Of these industries in France, only the typical Mousterian and the Charentian are believed to be associated directly with burials of the classic Neanderthal type.

The Mousterian groups of western Europe were perhaps the first to bury their dead deliberately. At La Chapelle-aux-Saints, an adult male with severe osteoarthritis was buried in a pit with head to the west, feet to the east with legs bent, and arms partly extended; the head was protected by animal bones. Flints and quartzite and crystal rocks, and remains of reindeer, bison and aurochs, accompanied the body. An 18-year-old male was buried at Le Moustier, contracted, and apparently had his head cushioned on a pile of flints. The shelter at La Ferrassie contained burials of two adults, one male and one female, placed head to head in shallow pits 50 cm. apart. The contracted male was protected by flat stones on head and shoulder, and flint flakes and bone splinters had been thrown into the grave. The female body lay on its right side with the legs bent up against the body, and with hands on knees. Near these graves were the remains of two children, perhaps of 5 years of age, buried in a conical grave. These remains, typified particularly by the La Chapelle-aux-Saints skeleton, are generally regarded as of extreme Neanderthalers.

Homo sapiens neanderthalensis is noted particularly for his heavy brow-ridges, retreating forehead, large jaws and rather heavy limb bones. In these, particularly in the limb bones, he is less like modern man than some of the *Homo erectus* finds. Neanderthal man rarely exceeded 5 feet in height, and had a rather large and thick-walled skull, with a cranial capacity of about 1450 c.c. The brow ridges were very large and overhung the orbits, the forehead receded and the brain case was flat. The orbits and nasal aperture were large. The lower jaw had a receding chin and the teeth were quite large. Although the position of the foramen magnum suggested to some authorities that the head was tilted forwards, it now appears that Neanderthal man did not have a stooping posture. It has already been suggested that many of the features associated with Neanderthal man fall within the range of variation for modern man.

In addition to burial of the dead, in certain areas Neanderthal man practised some form of cult involving the skulls of cave bear. In a cave at Les Furtins in eastern France, six bear skulls had been placed on limestone slabs, with two others near, and a bundle of long-bones on a slab laid against the north-west wall. This cult has more spectacular evidence in high-level Swiss and Bavarian caves (p. 286).

The industries stratigraphically succeeding the Mousterian industries in the west have been subjected to many analyses and descriptions, and the sequence proposed for this area is remarkable not only for its detail but also for the different interpretations placed upon it (Breuil 1912; Breuil and Lantier 1965; de Sonneville Bordes 1960).

The classic sequence of Upper Palaeolithic industries in the west is provided by the Dordogne sites of La Ferrassie, Laugerie Haute and La Madeleine, and almost all of the more recently excavated sites in the region have tended to confirm the general industrial succession originally proposed on the basis of these three sites, although quite minor differences have been recorded.

Although there appears to be little evidence for transitional industries between the Mousterian and the earliest Upper Palaeolithic, such industries have been reported from several sites, including Arcy-sur-Cure and La Quina. Of greater importance than these, however, is the picture which is developing from the abundant radio-carbon dates for Mousterian and Upper Palaeolithic industries in France (fig. 2); this seems to indicate quite strongly that considerable overlap in time may have existed between the people with Mousterian industries and those using Upper Palaeolithic material. What this overlap signifies in terms of contact or evolution remains to be further elaborated.

One of the original sequences for Upper Palaeolithic industries in the area was proposed by Breuil, who provided sub-divisions for the Aurignacian, Solutrean and Magdalenian industries (Breuil 1912). Peyrony considered that the Lower and Upper Aurignacian were more closely united than either was to the Middle Aurignacian, and he proposed the term Perigordian for the industries stratigraphically earlier and later than the Middle Aurignacian. Peyrony then sub-divided the Perigordian further, believing that there had existed two groups using different industrial traditions. At perhaps its most complex, the scheme appeared as follows:

PERIGORDIAN 1st group	I Chatelperron La Ferrassie E	II	III Laugerie Haute B	IV La Gravette sup.	V La Ferrassie J & K
PERIGORDIAN 2nd group	I	II Bos del Ser La Ferrassie E′	III La Gravette moy.	IV	V La Ferrassie L
AURIGNACIAN		I La Gravette inf. La Ferrassie F	II La Ferrassie H	III IV La Ferrassie H′ H″	V Laugerie Haute D

The first Perigordian group was characterized by Chatelperron backed points (as seen at Chatelperron and La Ferrassie E), truncated forms (Laugerie Haute B), Gravettian backed blades (La Gravette, sup.), Font Robert tanged points (La Ferrassie J), and finally, truncated forms (La Ferrassie K). The second group contained strong Aurignacian influence, with reverse backed bladelets of Dufour type (Bos del Ser and La Ferrassie E′), Gravette points (La Gravette moy.), Font-Yves points and Noailles burins (La Ferrassie L). Peyrony's structure has not been accepted, as it was based primarily upon a theory of industrial development rather than on stratigraphical realities, and, in fact, not only has the dual role of the Perigordian culture been dismissed but also the idea of parallel Aurignacian-Perigordian 'peoples' has not met with much approval. Perigordian II has been grouped with Aurignacian traditions, and Perigordian III (Laugerie Haute B) combined with developed La Gravette (and renumbered Perigordian VI). Currently the most economical view is that there exists an early industry with curved back blades, called Chatelperronian (La Ferrassie E, p. 273), which is succeeded by Aurignacian industries (former Middle Aurignacian of Breuil) as at La Ferrassie (F, H, H[1], H[11]), which are themselves succeeded by Gravettian industries (La Ferrassie J, K, L; Laugerie Haute B). However it may well be that such a simple unilinear approach is masking a more diverse situation. The radiocarbon dates from French Palaeolithic industries (fig. 2), if taken at their face value, indicate that Mousterian material was being produced at the same time as Chatelperron and Aurignacian material in a restricted area. Similarly, it can be said that the absolute dating evidence suggests an overlap in time between the Aurignacian and the Gravettian and between the Gravettian, proto-Magdalenian and Solutrean. Arguments against this interpretation would seem to fall on the lines of the relative coarseness of the radiocarbon dating method, the limited quantity of dates, and the fact that stratigraphically the unilinear sequence is supported. Yet we might be wise to assess carefully the quality of our stratigraphical detail, which rests upon interpretation of sections excavated in the early part of this century if not in the preceding one.

The Chatelperronian industries are characterized by flakes, end scrapers, burins, and blades with curved blunted backs (fig. 86, 1–18). At La Ferrassie E there is little evidence of a true punched blade technique, and at a number of sites there is reason to believe that the 'Chatelperronian' is a mixed industry containing Mousterian and Aurignacian material. Its status as an independent tradition is uncertain, and it may not represent anything more than a local development of limited extent in time and space. At La Roc de Combe Capelle an extended inhumation was discovered on a slab surrounded by shells; the right leg was bent outward, the left leg had been

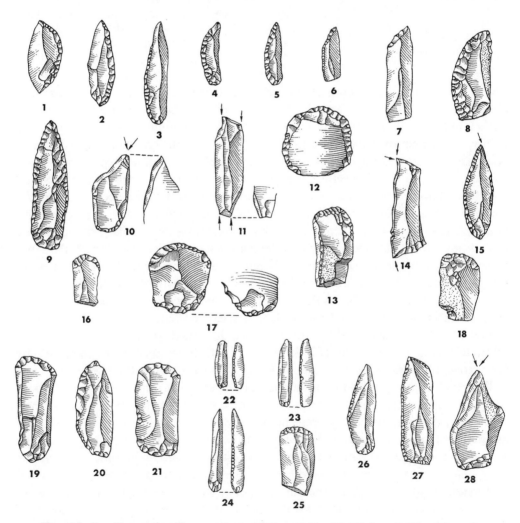

FIG. 86. La Ferrassie, France $\frac{2}{3}$; 1–18 Level E; 19–28 Level E[1]. *After de Sonneville-Bordes 1960*

disturbed. At the feet were several flake tools. The burial probably lay within a Chatelperronian deposit, which was covered by a sterile deposit followed by an Aurignacian level, but considerable uncertainty exists about the position of the skeleton, and it cannot be used in discussions of the origin of the Upper Palaeolithic in the west. At Arcy-sur-Cure (Yonne) the series of industries transitional between Mousterian and Chatelperron represent strong evidence for a local origin of this unsatisfactory group. Radiocarbon dates for industries of Chatelperronian character from central France range from *c.* 35,000 to 25,000 B.P.

The industries at La Ferrassie which succeed the Chatelperronian are 'Aurignacian', and are well represented at this site where four levels (F, H, H^1, H^{11}) were distinguished (fig. 87–88). Level E^1, called Perigordian II, has also been described as Aurignacian; the status of Perigordian II is uncertain (fig. 86, 19–28; p. 274). The Aurignacian industries of the west are characterized by the presence of punch-struck blades with flat skimming or scaly retouch on the edges of the dorsal face (fig. 87, 1–7), strangulated blades (fig. 87, 2, 7), high-backed carinated and nosed scrapers (fig. 87, 21, 23), and solid-based (fig. 87, 22, 27) and split based bone points. Burins including busqué forms are relatively insignificant in quantity. La Ferrassie F and H provide the classic Aurignacian I and II succession; levels H^1 and H^{11} are Aurignacian, although the flat retouch is rarely seen, but these industries are exceptional for western Europe.

The upper three Aurignacian deposits at La Ferrassie contain traces of artistic work, on slabs painted and engraved with animal outlines (fig. 88, 9, 14, 25), and symbols of female genitalia (fig. 88, 2, 3, 24; cf. fig. 90, 6). As such this represents the earliest known art in the west, and perhaps in the world. There is little other cave art in France that may be dated to the Aurignacian by any means other than stylistic. The collapsed wall fragments at the Abri Blanchard in the Dordogne had fallen onto Aurignacian deposits, and might therefore be considered as of Aurignacian age. The fragments bore black outlines of bison on a reddish background; the legs are straight, and one animal has a sagging abdomen. At Hornos de la Peña in Santander a group of horses engraved near the entrance to the cave have been considered to be of Aurignacian age because one of these figures is said to resemble an engraving on a horse bone discovered in the cave in an Aurignacian deposit; the artistic correlation is doubtful. Without doubt many cave and shelter sites were decorated by Aurignacian man, but in the absence of stratigraphical evidence these sites cannot be dated with precision. On stylistic grounds, and on the basis of superpositioning of the art, it has been suggested that the earliest forms included hand prints, both negative and positive, and animal outlines showing the body in side view, with two legs only, but with horns shown full-face. Such a style, often called twisted perspective, seems to have been employed during Aurignacian and Gravettian times but there are few sites where such early dating can be demonstrated (p. 230). Another profile that is considered as early is the elongated and emaciated 'duck-bill' style, documented at Gravettian sites (p. 230).

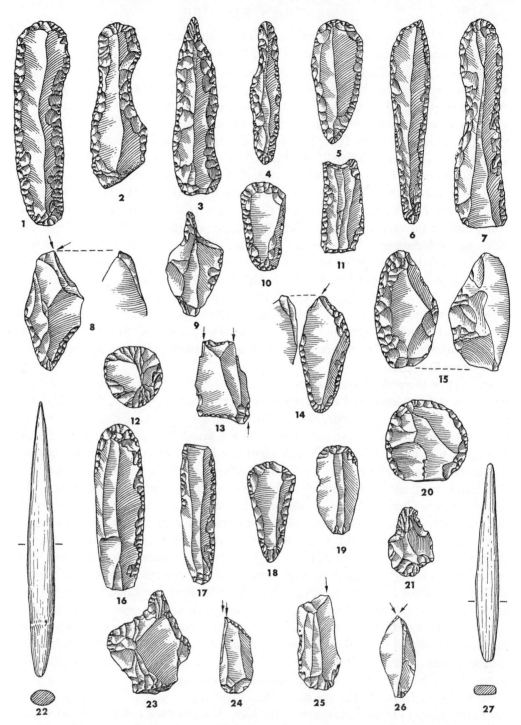

FIG. 87. La Ferrassie, France ⅔; 1–15 Level F (Aurignacian 1); 16–27 Level H (Aurignacian 2). *After de Sonneville-Bordes 1960*

PL. V. Clacton, England. Wooden spearhead. British Museum (Natural History). By permission of the Trustees.

PL. VI. Grotte des Enfants, Grimaldi, Double burial

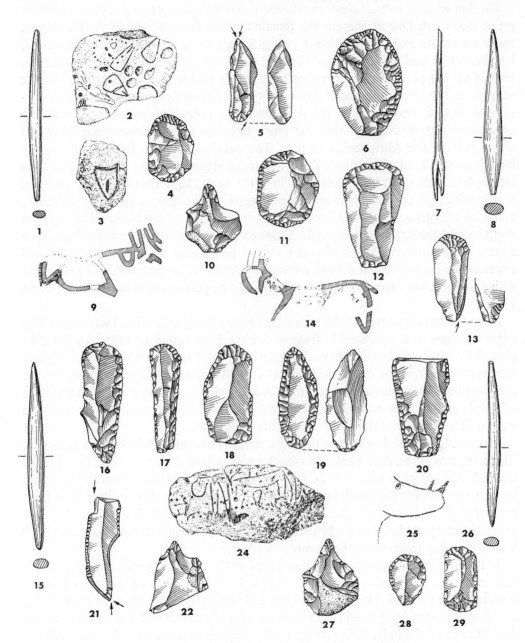

FIG. 88. La Ferrassie, France; 1–14 Level H¹ (Aurignacian 3); 15–22, 24–29 Level H¹¹ (Aurignacian 4); Scale $\frac{2}{3}$ except 2, $\frac{1}{12}$; 3, 9, $\frac{1}{6}$; 14, $\frac{1}{4}$; 24, 25, $\frac{1}{10}$. *After de Sonneville-Bordes 1960*

The Aurignacian culture cluster of the west also includes certain pieces of mobiliary art or home art. One of these is the female figurine from Sireuil in the Dordogne, made on calcite and representing a young female body with protruding buttocks, legs bent back and arms extended forward beneath the conical breasts; the head is broken off but part of a headdress or long hair is visible down the back below the shoulders. The circumstances of discovery of the Sireuil figurine are not well documented, but its attribution to the Aurignacian is probably correct in view of the apparently certain evidence that the ivory figurines from Brassempouy (Landes) are a part of the Aurignacian culture. The surviving figures from Brassempouy include a small head with delicate facial features and long hair (fig. 90, 8), and various incomplete bodies lacking heads and, in some cases, legs. One torso represents a female with high plump thighs and large breasts overhanging a (broken) abdomen, and with exaggerated details of the sexual organs. Two of the bodies with legs are slighter, and the sex might be male although this has not been emphasized. Two figures are little more than sticks, one carved to indicate head, bust and legs. All apparently were found in a deposit covered by Aurignacian material, and associated with a long backed blade considered by Breuil to be perhaps related to Chatelperron blades.

At La Quina (Charente) a limestone slab from an Aurignacian level was covered by engraved lines, and comparable fragments have been found at other Aurignacian sites. A bone splinter bearing an outline of a bison, and another with a human figure, were recovered from the Aurignacian site of Cro-Magnon (Dordogne). These, and the art sites noted above, indicate that during Aurignacian times there existed a tradition of artistic activity; it is not certain whether this was an indigenous development in the west, or introduced into the area from farther to the east.

At several Aurignacian sites in the west, musical instruments have been recorded. There are two types, deer phalange whistles with a hole on one surface (fig. 123, 4) and hollow bone pipes (fig. 147, 2). A whistling noise is produced from the phalange by blowing between the condyles over the hole; objects of this character have been recovered from many late glacial sites in western and central Europe. They are generally interpreted as decoy whistles, or hunting signalling instruments, but another view is that they represent anthropomorphic idols.

At Isturitz in the Pyrenees, bone pipes were found in late Aurignacian deposits. This instrument, in its simplest form, is a hollow long bone with ends removed and a perforation at one end. The position of this hole indicates that a fipple or plug of clay or other substance was placed to constrict the player's breath and to direct it upon the farther edge of the hole. This sets up a vibrating air column and the musical note results. More developed forms of this end-blown flute also occur in Palaeolithic contexts, from Aurignacian times to near the end of the Pleistocene. These have a varying number of holes along the length of the bone on one or on opposed sides of the instrument. The position of the end hole on certain of these, such as one from Istallosko in Hungary suggests its use as a form of notched flute. The variety is considerable, and a study of the musical notation of these instruments sufficiently preserved for blowing indicates that no claims at all can be advanced for an established tonal system at such an early time. The important elements of a flute or pipe are its length and internal diameter, and overblowing and partial covering of the finger holes would produce a large number of variations in pitch (Megan 1960).

We know neither the music played on the wind instruments nor their significance to Palaeolithic man. It is probable that the most personal of all music, singing or whistling, provided the inspiration for the appearance of the phalange whistle which itself may have encouraged the development of the more variable flute or pipe. Or it may have been the wind in reeds that prompted man to make a copy, using a stronger material. There is no evidence for reed pipes, but it is hard to visualize any conditions under which these would survive in recognizable form.

The function of these instruments is unknown, but probably both a personal appreciation of the sounds made by oneself, and a group participation in ceremonial activities, enter into this. The flute is by its nature an intensely personal instrument, and must have been used as part of human expression, but equally it may have played its part in ritual and ceremony. At Les Trois Frères (Ariège), a semi-human figure seems to be playing either a musical bow (although musically this is not in the correct position) or a flute (fig. 103). The association of the semi-humans at this site, with grouped animals, seems to indicate some ceremonial activity, whether it be sympathetic magic or not (p. 251) and music by this time had been in existence for some thousands of years.

Aurignacian burials are also known, including the Cro-Magnon group of five adult skeletons, infant and foetal bones, buried near the back of the shelter and associated with Aurignacian stone tools and perforated shells. One of the adults was a male approaching 50 years in age at the time of death. The skull is large and long, with a rather flattened vault; the face is broad and short with rectangular orbits, and the forehead is steep. The cranial capacity is 1,590 c.c. The limb bones indicate that Cro-Magnon man was tall and muscular. Skeletal remains possessing these features have been grouped as the 'Cro-Magnon race', and are believed by some authorities to be distinct from other Upper Pleistocene groups in the west such as Chancelade and Grimaldi.

Aurignacian industries in western Europe have been recovered from many sites extending from Gibraltar to Britain. Radiocarbon dates indicate a range in time from c. 34,000 to c. 29,000 B.P. In general, early Aurignacian industries in northern areas are found in cold cryoclastic deposits with arctic fauna. A later stratigraphical stage of Aurignacian has been considered to have occurred during a more temperate period, perhaps a slight oscillation only recorded in certain areas.

The Aurignacian industries of the Riviera region, and western Italy, are probably more closely related to traditions in western Europe than in central Europe. Sites in western Italy such as Fossellone, and along the Riviera at Riparo Mochi, have yielded characteristic material of Aurignacian I type; the Grotte des Enfants probably had both Aurignacian phases represented in its extensive deposits. At Riparo Mochi, the

Aurignacian was stratified above a deposit with nibbled bladelets recalling the industry of La Ferrassie E[1].

The Gravettian industries of western Europe are distinguished from the Aurignacian by a decrease in flat edge-retouch on blades, high-backed scrapers, nosed scrapers and burins busqués, and an increase in other forms of burin, ordinary end scrapers and in the appearance of backed blades. The increase in burins may reflect a growing interest in bone and antler work. Within the western area, regional differences in Gravettian industries occur; among the most marked are Gravettian industries of the Pyrenees in which considerable Aurignacian elements persist. The Charente, too, has its local variant.

At La Ferrassie, three levels contained Gravettian industries (fig. 89; p. 273), the first characterized by the Font Robert tanged point (fig. 89, 10–15) as well as straight backed blades (fig. 89, 1–4), end scrapers, burins of angle, polyhedric and ordinary types, and awls. The tanged point appears to be restricted to south-western France, with rare examples found in Spain and to the north. The succeeding industry at La Ferrassie contained truncated backed blades (fig. 89, 27), and the final Gravettian deposit here had quantities of small multiple angle burins called Noailles burins (fig. 89, 35–36). Sterile deposits separated these three Gravettian industries. A final stage of the Gravettian in this area may be represented by Laugerie Haute B (fig. 91, 1–24; p. 276), which continues the tradition of backed blades. Bone and antler artefacts were not well represented in the Gravettian levels at La Ferrassie; elsewhere, including Laugerie Haute B, bone points, awls, rods and half-rods (split longitudinally) are a feature of western Gravettian industries (fig. 91, 6–8, 21). Perforated bâtons of antler occur, at Isturitz for example; decorated bâtons are characteristic in Magdalenian industries, but plain bâtons appear first in the Aurignacian at La Ferrassie. Body decoration with perforated teeth and shells was probably common. An early Gravettian deposit at Pair-non-Pair yielded a representation of a cowrie shell carved in ivory.

Decoration played an important part in Gravettian traditions of western Europe. Engraved plaques at Gargas in the Pyrenees depict bison and horse, in a Gravettian deposit with Noailles burins. In the Labattut shelter (Dordogne), several blocks had fallen into Gravettian levels; the decoration consisted of a horse in high relief whose elongated head ends in a snout (fig. 102, 1), a hand stencilled in black, and a palimpsest with an underlying black and red figure overlaid by black line drawings of animals including a red deer with long neck and thin head bearing antlers only partly depicted in profile. The Labattut shelter provides important dating evidence for cave art; all of the slabs were sealed between Gravettian deposits and must therefore date at latest to a phase within the Gravettian culture in this area. At Laugerie Haute, limestone blocks were engraved with male and female symbols, and animal forms (p. 277). The Gravettian level at Parpallo (Valencia) contained a number of engravings of heads of deer (p. 280). Many other Gravettian sites have yielded comparable material in western France including Laussel with human and animal representations (fig. 90,

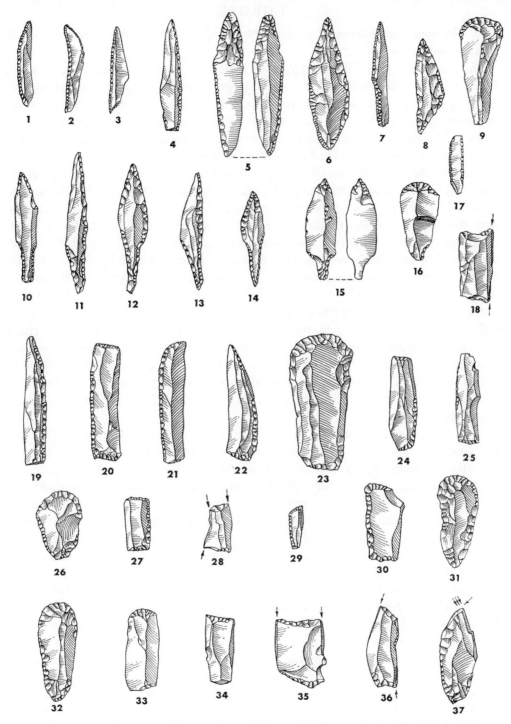

FIG. 89. La Ferrassie, France $\frac{2}{3}$; 1–18 Level J (Gravettian); 19–31 Level K (Gravettian); 32–37 Level L (Gravettian). *After de Sonneville-Bordes 1960*

1–5). The engraved pebbles of La Colombière (Ain) indicate the same tradition in adjacent regions to the east.

The representation of human figures is a feature of the Gravettian industries of Europe. In the west, the ivory Venus of Lespugue (Haute-Garonne) is one of the outstanding pieces of sculpture in the round (fig. 90, 7). The head of this figure is small and oval and is bent forward over the thin arms which rest in enormous pendulous breasts. The buttocks, breasts and abdomen are strongly emphasized. The Venus wears a grooved apron over the backs of the legs which are without feet.

Many of the cave art sites of France and Spain are believed to be of Gravettian date, a few sites dated stratigraphically, others stylistically (Breuil 1952; Ucko and Rosenfeld 1967). In view of the problems of dating by art styles, it seems better to limit this brief discussion to sites the age of which is in little doubt. At La Grèze (Dordogne) a deeply engraved bison was recognized on the wall of a small shelter; the figure had apparently been covered by a deposit containing a Font Robert point among the other Gravettian artefacts. The bison is a classic example of the twisted perspective style, the body shown in side view, with only two legs visible, and the horns seen full-face. At Pair-non-Pair (Dordogne), a series of animal figures on the walls of a cave were covered by archaeological deposits containing Gravettian material, and were above those deposits of Aurignacian age; the engravings must have been executed by Aurignacians or early Gravettians. The animals consist of horses, aurochs, deer, ibex and mammoth. Many are rather crudely drawn, but a number of horses have slender necks and protruding muzzles, in so-called 'duckbill style' (fig. 94).

Of the scores of cave art sites in the three major provinces, Dordogne, Pyrenees and Cantabria, a considerable proportion are probably of Gravettian age, but it is virtually impossible to segregate these from those believed to be of Solutrean and Magdalenian age; in many ways this is a satisfactory state of affairs, because the evidence available points to a continuity in the decoration of art sites, as in the development of industrial traditions that are divided into 'cultures'. Although phases in art styles may be distinguished through detailed analyses of the sites, there is no real evidence that basically the cave art of the west was not an overall continuous development, although this itself raises certain problems (p. 251–2).

Radiocarbon dates for the Gravettian of France indicate a time range between c. 28,000 and 21,000 B.P. with considerable overlap both with Aurignacian and proto-Magdalenian industries (fig. 2). This situation is bound up with the problem of the origins of the Gravettian of western Europe; postulated connections with backed blade industries in central Europe and European Russia remain to be documented.

In the French and Italian Riviera, Gravettoid industries succeed the Aurignacian. These industries appear to represent a local facies. At the Riparo Mochi, overlying an Aurignacian industry, two industries containing backed blades have been recovered. Some of the blades have backing retouch on both edges, to form a pointed implement. Burins are common, small Noailles types among them, and end scrapers,

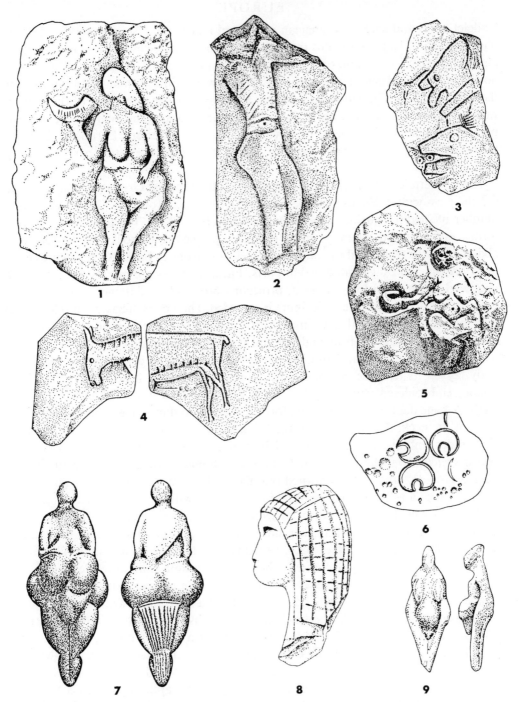

FIG. 90. Aurignacian and Gravettian art; 1–5 Laussel (Gravettian); 6 Laussel (Aurignacian); 7 Lespugue; 8 Brassempouy; 9 Grimaldi; Scales 1, 2, 5, *c.* $\frac{1}{8}$; 4, $\frac{1}{5}$; 3, 6, *c.* $\frac{1}{10}$; 7, *c.* $\frac{1}{2}$; 8, *c.* $\frac{3}{2}$; 9, $\frac{2}{3}$. *From Müller-Karpe 1966*

bladelet cores and some Aurignacian retouched blades are also represented. Micro-burins appear. The bone work is rather indeterminate. These industries of the Riviera may be taken as representative of a series of rather small Gravettoid industries in northern Italy, and may be related in a general way to the Romanellian industry of the south (p. 321). Gravettian material as a whole is rather rare north of the Alps, a situation probably brought about by the cold conditions of the Würm. The western part of Italy seems in general to have participated in western European developments including Aurignacian and Gravettian traditions, the latter perhaps rather later in time.

The Gravettoid industries of the Riviera, sometimes called Grimaldian, are notable for their associated Venus figurines and their burials. From the Grimaldi caves a number of steatite figurines have been recovered (fig. 90, 9). The females are of two forms, one flattened laterally which produces projecting buttocks to the rear and abdomen to the front, and the other flattened from front to back. All the figures have large breasts and exaggerated sexual parts. Facial features are not shown except for one head which has a low forehead, projecting brow-ridges, flattened nose and criss-crossed hair markings. One male figure is recorded. The Venus of Savignano (Modena) may not be related to this Grimaldi group; the thighs, abdomen, buttocks and breasts are large, and the head and legs end as conical projections.

In the Cavillon cave at Grimaldi, a contracted burial of a male was found. The body lay on its left side and was smeared with ochre. The head was covered by a bonnet embroidered with over 200 *Nassa* shells, with a crown of perforated stag teeth. A bone dagger lay against the forehead, and two flint knives were placed at the back of the neck. A garter around the left knee was made of 41 *Nassa* shells. In the Grotte des Enfants, two children had been buried side by side, with a covering of *Nassa reticulata* shells extending from their stomachs to their upper thighs. At Barma Grande, other richly adorned burials had been made, one a triple burial on a bed of ochre; a tall male had been laid on his back with a young woman and a boy on their sides facing him with arms raised and folded. The man had a necklace of fish vertebrae and stag teeth, with other similar objects placed on skull and thorax, and with two large *Cypraea* on the knees; he held a flint knife in his left hand. The female body was less elaborately decorated; she also had a flint knife in her left hand. The boy had a necklace of front vertebrae, shells and stag canines, with pendants and a headdress of similar objects; beside his head lay a flint blade. Other burials in the same group of caves included bodies laid over hearths, one of which had still been hot enough to partially burn the body. One body, of a boy of fifteen, lay face down without any grave goods. At the Grotte des Enfants, an adult male of Cro-Magnon type had been placed on his back, head on an ochre-covered slab, with a necklace of shells and teeth. A double burial (Pl. VI) lay stratigraphically beneath this, in a shallow grave; the ochre-covered body of a young man lay on his right side with legs bent back so that the heels lay under the buttocks, and on top of this body lay the body of an elderly female, her skull touching the male's face, her knees drawn up under her chin, and wearing shell bracelets. The last burial to be noted was discovered at Arene Candide to the east, in which a youth lay holding a large flint blade in his right hand. Ochre covered the body, and quantities of small perforated *Nassa* shells lay near the head and upper left arm. Elk antler stemmed and perforated discs lay in pairs on the left and right arms, pointing downwards on the left and upwards on the right. Stones protected the feet and hands and the head.

These burials in Mediterranean France, Monaco and Italy are generally associated with Gravettoid industries of this region, but there is some evidence that these industries extend in time over a considerable period, succeeding the Aurignacian industries and contemporary in part with the western Solutrean and Magdalenian industries.

The human remains from the Grotte des Enfants have been considered to represent two distinct groups, one of typical Cro-Magnon form, the other of Grimaldi form. The evidence for the latter is the double burial, of a male and older female. Both were short in height, the youth 5′ 1½″, and the woman 5′ 3″. The skulls are elongated, hyperdolichocephalic, with flattened parietals; the forehead is vertical and the supra-orbital ridges are slight. The nose is broad and the upper jaw projects forwards. These features have been regarded as negroid, and certain of the Venus figurines from Grimaldi have also been compared with negroid characteristics.

Using these and many other burials, it has been shown that about ⅓ of Upper Palaeolithic individuals died before the age of 20 and that only 1 in 10 reached 40 years of age. Neanderthaloid burials indicate that over ½ died before age 20 and only 1 in 20 reached 40 years of age.

The industrial succession in western Europe is continued at Laugerie Haute, where the industry found stratigraphically above the Gravettian is the Proto-magdalenian (fig. 91, 25–38), a backed blade industry with scrapers, awls, burins and other elements including high-backed scrapers and blades with flat retouch (fig. 91, 25, 37–38). Bone and antler artefacts occur (fig. 91, 30, 31, 34, 36), including a perforated bâton with engraved mammoths. A comparable industry is recorded from one or two other sites in western France. Radiocarbon dates from this industry range from *c*. 22,000 to *c*. 19,000 B.P. The overlying industry at Laugerie Haute is the so-called Aurignacian V, characterized by high-backed scrapers, burins of various types, bone points and pins. This industry too has been recognized at other sites; in view of the succeeding developments in this region, it might be said that such industries as these indicate the existence of varying industrial traditions, perhaps employed by different groups or perhaps merely seasonal and/or functional variations, at a particular time when new indigenous ideas were being actively developed. A principal result of such ideas was the gradual emergence of an industry called Solutrean.

The Solutrean industries are restricted geographically to central and south-western France, and limited areas in Iberia (Smith 1965, 1966). Typologically, an early phase appears in northern France, Belgium and England, but more developed Solutrean industries in these regions are rare or absent. Little Solutrean is known

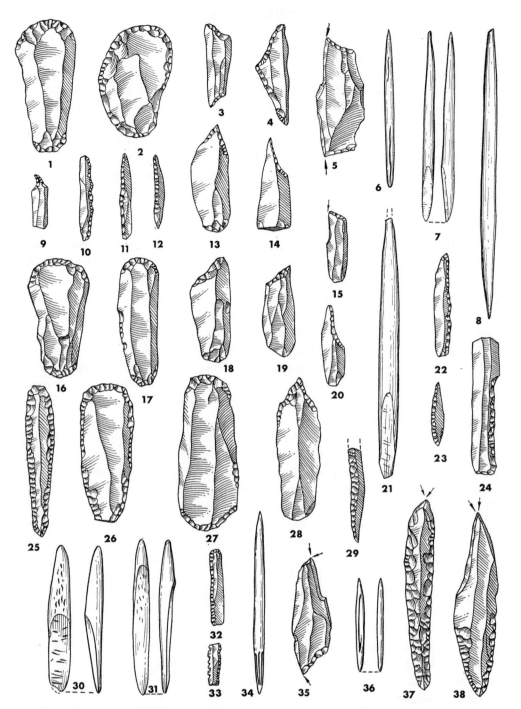

FIG. 91. Laugerie Haute, France $\frac{2}{3}$; 1–14 Level B(III¹) Perigordian 3; 15–24 Level B(III²) Perigordian 3; 25–38 Level F Proto-Magdalenian. *After de Sonneville-Bordes 1960*

from the Pyrenees, and most of this appears to be late. The marginal Solutrean areas in the Pyrenees, Landes, in the area north of the Charente, at Solutré itself in Saône-et-Loire and in the Lower Rhône Valley, appear not to have participated in all the classic development phases of the Solutrean in south-western France.

These variations are important for the problem of the origin of the Solutrean. The former views that the Szelethian and Altmühlian leaf-point industries of central Europe (p. 287) were the source of the Solutrean is not now accepted because it is only the middle Solutrean laurel leaves that recall the Szelethian, and the former may be seen to evolve from an early Solutrean phase; the time gap, too, is an argument against any central European contribution, the Szelethian of the order of 32,000 B.P., the early Solutrean dated to *c.* 21,000 B.P. at Laugerie Haute. A north African source is also denied, partly because of the absence of any early Solutrean industries in Spain. Typologically, the Gravettian industries of south-western France are considered to differ so markedly from the early Solutrean that these too have not been accepted. A recent view suggests that the Aurignacian industries of the lower Rhône valley may have developed into an 'early Solutrean' stage, and spread to south-western France where the subsequent developments occurred. The early Upper Palaeolithic phases in the north too may have played a part.

The Solutrean industries of the central area, as characterized by Laugerie Haute (fig. 92; p. 278) may be broadly divided into three phases, an early phase characterized by the pointe à face plane (fig. 92, 2, 4, 7–9), a middle phase with bifacially-worked leaf-shaped points called laurel leaves (fig. 92, 15–16), and a late phase with willow leaves and shouldered points which may be pressure flaked (fig. 92, 22–24). Pressure flaking is the technique generally associated exclusively with the Solutrean in western France. The fact that these three artefacts occur in roughly comparable proportions throughout Solutrean industries suggest that they all served the same function or functions. In addition, quantities of finely-finished specimens of shouldered points and laurel leaves in some sites suggests an interpretation in terms of over-production for trade. Less distinctive are burins, often of angle type, end scrapers, awls, bevelled bone points, bone rods, pins and needles; backed blades are relatively well-represented in the late Solutrean. Radiocarbon dates indicate that the Solutrean industries existed for little over 1000 years, from *c.* 21,000 B.P. to *c.* 20,000 B.P.

In eastern Spain, the site of Parpalló provides several phases of the Solutrean (fig. 95–97; p. 280); the Solutrean in this area differs from the French sequence in certain details, particularly in the presence of the tanged point, with bifacial or unifacial pressure flaking, in a late phase (fig. 97, 1–7). In northern Spain, a variant industry is characterized by bifacial points with concave bases (e.g. fig. 97, 10). The distribution in Iberia is restricted to Cantabria and Asturias, Portugal, the Madrid region, Catalonia and the south-east; there is no evidence of an early Solutrean, and little for the middle Solutrean, in the French sense, in these regions.

Solutrean burials are rare, apart from some dubious burials from Solutré. A female

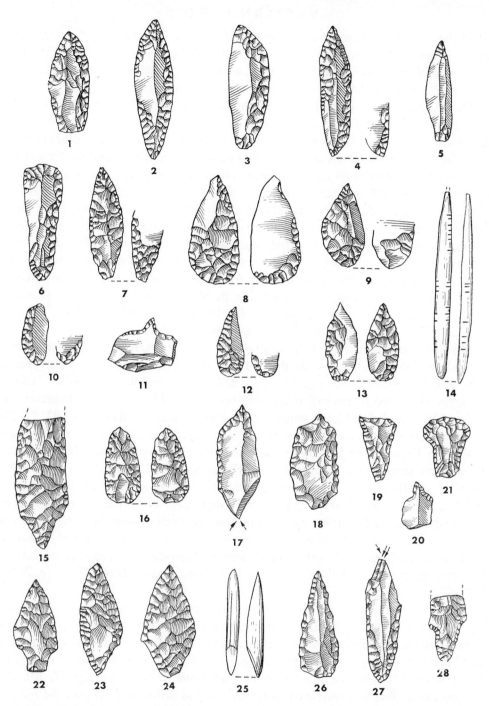

Fig. 92. Laugerie Haute, France ⅔; 1–5 Level G Proto-Solutrean; 6–14 Level H^I Early Solutrean; 15–21 Level H^{II} Middle Solutrean; 22–28 Level H^{III} Late Solutrean. *After de Sonneville-Bordes 1960*

skull was found at Parpalló, and there are a number of fragments from other sites, some of which had been scratched and charred. The Parpalló remains are said to be of Cro-Magnon type. At Solutré the remains of several individuals including children and a foetus were recovered; one body had been affected by fire; the evidence suggests that these burials may have been of Gravettian rather than Solutrean age. The inhumation at La Terre Sève lay inside an oval penannular ring of stones; it is said to have been associated with laurel leaf-shaped points, shells, perforated stone discs and limestone figures of animals; reindeer antlers were piled around the wall. This site was excavated a century ago and the burials are sometimes not accepted as of Solutrean age.

Small portable decorative objects occur in some Solutrean industries. At Solutré, in the middle Solutrean level, several limestone blocks had been carved into representations of animals, a reindeer in high relief, another with four legs shown under the body. From Isturitz in the Pyrenees, sandstone figures of animals were recovered from Solutrean and Magdalenian deposits. Engravings of animals on slabs were found in Solutrean deposits at Badegoule and painted and engraved slabs at Parpalló (figs. 95–97). Scarcely any human figurines are known from Solutrean sites, which is rather surprising in view of the considerable evidence for depiction of the human form in both the Gravettian and Magdalenian traditions.

Formerly, the view was widespread that the Solutrean phase marked a hiatus in cave art, but the evidence of painted and engraved slabs in Solutrean deposits suggests that there probably was no break in the decorating of cave and shelter sites; in fact, it has been suggested that sites such as Lascaux, La Pasiega and Pech-Merle are of Solutrean age. It is possible to prove or disprove this view on purely stylistic grounds. In the lower Rhône valley, sites such as La Figuier and Chabot are considered to be of early Solutrean age by reputed associations at the sites. At Chabot, deep engravings of horses and mammoths were found, comparable in style to those at Le Figuier; Solutrean deposits are considered contemporary.

Nearer to the central Solutrean area, there are a small number of sites in which decorated areas may also be considered as Solutrean. At Le Roc de Sers near Angoulême, a series of decorated rocks were recovered from positions stratified within later Solutrean deposits; they must therefore be of Solutrean or earlier age. The decoration consists of animals in low relief, a number of horses, bison, ibex, ox and deer; several human figures are also present. At La Chaire à Calvin in the same region, comparable pieces were found under early Magdalenian deposits.

At Laugerie Haute the Solutrean industries are succeeded by industries of the Magdalenian culture which show an abrupt change in stone-working (fig. 93; p. 276). The flint flakes are rather heavy and bear steep retouch of poor quality (fig. 93, 1–5). Tools of chance such as awls, burins and notched flakes are common. The developed blade technique, and pressure flaking, of the Solutrean are no longer present. However, the bone and antler work is comparable to that of the Solutrean; ivory eyed needles and bevelled bone points occur, as well as perforated teeth, ivory beads and

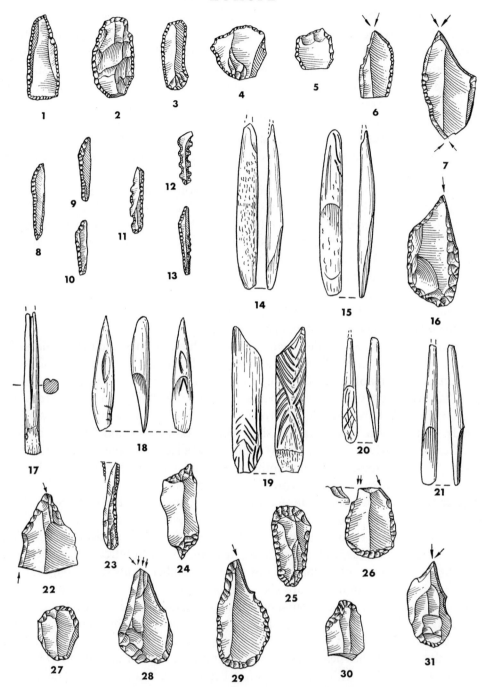

FIG. 93. Laugerie Haute, France $\frac{2}{3}$; 1–7 Level I^I Magdalenian 1; 8–16 Level I^{II} Magdalenian 2; 17–31 Level I^{III} Magdalenian 3. *After de Sonne-ville-Bordes 1960*

FIG. 94. Pair-non-Pair, France. *After Breuil 1952*

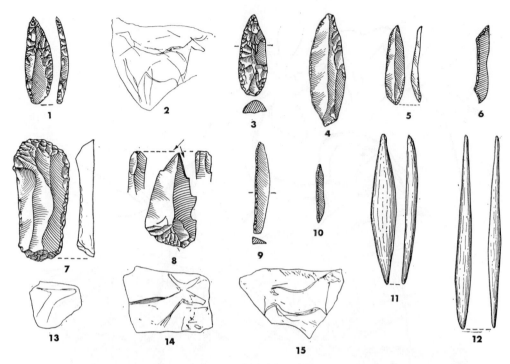

FIG. 95. Parpalló, Spain; 1–2 Proto-Solutrean; 3–15 Early Solutrean; Scale $\frac{2}{3}$ except 2, 13–15, $\frac{1}{3}$. *After Pericot Garcia 1942*

shells. The succeeding stages of the Magdalenian include the development of backed blades and triangles and increasing use of bone, antler and ivory for small articles. Decorated bâtons appear, continuing the Gravettian development. Half-rods, eyed needles and bone points were produced. The Magdalenian sequence of development in the Dordogne is continued by the site of La Madeleine (figs. 100–101; p. 281). Burins become increasingly common in the middle and later stages, with end scrapers, backed blades, and awls also important. In middle Magdalenian, the spearthrower makes its brief appearance (fig. 100, 13; fig. 101, 1, 12), to be succeeded by single-rowed and double-rowed harpoon heads in the late Magdalenian (fig. 100, 9–10; fig. 101, 13). The bow is attested only from final Magdalenian times, and this only by a report of the destruction of one during its excavation at Teyjat (Dordogne).

In Spain, the Magdalenian sequence at Parpalló is broadly similar to that of the Dordogne although there are no perforated bâtons or spearthrowers at the Spanish site (fig. 98–99). The decorated stone slabs at Parpalló represent the persistence of local traditions, begun in Gravettian times, and including a certain amount of curvilinear and geometric shapes. In northern Spain, the Magdalenian industries appear to represent late phases of this culture; some of the harpoon-heads are perforated, unlike the French heads.

PL. VII. The cave of Asprochaliko, Epirus

Pl. VIII. Semicircular ring of postholes around a hearth at Kastritsa, Epirus

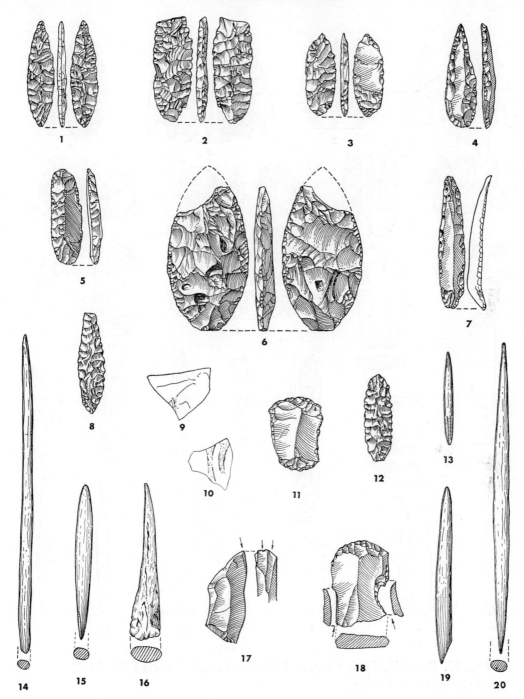

FIG. 96. Parpalló, Spain; Middle Solutrean; Scale $\frac{2}{3}$ except 9, 10, $\frac{1}{3}$. *After Pericot Garcia 1942*

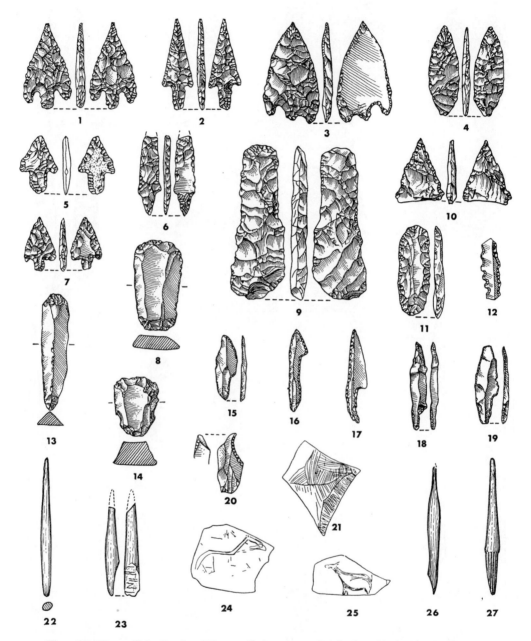

FIG. 97. Parpalló, Spain; Upper Solutrean; Scale $\frac{2}{3}$ except 21, 24–25, $\frac{1}{3}$. *After Pericot Garcia 1942*

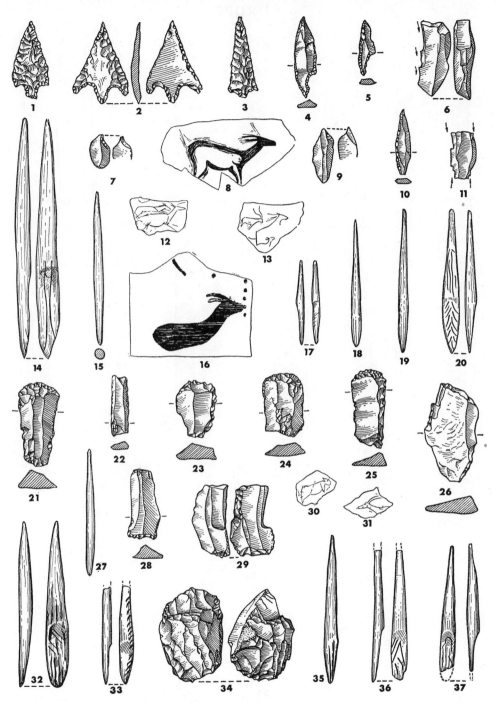

FIG. 98. Parpalló, Spain; 1–20 Solutreo-Aurignacian Final (Gravettian); 21–37 Magdalenian 1; Scale $\frac{2}{3}$ except 8, 12, 13, 16, 30–31, $\frac{1}{3}$. *After Pericot Garcia 1942*

243

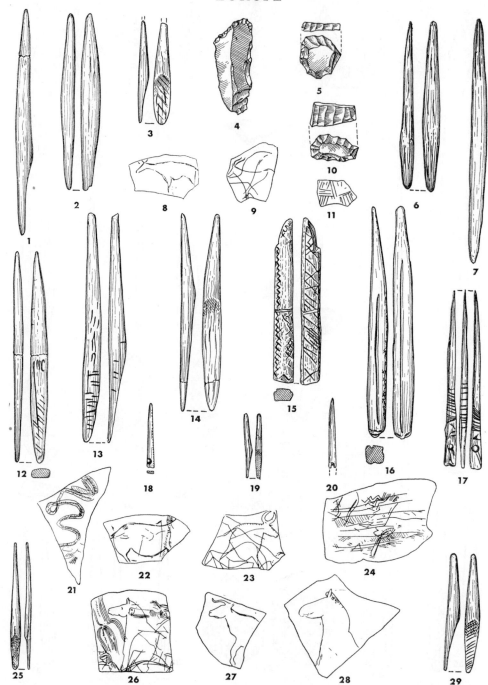

FIG. 99. Parpalló, Spain; 1–11 Magdalenian 2; 12–25, 29 Magdalenian 3; 26–28 Magdalenian 4; Scale $\frac{2}{3}$ except 8, 9, 11, 21–24, 26–28 $\frac{1}{3}$. *After Pericot Garcia 1942*

Decoration of equipment played an important part in Magdalenian industries. In the early phases, bone points often bear simple designs representing parts of animals. Animal carvings in ivory, bone and antler are common in middle Magdalenian times. The pair of reindeer from Bruniquel carved on ivory and the Espélugues (Lourdes) horse are superb examples. The weighted spearthrowers often have an entire animal figure carved at the end, attached by the legs or head to the shaft (fig. 100, 13; 101, 12). Bison and ibex figures are the most common on such throwers. The bison with turned head from La Madeleine (fig. 100, 13) and the similar goat from Mas d'Azil represent such carving at its most sophisticated; occasionally bird beaks, as on the St. Michael d'Arudy thrower, served as the hook to engage the spear shaft (Garrod 1955).

Bâtons were decorated in naturalistic style from middle Magdalenian times (fig. 100, 11; 101, 3); some of the later art, engraved around the body of the bâton, appears in perfect proportion when 'unfolded'. The Montgaudier (Charente) bâton, with two seals, two snakes, a fish and other figures, is a fine example from the late Magdalenian, as is the Teyjat (Dordogne) bâton with shaded mare and foal, swans and the 'mosquito' figures with hairy bodies and chamois heads. At Lorthet, stags and salmon are depicted, perhaps as a commemoration of a successful food quest; the stags appear to be lying on the ground (p. 251). There are many other examples of this superb art, on bâtons and other objects (fig. 7).

The human figure is not uncommon; at Isturitz a middle Magdalenian rod depicts a man following a woman who has an arrow in her thigh. Of the same age is the female figurine from Laugerie Basse, made on ivory, and representing a cylindrical torso and thin long legs with the sexual organ emphasized; probably the figure was completed by the addition of head, arms and breasts in another material. The Gourdan (Haute Garonne) spear thrower is topped by two sub-human heads with masked faces and sockets for eyes. The Le Placard 'sardonic' face on a bâton is also of middle Magdalenian times. A bone panpipe of 4 holes is reported from this site.

The representation of animals in low relief is common in middle Magdalenian times, and among the human figures executed in this manner are a hunter throwing a javelin at a bison from Laugerie Basse.

Engravings on stone slabs and unworked bone are abundant at some Magdalenian sites, rare at others. At La Marche (Vienne), a middle Magdalenian deposit yielded quantities of engraved limestone slabs, some of which had been used as hearthstones. The animals depicted on these slabs from La Marche include bears and lions as well as the more usual forms such as reindeer, horse and bison; human figures also occur, including obese females, male heads with hooked noses, a man standing and shouting, waving his arms and surrounded by strange faces. Slightly later in age are the slabs from Bruniquel, and of the late Magdalenian are those from La Madeleine and Limeuil; the latter site and Parpalló have yielded large numbers of such decorated slabs. At Parpalló, the slabs occurred in the Gravettian, Solutrean and Magdalenian levels (figs. 95–99). The engraved mammoth from La Madeleine, in a middle

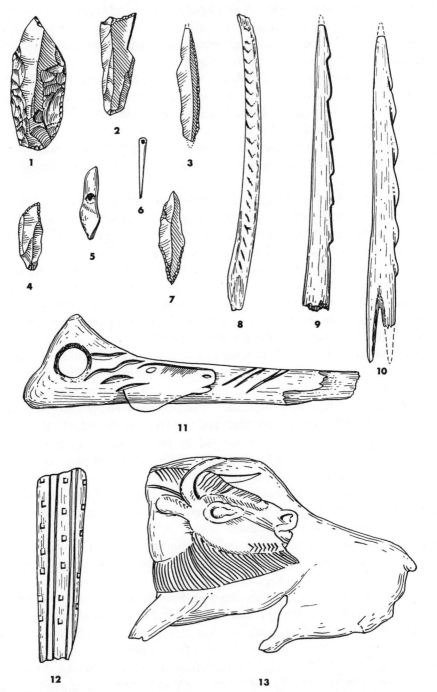

FIG. 100. Magdalenian $\frac{1}{1}$; La Madeleine, France; 1–13 Magdalenian 4. *After Capitan and Peyrony 1928*

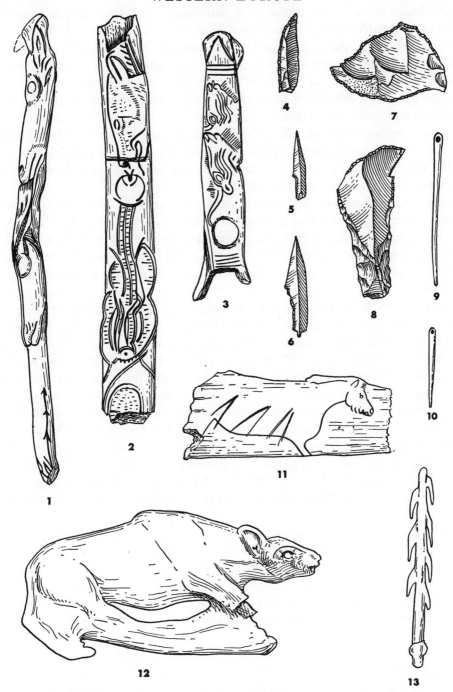

FIG. 101. Magdalenian $\frac{1}{1}$; La Madeleine, France; 11–12 Magdalenian 4; 1–3, 5, 9 Magdalenian 5; 4, 6–8, 10, 13 Magdalenian 6. *After Capitan and Peyrony 1928*

Magdalenian context, was drawn on a mammoth's tusk fragment; reindeer antler palms, and shoulder-blades, were other sources for such engravings. At Mas d'Azil, in a late Magdalenian deposit, a number of decorated shoulder-blades set in a small space apart from other artefacts may represent a portable shrine or an art school.

Schematic art is another feature of the Magdalenian. Chevrons and other linear designs have been considered to represent various animals as pictograms, but this interpretation is difficult to demonstrate. It was from the naturalistic art that certain patterns were extracted and elaborated into curvilinear designs; bison horns and eyes are considered to lie behind the ocellate and spiral decoration of Magdalenian objects in the Pyrenees, as seen at Isturitz on deeply carved half-rods, although a similar motif occurred in earlier times on a bâton from Laugerie Haute.

Cave art sites demonstrably of Magdalenian age are rare, but stylistic typological studies claim to indicate that a large proportion of sites in southern France and northern Spain were decorated by Magdalenians. Such studies depend upon analogies between mobiliary art and mural art, but it is a fact that evidence of exact matching between animals on cave walls and animals on portable objects is practically non-existent.

At Isturitz in the Pyrenees, animal outlines cut into a stalagmitic cone in the centre of a chamber were covered by late Magdalenian deposits (fig. 102, 3). Solutrean occupation debris did not hide any of the figures, and this art may therefore be dated to either late Solutrean or Magdalenian times. There is little evidence of early Magdalenian occupation in the Pyrenees, and probably the Solutrean industries here were long-lived. The animals represented at Isturitz include reindeer and horse.

At Angles-sur-L'Anglin, a remarkable sculpted frieze of animals and humans was partly covered by late Magdalenian deposits; the human representations consist of female bodies, shown from the upper abdomen down to below the knees, with the sexual triangle emphasized (fig. 102, 5). In the deposits of the Reverdit shelter in the Dordogne, fragments of a sculpted frieze were found with middle Magdalenian material; the animals represented in the deposits include bison, and on the shelter wall are horse and bison.

At Teyjat, engravings of oxen, reindeer, horses, and bison and bears had been made on stalagmitic flows and on blocks of the same material (fig. 6). Several of these engravings were recovered from late Magdalenian deposits. Stylistically, the animals from Teyjat have been used to date other art sites where stratigraphical evidence is unavailable. Other sites believed to be of Magdalenian age such as Les Combarelles and Cap Blanc possess Magdalenian occupation debris, but this is not physically associated with the art.

Not only can little of the cave art of late glacial times be dated stratigraphically, but our understanding of its significance is also extremely vague and insecure. It has been studied endlessly since its recognition in 1895 as the earliest mural art in the world, but today its meaning to late glacial man remains beyond our comprehension (Graziosi 1960; Ucko and Rosenfeld 1967).

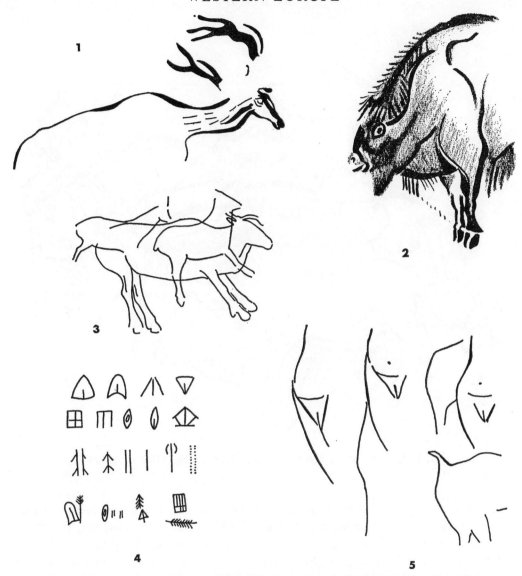

FIG. 102. Art from Upper Palaeolithic caves. 1. Labattut; 2. Altamira; 3. Isturitz; 4. Signs interpreted as (upper) female, (middle) male, (lower) coupled; 5. Angles-sur-L'Anglin. *After Breuil 1952, Ucko and Rosenfeld 1967, Leroi-Gourhan 1967*

The stylistic development of cave art rests upon ideas about advances in technical achievement and superpositions of animal upon animal in some caves (fig. 103). A number of schemes have been produced which purport to show the progression of art styles, and some authorities claimed to be able to date individual paintings or engravings by their knowledge of the treatment of such features as horns and legs. One of

FIG. 103. Les Trois Frères, France. Engravings. *After Breuil 1952*

these schemes involved a twin cycle of art development, but more recent schemes have tended to a unilinear sequence. The point has been made, however, that there may well be initial periods of art experimentation not represented in the archaeological record, that periods of 'regression' may have occurred, and that external influence may have accelerated or held back artistic activities.

The art itself consists of paintings and engravings of animals, the former executed in shades of yellows, reds, browns and blacks, the latter carved in limestone by burins or drawn on clay surfaces with sticks or fingers. Representations occur at the entrances to some caves, or in the middle or terminal regions of some caves. A number of these caves and shelters were occupied in late glacial times.

The animals represented are predominantly bison (fig. 9; 102, 2) and horse (fig. 94), but other beasts included are aurochs (fig. 6), reindeer (fig. 7) and red deer (fig. 8), mammoth (fig. 4), rhinoceros (fig. 5), ibex and chamois, boar, wolf, lion and bear. Some unidentified creatures occur, as well as 'sub-humans' (fig. 103), birds and fish,

250

human hands and a great variety of signs and symbols. In some caves animals are superimposed upon each other. Scenes presumably showing an event or events are extremely rare, but one such event is recorded at Lascaux where a male human appears to be associated with a wounded bison, a broken spear and spearthrower.

The theories which purport to explain the art are varied, but none are universally accepted today, and it seems evident to us that although none explains *all* the art, each may help to indicate a possible meaning for certain sites.

Sites such as Laussel, Pair-non-Pair and Teyjat indicate that mural art was being engraved or painted during a period when these caves were occupied. We do not know if the walls were decorated during an actual period of occupation, or during a temporary abandonment of the site, but the art was not hidden and could be viewed by anyone camping there.

Animal representations in other sites are not positioned at the entrance, and indeed some of it is barely accessible. Many representations occur near the innermost parts of caves, where domestic occupation never took place. Much of this art is engraved, and could only be viewed with special light-positioning. This art may be classed as hidden art, the position of which would not be readily known except by deliberate communication.

A small proportion of the animal figures, generally those not at cave entrances, have lines drawn upon or approaching their bodies (fig. 8). A few beasts, engraved upon inner cave walls, have circles drawn upon or holes prodded into their bodies. Other animals seem by their appearance to be dead in that their tongues and tails are raised, their bellies are exposed, their nearside legs are shorter than offside legs, and their feet are pointed down in a tiptoe position (fig. 102, 2); they seem to have been drawn as if lying upon the ground (Leeson 1939). Other animals have been considered to be pregnant. These animals, believed to be wounded, dead or pregnant, are the basis of the 'sympathetic magic' theory (Burkitt 1933), to which have been added representations of the sorcerer or magician (fig. 103, right) as the leader of the cere-monies involving the magical control over the animals. A recent theory about cave art has claimed to dispose of the 'sympathetic magic' hypothesis, but in fact is little more than a new version of the same. In this new scheme, each cave represented a composition, in which each animal had a special position and part to play (Leroi-Gourhan 1967). Each animal represented either the male (horse, ibex and deer) or female (bison, cattle and mammoth) sex, and each sign or symbol also was either male or female (fig. 102, 4). The male symbols and animals were placed in the depths and entrances of caves, female representations in the central area where some males were also present. This theory has not yet been fully explored but a number of difficulties exist, principally, as in all the other interpretive schemes, because the theory is too general and is applied to all sites.

The facts remain that about 100 cave art sites have been found in south-western France and northern Spain, with outliers of different character in southern Spain and Sicily, and that in these 100 sites several thousand representations occur. Under a unilinear scheme of practice and development, which is based upon the overall evidence for few if any major intrusions of people into this area from *c*. 33,000 to 10,000 B.P., and on the evidence of dated sites in each major industrial group, the number of art sites and representations are very small indeed, and this must be taken into account in any interpretative effort.

A number of burials of Magdalenian man have been found. At Chancelade, the body of an adult male had been compressed into a pit measuring 16 by 26 inches; he had been tightly flexed, with the legs brought up so that the feet were on a level with the pelvis, the knees touching the nose. Ochre had been smeared over the body. The Chancelade man stood originally 5′ 3″ high, and this has been contrasted often with the 5′ 11″ height of Cro-Magnon man. The differences between these two adult males has led to the idea of two races, Cro-Magnon and Chancelade. Both men had a broad face, but Chancelade man's face was longer than that of Cro-Magnon man and had a broad high forehead and narrow nose. The orbits of the Chancelade face are quadrilateral, the height approximating to the breadths; the Cro-Magnon orbits were more elongated transversely. Chancelade man has been compared with present-day Eskimos, although there are important differences in facial features.

Other early Magdalenian burials (Breuil and Lantier 1965) include a tightly flexed and ochre-covered body from Saint-André-de-Cubzac (Gironde), and a body in Cap Blanc (Dordogne), protected by stones on the head and feet; the latter were pressed up to the pelvis. At Laugerie Basse a crouched body was decorated with *Cypraea* shells from a Mediterranean source. An extended inhumation of a youth, at Les Hoteaux (Ain), was accompanied by ochre, a decorated perforated bâton, flints and stag canines; some disturbance of the body had occurred before or after burial, as the femurs were exchanged. At the Duruthy cave (Landes), the body was decorated with bear and lion canines, all engraved with pictures of seal, pike, bear and darts. A late Magdalenian burial at the type site was of a child laid out on its back in a hollow, accompanied by perforated teeth and shells which probably had formed a headband, necklace, bracelets, anklets and knee circlets.

Radiocarbon dating of Magdalenian industries is at the moment uneven. No dates for the early Magdalenian have been published, but late Solutrean dates *c*. 20,000 B.P. may be significant. Dates for middle Magdalenian industries in France range from *c*. 16,000 to 13,000 B.P., in Spain *c*. 15,400 B.P. Other dates for this phase, and for late Magdalenian industries, are generally not accepted, although a late industry at La Vache, *c*. 12,800 B.P., appears to be reasonable. Pollen analyses of cave deposits have indicated that the final Magdalenian in France is of zone Ib or II (p. 42). By fauna, it has been indicated that late middle Magdalenian existed during a more temperate climatic episode in France, and it is only at this time that Magdalenian industries began to appear in quantity outside south-western France. There is little evidence of early Magdalenian industries in central or eastern France, or in Switzerland or further east (p. 299).

The climatic amelioration following the recession of the ice had the consequence that the traditional cave sites were no longer necessarily in an optimum situation conducive to human survival, and with the increase in the forested area the territories occupied by the human groups apparently changed (J. G. D. Clark 1962). The Magdalenian type of assemblage in northern Spain and the Pyrenees was followed in the caves, however, by assemblages named after the site of Mas d'Azil, the Azilian, characterized by the Azilian harpoon (Thompson 1954), painted pebbles and small microliths. Similar industries have been found in eastern Spain, Provence and as early as the ninth millenium B.P. in Italy.

Microlithic flint implements (fig. 110) developed perhaps largely owing to changes in hafted and composite tools which were rendered necessary by changes in economic exploitation and the nature of the terrain involved. These microlithic industries, the Sauveterrian with geometric microliths and narrow small backed blades, and the succeeding Tardenoisian with trapeze arrowheads, occupied inland areas in western Europe and sometimes the coasts (J. G. D. Clark 1958). The blades and trapezes lasted at least from 7,500 B.P. to *c.* 4,000 B.P. This general period shows increasing evidence for the occupation of coastal areas, but this apparent economic change is perhaps due to the fact that coastal exploitations earlier, and in the glacial period, have been hidden or destroyed by the rising level of the sea.

The coastal cultures may represent, as some authorities think, strand-loopers forced there by the growth of the European forest. The shell middens, however, were most probably sites occupied by bands which also exploited the hinterland, but used on the shores tools appropriate to that form of economic exploitation. They are, in fact, evidence for the integration of resources into the economic unit which exploited the area.

Perhaps in a similar situation is the culture called the Maglemose (fig. 105–109) or the Big Bog culture of the area at present covered by the North Sea. The sites are as a rule found below the 200 metres contour adjacent to water, although recently some of the tools usually associated with this culture have been found in Britain in the highlands of the Pennine range. An examination of the industries of the Pennines in Britain has suggested that there are two cultural groups characterized by broad and narrow blades, the first undated and allied to the Sauveterrian and the second to the Maglemose (Radley and Mellars 1964). If the customary equation of a culture with a people is made, it would appear initially that the Maglemoseans would have inhabited the lowlands and the Sauveterrians the mountain range of the Pennines. Such a habitat as the Pennines in a pre-Boreal or even Boreal winter would seem unlikely to lead to the survival of human groups. Indeed, such a distribution of economies between highland and lowland would appear to be the least advantageous method of exploitation. It would appear at least as reasonable to associate the two types of industry concerned into economic units, the unit being based on the most advantageous way of exploiting the terrain according to season, rather than assigning human groups to ecological zones. It would appear more likely, in fact, that the situation is as in Epirus (p. 71), where groups practising mobile economies travelled

FIG. 104. Some important sites in late glacial Europe. 1. Parpalló; 2. Altamira; 3. Isturitz; 4. Brassempouy; 5. Lespugue; 6. Les Trois Fréres; 7. Niaux; 8. Mas d'Azil; 9. Font-de-Gaume; 10. La Ferrassie; 11. Laugerie Basse, Laugerie Haute; 12. La Madeleine; 13. Pair-non-Pair; 14. Angles-sur-L'Anglin; 15. Solutré; 16. Arene Candide; 17. Petersfels; 18. Vogelherd; 19. Ahrensburg; 20. Romanelli; 21. Willendorf; 22. Dolni Věstonice; 23. Brno; 24. Pekarna; 25. Předmost; 26. Kiev; 27. Mezine; 28. Kostienki; 29. Gagarino; 30. Malta

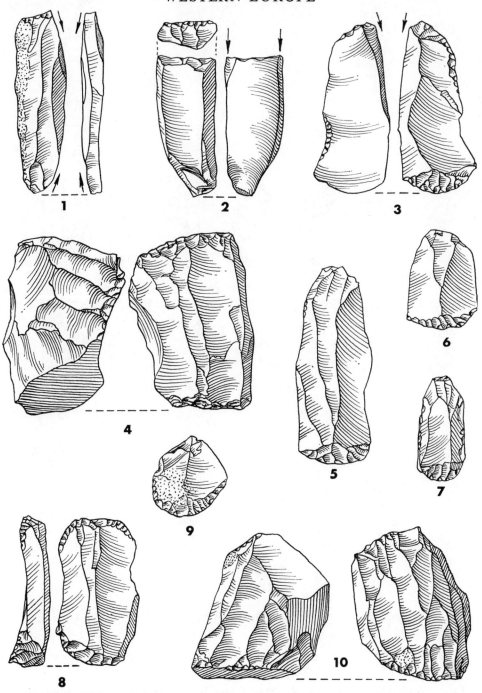

FIG. 105. Early Maglemose $\frac{1}{1}$; Star Carr, England; 1–3 burins; 5–9 scrapers; 4, 10 cores. *After Clark 1954*

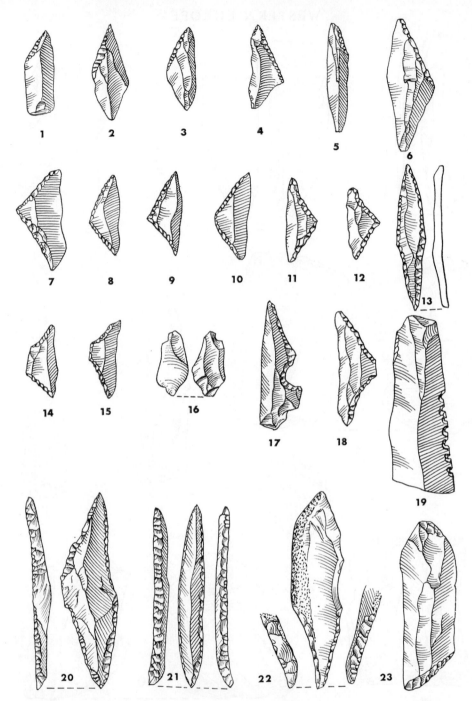

FIG. 106. Early Maglemose $\frac{1}{1}$; Star Carr, England; 1–6 oblique blunted points; 7–12 triangles; 14, 15, 18 trapezes; 16 microburin; 17 microburin not detached; 19 saw; 20, 22 tanged flakes; 13, 21 awls; 23 oblique truncated blade. *After Clark 1954*

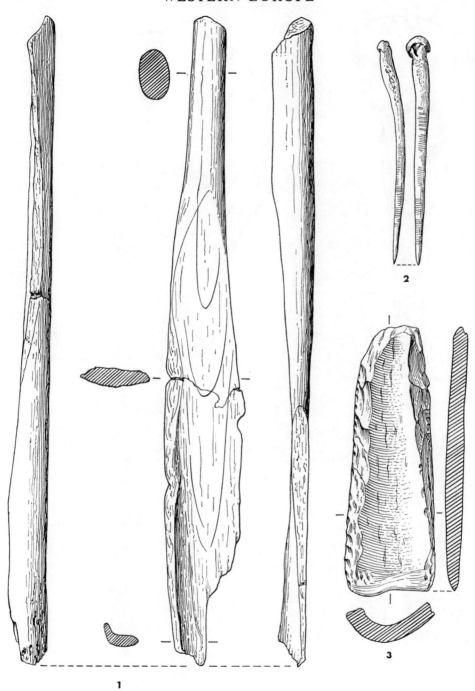

FIG. 107. Early Maglemose ½; Star Carr, England; 1 wooden paddle;
2 bone point; 3 bone scraper. *After Clark 1954*

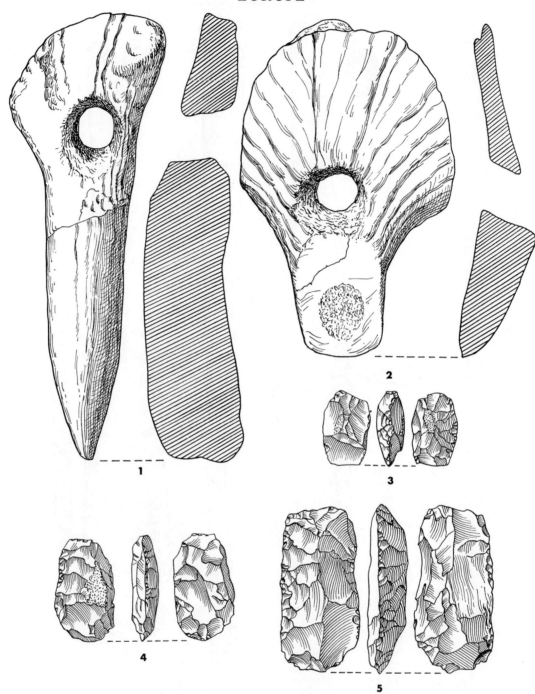

FIG. 108. Early Maglemose ½; Star Carr, England; 1–2 elk antler mattocks; 3–5 core axes. *After Clark 1954*

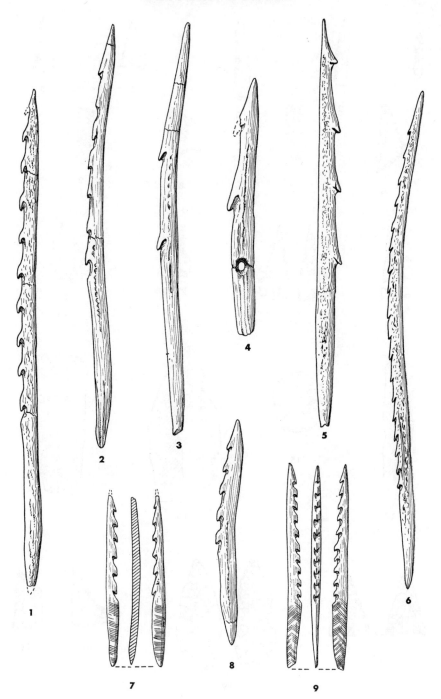

FIG. 109. Early Maglemose ½; Star Carr, England; Barbed points. *After Clark 1954*

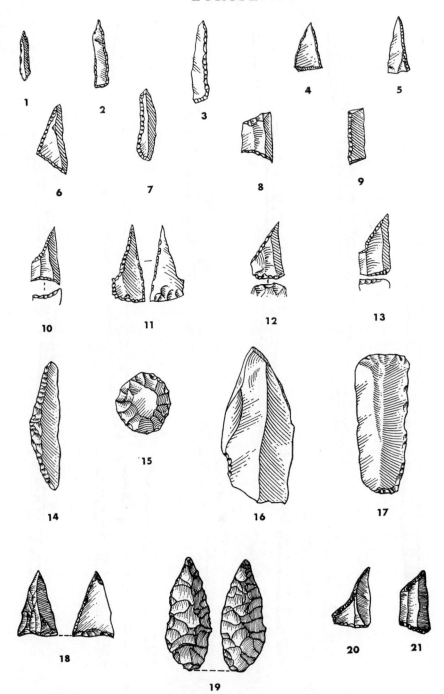

FIG. 110. Cuzoul, France ⅟₁. *After Lacam* et al. *1944*

between highland and lowland. It is perhaps significant in that at both Peacock's Farm, Cambridgeshire, and Hail Mary Hill near Sheffield the two types of industry appear together in a single assemblage.

A similar situation is also evident with the Ertebølle shell midden group of the Baltic, where shell midden sites are in close association with domestic animals. At this time the 'cultures' practised in the Sub-Boreal period in the Baltic include Maglemose, Ertebølle and Neolithic farmers, forming a combination of economic factors necessary for the full exploitation of the resources of the area into an overall economic unit. The farming communities in fact exploited also the sea shores.

The painted rock shelters of eastern Spain are probably to be associated with this general period of post-glacial activity, representing activities of groups who are unlikely to have been restricted only to the immediate area of the art sites. This art occurs in a hilly area extending from the Pyrenees to the Sierra Nevada (fig. 111), and is not coastal in distribution or in content. The art occurs in rock shelters, often at the base of cliffs above scree-slopes (Bandi 1961; Almagro Basch 1962).

Engravings are rare, and almost all the paintings are monochrome, generally red, although black and white pigments were used on occasion. The subjects are human and animal, and the figures may be isolated or grouped in scenes of activation (fig. 111–112). Most of the figures are small, 6–8 inches in length, although some animals were drawn as large as 30 inches in length. The animals are naturalistic, but the human form was painted in several styles, naturalistic (fig. 112, 3), long-bodied (fig. 112, 4), short-bodied (fig. 112, 5) or linear (fig. 112, 1). The groupings of animals and humans generally depict a hunting scene, tracking, chasing, shooting; one appears to show a wounded beast turning on a hunter (fig. 112, 2). Human groups are shown in battle (fig. 111, 1), or marching to battle (fig. 112, 3). More peaceful scenes include the collection of honey, women clapping or dancing, mother and child.

The equipment of the hunters represented in the art is predominantly the bow and arrow. Men generally appear naked, but some wear loin-cloths or breeches, and most have headdresses of feathers, or a cap. Ornaments were worn around the knees, sometimes on the arms. Males occasionally have beards and moustaches. Females were dressed in long skirts, with the upper body naked (fig. 111, 2).

The dating of this art is a difficult problem. The animals represented are forms which were present in this area in early post-glacial times, and which survived until a relatively recent period; deer, goat, boar and aurochs are among those represented in the art. The evidence of domesticated animals in the art remains uncertain, but all of the activities shown are those of a hunting or gathering community. A dog seems to be depicted in one stag-hunting scene. The art occurs in the mountainous area away from the coast, where hunting groups might well have survived undisturbed by agriculturalists along the coast. In the immediate areas of the art, flint assemblages have been recovered, in which geometric microliths occur. It is also possible that the makers of these industries were agriculturists, occupying the coastal plain, but who also utilised the mountainous areas for hunting activities.

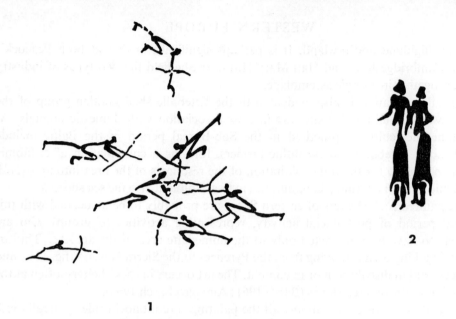

FIG. 111. Rock shelter art, Spain. 1. Morella la Vella, Castellón. Red ⅔;
2. Cogul, Lérida. Black ⅛; (bottom) Area distribution of Mesolithic ●;
Upper palaeolithic ○, cave and shelter art in Spain and Pyrenees. *After
Bandi 1961*

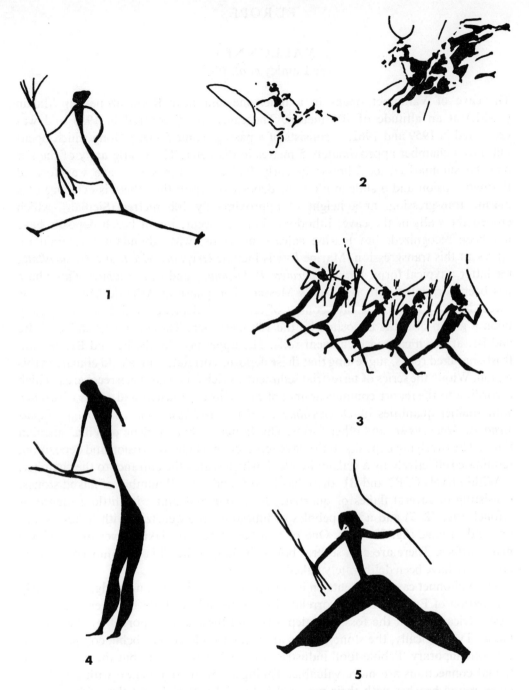

FIG. 112. Rock shelter art, Castellón, Spain. 1. Cueva de los Caballos. Red
c. $\frac{1}{2}$; 2. Cueva Remigia. Red $\frac{1}{3}$; 3. Cingle de la Mola Remigia. Grey-black
c. $\frac{1}{3}$; 4. Cueva del Civil. Black c. $\frac{1}{4}$; 5. Cueva de los Caballos. Red c. $\frac{1}{4}$. *After
Bandi 1961*

263

VALLONNET
(de Lumley *et al.* 1963)

The cave of Vallonnet opens in a limestone cliff near Roquebrune-Cap-Martin (A.-M.) at an altitude of 106 metres. The cave was discovered in 1958 and was excavated in 1959 and 1962. It consists of a passage some 5 metres long which opens out into a chamber approximately 5 metres in diameter. The stratigraphy of the site may be summarized as follows: in early Pleistocene times the cave was formed through erosion and a stalagmitic floor deposited. Upon this, there is evidence of a marine transgression, at a height of approximately 108 metres (Sicilian), which eroded the walls of the cave; lithodome borings occur. Fossil beach deposits have not been recognized, but marine calcareous sands, with abundant foraminafera, represent this transgression. Marine fossils include *Gryphaea virleti* and *G. cucullata*, the latter a typical form, *Patella caerulea*, *P. lustianica* and *P. ferruginea*. This phase has been correlated with Biberson's Messaoudien phase in Atlantic Morocco. The succeeding deposits in the cave consist of terrestrial elements, laid down principally upon a group of rocks deposited by the 108 metre sea. These deposits called C, B2 and B1, are each capped by ancient soils. The uppermost levels, B2 and B1, contain frost-shattered rocks, suggesting that these deposits correlate with a cold climate in this region. Within the series of terrestrial sediments, a rich fauna has been recovered, which according to the report contains abundant *Leptobos* cf. *etruscus* and *Ursus* cf. *arctos*, with smaller quantities of *Dicerorhinus etruscus*, *Archidiskodon meridionalis*, *Equus stenonis*, *Macacus sp.* and other forms. This fauna is characteristic of Villafranchian times. The overlying deposits in the cave represent episodes of erosion and deposition, terminated effectively by a stalagmite block which sealed the entrance to the chamber.

Within levels C, B2 and B1, there has been found a small number of flaked stones, consisting of several flakes of quartzite, limestone and flint with little evidence of retouch (fig. 72, 7) and a few pebbles of limestone and quartzite with flake-scars at one end or edge (fig. 72, 6, 8). One or two bear traces of flaking over much of one main surface. There are also several bones, including the tibia of rhinoceros, which are said to have been deliberately flaked.

The Vallonnet cave represents an important advance in our knowledge of the early occupation of Europe. Direct correlations are possible with developments in north-west Africa through the fossil sea deposits, and these are supported by the archaic fauna. Typologically, the stone objects are recognizable only as being comparable to the contemporary 'Pebble-tool' industries of north-west Africa, but the eustatic and faunal connections are more valuable. Taking them in conjunction with the Portuguese raised beaches with their reported industrial material, and the evidence from the upper terraces of the Somme and Garonne Rivers, there seems now to be little reason to doubt that man had penetrated into western Europe by the beginning of Middle Pleistocene times.

THE SOMME RIVER TERRACES
(Breuil 1939, Bordes 1956)

The river terrace formations of the Somme have been the subject of many studies by geologists and archaeologists since the beginning of this century. One of the first to attempt to correlate the deposits of the Somme terraces was V. Commont, who studied the terraces near Amiens. Commont defined these terraces by the heights of their benches relative to the floor of the buried channel below the terrace exposure. His terraces were named High or 45 m. Terrace, Middle or 30 m. Terrace, and Low or 10 m. Terrace. De Lamothe's study of the Somme deposits was based on the height of the uppermost fluviatile deposit on each terrace, which de Lamothe believed he could project to hypothetical high sea-levels. The correlations he made linked the fluviatile deposits resting on the 45 m. bench of Commont with a sea-level of 57–58 m. above that of the present day, the deposits on the 30 m. bench with a sea-level of 32–33 m. and deposits on the 10 m. bench with a sea-level of 18–19 m.

Breuil and Koslowski, working on the terrace exposures in the early 1930's, based their studies on reinterpretations of Commont's pioneer research, and much of the criticisms of Breuil's approach, made by F. Bordes, have been directed at his and Koslowski's study, made at a time when sections in the terrace deposits of the Somme were particularly well-exposed. Breuil published another survey of the terrace formations in 1939, in which he altered both his interpretations and certain elements in the recorded sections.

Recent work on the Somme gravels near Montières has indicated that the sequence of terraces hitherto proposed is over-simplified. Here, the 32–38 m. gravels are called the lower middle terrace, and the upper middle terrace is believed to lie at 42–45 m. above the river. Above is the lower high terrace, at 50–55 m., from which there has been recovered a few flakes including one coarse biface. The upper high terrace, 61–66 m. above the river, consists of a series of coarse fluviatile gravels with water-rolled flints, capped by an ancient land surface itself covered by sand, clay and silt. Heat-crazed flint flakes have been recovered from the uppermost levels of the gravel, and represent the earliest reputed traces of man's presence in this area. The stratigraphical position of the gravels, and the discovery in them of a tooth of *Equus stenonis*, has suggested an early Pleistocene date for these flints (summary in Coles 1968).

Although interpretative difficulties exist, the Somme terraces provide unique evidence for the existence and dating of several industrial traditions of the Middle and Late Pleistocene.

The 45 m. terrace of the Somme is represented by sections at Abbeville (Carrière Carpentier) and at St. Acheul (C. Fréville). These two series of deposits exhibit sufficient elements in common to allow a composite, generalized, section to be described here. On the bench, cut by an erosion phase of the river, lies a series of gravels, the basal portion apparently of coarse angular material with coombe rock and representing a cold climatic phase. This soliflucted material merges with less angular gravels and sands of fluviatile origin, overlaid in places by a marl of chalky white sands. Associated with the marl at the Carrière Carpentier was a fauna reported to consist of *Elephas* (*Archidiskodon*) *meridionalis*, *Rhinoceros* (*Dicerorhinus*) *etruscus*, *Equus stenonis*, *Machairodus*, *Bos priscus*, *Cervus somonensis* and other forms, the assemblage as a whole indicative of temperate conditions and considered as belonging to the Cromerian faunal assemblage. No stone industry was found at this particular section, but Commont, followed by most authorities, believed that an Abbevillian industry was associated with a similar fauna elsewhere at the same level, and at Carrière Fréville an early industry of this character was recovered from gravels corresponding to the fluviatile series at C. Carpentier. The association seems to be reliable, although in later reports on these sections, the industry was divided into one with early handaxes, mostly from below the marl, and another with flakes mostly from the top part and above the marl.

According to recent work on the Somme gravels at Montières, some 40 km. from Abbeville, the marls containing the Cromerian fauna and archaic industry represent a deposit intermediate between the upper middle terrace and the lower high terrace.

Above the fluviatile series on the 45 m. terrace is an erosional disconformity, succeeded by a second partly fluviatile series, mainly of sands, containing a more evolved faunal assemblage and industry. The fauna from several exposures includes *Elephas antiquus*, *Bos*, *Equus*, with *Hippopotamus* and *Rhinoceros kirchbergensis* (*merckii*). An industry of Acheulean facies belongs to this series, which are overlaid by a complex of loessic deposits, containing handaxes in a weathered Older Loess, and Levallois directly above in a pebble layer at the base of Younger Loess.

The importance of the 45 m. terrace lies in its evidence for the association of an industry with a faunal assemblage of Cromerian affinities, that is, a fauna which relates to that found at Cromer which is believed to be of Günz-Mindel interglacial age. It has, however, been pointed out that certain animals of the Cromerian assemblage continued to exist and are recorded in late Mindel times, so that on this basis we cannot date the Somme Abbevillian industry to the Günz-Mindel interglacial without some doubt. Allied to this is the view that the high sea-level with which the top of the 45 m. terrace fluviatile series correlates is of the order of 57–58 m., called the Milazzian or Sicilian II sea. Such a sea-level as this has been considered to represent a Mindel 1–Mindel 2 interstadial sea although the correlation is uncertain. It is believed that the fluviatile series overlying the disconformity represents some stage of the Mindel–Riss interglacial, as it directly underlies Rissian Older Loess.

The 30 m. terrace of the Somme has also been the subject of several interpretations, although most authorities agree to a considerable extent on the actual stratigraphy of the numerous sections. The most important exposures occur at St. Acheul, in the Carrières Bultel and Tellier, and at Cagny in the pit of Cagny-la-Garenne. These sections are uniform enough to allow a composite stratigraphical series to be presented.

Overlying the bench of the terrace, presumably cut during a phase of downcutting of the river, is a deposit of coombe rock with angular gravels and coarse sand, probably soliflucted, which has yielded rolled handaxes, of various forms, from crude Abbevillian to cylinder-hammer Acheulean forms. This deposit is overlaid by fluviatile gravels and sands, containing an Acheulean industry, mostly rolled, and including flake tools, associated with an important faunal assemblage of *Elephas antiquus*, *Dicerorhinus merckii*, *Cervus elaphus*, *Bos* and *Equus*. Industrially important is the report of 'proto-Levallois' near the top of this fluviatile series, with Acheulean axes. Most authorities agree that this deposit is of the Mindel–Riss interglacial; the aggradation of these sands and gravels indicates a flooding episode due probably to an interglacial high sea of the order of 32 metres.

Overlying this series is a major episode of soliflucted coombe rock (*prèsle*), deposited before the fluviatile aggradation had completely ended. Breuil and Koslowski barely recognized this cold episode, although Breuil in 1939 considered it to be representative of Riss 1. The entire series containing the fluviatile and soliflucted deposits were interpreted differently by Breuil over the relatively short period between 1932 and 1939 (fig. 77). In the coombe rock an abundant industry of handaxes, Levallois flakes and cores, and other flakes, has been found, mostly in fresh condition. Many of the axes are lanceolate, and from the differing industrial levels within this solifluction it is evident that Acheulean man visited the area sporadically, perhaps to gather fresh supplies of raw materials and to produce various tools.

Above this coombe rock is a shell-bearing deposit of fine sand and silt, generally blue-grey yellow in colour. The shells combine freshwater and terrestrial forms, and the whole deposit may represent a washed material from adjacent higher ground. Breuil and Koslowski considered this deposit as of Great Interglacial age, but in 1939 Breuil believed that its underlying solifluction was of Rissian 1 age, hence the warmer shell-bearing sands were also Rissian. Most authorities agree now that there is little if anything of a truly fluviatile nature about this deposit.

A further solifluction separates this from overlying reddish sands (*sables roux*), again probably of hill-wash character, in which have been found Acheulean workshop sites and a fauna containing *Bos* and *Equus*, with some traces of *Elephas antiquus*. These workshop sites include the famous *Atelier de Commont*, with finely-flaked handaxes of ovate, lanceolate and other forms, as well as flakes with secondary retouch (Bordes and Fitte 1953). The stratigraphical sequence is completed by a series of loessic deposits, separated by pebble bands, and yielding various Palaeolithic industries. Immediately above the reddish sands is a solifluction deposit, followed by, in some exposures, three separate levels of Older Loess, yielding Acheulean and Levallois artefacts. Above these is a truly interglacial soil, near the top of which have been found handaxes of Micoquian character. Younger Loess, divisible into three phases, complete the Pleistocene deposits, with intervening solifluction traces and some evidence of Levalloisian-type industries extending in time to Younger Loess 2.

The importance of the 30 m. terrace deposits lies in its evidence for a sequence of industries in the handaxe tradition with Levalloisian technique appearing and developing into an evolved form. The precise dating of these industries is not at all certain, because on the one hand there is very little evidence that the reddish sands and their underlying shell-bearing sands represent in fact one climatic episode, separated as they are by soliflucted deposits, nor are they certainly of fluviatile origin and of full interglacial age. If they were so, then the underlying major coombe rock stage, near the base of the sequence, would indicate an appreciable cold climatic fluctuation within the Great Interglacial; such a cold episode is indicated elsewhere, but there is little direct evidence of correlation. On the other hand, the acceptance by most authorities that the major coombe rock stage marks the end of the Great Interglacial means that a quite wide and varied range of deposits of Rissian age were laid down before the first phase of (Rissian) Old Loess. The most economical theory is to call the coombe rock 'pre-Rissian', yet to separate it from what we are accustomed to call the Great Interglacial. At the moment there seems nothing between this solifluction and Older Loess that need be representative of a warm climatic episode. The significance of this is the positioning of the *Atelier de Commont*, with its well-developed handaxe industry (fig. 78–80), in a cooling climatic phase before the onset of full periglacial conditions and the deposition of Loess.

The Lower terraces of the Somme are two in number, and are often called the 10 m. and the 5 m. terraces. These two terraces have been the cause of almost diametrically opposed viewpoints, by Breuil and Koslowski on the one hand, by Bordes on the other. Breuil did not help his case by quite drastically altering not only his interpretation but also his sections in 1939. It now seems clear that the ancient dating of some of the low terrace deposits to the Hoxnian is without foundation and we can present here a generalized sequence that may be accepted by most authorities today.

At the time when the major coombe rock was being deposited on the 30 m. terrace, the river down-cut and formed the bench on which the 10 m. low terrace deposits now lie. Upon this bench, soliflucted gravels were deposited containing a cold fauna with *Mammuthus primigenius*, *Rhinoceros antiquitatis* (*tichorhinus*), and *Megaceros*, and rolled Acheulean material. Above is a gravel and sand aggradation which is believed to grade into a sea-level of the order of 18–20 m. Associated with these gravels are a warm fauna with *Elephas antiquus* and *Hippopotamus* and an industry of developed Levalloisian character. A Younger Loess series overlies this Last Interglacial deposit.

The lower terrace, at 5 metres, is entirely Würmian in date according to most authorities, with bench cut in early Würm times, covered by solifluction gravel and coombe rock with mammoth, woolly rhino and reindeer associated with Levalloisian flakes, cores and small handaxes. Younger Loess deposits complete the sequence.

THE THAMES RIVER GRAVELS
(King and Oakley 1936, Wymer 1961)

The river Thames has often been considered as an example of the interacting agencies of erosion and deposition under Pleistocene conditions, but that difficulties in interpretation still exist can be judged from the variations in climatic dating that have been suggested. Three exposures will be considered here, the Caversham channel, the Boyn Hill gravels and the Clacton channel.

The *Caversham channel* is an ancient course of the river Thames between Caversham and Henley (Treacher *et al.* 1948). The channel was cut through pre-existing gravel deposits at a time when the Thames flowed to the north-east, through a gap at Finchley. The channel is filled with fluviatile gravels, and the top of these lie at a height of about 160' above the modern Thames at Caversham, or 271' above present sea-level. No significant faunal remains have been recovered from the gravels, but a great number of flint implements, both handaxes and flakes, have been found in varying states of preservation, fresh to rolled, throughout most of the gravels (fig. 74–75). At Caversham, a bluff separates the channel deposits from the gravels of the Boyn Hill terrace, and the Caversham channel gravels therefore appear to run into a higher sea level than do the Boyn Hill gravels. If so, the Caversham gravels should be of an earlier date, but the association and contemporaneity of the artefacts with the river gravels remain to be re-examined.

The *Boyn Hill* terrace, at a lower level, is generally considered to be of the Hoxnian interglacial. Exposures of this terrace are visible from Taplow, near Maidenhead, for about 50 miles to Swanscombe, near Gravesend. The surface of the fluviatile deposits on this terrace lies at approximately 30 metres above the floodplain level over most of this distance. By comparison with the modern floodplain's gradient, it has been estimated that, at the time of the formation of the 100' gravels, the estuary of the river must have been not much more than 15 miles downstream from Swanscombe.

On the basis of the height of the Boyn Hill terrace gravels it has been considered that the Thames flowed into a sea of *c.* 32 metres (107'). This sea, the Tyrrhenian, is believed to be of the Hoxnian interglacial. Archaeological evidence is not considered to be valid in dating the Boyn Hill gravels to any specific Pleistocene climatic phase, but it has been considered that the comparable Acheulean industries from the Boyn Hill gravels and from Hoxne (West and McBurney 1954), not far away, suggest a degree of contemporaneity during the Hoxnian interglacial through pollen and morainic stratigraphy at the latter site.

The best known exposure of the Boyn Hill gravels is at *Swanscombe*, where the Lower Gravels rest on Thanet Sand at a bench level of 75' O.D. (Ovey 1964). The gravels contain a flake industry without handaxes, comparable in character to an industry in fluviatile gravels, overlaid by estuarine gravels, at *Clacton-on-Sea*. These

269

gravels lie at 15' below O.D. and this is too low to be connected to the bench level at Swanscombe (Oakley and Leakey 1937).

It has been suggested that a period of low sea-level occurred after the deposition of the Lower Gravels at Swanscombe, during the formation of the Lower Loam. The fall in sea-level is marked by the channel at Clacton, and the estuarine gravels over-lying the fluviatile implementiferous (fig. 76) gravels at Clacton mark a subsequent rise in sea-level, flooding into the channel and contemporary with the Middle Gravels at Swanscombe. Polleniferous deposits at Clacton indicate a time late in the Hoxnian interglacial. The spearhead of yew from Clacton (Pl. V) is one of the few organic artefacts surviving from this period. The Middle Gravels at Swanscombe are of Thames origin, and their top, at *c.* 107' O.D., is taken to mark the maximum Tyrrhenian sea of the Hoxnian interglacial. The Middle Gravels (Pl. IV) contain handaxe industries, a rich fauna, comparable to that at Clacton, and fragments of human skull. The division of these gravels into a Middle and Upper Middle may or may not indicate a significant chronological difference; the similarity of their indus-trial remains cannot be used as a guide in this. Over the Middle Gravels is the Upper Loam, with developed handaxe industries, and above this is the soliflucted Upper Gravel with derived tools.

FONTÉCHEVADE
(Henri-Martin 1957)

The cave of Fontéchevade lies in the valley of the Tardoire, near Montbron (Charente). The first excavations of the cave deposits yielded evidence of occupation of Upper Palaeolithic and Mousterian character, but deeper soundings revealed the presence of earlier industrial material with associated human remains.

The stratigraphy of the site may be summarized as follows: beneath the Upper Palaeolithic Aurignacian occupation, and separated by a slight sterile deposit, was a flake Mousterian industry (C1), which itself was stratified above an industry of Mousterian tradition containing handaxes (C2). The deposit containing the Mous-terian material rested upon a thick rock and stalagmitic layer (D), and the fauna from the deposit above this stalagmite is said to contain arctic forms including reindeer and possibly *Rhinoceros tichorhinus*.

Beneath the stalagmite is a deposit (E) containing a flake industry of varied character, a fauna indicating a warm temperate climate, and parts of two human skulls. The fauna includes rhinoceros (*Rhinoceros merckii*), deer (*Dama clactonianus*), tortoise (*Testudo graeca*) and bear (*Ursus sp.*), a few *Bos primigenius* and horse, and *Castor fiber* and *Cuon alpinus mediterraneus*, indicating in general a temperate forested environment.

The application of fluorine analysis has established the contemporaneity of the fauna and the human remains which were near the top of layer E. These include the parietals and part of the frontal bone of one individual, and a fragment of the frontal bone of a second person. The bones apparently have been subjected to fire. In general, the features of the skull recall those of *Homo sapiens*, particularly in the forehead and parietal bones, but the thickness and other features indicate some relationship with the Swanscombe skull and Neanderthal specimens. The Fontéchevade remains have been termed 'Praesapiens' and linked with Swanscombe, although the dates of these two finds are widely separated, Swanscombe of the Mindel-Riss, Fontéchevade of the Last Interglacial (Eemian).

The industry associated with the human remains has been called Tayacian, but it seems to exhibit certain specialized characters of its own (fig. 82–83). The flakes represented include irregularly shaped plain-platform flakes with retouched edges, some quite large in size (fig. 82, 8), and flakes with prepared platforms, some with only 2 or 3 preparing scars, but others with multiple facets on the platform and bearing traces on the dorsal surfaces of a prepared core technique (fig. 82, 1–6, 9). There are a few flake-blades with plain platforms (fig. 82, 7), and a few finely retouched flake scrapers (fig. 83, 4, 6) and notched flakes. The cores include tortoise cores, mostly rather irregularly prepared and with an uneven main flake scar, and discoid cores (fig. 83, 5). A relatively high proportion of the material consists of coarser and larger objects, including large block-like cores, an abundant group of irregularly flaked lumps bearing cortex and called 'chopping tools' (fig. 83, 3), pointed pick-like implements, and some cores that bear retouch in blade-like fashion, and may have been employed as heavy scrapers. In addition there is a group of quartz nodules which have been roughly flaked.

LA MICOQUE
(Bourgon 1957)

La Micoque is the name of a farm near Les Eyzies, and lies some 500 metres from Laugerie-Haute. The rock shelter itself overlooks a broad plain of the Vézère river and is situated quite low in the gentle slope leading up from this terrace. Excavations began in the shelter in the late 19th century, and continued into the first decade of the 20th. Capitan, Coutil, Cartailhac and Hauser operated from 1896 to 1907, and were succeeded by Peyrony who excavated from 1929 to 1932.

The deposits at La Micoque are some 6 metres thick, and have yielded six industrial assemblages. The shelter roof has been eroded away so that the prehistoric deposits have not only been subjected to percolating water, forming almost total patination of the flints, but have been so eroded that the slope of the land is hardly interrupted by the shelter and its filling.

The fauna associated with the industries at La Micoque is poorly represented. Bovids and horse are reported from the lower industrial deposits, with horse more abundant in the upper levels. Traces of reindeer and woolly rhinoceros were recognized in the top industrial horizon.

The six industries of La Micoque occur in separate stratigraphical deposits, but there is remarkable overall uniformity about the character of the flint working. Most of the flakes are thick and irregular in shape, with inconsistent retouch and heavy utilization. Globular cores were used for direct hammer percussion, or were subjected to the anvil technique of flaking. One of the industries, fourth from the base, consists of thinner flakes with flat faces struck from prepared cores. Retouch is more consistent, and the industry as a whole has been compared with true Mousterian. The industry above this reverts to the previous traditions. At the top of the deposit is an industry with bifacial pointed axes as well as unifacially worked flake tools.

LE MOUSTIER
(Peyrony 1930, Bourgon 1957)

The small village of Le Moustier lies some 10 km. from Les Eyzies, on the bank of the Vézère River. The site itself consists of two rock shelters, an upper shelter some 13 m. above the more important lower shelter. Bourlon and Peyrony excavated in the lower shelter in 1928; both shelters were almost completely filled by Pleistocene deposits including Middle Palaeolithic and early Upper Palaeolithic occupation debris. The lower shelter yielded a sequence of Mousterian deposits that generally serve as a basis for some of the stages of industrial development in the Mousterian tradition. Unfortunately the dating of this site is difficult, as the fauna is not particularly well-defined in the lower deposits.

The sequence of deposits in the lower shelter at Le Moustier is complex, consisting of sands, clays and gravels as well as brown earth occupation soil. The fauna contained within the sequence commences with bovid, horse, *Cervus elaphus* and ibex, associated with the flake and discoid core tradition (fig. 84, 1). Retouch tends to be of the step variety, and the tools produced include triangular points and edge-tools with concave or straight retouched edge. Above are generally sterile deposits underlying occupation levels with bovid, reindeer, ibex and woolly rhinoceros, and a flint industry consisting basically of utilized flakes and cores, but with bifacially trimmed cordiform axes (fig. 84, 2–5). Traces of manganese oxide were recovered. Immediately above this is a deposit yielding bovid remains, with fewer *Cervus elaphus* and horse. The ratio of bovid to *Cervus elaphus* is 10:1, bovid to horse 15:1. The industry contains many cordiform axes, flake points and scrapers or knives (fig. 84, 6–8). Flake-blades occur, as well as pieces of manganese oxide and a limestone block used for grinding this colouring matter. Hearths above this deposit were associated with bovid, deer and horse remains again, and an industry mainly of unretouched flakes, but including convex scrapers or knives, small flake and flake-blades.

Fluviatile sands cover this deposit, and are then succeeded by a further cave earth yielding bovids, deer, horse and reindeer as well as a flake industry. Cordiform axes are rare, but discoid cores and broad flakes with side retouch are well represented (fig. 84, 9–11). The burial of a young child in a pit 20″ wide and 16″ deep was associated with this occupation. The upper part of this deposit contained few bovid remains, and reindeer and horse were more abundant. Subsequently the reindeer predominates, and bovids may have been no longer available to the occupants. The associated lithic material of this presumed colder episode combines Mousterian implements and blades. A true Upper Palaeolithic industry, in Aurignacian tradition, lies in sands above with a reindeer fauna.

One of the original interpretations put on this sequence at Le Moustier assumed that the deposits spanned the final Eem and early Würm, the latter with a mild oscillation (fluviatile sands) in the middle. The geological and faunal evidence is not now capable of re-interpretation.

LA FERRASSIE
(Peyrony 1934)

The rock shelters of La Ferrassie are situated five kilometres west of Les Eyzies; each of the three habitations here have yielded Pleistocene deposits with evidence of human occupation, the smallest shelter with Mousterian, the cave with Upper Palaeolithic, and the largest shelter with a long succession of industries described below. This site was excavated in the late nineteenth and early twentieth century, but our knowledge of the stratigraphy comes from the work of Peyrony in the 1930's.

Two sections of the deposits were published by Peyrony, both running approximately north to south through the shelter filling, one to the west side, the other nearer the east side of the shelter. The sequence of deposits is basically identical in each except that subdivision of certain layers, running in alphabetical order from the base upwards, is claimed principally in the eastern section. No horizontal spread is given. The rock floor of the shelter is horizontal and the lower deposits rest more or less horizontally upon this. Above, the upper deposits slope more obliquely from the back of the shelter downwards. The fauna of the deposits shows little change in its general composition throughout the sequence. Bovids are abundantly represented from the basal deposits to near the top. Horse and deer (*Cervus elaphus*) are present at all stages. Reindeer is sparsely represented in the lower deposits and becomes predominant only in the earliest Aurignacian deposits, thereafter maintaining a steady representation although not as abundant as horse, bovid or deer. Other forms present are wolf, fox, hyena, cave bear and lion. Traces of *Rhinoceros tichorhinus* are reported from the Mousterian levels, not above. In general, the fauna indicates cold conditions prevailing in the area.

On the rock floor is a conglomerate of limestone blocks with a sparse industry of plain platform flakes, some with irregular retouch (layer A). On the surface of this layer a few cordiform axes were found. The flake tools include those with retouched longer sides, thick sectioned tools and miscellaneous pointed objects. Above this are two industries in a deposit of fine-grained loams which is divided by a group of

Neanderthal burials. The lower industry (C) is a pure flake Mousterian, without certain axes and with many points, side scrapers and some faceted platform flakes (fig. 85). The disc cores as well as the flakes are remarkably thin. The tools represented include points on elongated triangular flakes, some with narrowing at the base, triangular and oblong knives, broadside scrapers some with a sort of tang, saws and pointed awls, some burin-like flakes and many utilized flakes. A few examples of plano-convex retouch are known, in which the bulb was removed from side scraper flakes and from points by flat flaking across the face (fig. 85, 3). Some compressors occur along with utilized bone points. A number of burials are associated with this layer, two adults and four children with accompanying artificial humps and pits.

The succeeding layer was effectively separated from this by a flooring of slabs placed over an area of approximately 5 by 3 yards. Otherwise there is little difference between layers C and D. The industry of D is similar to that of C but in general it is smaller in artefact size. Points with fine even retouch occur, as do side scrapers and truncated flakes (knives or saws). The disc cores are small in size and there are a number of utilized flakes. The plano-convex retouch is present on points. Utilized bone objects, and one slightly incised bone, are reported. The industries of layers C and D are closely related.

An abrupt change in the archaeological record occurs in the overlying loam of layer E, which is slightly redder in colour. Peyrony suggested that some mixture with the underlying layer D may have occurred. Although layer E is thin, it is divided into two separate deposits by a sterile lens in places. The lower layer is called E and the upper is E'. Two industries have been claimed, the lower called Chatelperron or Perigordian I. Its direct contact with the underlying Mousterian deposit may account for the presence of discoidal flakes, but some of the flint tools may indicate a new technology (fig. 86, 1–18). Blades are common, some retouched into end scrapers and burins, often of the angle type. Truncated blades with retouch occur, and a variety of miscellaneous retouched and utilized blades and flakes. Characteristic are curved backed blades or Chatelperron points (fig. 86, 1–6). Although this layer apparently lies directly on top of the Mousterian deposit (D), this need not indicate a sudden and abrupt interruption of the Mousterian occupation of the site, because we cannot be certain that sedimentation need have continued during an abandonment of the shelter. The upper part of E, called E', is marked by the disappearance of typical Chatelperron points. Some curved backed blades are present, but these are atypical, and the characteristic piece is the nibbled blade, a narrow blade with marginal retouch on the bulbar face (lamelles Dufour) (fig. 86, 22–24). Associated are retouched flakes of Mousterian tradition, end of blade scrapers, ordinary burins and some fairly thick flake-blades with retouch. A few bone points and an ivory rod are reported. This industry is often called Perigordian II, but it has also been considered as part of the Aurignacian tradition.

Overlying this deposit is the first of the true Aurignacian industries, in a brown-red earth (F), which itself is partly separated from the principal Aurignacian deposit in

H by a pebble layer. Layer H was subdivided by Peyrony in the eastern part of the shelter into 3 components distinguishable by intercalated sterile layers. The Aurignacian here then has 4 parts, and their respective containing deposits are F, H, H' and H". All four industries exhibit the same basic characteristics, with long blades and bone tools. These peripherally retouched blades (fig. 87, 1–7, 16–17) are occasionally waisted (fig. 87, 2, 7), and are particularly abundant in Aurignacian I and II at La Ferrassie. Another characteristic piece is the thick carinated scraper, made on a flake with a high ridged back, and which is present in all 4 layers (fig. 88, 4, 11). An allied form is the nosed scraper which is marked in Aurignacian II (fig. 87, 21, 23). End of blade scrapers are common, as are burins, the angle type throughout the series, while the ordinary type is partly superseded by polyhedric burins especially in Aurignacian IV. A specialized type, the burin busqué, with stop-notch, is important only in stage II. Various notched blades and awls are also sporadic in their appearance.

Implements of bone and antler are an important component of the Aurignacian industries. A form which is characteristic of the first stage is the split base bone point, which does not appear in stage II where the flattened lozenge-outlined point has replaced it (fig. 87, 27). This form continues in use in the following stage, although at La Ferrassie the bone points of Aurignacian III are less flat in cross-section. By Aurignacian IV the points are oval-round in cross-section, and are generally smaller in overall size. Other organic objects in the Aurignacian at La Ferrassie include needles, with heads or with perforations, fish-gorges, various notched rods, bone spatulae and compressors, and, in Aurignacian I, a perforated bâton of antler, the earliest known. Decorative perforated teeth, pebbles and shells also are known, from all stages.

A limestone bowl or mortar, probably used as a lamp, was recovered from layer F. The first evidence of animal representations occurs in layer H, where a palimpsest of grooves, irregular animal outlines, and symbols of female genitalia are distinguishable. The last is also associated with layer H' (fig. 88, 2–3), with indistinct painted outlines of animals (fig. 88, 9, 14), and the tradition is also present in the final Aurignacian layer here. The Aurignacian I and II at La Ferrassie represent two successive stages in the development of this characteristic industrial tradition, and this succession of flint and bone tools is represented elsewhere in central and west Europe. The split base point, in particular, serves as a type fossil for the early stage of the Aurignacian industries, but the relative proportions of flint tools, the peripherally sharpened blades, carinated scrapers and nosed scrapers, in the differing layers of the Aurignacian at La Ferrassie are not necessarily valid for other Aurignacian sites. The associated art at La Ferrassie represents, so far as present information extends, the earliest evidence of the beginnings of artistic expression.

To the west, a thick pebble and stone deposit rests upon layer H with its Aurignacian industries, but at the back of the east side of the shelter this sterile deposit is scarcely evident, and a direct superposition exists of layer J with its Gravettian (Perigordian) industry upon the underlying Aurignacian. To the west, this Gravettian deposit rests more or less horizontally upon the stony layer, but its upper surface is oblique, sloping down from the back wall of the shelter. Certain stone placements led the excavators to believe that a windbreak had been constructed at this time to close off part of the occupied area.

The industry of layer J represents a new tradition at La Ferrassie. In general, there seems to be a greater emphasis upon flint tools and less upon artefacts of bone and antler. Characteristic of this industry is the backed blade, with straight or slightly curved back (fig. 89, 1–4) and the Font Robert tanged point (fig. 89, 10–15). End scrapers and burins on flat flakes are abundant, and there are a number of half rods. Bulbar flat flaking occurs on a few pointed flakes (fig. 89, 5), but the characteristic Aurignacian forms are rare or absent. Slabs with crude animal and human aspects indicate the continuance of the artistic tradition. To the east, a thin sandy deposit (K) overlies directly the Font Robert Gravettian layer. The contained industry is typified by the backed blade, but many of these are squared off to produce rectangular or roughly triangular shapes (fig. 89, 20, 27, 29). There are a number of burins which must indicate some dependence on bone and antler work although no evidence of this was recovered, in contrast with indications from other Gravettian sites (p. 228).

Overlying this Gravettian deposit in the eastern side of the shelter is a red-earth layer with another Gravettian industry (L). The forms include backed blades, end scrapers, many small multiple angle burins (Noailles burins) (fig. 89, 35–36) and some evidence of grooving of antler.

LAUGERIE HAUTE
(D. & E. Peyrony 1938)

The prehistoric site of Laugerie Haute lies 2 km. from Les Eyzies on the right bank of the Vézère, with its base about 5 m. above the level of the river. Excavations have taken place here since 1862 but the most complete examination to date was made by Peyrony. More recent work by Bordes has resulted in a slight alteration to the stratigraphy as published by Peyrony. The shelter opens over a distance of 180 metres, and the deposits range between 4½ to 5 metres in depth. As the shelter is so large, it is evident that traces of occupation will not necessarily be uniform in their character or thickness over all the area available. Peyrony published two major sections, based upon a western and an eastern cutting through the deposits. These are consistent within each other although certain layers are represented only at one or the other. There are a large number of sterile deposits which effectively separate the successive occupations.

The fauna of Laugerie Haute in general indicates cold conditions existing through-out. Reindeer remains are predominant and generally abundantly represented in all the occupation deposits except layer G where there is little faunal material. Horse is well represented throughout, in proportions of about 1 horse to 10 reindeer in the

Magdalenian layers. Peyrony noticed an increase in the horse remains between his layer B and D, accompanied by a decrease in ibex. The latter becomes less evident in the upper (Solutrean and Magdalenian) layers.

Bovids and red deer are present throughout the series and there are also some traces of fox, wolf, mammoth and other animals. Antelope is only recorded from the upper Magdalenian layers.

In general terms, this site shows a number of backed blade industries underlying a series of layers which shows increasing use of 'pressure flaking', and which itself is succeeded by a Magdalenian sequence. The terminology of the industries recovered by Peyrony has given rise to considerable difficulty in interpretation, and recent excavations at Laugerie Haute and elsewhere have not succeeded in clarifying the problems, although the stratified sequence of industries at Laugerie Haute itself is now well established.

The basal industry is called Perigordian III and consists of a composite deposit which has been partially subdivided (fig. 91). Basically, however, it consists of a series of slender backed blades (fig. 91, 10–12), including geometric forms, such as a few triangles (fig. 91, 4) and a number of obliquely retouched blades (fig. 91, 14, 19). End of blade scrapers and round scrapers are present, as well as angle burins and other burin forms including multiples. The bone work is important, and consists of bevelled bone points of cylindrical section (fig. 91, 7, 21), bone lissoirs and headed bodkins, double pointed gorges and curved and grooved bone points. Decorative objects include perforated teeth of reindeer and fox and abundant red ochre, while artistic objects consist of two limestone blocks engraved with male and female sexual symbols, and a number of slabs with inscribed representations of parts of animals. Some evidence of former ochre drawings was recovered as well.

Above this Perigordian occupation is a sterile deposit, and resting upon this Peyrony believed he found his layer D (Aurignacian V) which was only represented on the western side of the shelter. More recent work has indicated that in fact this industry is intercalated between layers F and H, and that the next archaeological deposit is that of Peyrony's F, called Protomagdalenian (fig. 91, 25–38). The industry of this is basically of backed blade tradition, small narrow blades (fig. 91, 29) and larger blades with blunting retouch down one side. Also present are blades with a form of sharpening retouch down all of one or both edges (fig. 91, 25, 37). End of blade scrapers and burins of angle and ordinary types are present as well as awls and a form of carinated scraper reminiscent of the Aurignacian industry. The bone and antler artefacts include bevelled-base bone points (fig. 91, 30–31), and headed pins as well as engraved fragments of antler. A perforated bâton de commandement has two facing mammoths engraved on its side; this object, and the evidence for groove and splinter technique in the working of antler, led Peyrony to suggest that this industry, foreshadowing Magdalenian traits, should be called Protomagdalenian. Basically, however, it is an industry characterized by small backed blades, and not so unlike the underlying industry found by Bordes (in his layer 38) called Perigordian III[2].

Overlying this Gravettoid industry is Peyrony's Aurignacian V, found only on the Western side of the shelter. In this industry there are no typical backed blades, and the characteristic forms are carinated scrapers including the nosed type, associated with many burins including angle and a sort of parrot beak form. The bone points are bevelled at their base or midway along their length, and there are also headed pins, gorges and other types. The industry is very small and there seems to be insufficient material to allow a definitive diagnosis, although this has been attempted several times.

Another problematical industry is that recovered from a small deposit in the western area of Laugerie Haute in Peyrony's layer G, directly overlying layer D but found only near the back of the shelter; Peyrony called this Protosolutrean. The most important elements here are the double-pointed leaf-shaped flint blades (fig. 92, 2–4) with squills skimmed over the surface, technologically an early stage in the appearance of 'pressure flaking'. The central ridge on the dorsal surface of the blades remain unretouched. Angle burins, end scrapers and retouched 'mousteroid' flakes also occur. Little bone work was found. The retouched blades of Aurignacian industries might be said to lie behind this industry and it may be important that the industry also contains some traces of carinated scrapers, but the 'pressure flaking' technique makes it first appearance in this deposit.

The overlying layers, Peyrony's H, form a composite series of industries separated by sterile deposits. Three phases were recognized by Peyrony, in his H^I, H^{II} and H^{III}, and these provide the basic divisions of the Solutrean tradition. The recent excavations at Laugerie Haute have yielded evidence of some ten industries of Solutrean character, but the basic divisions remain.

The first deposit is characterized by pointes à face plane, long blades with pressure flaking over almost all of the dorsal surface and sometimes invading the bulbar surface (fig. 92, 7–9, 13). Curved backed blades are common, as are angle burins and rather steep scrapers. The bone tools include single-bevelled bone points with roughened surfaces, and there are antler rods and part of a bâton.

The second major industry in this series of deposits is typified by fragments of large bifacially-pressure flaked leaf points, called laurel leaves. The industry in fact is not particularly well-defined, but it does indicate the place of the laurel leaf facies in the Solutrean development. The leaf points are coarsely retouched (fig. 92, 15–16), and are as much as 8″ in length. They may not have been pressure flaked, as their irregular retouch could have resulted from percussion. Other flint forms include straight backed blades, small scrapers and burins (fig. 92, 17–20). There are a number of bone points and club-headed pins.

Above is the Solutrean with shouldered points, associated with fine pressure-flaked willow leaf points. Some of these latter have been thinned by flaking to a thickness of 2–4 mm., and a certain number of the former have also been pressure-flaked over much or all of the dorsal surface. Among the range of projectile heads are shorter tanged points (fig. 92, 22–24), again with pressure-flaking, and these are reminiscent of the much more evolved points in the Parpalló Solutrean. Small backed blades (some denticulated), fine awls, end scrapers and burins complete the basic flint equipment, which was augmented by single-bevelled bone points (fig. 92, 25) and at least one eyed needle, the first noted from this site. Perforated teeth and shells, manganese oxide and red ochre indicate some attention to personal decoration, and a limestone block engraved with animal designs was also recovered from this industry.

The importance of Laugerie Haute for the Solutrean industries is in its undoubted stratification into three main stages, the pointe à face plane, the laurel leaf and the shouldered point stages. This sequence is confirmed elsewhere, at Badegoule for instance, and further subdivision of the later stages are indicated at Bourdeilles.

Directly superimposed on the late Solutrean layer in the western section of Laugerie Haute, but separated from it to the east, is a deposit that Peyrony subdivided into three major horizons, and which he called I^I, I^{II} and I^{III}, all representing the Magdalenian industry (fig. 93). Bordes has identified at least nine such deposits in his excavations. The industry found in the lowest of Peyrony's deposits shows a distinct and abrupt change from the fine technological stage represented in the Solutrean layers beneath. In H^I there are no contemporary pressure-flaked tools, and the characteristic flint forms are flakes of irregular shape with steep marginal retouch (fig. 91, 1–5). There is also a high proportion of burins, mostly angle burins, end scrapers, and steep scrapers. Awls, peripherally sharpened flakes, and a few backed blades make up the rest of the flint equipment. The bone, antler and ivory work includes single-bevelled points, awls and eyed ivory needles, part of a bâton and rare bone snow knives, and there is some evidence of animal representations scratched on certain objects.

The second Magdalenian occupation shows many of the same elements, with end scrapers and burins common, awls and composite tools present, and bevelled bone points, eyed needles and awls, perforated bâtons and bone daggers or knives. However, certain elements have altered, and the irregular flakes, called raclettes, are rare, steep scrapers are rare as well, while backed blades are much more numerous (fig. 93, 8–10), and include small or large scalene triangles and denticulated blades (fig. 93, 11–13). Biconical bone points occur, and the characteristic decoration of objects includes deep grooving rather than the line and dot of the preceding industry.

The third Magdalenian occupation is again separated to the west from the preceding by a slight and sterile deposit. The basic flint tools in an industry (fig. 93, 17–31) dominated by bone and antler work continue to be burins, many of the angle type, and there are also awls and composite tools, many end scrapers most of which are double-ended, backed blades now mostly straight-backed with few triangles and a few denticulated. The bone and antler work is abundant, with wider and shorter bevelled bone points decorated with deep grooves, chisel-ended points, awls and eyed needles and perforated bâtons decorated by grooving in geometric designs. Bone half-rods occur; these are up to 2′ in length, and it might be that they formed part of composite weapons, perhaps bows. Bone knives and spatulate objects are also known in this prolific industry. Certain of the objects are decorated with animal figures, including horse and bison. A number of stone lamps were also recovered.

Well separated from this third Magdalenian deposit is the final Pleistocene occupation layer in Peyrony's K. The archaeological evidence consists of a sort of cache of implements with bone and antler points, finely backed, a decorated rod and forked points.

PARPALLÓ
(Pericot Garcia 1942)

The cave of Parpalló is 10 kilometres to the west of the town of Gandia in the province of Valencia in Spain. Situated at 39° of latitude it is more southerly than, for instance, the cave of Romanelli in southern Italy (p. 321).

The cave is on the side of a gorge 450 metres above sea level in the rugged limestone uplands and below the mountain peak of Mondahes which rises to 836 metres above the sea. Between the mountains and the sea there is a narrow coastal plain, but so sharp is the fall from mountains to sea level that the coastal plain is not likely to have taken any great part in the economy of the hunters of Parpalló.

The fauna from the cave consists of ibex (*Capra pyrenaica*), horse (*Equus caballus*), cattle (*Bos primigenius*) and rabbit (*Lepus cuniculus*) which are present in all levels. In the upper levels of the cave in the Late Solutrean there is roe deer (*Cervus capreolus*), and fallow deer (*Cervus dama*) in the Magdalenian levels. The fauna therefore is primarily of grassland type but some increase in woodland is suggested during the Late Solutrean and Early Magdalenian times. Chamois (*Rupicapra*), red deer (*Cervus elaphus*), pig (*Sus scrofa*), rabbit (*Lepus cuniculus*), fox (*Canis vulpes*), and lynx (*Felis lynx*) also occur.

The excavation is recorded at levels below datum and no stratigraphy is recorded. It is stated however that the industrial levels are distinct and separate entities.

The tool succession (figs. 95–99) indicates a striking similarity with the tool succession at Laugerie Haute in the Dordogne. The basal level contains characteristic Gravettian type backed blades, burins, end scrapers and blade cores. There are some crude bone points and painted and engraved plaques with representations of animals including horse and cattle. Above there are, as at Laugerie Haute in the Dordogne, ascending layers of Solutrean beginning with the pointe à face plane (fig. 95, 3–4) and passing through the typical willow leaves and laurel leaves (fig. 96, 1–3, 6, 8) to an Upper Solutrean with barbed and tanged arrowheads (fig. 97, 1–3, 5–7), micro-burins and shouldered points (fig. 97, 15–19).

Overlying the Solutrean is a level which contains an industry which has been called Solutreo-Aurignacian Final (Solutrio/Gravettian) and which contains barbed and tanged arrowheads, shouldered points and Gravettian type backed blades (fig. 98, 1–20).

LA MADELEINE

Finally there are four layers described as Magdalenian I to IV. In Magdalenian I the bone tools are relatively more important but they are similar to those in the layers below except for a slight increase in scoriation and decoration. The tools consist largely of scrapers and burins. The bifacially-worked arrowheads, laurel leaves, willow leaves and even backed blades are no longer present. This layer represents a diminution in flint tool types without a corresponding increase in bone and antler tool types (fig. 98, 21–37); there is in fact an overall decrease in tool types and, unless one regards it as fortuitous, it possibly indicates at this point an increase in technological specialization in the sense that increased reliance is placed upon fewer tool types. There is an increasing diversification in the bone tools and some increase in tool types including needles in Magdalenian II (fig. 99, 1–11) and III (fig. 99, 12–25, 29) and uniserial harpoons in Magdalenian IV. In Magdalenian III there is an increase in the use of microliths which develops into a more general use of flint types by the introduction of various types of backed blades and triangles. The painted and engraved plaques which are common throughout the layers do not show any great stylistic changes and it has been suggested this may indicate a static population receiving external cultural influences.

LA MADELEINE
(Capitan and Peyrony 1928)

The rock shelter of La Madeleine is the type site of the Magdalenian. The cave is situated in the Dordogne on a loop of the Vézère and is at a few metres above the present level of the plain. There are three occupation levels which in one cutting are separated by sterile layers.

The fauna shows some evidence for climatic change. At the bottom of the deposits reindeer predominate and there is also a considerable quantity of horse bones in the sand deposits which compose the bottom layer and the lower part of the second layer. Subsequently the horse remains decrease and the reindeer becomes even more predominant in the stony deposit without water-laid sand. Chamois, pika and snow partridge confirm the suggestion that colder conditions prevailed at the time of their deposition which may have been contemporary with a Dryas pollen zone. In the upper layer milder conditions perhaps associated with the Bølling or the Allerød oscillation (p. 42) are suggested by the decrease in reindeer and the presence of red deer and pig.

At the base of the deposits are several flint artefacts which include a Solutrean laurel leaf. The lowest level, which is regarded as Magdalenian IV in the French classification, contains primitive harpoons (fig. 100, 9–10), forked base bone points, numerous single-bevelled base bone points and a variety of bone tools. There are numerous engravings and bas-reliefs on bone, stone and antler, and some fine sculptured animal figures in ivory and antler including spearthrowers (fig. 101, 12;

281

Garrod 1955). The flint work (fig. 100, 1–4, 7) includes a variety of backed blades, some tanged blades and burins resembling the parrot beak type.

The middle layer is regarded as Magdalenian V with a subdivision into Va and Vb (fig. 101, 1–3, 5, 9). It is characterized by a considerable number of uniserial harpoons, spearthrowers and double-bevelled bone points. There are parrot beak burins and shouldered points. In the upper part of the layer tridents occur. Throughout there is a considerable number of tools in bone, ivory and antler. The art forms appear to be more stylized and more sophisticated than those in the layer below.

In the upper layer of La Madeleine harpoons are commonly biserial and are classed as Magdalenian VIA in Breuil's succession (fig. 101, 13). There are a number of needles (fig. 101, 9–10) and a great variety of decorated bone points, bâtons de commandement or arrow straighteners, bone daggers and a proliferation of decorated bone and antler tools with animal representations (fig. 101). The lithic industry contains true parrot beak burins (fig. 101, 8), shouldered and tanged points (fig. 101, 5–6) and a number of small points with a curved and retouched edge (fig. 101, 4).

The succession may be continued by referring to the Abri Villepin in the same district where a Magdalenian VIa layer is associated with many reindeer, whereas in Magdalenian VIb above the reindeer decrease and the red deer increase (Peyrony 1936). Above this there is an Azilian layer in which reindeer is rare, horse decreases and red deer shows a marked increase, which is evidence for a climatic change and may indicate the onset of warmer post-glacial conditions.

STAR CARR
(J. G. D. Clark 1954)

The site of Star Carr is five miles south of Scarborough in Yorkshire. The settlement, some 220–240 square yards in extent, consists of an area of swamp stabilized by stones and brushwood. Pollen analysis shows that it was formed during the pre-Boreal (Zone IV). A radiocarbon determination gave a date of 7,358 ± 350 B.C. The food eaten by the inhabitants is indicated by the presence of a number of seeds of various plants and the remains of 80 red deer, 33 roe deer, 11 elk, 9 cattle and 5 pigs. There were no fish and only a few birds. From the shed and unshed antlers it is evident that the site was occupied appropriately enough in the winter season and possibly in the spring and autumn. There are also the remains of what was at one time considered to be a wolf but is now regarded as being the earliest known dog in the Old World. The flints included two-platform (fig. 105, 10), three-platform (fig. 105, 4) and various other types of cores, and long (fig. 105, 5, 7), medium (fig. 105, 6) and short (fig. 105, 9) single-ended scrapers, double-ended scrapers (fig. 105, 8), and burins (fig. 105, 1, 2, 3). Fig. 106 illustrates a variety of microliths, awls which are characteristic of the industry and obliquely truncated blades. Bone pins and scrapers (fig. 107), mattocks made of elk antler (fig. 108), and barbed points of antler (fig. 109) indicate the importance of organic materials. The points may have been used in compound tools for fishing. The flint axes (fig. 108) probably served as chisels. A feature of the finds was a number of stag frontlets with antlers attached, smoothed inside so that they might be worn as a head-dress for presumably either ceremonial or stalking purposes or both. In addition there were shell and amber beads and a perforated deer canine. The presence of resin on one of the flint points, the well-preserved wooden objects, the cut timber, the use of birch bark containers and the paddle (fig. 107) give an unusual account of the techniques and way of life of pre-historic man at this time.

CUZOUL
(Lacam *et al.* 1944)

This site in France is 4 kilometres south-west of Gramat. It is a cave which contains a Sauveterrian industry in the lowest layers with bones of *Equus caballus*, *Sus scrofa*, *Cervus capreolus*, *Cervus elaphus*, a large bovine, beaver and some small carnivores. Superimposed on this are two layers of an industry which is regarded as the first stage of the Tardenois. These layers contain much the same fauna as the Sauveterrian layer and a sheep or goat molar. There are the remains of large bovines but whether or not they are of *Bos primigenius* or bison is not clear. Some are said to be of small size and perhaps of females. Above this there are two layers which contain a final stage of the Tardenois industry. The fauna is much as before and includes an astragalus of sheep or goat of the size of domestic sheep. Higher up there is a further Tarde-noisian layer (Tardenoisian III) again associated with a similar fauna. The faunal remains suggest the possibility that a domestication of animals may have taken place in France at an early date. The Sauveterrian tools include backed blades (fig. 110, 1–3, 7, 9, 14), bec-de-flute burins (fig. 110, 16) and scrapers (fig. 110, 15, 17).

The Tardenois layers contain microlithic tools (fig. 110, 8, 10–13, 18–21), Tardenois points (fig. 110, 11), some à base récurrente (fig. 110, 20) and trapezes (fig. 110, 8, 10, 21). The Sauveterrian industries are characterized by their small size. At Sauve-terre La Lémance (Lot et Garonne), the cave of Le Martinet has a Sauveterrian industry which includes a variety of triangular forms of microliths, as well as the very small backed blades. It is said to overlie an industry which is regarded as being late Magdalenian in type. Superimposed upon the Sauveterrian industry are also layers containing Tardenois industries (Coulonges 1935).

15

Central Europe

THE evidence for industrial activity contemporary with the developing Acheulean-Levalloisian traditions of western Europe is sparse, apart from a concentration, if it may be called this, between the Weser and the Elbe rivers in north-eastern Germany (McBurney 1950). The most important site in this area is Markleeberg, where a quantity of flakes and a few bifacial tools were recovered from gravels sometimes believed to be of Eemian age. The lack of evidence for preparation of cores demonstrates that this industry is not of Levalloisian character, and it has been suggested that it may be related to the Clactonian industries of southern England. Such a relationship remains to be demonstrated, but an alternative source, ultimately in the Buda industries of central Europe, is equally as difficult to maintain in the absence of linking finds. The solution may in fact be simpler, that these flake industries represent an inland facies of a more westerly tradition, either of handaxe or Levalloisian character, and of temporal (including seasonal) and functional variation.

In central Europe, the archaeological record of occupation during the Middle Pleistocene is limited to a few sites such as Vertesszöllös (fig. 72; p. 303), and during the earliest part of the Upper Pleistocene (Saale in terms of the glacial sequence) there continues to be little evidence of widespread settlement in the area. By Eemian times, however, there had appeared a developed Mousterian industry typified by the site of Ehringsdorf near Weimer (fig. 113; Behm-Blancke 1960). The industry here appears to be wholly characteristic of the Mousterian traditions that occur from Eemian times in areas east of the Rhône and Rhine rivers, including Italy, and it is associated with a fauna including *Elephas antiquus* and *Rhinoceros merckii* and the remains of several humans. The skull of a young male has prominent brow-ridges with a slightly receding forehead and a flattened vault.

The Mousterian occupation of a rock shelter at Krapina in Croatia may also be of this late Eem date; the associated fauna included *Rhinoceros merckii* as well as *Cervus elephus, Bos primigenius* and *Ursus spelaeus*. The shelter also contained the remains of at least 13 humans, the bones badly fragmented and sometimes burned. The post-cranial bones are essentially of modern type, and do not show the large joints and heavy muscular marking of the Neanderthal skeletons from western

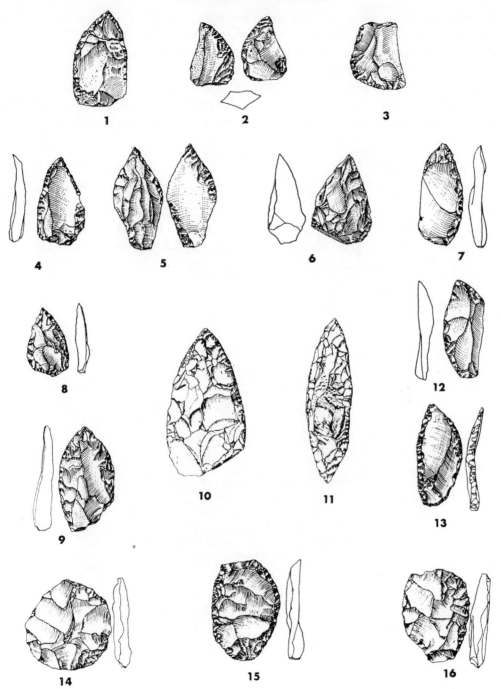

FIG. 113. Mousterian $\frac{1}{2}$; Ehringsdorf, Germany $\frac{1}{2}$. *From Müller-Karpe 1966*

Europe. The skulls are considered to be more archaic in that they possess a pronounced supra-orbital torus, and the mandible has a receding chin. The Krapina remains are often considered to demonstrate the existence of cannibalistic practices, in that they are broken and burnt (Gorjanovic-Kramberger 1906).

In high-level caves of Switzerland, Bavaria and Croatia, evidence exists of a cult of bears involving the deposition of bear skulls and bones in certain caves (fig. 114). In a chamber of the Drachenloch in Switzerland, a stone cist had been built to house

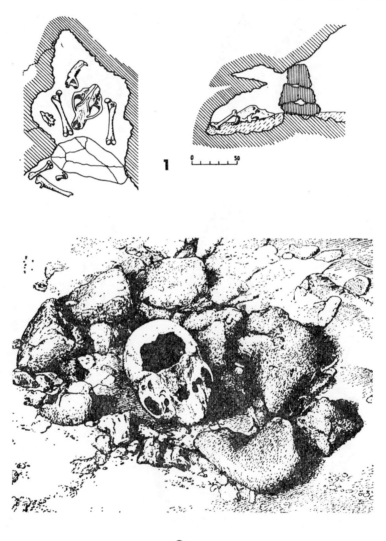

2

FIG. 114. 1 Veternica, Yugoslavia; Crevices with deposits of cave bear bones (scale in centimetres); 2 Monte Circeo, Italy. Human skull. *From Müller-Karpe 1966*

stacked bear-skulls; piles of sorted long bones were laid along the walls of the cave. Another heap of bones contained the skull of a bear through which a leg bone had been forced, the skull resting upon two other long bones; each bone was from a different beast. In the Bavarian Petershöhle, ten bear-skulls had been laid on a platform.

In addition to this cult of bear-skulls, there is some evidence of particular attention paid to human skulls. In a small cave at San Felice de Circeo, a human skull lay, with a mandible from another individual, at the centre of a circle of stones (fig. 114, 2); bones of many animals had been heaped around the cave. The skull had a large hole in the right occipital and the foramen magnum had been cut away, perhaps to allow extraction of the brain (Müller-Karpe 1966).

The east Mousterian is documented through the early phases of the Last Glaciation; a typical industry of this time is that from the lowest level in the cave complex of Mauern, west of Regensburg (fig. 115; p. 305). Characteristic forms include straight-line retouch and thinning of the bulbar surface (plano-convex retouch) on flakes from discoidal cores. The open station of Salzgitter-Lebenstedt in north-western Germany is less typical, containing some forms considered characteristic of western areas as well as a basic eastern Mousterian industry (p. 306). The Mousterian from Tata in Hungary has been radiocarbon dated to c. 53,000 B.P., and other dates in the same area extend as late as c. 35,000 B.P.

Stratigraphically later is the Altmühlian industry from Mauern, which marks a culmination of thinning bifacial retouch on leaf-shaped points, associated with flake scrapers and points (fig. 116; p. 305). Such bifacial leaf-shaped points are generally considered a characteristic feature of late eastern Mousterian industries, but the type is also known in western Europe, not only from eastern French sites such as La Baume Bonne, but also in certain contemporary Mousterian assemblages from as far west as La Quina in the Charente. In Italy the foliate point is not well represented, and developed Mousterian industries tend to become miniaturized, partly due to limited sources of raw material in certain regions. Mousterian industries containing variants of leaf-shaped points occur in Epirus (p. 312), Rumania and Bulgaria, and to the north in Hungary and Czechoslovakia. The Czechoslovakian Mousterian industries, in common with those of other regions in central Europe, demonstrate the existence of several different facies, from finely-finished industries to coarse and irregularly-retouched material reminiscent of 'Tayacian'.

The type site of the Hungarian facies is Szeletha, a cave in which three industrial deposits are recorded (p. 306); these appear to demonstrate the development of round-based bifacial leaf-points within a flake tradition. At Szeletha, there is evidence of association with Upper Palaeolithic artefacts, and at Istallosko in the same area industries of Aurignacian character contained traces of Szelethian leaf-points. Radio-carbon dates from Czechoslovakia and Poland indicate an age between 35,000 and 40,000 B.P. for leaf-point industries. Dates from Istallosko are as late as c. 31,000 B.P. for the association of leaf-points and Upper Palaeolithic material.

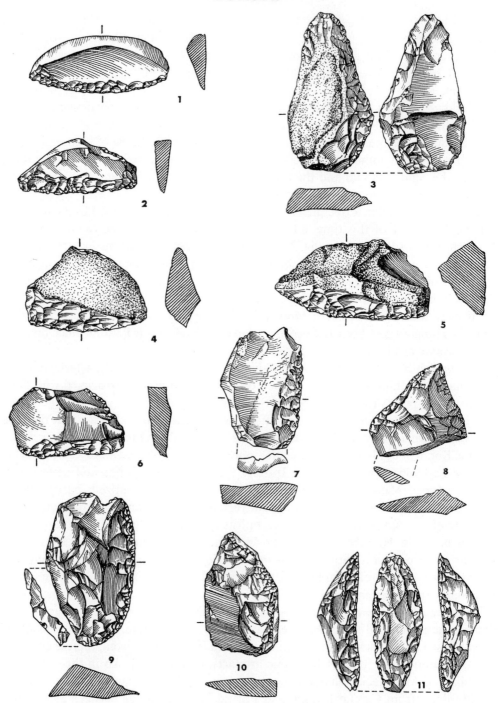

FIG. 115. Mousterian ⅔; Mauern, Germany. *After Bohmers 1951*

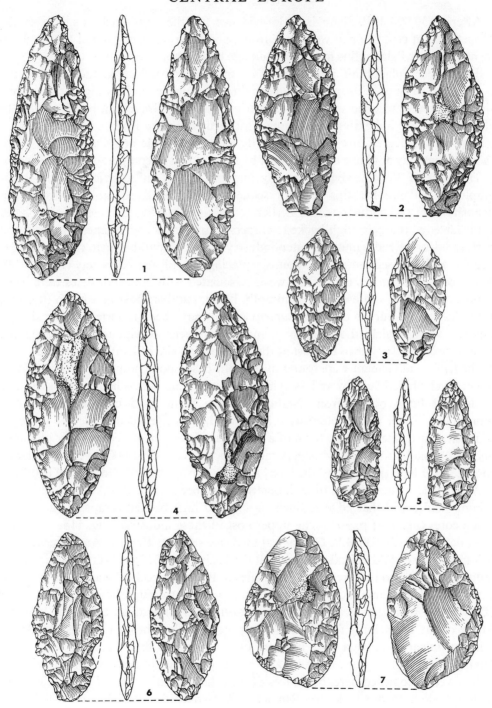

FIG. 116. Mousterian $\frac{2}{3}$; Mauern, Germany. *After Bohmers 1951*

After *c.* 30,000 B.P. there is little evidence for the continued existence of the Mousterian in central or in western Europe, and it has been suggested that replacement by Upper Palaeolithic man was complete by, or shortly after, this time.

The Upper Palaeolithic industries of central Europe reflect, in their names, the dominance of west European influence in Palaeolithic archaeology; typological similarities have resulted in the terms Aurignacian and Gravettian being applied to almost all of the industries in this area, eastwards from the Rhône. The use of such terms infers a degree of cultural similarity over these wide areas, a community of thought that may not have existed except by the accident of comparable conditions.

The sites of Vogelherd in Germany and Willendorf in Austria provide stratigraphical evidence for this twofold sequence. At Vogelherd, above Mousterian deposits were two industries, the earlier containing split-based bone points, blades with flat edge retouch, high-backed scrapers, burins and end scrapers, incised and perforated bone rods, and the later industry with comparable material except for circular and oval-sectioned bone points replacing the split-based variety (Riek 1934). The succession matches that of the west. Associated with both industries were ivory figures of animals, representing mammoth, horse, panther, bear and bison (fig. 117, 1–6). Associated burials of *Homo sapiens sapiens* have been reported. Other sites in this region have yielded Aurignacoid material associated with leaf-shaped points, such as occurred farther to the east at the Aurignacian site of Istallosko, where traces of the leaf-point element were found in the split-based bone point industry and in an upper level where blades were less evident and the bone points had solid bases. The split-based bone points from Istallosko range from 5–25 cm. in length, and biproducts of their manufacture were also found. This site has also yielded evidence of musical instruments in the form of a whistle made of perforated reindeer phalange and a flute made from a long bone. A radiocarbon date of *c.* 31,000 B.P. was obtained for the upper level (p. 307), but the basal Aurignacian has been dated to *c.* 44,000 B.P.

At Willendorf in Austria, three industries have been classed as Aurignacian, containing blades with flat edge retouch, nosed and high-backed scrapers, burins and blade cores (fig. 118; p. 307). The uppermost of these industries (fig. 118, 8–12) has been dated to *c.* 31,800 B.P. Geological evidence suggests that the Aurignacian here belongs to a wet cold episode, perhaps at the beginning of Main Würm. Aurignacian industries have also been recorded from sites in Poland, Czechoslovakia, Yugoslavia, Bulgaria and Rumania. At Potočka Zijalka, in northern Yugoslavia, a cave at over 2000 metres represents a high-level occupation by Aurignacian cave-bear hunters. Many of the bear skulls found in the deep deposits had broken snouts. At Bacho Kiro in Bulgaria, above a flake industry on poor quality flint was an industry containing peripherally-trimmed blades and nosed scrapers. No certain split-based bone points were recognized here, but traces of these have been recovered from other sites in this region. In north-eastern Rumania, Aurignacoid material is recorded from loess sites, the industries containing rough steep scrapers, edge-retouched blades and burins.

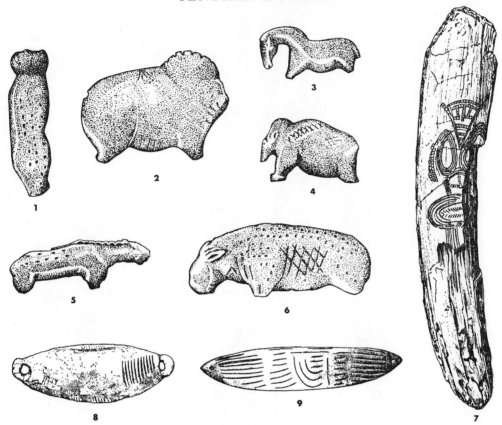

FIG. 117. 1–6 Vogelherd, Germany; 7 Predmost, Moravia; 8–9 Pavlov, Moravia; Scale 1–6, 8, $\frac{1}{2}$; 7, $\frac{3}{4}$; 9, $\frac{1}{3}$. *From Müller-Karpe 1966*

The second major Upper Palaeolithic tradition in central Europe is the Gravettian, which is generally considered to have abruptly replaced the Aurignacian. At the site of Willendorf, there is a typological change between industries 4 and 5; small backed blades and pointed blades appear in significant quantities in industry 5 (fig. 119, 1–8), which has been dated to *c.* 32,000 B.P. although Aurignacian retouched blades are still well represented. Succeeding industries (figs. 120, 121) demonstrate the development of the backed blade element, but there is a considerable body of material common to both groups of industries; the insignificant quantities of bone and antler work leave a large gap in our knowledge of the industries of Willendorf. A characteristic tool of the Gravettian industries of central and eastern Europe is the shouldered point, with a wide tang and slight shoulder (fig. 121, 6–7). Other stone artefacts include angle burins, end scrapers, lames écaillées, and backed blades; bones and ivory points appear in a developed form only in industry 9, accompanied by figurines. The Venus of Willendorf (fig. 121, 8), carved in limestone, is a short, fat figure with

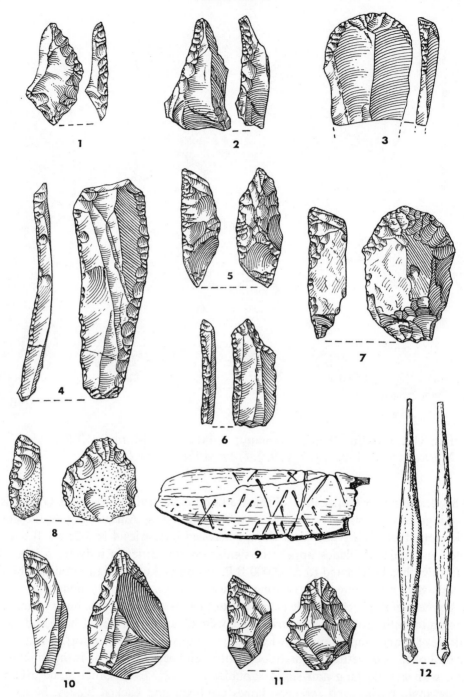

FIG. 118. Willendorf, Austria $\frac{1}{1}$; 1–3 Level 2; 4–7 Level 3; 8–12 Level 4.
After Felgenhauer 1956–9

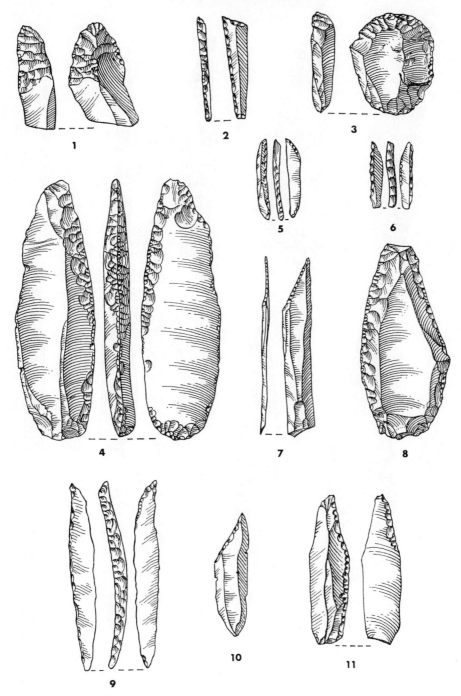

FIG. 119. Willendorf, Austria $\frac{1}{1}$; 1–8 Level 5; 9–11 Level 6. *After Felgenhauer 1956–9*

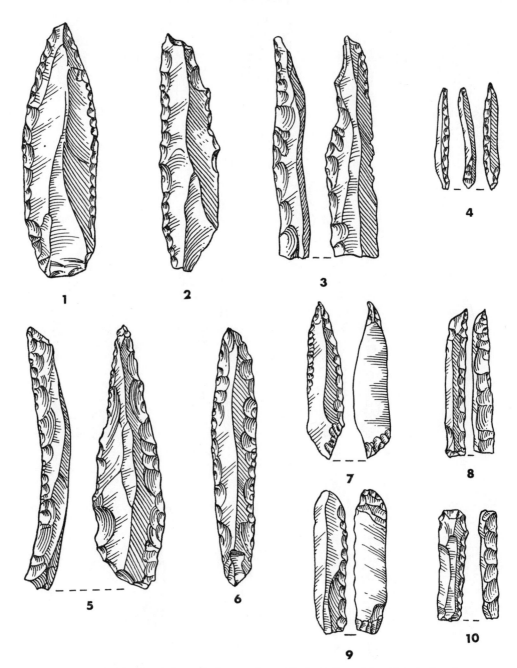

FIG. 120. Willendorf, Austria $\frac{1}{1}$; 1–4 Level 7; 5–10 Level 8. *After Felgenhauer 1956–9*

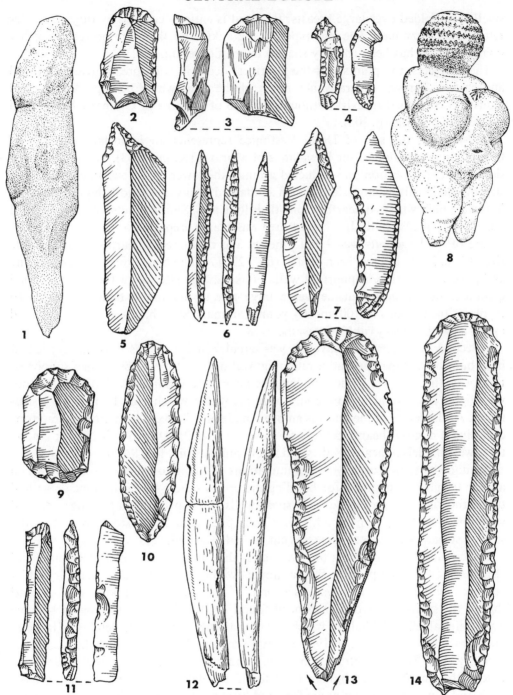

FIG. 121. Willendorf, Austria; Level 9; Scale $\frac{1}{1}$ except 8, $\frac{3}{4}$; 1, $\frac{1}{2}$. *After Felgenhauer 1956–9, and Müller-Karpe 1966*

small arms folded over large breasts; the head is entirely covered by ridged grooves resembling frizzy hair. The legs taper to the ankle and there are no feet. Another pointed pebble has been roughly shaped into a figure (fig. 121, 1).

These objects, the points and the figurines, occur in widespread areas of central and eastern Europe, generally not north of the Alps where perhaps Aurignacoid industries continued to exist, although the site of Mauern in Germany has yielded Gravettoid material (p. 305).

In Moravia, the site of Dolni Vestonice represents an important example of Gravettian occupation of the loess-lands of Moravia (Klima 1963). The site lies on a slope, the upper portion on soliflucted ground, the lower part a swampy area with a stream. Beside this depression, which contained many mammoth bones, tent-like huts were built with two hearths along their long axis. Summer huts, of large size and unroofed, were also built. In a central area was a large fireplace.

One of the large huts was 9 × 15 metres and contained 5 hearths; in view of its size, it is unlikely to have been roofed (fig. 122, 17). The base probably was of stone and post construction, supporting walls of skins. The interior of the hut contained quantities of artefacts; outside was a large pile of mammoth bones estimated to represent the remains of 100, mostly young, animals. Such bones would have served as fuel as well as heavy rubble for walls.

A second hut, recently excavated, was circular and 6 metres in diameter; it had been built on a slope and had a retaining wall of limestone blocks which supported roof posts (fig. 122, 16). Inside the hut, the normal accumulation of tools and bones was slight, but several hollow bones were recovered which may be musical instruments. At the centre of the hut was an oven made of soil mixed with ground limestone enclosing a dug-out hearth containing soot and over 2,000 fired clay lumps; among these were models of heads, bodies and feet of animals (fig. 122, 8–12).

Around the settled area were accumulations of mammoth bones, some of which appear to have been stored for building materials, others for fuel. Some areas had tusks stuck into the ground to form slight walls; these provided a boundary beyond which no huts have been found. Other bone piles, and heavy stone tools near the stream, suggest areas where game was cut up and prepared.

The circular hut containing the oven lay higher up the slope than other huts, and clearly served another purpose than a simple dwelling. In a hut below, an ivory tablet engraved with a human face was discovered in 1948 (fig. 122, 4); both this face, and that of the small sculpted human head found in 1936 (fig. 122, 6), appear to have asymmetrical left facial halves, which has been thought to indicate debility of muscles and paralysis of the nerve. In 1949 a burial was found in a pit within the settlement area (fig. 122, 7); the contracted body lay under two mammoth scapulae, and was that of the small sculpted human head found in 1936 (fig. 122, 6), appear to have teeth and some bones of an arctic fox, and near her head was a flint point. The left half of her face is considered to have been deformed through peripheral paralysis of the cheek nerves, indicated by pathological processes of the left maxillary joint. It is

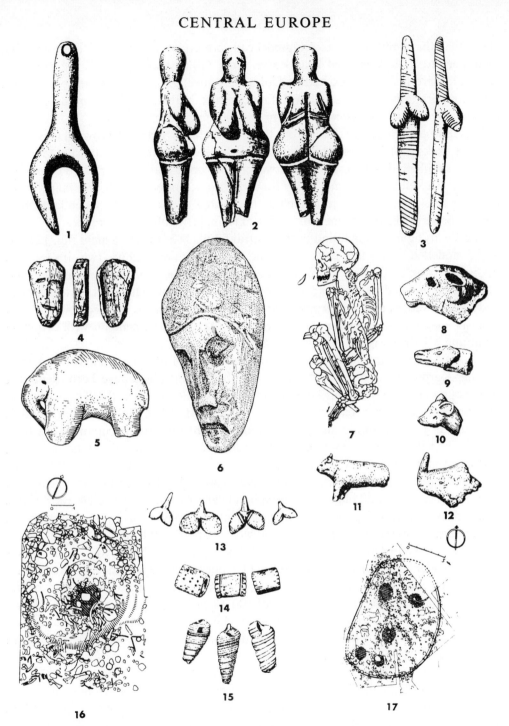

FIG. 122. Gravettian; Dolni Vestonice, Moravia; Scale $\frac{1}{2}$ except 1, $\frac{2}{3}$; 3, $\frac{2}{3}$; 6, $\frac{3}{2}$; 7, 16, 17. *After Müller-Karpe 1966*

297

likely that this body, and the sculpted head, are contemporary and represent the same person; if the engraved head on an ivory tablet also represents the same individual, there must have existed at Dolni Vestonice a tradition or memory of this person generations after she had been first commemorated. Radiocarbon dates from the site suggest that it was occupied from *c.* 29,000 to *c.* 25,000 B.P.

The industrial material found on the site includes many narrow blades with blunted backs, notched and denticulated blades, end scrapers and burins, few and atypical shouldered points. Tools and weapons of bone and ivory are also common; awls, needles, knives, mammoth ribs for lanceheads, antler shovels and many other forms occur. Decorative objects include perforated shells and other pendants, and tubular beads; bone tubes, one with a plug of resin, probably were panpipes.

The Venus figurine was found in the central fireplace of the settlement (fig. 122, 2); it was modelled in clay and powdered bone, then fired; the head has two slits for eyes but is otherwise featureless except for four grooves in the top. The body is wide and the breasts long and pendulous; the arms end at the elbow. The junction of legs and body is grooved, and paired grooves extend across the back. A striated rod with two 'breasts' may represent a schematic Venus (fig. 122, 3), and a pendant with drooping point may also be designed in the same way (fig. 122, 1).

Also in Moravia are the important Gravettian sites of Předmost, Pavlov and Brno (Müller-Karpe 1966). At Pavlov a large number of hut plans have been identified, oval, round and five-sided in shape, with some postholes and hearths. The associated industry included decorated bone and ivory objects (fig. 117, 8–9) including animals and human figures, and a number of phalange whistles; the occupation has been radiocarbon dated to *c.* 25,000 B.P. At the Předmost mammoth-hunters' open site, decorated mammoth ivory was associated with other pieces of hatched and curved decoration (fig. 117, 7), as well as an industry containing backed blades, shouldered points, end scrapers, and blades with peripheral flat retouch. An oval pit 4 × 2·5 metres and 0·5 metres deep lay within the settlement, covered by a layer of stones and surrounded by mammoth bones; in the pit were the bodies of 8 adults and 12 children, mostly in a crouched attitude. One of the children had a necklet of ivory beads. Mammoth shoulder blades protected other smaller piles of bones on the site. At Brno, a grave under a heap of mammoth tusks and rhinoceros bones contained an ochre-covered adult male wearing a necklace of 600 *Dentalia* shells and accompanied by 2 perforated discs and 3 roundels of limestone, 3 flat discs of mammoth tooth, 3 discs of mammoth rib and 5 others of ivory, and a male figure of ivory, legless and with only one arm, 25 cm. in height.

A number of other sites in Moravia and Slovakia have yielded material of Gravettian character, including female figurines, and on the basis of known finds there can be little doubt that Moravia in particular was extensively occupied by Gravettians compared to other neighbouring regions. Many sites to the south, for example, appear to represent leaf-point and Aurignacoid traditions rather than Gravettian.

Industries of Magdalenian character can be recognized in parts of Germany and

Switzerland, and farther eastwards in Moravia. If these can be considered as made and deposited by Magdalenians, they may indicate a migration of people from the west French area. Almost all of these industries contain material which belongs typologically to the late Magdalenian in France. In southern Germany and Switzerland, the caves of Schweizersbild, Kesslerloch and Petersfels provide geological evidence indicating Magdalenian occupation during cold conditions, with some indication of a more temperate episode at the Kesslerloch during the earlier part of the occupation. At Petersfels, harpoon-heads with double row of barbs, bevelled bone points, needles, burins, awls, end scrapers and backed bladelets were found, as well as bâtons with one, two or four holes (fig. 123, 4–7; Peters 1930). Decoration was both naturalistic and conventionalized, and included a number of jet objects said to resemble female figurines.

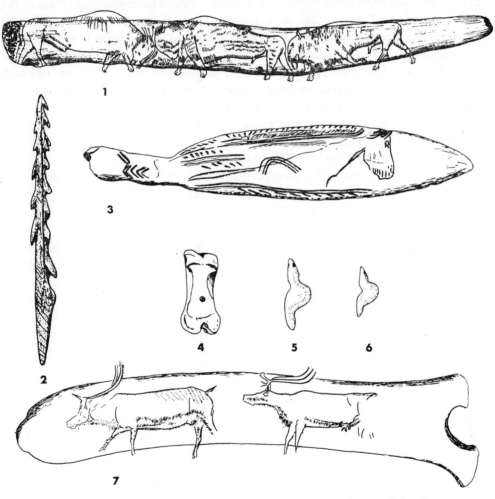

FIG. 123. 'Magdalenian' ½; 1–3 Pekarna, Moravia; 4–7 Petersfels, Germany. *After Müller-Karpe 1966*

In the valley of the Rhine, the weathered portion of a loessic deposit at Andernach contained an industry with a double barbed point and single-rowed harpoon heads, bevelled points and needles, end scrapers, burins, awls and backed blades as well as some larger and coarser flints (R. Schmidt 1912). The loess was covered by volcanic pumice dated by pollen in the area to the Allerød oscillation.

In Moravia, one of the easternmost sites reputedly of Magdalenian affinities is Pekarna, with an industry of backed blades, rectangles, burins and awls, a forked bevelled bone point with crescentic engraving, a bone flute, harpoon-head with triple rows of barbs, bâton, linear decorated half rods, eyed needles and antler clubs. Decorated pieces bear engravings of horse, chamois and bison (fig. 123, 1–3; Müller-Karpe 1966).

In northern Germany a number of industries have been recognized which mark the earliest evidence of Late Glacial occupation of the region, contemporary with the Magdalenian of France and Spain. The open landscape of the north European plain was particularly suitable for animals such as reindeer, bison and horse; sedges, dwarf birch and willow, and some steppe types of vegetation too, formed a grassland with tree 'islands' in sheltered spots. In Schleswig-Holstein and other areas, tunnel valleys existed, formed by melt waters at the edges of the ice sheets and left as valleys after the withdrawal of the ice; lakes and ponds existed in these valleys which provided rich pasture for reindeer and other animals.

At Stellmoor, stratified muds and peats have yielded evidence of two related traditions, called Hamburgian and Ahrensburgian (Rust 1943). The lower industry, so-called after a group of sites in the neighbourhood of Hamburg, was associated with pollen of Oldest Dryas character. The economy at Stellmoor was directed upon the reindeer, and most of the equipment was based upon this animal (fig. 124, 7–10; 125, 2, 6). Flint tools include heavy scrapers, blade scrapers, burins, small obliquely-blunted blades, awls of which a twisted form is characteristic, and shouldered points; a few microburins occur on Hamburgian sites. The burins and awls appear to have been used in antler work, after the antler had been softened by water and heat. The points are small, about $1\frac{1}{2}''$ long, and were used as projectile tips; fragments have been found in reindeer ribs. The bone and antler work contains bone knives, long points about 10″ long, and curved antler pieces with a hole at the curve for the insertion of a flint flake; these implements are often decorated with simple linear designs, and are believed to have been used in the cutting of hide (fig. 125, 6). At the site of Meiendorf, a single-rowed harpoon-head was found (Rust 1937). Present on both sites were shoulder blades of reindeer, each with a hole, perhaps representing a ceremonial activity rather than expert marksmanship during hunting (fig. 125, 2). Certainly of ceremonial practice are the skeletons of young reindeer, two at Stellmoor and one at Meiendorf weighted down by large stones, and believed to have been deposited in the lake; one of the reindeer at Stellmoor had a perforated shoulder blade. Art on Hamburgian artefacts is rare; at Meiendorf several rather simple outlines of animal heads, including horses, were found, and grooves and incised lines occur on antler fragments.

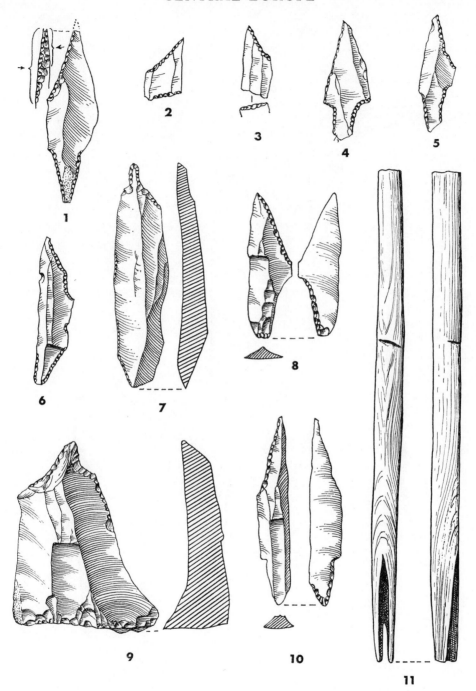

FIG. 124. Stellmoor, Germany $\frac{1}{1}$; 1–6, 11 Ahrensburgian; 7–10, Hamburgian. *After Rust 1943*

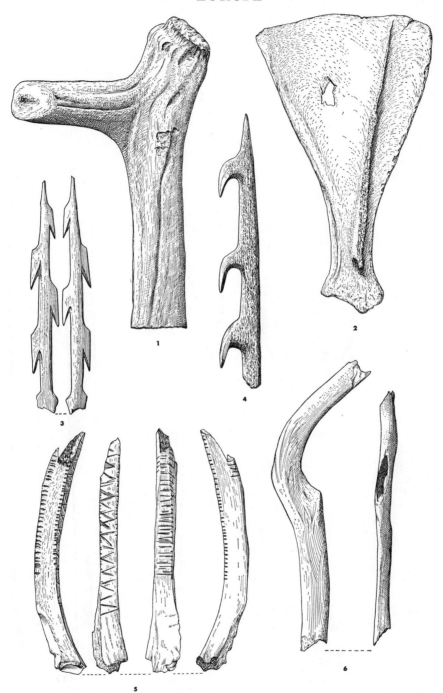

FIG. 125. Stellmoor, Germany $\frac{1}{2}$; 1, 3–5 Ahrensburgian; 2, 6 Hamburgian. *After Rust 1943*

Stratified above the Hamburgian at Stellmoor in the Younger Dryas phase (Zone III) was a second occupation deposit, which also represents a temporary settlement during the summer season of reindeer hunters; a very high proportion of the bones recovered are of reindeer. Of these, a gap in size exists between bones of calves, indicating that these animals were elsewhere during the winter months. The rarity of shed antlers suggests that it was in the summer that this area was favoured by the reindeer and their hunters or herders.

The Ahrensburgian industry at Stellmoor consists of flint scrapers, burins, obliquely-blunted flakes, and tanged points; no microburins occur (fig. 124, 1–6, 11; 125, 1, 3–5). The points served as arrowheads; two-piece pinewood shafts were found, the forked joint of the short foreshaft bound onto the longer shaft (fig. 124, 11). Harpoon heads with single or double rows of barbs (fig. 125, 3–4) and antler clubs also occur (fig. 125, 1); the industries at Pekarna and Pavlov contain similar clubs. Reindeer skulls at Stellmoor show holes into which the club heads fit; these clubs were used for killing, perhaps after the animal had been disabled. Sacrificed reindeer skeletons were found at Stellmoor, as well as evidence that a head with antlers had been set upon a post. Reindeer skin tents were used, and held down by large stones; a number of such pear-shaped stone settings have been recognized from both Hamburgian and Ahrensburgian sites. The distribution of Ahrensburgian industries extends from Schleswig-Holstein westwards to northern Holland, and eastwards to central Germany, eastern Prussia and Poland. Radiocarbon dates indicate that the Ahrensburgian existed in the ninth millennium B.C., a date some four or five thousand years after the Hamburgian traditions.

Of approximately the same age as the Ahrensburgian industries is a large group from the north European plain and known collectively as the *Federmessergruppen*. A number of variant regional industries have been identified. Characteristic forms include curved backed blades and narrow straight backed blades, blade scrapers and burins. To the north, an industry from Bromme dated to the Allerød (Zone II) represents an early occupation of Denmark. Scrapers, burins, heavy tanged flakes and lighter tanged points occur. Elsewhere, developments similar to those of western Europe took place. There is a proliferation of small tool industries arising out of earlier Upper Palaeolithic techniques. In Switzerland a microlithic industry developed out of the local Magdalenian. The trapeze became ultimately a common artefact which continued in some areas into Neolithic times, and Tardenoisian-type industries extended as far eastwards as the Dniepr (Schwabedissen 1954; Taute 1963; J. G. D. Clark 1958).

VERTESSZÖLLÖS
(Kretzoi and Vértes 1965)

The prehistoric site of Vertesszöllös, 50 km. to the north-west of Budapest, consists of a stratified deposit of calcareous muds and loessic elements with travertines. At the base is a series of detritus cones surrounded by grey travertine and capped in places by grey lime muds. A disconformity separates this complex from an overlying yellow loess which contains a reddish calcareous mud. Grey travertine and soil cap the entire deposit. Geologically this site indicates the end of a warm period and the onset of colder loess-forming conditions, but the rich macrofauna enables a more precise date to be assigned to the industrial remains. The faunal sequence for Hungary is well established, and its Middle Pleistocene stage is called the Biharian. This is considered to represent the Günz–Mindel interglacial and the Mindel glaciation. Kretzoi and Vertes, who excavated at Vertesszöllös in 1963–5, believe that the site belongs to their stage *e* of the Biharian, that is, a slightly warmer phase between stages *d* and *f*. The Mauer fauna indicates a position in stage *c*, in late Lower Biharian times, while the Vertesszöllös assemblages must fall within Upper Biharian times, in glacial terms the Mindel interstadial and Mindel 2.

The relative decrease in numbers of *Pitymys arvalidens*, and the increase of *Microtus conjungens*, from the base of the fossiliferous deposits at Vertesszöllös upwards, point to a deteriorating climate during the deposition of the upper layers. The pre-loessic deposits then may be considered to be of Mindel interstadial age, while the loessic strata represent Mindel 2 glacial conditions.

Four separate industrial levels have been recovered from Vertesszöllös, two in the solid travertine and the lime mud of the lower complex, and two within the loess, one at the base and the other near the top. Although this physical separation must indicate a considerable period of time, the four industries are remarkably alike in general character.

Represented in these levels are actual occupation sites, with unrolled quartzite and other stone tools, waste flakes and cores, fragments of animal bones including burnt bones, and traces of hearths. The lithic industry is mainly on pebbles, some on limestone boulders, and about half are quartzite with the remainder of flint, chert and radiolarite. Cortex remains on most of the tools. In size these average 24 mm., with a range from 11 to 62 mm. in length, and the excavators believe that smaller tools were more evident in the lowest level than in the loess levels. Most flakes have plain platforms and deep scars, although a few diffuse (soft hammer) scars are visible. Although the angle of these platforms is of the order of 110° or 120°, the small size of the nodules probably prevented a true anvil technique. Retouch occurs on about 25% of the tools, and is rather steep, occasionally producing a denticulated effect. The tools are clearly unspecialized, but can be divided into heavier chopping forms (fig. 72, 1) and lighter, smaller flake tools (fig. 72, 2–5). The industry as a whole belongs to the Buda pebble industries of the immediate area, also of Upper Biharian age. Correlations with other unspecialized flake industries of central and eastern Europe are premature.

The importance of Vertesszöllös lies in the undoubted later Mindel dating for this primitive industrial series, contemporary with the development of handaxe traditions farther west. Of equal importance is the discovery in the lowest industrial level at

MAUERN

Vertesszöllös of remains of hominid teeth and occipital bone said to be in the *Homo erectus* pattern, and recently classified as a primitive *Homo sapiens*.

MAUERN
(Bohmers 1951, Zotz 1955)

The stratified site of Mauern lies in a limestone cliff overlooking a small valley, once a tributary of the Altmühl river which flows into the Danube west of Regensburg. The site itself lies near the Danube river, and consists of a small series of interlocking caves. The sequence of deposits in the major cave consists of a series of loams resting on the rock floor, the upper layers of which contain developed Mousterian material in a stratified succession. Above these are loessic deposits, the top of which contains a Gravettian-related industry separated from the Mousterian by several feet of sterile deposit.

The deposits are climatically dated on the basis of their pollen, fauna and sediments. In general terms, deposits associated with much frost-shattered rock indicate a cold phase, while the major rock fall-free deposits beneath, with their contained Mousterian industries, represent milder conditions at an earlier time. Faunal and pollen studies support this general conclusion.

The lowest industry (fig. 115) is characterized by limace-shaped scrapers up to 10 cm. in length with plano-convex technique and rather coarse retouch. There are also flake points and rather thick side scrapers with coarse trimming. The scrapers, however, exhibit great variety in their treatment, including the straight edge type. There are other retouched flakes, with faceted platforms. Basically this is a typical East Mousterian industry. The technique of plano-convex retouch as seen on certain of the flake tools here consists of ordinary step flaking on one side, and larger thinner facets on the other. Apparently when a tool became dull through use, flakes would be skimmed off the central face to produce a fresh intersection.

Above this industry a specialized tradition is represented, a tradition involving the use of leaf-shaped points. These Mauern or Altmühl points are 10–11 cm. long, a few up to 15 cm., rather pointed at both ends, and either retouched in plano-convex fashion as before, or bifacially-trimmed (fig. 116). The technique is not pressure-flaking, but ordinary percussion was used although effective damping of the blow could have been required. The points are very thin in section, and have been called Solutrean on occasion, although they are distinct from the fully-evolved Solutrean laurel leaf points.

Other material in this Altmühl layer includes side scrapers of various types, straight-edge tools and rather coarse scrapers called handaxes on occasion. A few points, faceted flakes and disc cores complete the assemblage.

EUROPE

SALZGITTER-LEBENSTEDT
(Tode *et al.* 1953)

The open site of Salzgitter-Lebenstedt was found to the south of Brunswick, about 40 miles east-southeast of Hanover. The area of occupation was approximately 15 metres in diameter, resting upon a fossil soil developed on sands. Covering the occupation horizon were further sands, sand with pebbles and loamy loess. The fauna recovered from the site was predominantly reindeer, with mammoth and a relatively small amount of bison and horse also represented. Pollen from the area indicated a sub-arctic climate with grass-tundra vegetation, and with pine the dominant tree; birch, willow and spruce were also present somewhere in the region. No trace of interglacial deposits was recovered from above the occupation level, so the latter must date to the last glacial episode. A radiocarbon date for the site suggests the occupation is of the order of 50,000 years old. The industry associated with this environmental detail is predominantly in the flake tradition. Of some 2000 pieces, most of Baltic flint, 200 are identifiable as tools. The flakes have plain or faceted platforms, and the predominant tool is the convex-edged scraper; others have straight-line retouch. There are also bifacially-worked leaf-points and pointed handaxes which are rather thick in section. Some 10 points made on mammoth rib, about 60–70 cm. long, were found, as well as a small barbed bone point and a club made of reindeer antler.

SZELETA
(Gabori 1953, Freund 1952)

The cave of Szeleta in Hungary is within 20 kilometres of Misholc, in the hills flanking the river Theiss. The numerous caves in this area show ample confirmation of the data acquired from the excavations at Szeleta. Throughout the deposits cave bear predominates and there is a little reindeer. Arctic rodents are present in the upper layers, which has been taken to indicate the onset of colder conditions. In the earlier excavations which were published in 1923, three layers were observed. The lowest layer contained eleven bifacials which were thick and irregular in shape. They have been regarded as small handaxes evolving towards foliates. A subsequent investigation showed that the lowest layer also contained split base bone points.

The middle layer contained 82 laurel leaves which are similar in workmanship to those below but two show fine flint workmanship similar to those in the layer above.

The upper layer contained 63 bifacials of which 8 only are of the crude type characteristic of the lower layers. The remainder are of fine workmanship with a rounded base. The upper layer also contains, besides peripherally sharpened blades similar to those of the Middle Aurignacian, a few backed blades.

The interest of this cave is in the association of Upper Palaeolithic artefacts with an

306

evolving series of bifacial implements which are thought to have been derived from a Middle Palaeolithic source within the area.

In this connection the site of Istallosko 16 kilometres away is of interest. Here there are two superimposed layers both containing bone points comparable with those of the Middle Aurignacian in Western Europe and each layer contains a single bifacial piece. The upper layer is dated to *c.* 31,000 B.P. From the evidence it is concluded that the eastern European Middle Aurignacian and the Szeletian were approximately contemporary in the area and that there was a cultural admixture at this early date. Some authorities consider that the bifacial element in the Middle Aurignacian layers in this area is so small that it was not a component of these industries but was carried into the cave from Szeletian sites elsewhere.

A further point of interest is the association of backed blades with the upper layers of the Szeletian, a circumstance which may be interpreted as an early intrusion of the Gravettoid cultures of Russia into eastern Europe.

WILLENDORF
(Felgenhauer 1956–9)

Willendorf lies on the left bank of the Danube in Lower Austria. There are a number of Pleistocene sites in this area, all called after the village of Willendorf, but of these sites only Willendorf II has a relatively long stratigraphical sequence of deposits. Willendorf II is on an eastern slope of the Nursberg, and was discovered during road excavations in the first decade of this century. Subsequent soundings up to 1955 have defined the cultural succession revealed by the earlier work. The sporadic nature of these excavations, the absence of any proper recording of the deposits exposed during the first excavations, and the lack of well-defined terrace formations and former river gravels recovered in the investigations, make it difficult to obtain a complete record of the geological section at this site. The sequence of deposits may, however, be summarized as follows: at the base is a loessic sand and gravel deposit capped by a thick zone of red-brown loam. Above this is a relatively pure loess deposit within which cultural layers 1 and 2 have been identified. Overlying these are deposits of banded loess and loam, containing cultural layers 3, 4 and 5. At the top is another deposit of relatively pure loess which has yielded evidence of occupations 6 to 9. The cultural deposits in general slope gently down towards the river, dipping more abruptly to the eastern (riverward) side where in fact the earlier occupation layers are obscure. The individual sections of the nine areas exposed during the period 1909–1955 show that the complete cultural succession as published by Felgenhauer represents a composite reconstruction of the history of deposition along the river bank. The fauna recovered from the occupation layers at Willendorf II indicates, in general terms, a glacial climate, less marked in the lower layers than in the upper layers, where glacial conditions are particularly well marked in layers 8 and 9. The forms represented are all characteristic of central Europe during the last glaciation, including *Ursus* cf. *arctos*, *Panthera spelaea*, and *Elephas primigenius*, which occur only from layers 5 to 9. Such forms as *Alopex lagopus*, reindeer, mammoth, bison (*B. priscus*) and horse indicate tundra and steppe conditions, while *Vulpes*, Lynx and *Cervus elaphus* might be taken to represent an environment not without forested areas even if of limited extent. Nine industries have been identified from Willendorf II. In general, industries 2–4 are often grouped as Aurignacian, and 5–9 as Gravettian. Only the uppermost industry (9) has the single shouldered points and Venus figurines of the classic eastern Gravettian.

The basal industry (1) has some 200 stone objects, of which very few show any diagnostic signs of workmanship. This industry is culturally unidentifiable at the present time; it has been dated by radiocarbon to 30,310 B.P. ±250. Of about 1100 stone objects in the second industry, 10% have been worked. Of these, a majority (70%) are 'atypical' and few are illustrated in Felgenhauer's report. Present as recognizable forms are flakes and small blades with retouched edge, some pointed forms, blade scrapers and nosed scrapers, and a few core scrapers (fig. 118, 1–3). In general terms, this industry is described as Aurignacian because of the presence of peripheral sharpening retouch, the absence of backing retouch, and the presence of nosed forms of scraping tools.

The third industry is somewhat similar although only 100 worked stone objects are recorded from this level. No bonework here, or in the second industry, has survived. Small retouched blades, blade and keeled scrapers and core scrapers make up all the definable forms, although many other scraping tools are recorded in the 'atypical' group which makes up about half of the total (fig. 118, 4–7).

Above this is the fourth industry which has about 1300 stone and 40 bone objects. The unclassifiable forms make up some 70% of the total, but many of these, by their retouch, are to be grouped in the scraper class. Characteristic tool-types are small blades, few with retouch, several Krems points (slender blades with edge retouch leading to a point), a few burins of angle and single-blow types, and a high proportion of scrapers (fig. 118, 8–12). The latter include end-of-blade, and many keeled, nosed and other high-backed forms. The bone tools are undistinguished, and consist of simple points on split long bones, and round-ended and thicker forms; there is some evidence of decoration by crossed incised lines on small areas of long bone fragment.

The presence of high-backed scrapers in such numbers, plus the Krems point, has been taken as indicative of an Aurignacian tradition, and this industry (4) is generally linked with the two industries beneath. A radiocarbon date of 31,840 B.P. ±250 has been obtained for this fourth industry.

Industry 5 from Willendorf II shows some rather marked differences from the industries below. Although only 350 stone, and 12 bone, objects were recovered, most of the former have been classified as specific recognizable types (fig. 119, 1–8). Fine blades are very common, and a number of these have edge-retouch occasionally on both dorsal and ventral surfaces. Peripherally-retouched blades are rare, but the single retouched edge on blades is much in evidence. Backed blades are rare but present now, and pointed forms also occur. Diagnostic are minute backed blades with nibbled reverse retouch (fig. 119, 5–6). Burins of angle and ordinary types are present but are generally of rather poor quality. End scrapers and a few round and core scrapers occur, and there are still a few nosed and high-backed forms. Microlithic blades, some with retouch, are common. This industry exhibits distinct changes from the preceding traditions, particularly in the presence of microlithic and bladelet forms, and the appearance, although slight, of backed blades. However, the peripherally retouched blades and large fine single edge retouched blades are still in evidence. Unfortunately the bone element is without character. This industry also contains the first evidence in quantity for personal ornament, apart from one or two objects found in layers 2 and 4. *Dentalium* shells seem to have been among the most popular objects for personal decoration. A radiocarbon date from this level at the site is 32,000 B.P. ± 300.

The sixth industry at Willendorf II continues to represent the tradition of the fifth (fig. 119, 9–11). Only 250 stone objects, and none of bone, are recorded, and there are no data on unworked waste material. Untouched blades are common, and those with edge retouch are also not infrequent. Peripherally retouched blades are rare. Gravette points and microlithic points with backing retouch were found, although they are not at all common. A few burins, and scrapers of end-of-blade type, make up the remainder of retouched forms; atypical forms comprise about one half of all the lithic material.

Above this deposit is level seven, with about 450 stone pieces, and a few of bone. Unclassifiable forms total one-third of the surviving material, but again we have little knowledge of the waste material (fig. 120, 1–4). Retouched long and slender blades are very common, few peripherally retouched, but many with secondary trimming down all or part of one edge. These and unretouched blades make up over half of the total material. Scrapers of end-of-blade and irregular round types are remarkably scarce, as are the burins which make up less than 1% of the total. Microlithic forms are also very rare. Little is known of the bone-working element in this industry. The scarcity of burins suggests little interest in this aspect, as is borne out by the relatively poor quantity of bone recovered from the site.

The industry from the level above, 8, is more abundant, and we have information on some 1,100 stone pieces (little waste was saved) and 10 bone objects. Atypical forms represent one half of the known total (fig. 120, 5–10). Again, retouched blades, and fewer unretouched blades, form the bulk of the surviving material equipment, and a considerable number of the former have retouch down all or most of one edge. Gravette backed blades and points are rare, end-of-blade scrapers are more common than in the preceding industry, but burins remain unimportant. Microlithic forms again are present, although in small numbers. The use of reverse retouch on square-ended blades and other forms is not uncommon; a trace of this technique occurred in the underlying industry.

The industry from the upper level (9) at Willendorf II is said to be in the classic East Gravettian tradition (fig. 121). Slender retouched blades form one-third of the total, and although this retouch is rarely peripheral, many of the blades have been retouched down one edge and round the end. Backed blades and points are present although still in small quantities. End-of-blade scrapers and burins of angle, ordinary and polyhedric types occur. Burins are relatively more common than before. Microliths, generally short slender rods, form an important element, and there are a few, but only a few, shouldered points with reverse retouch on the 'tang'. The bone work is more extensive than before, with fairly heavy points and a few spatulate forms decorated by crisscross or zigzag incision. Several bone points have an incipient barb near the point. Also associated with this industry is the famous Venus figurine of limestone and an elongated figurine of the same general type made in ivory. An unfinished head from the same level recalls the finely modelled head from Dolni Vestonice.

As stated, the cultural succession at Willendorf II is often linked, first with the Aurignacian (layers 2–4), second, with the Gravettian (layers 5–9), and quantitative and qualitative comparisons have been made with industries of these two traditions in the French Dordogne. A number of differences have been listed, but in general the consensus of opinion seems to be that this site demonstrates the basic sequence of Aurignacian followed by Gravettian first worked out in western Europe. It may be however that the transference of established cultural names to an outside area is masking essential and basic differences in these regions.

16

Greece and Peninsular Italy

THE late development of archaeology in Russia and the absence of evidence from Greece led at one time to the conclusion that the industries of Italy were atypical appendages of the western European succession. It is now apparent that peninsular Italy, Greece and perhaps parts of Yugoslavia and unexplored Albania may be considered as a geographic, climatic and industrial unit, at least at times when there was a low sea level, forming a province which links western Europe with western Asia and the Levant.

Within this province the earliest known artefacts may be the crude flakes which in Italy have been found associated with *Elephas antiquus*, in gravels which may be slightly older or contemporary with a Milazzean sea level (p. 32). At Torre in Pietra, 26 km. south of Rome, Acheulean handaxes have been found which are later than 431–438,000 years ago (p. 316). The deposits which contain the handaxes are regarded as being earlier than the Last Interglacial and later than the Lower Pleistocene.

At Venosa in the province of Potenza there is a crude flake industry below a level with handaxes (Chiappella 1964). The flake industry with many retouched pieces is said to be Tayacian in type. By some authorities the industry is regarded as pre-Mousterian or pre-Tayacian. The lower layers contain *Elephas antiquus*, and *Equus* cf. *stenonis* and *Rhinoceros merckii* are also present on the site. It is regarded as of Last Interglacial date at the latest. There is also an undated Acheulean handaxe from Palaeokastron near Siatista and east of the central Pindhos range in Greece, and another at Kokkinopilos in western Greece which is not certainly associated with a Mousterian industry in a *terra rossa*.

In Italy there are numerous Mousterian industries which are later than a beach containing the mollusc *Strombus bubonius*; the beach is considered to date to the Last Interglacial. In both Italy and Greece, Mousterian industries occur commonly in red deposits (*terra rossa*). The Mousterian episode lasted, at least at Asprochaliko in Epirus, to some time between 40,000 and 24,000 years ago.

Mousterian industries have also been found in and on the banks of the Penios river in Thessaly, in the Peloponnese and at a number of sites in Epirus, particularly at Kokkinopilos between Arta and Ioannina, and Karvounari near Paramythia (Dakaris *et al.* 1964; Higgs *et al.* 1966, 1967). The Kokkinopilos industries have characteristic sidescrapers (fig. 126, 11), points (fig. 126, 8–10), disc and tortoise cores and a high percentage of faceted platforms (fig. 126, 7). A statistical analysis has suggested that the industry may perhaps in some aspects be comparable with an early phase of the Mousterian industries of France. On the other hand, the leaf-shaped bifacial points (fig. 126, 1–3, 5, 6)) suggest a relationship with the industries of the central German Highlands (p. 287).

The Mousterian industries (fig. 127) at Asprochaliko (plate VII) are succeeded by a smaller and cruder Middle Palaeolithic industry (fig. 128) which is superseded by tools of Advanced Palaeolithic type at some time before 24,000 B.P. and after 40,000

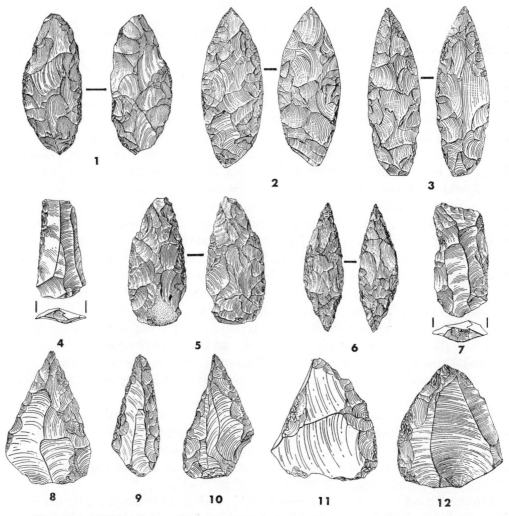

FIG. 126. Middle Palaeolithic ⅔; Kokkinopilos, Greece; Artefacts from the red clay

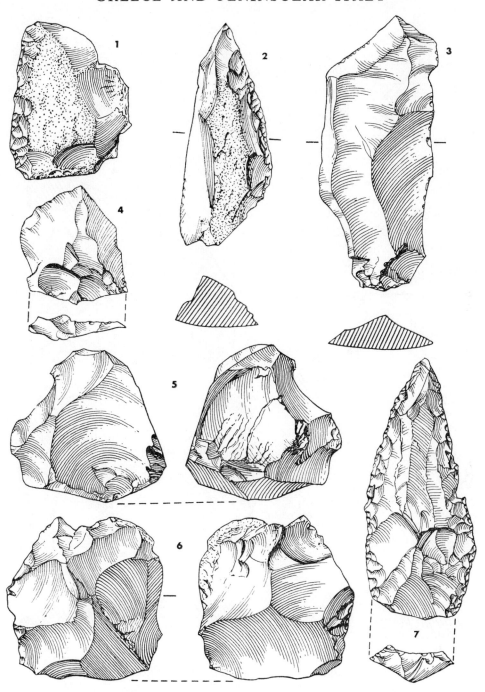

FIG. 127. Mousterian $\frac{1}{1}$; Asprochaliko, Greece; Artefacts from the base of
the deposits

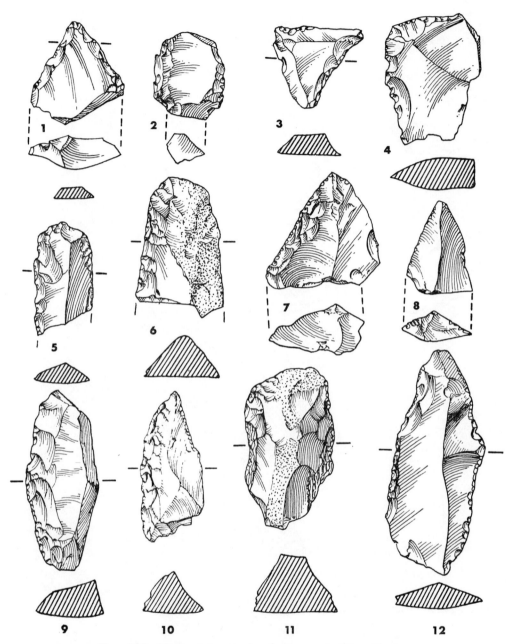

FIG. 128. Upper Mousterian $\frac{1}{1}$; Asprochaliko, Greece

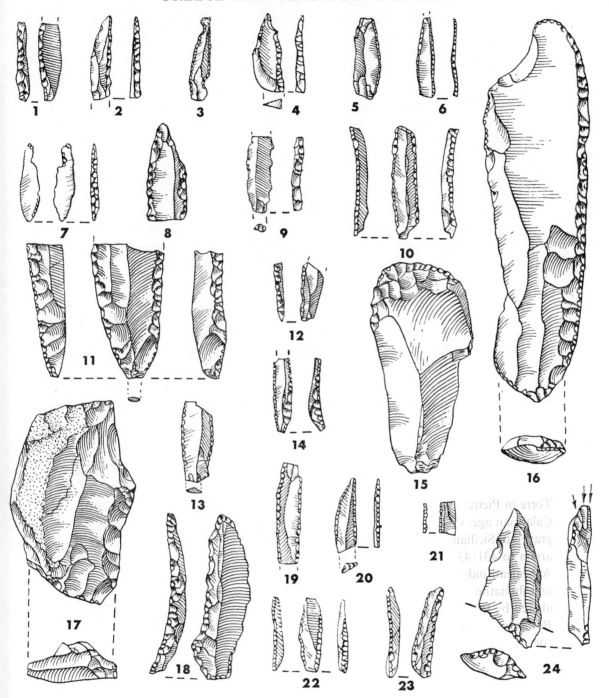

FIG. 129. Advanced Palaeolithic $\frac{1}{1}$; Asprochaliko, Greece; 1–16 artefacts dated by radiocarbon to *c*. 26, 100 B.P.; 17–24 artefacts below this level

B.P. (fig. 129, 17–24). The Advanced Palaeolithic industries contain narrow backed blades (fig. 129, 1–10) from their earliest phase here. East of the Pindhos range a few finds from the Penios river have been attributed to the Middle Aurignacian but there does not seem to be sufficient evidence to support this claim as all the types may be found with numerous backed blades from assemblages in this area. Similarly an early discovery of bone tools considered at that time to be Magdalenian in type has not been supported by further evidence. The Advanced Palaeolithic industries therefore appear to be entirely Gravettoid in character. Narrow backed blades continue to the end of the Last Glaciation both at the Seidi cave in Thessaly east of the Pindhos range (Schmidt 1965) and in the Epirus caves west of the Pindhos and in the Peloponnese. Eventually there is an appearance of geometric forms again with backed blades, in the final industry at Asprochaliko and in some open sites in the Peloponnese. They are remarkably similar to the upper industries at Romanelli across the Straits of Otranto in Italy where they are dated to c. 12,000 B.P. In Italy and Greece epi-Gravettian industries continued as late as the fifth millennium B.C. but west of the Apennines there is some suggestion of an infiltration of assemblages of Middle Aurignacian type, at an early date.

A microlithic industry has been found near Sidari on Corfu which on a radiocarbon date is in the early fifth millennium B.C. and is immediately prior to the appearance of pottery in that area. Elsewhere there has been noted at Volos in southern Greece, and perhaps on Crete, a flint industry of very small dimensions, which is almost characterless and which has been discovered in both cave and open sites. It has not so far been dated but appears to be either associated with early pottery or immediately antecedent to the pottery industries.

TORRE IN PIETRA

Torre in Pietra is a site 26 km. south of Rome. At the base there are marine clays of Calabrian age. Overlying them unconformably is a series of clays, marine sands and gravels of Sicilian age. Overlying are gravels and volcanic deposits dated by potassium/ argon to 431–438,000 years ago and of probably early Middle Pleistocene age. An Acheulean industry occurs at the base of the overlying sediments, which are sands and fluviatile gravels influenced by cryoturbation. Most of the artefacts have been altered by frost action. The faunal remains include *Equus caballus*, *Elephas antiquus*, *Bos primigenius*, *Dicerorhinus kirchbergensis* and *Cervus elaphus*. The deposits which contain the implements are therefore considered to be earlier than the Last Inter-glacial, and later than the Lower Pleistocene. They may be of Rissian age.

316

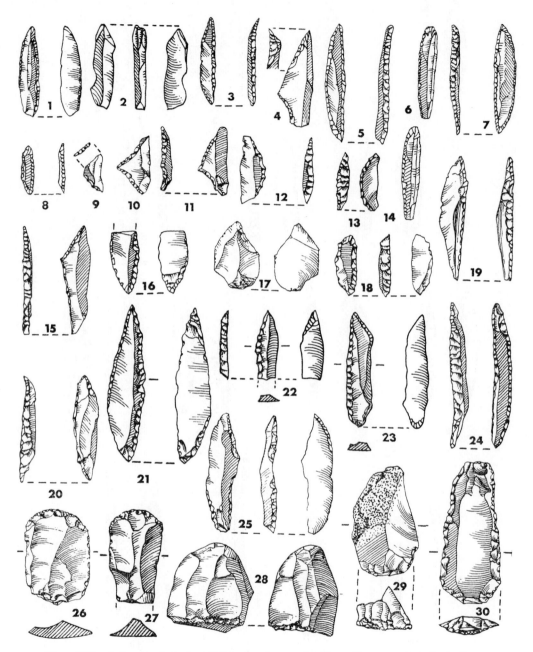

FIG. 130. Advanced Palaeolithic $\frac{1}{1}$; Asprochaliko, Greece; Artefacts from the upper layers

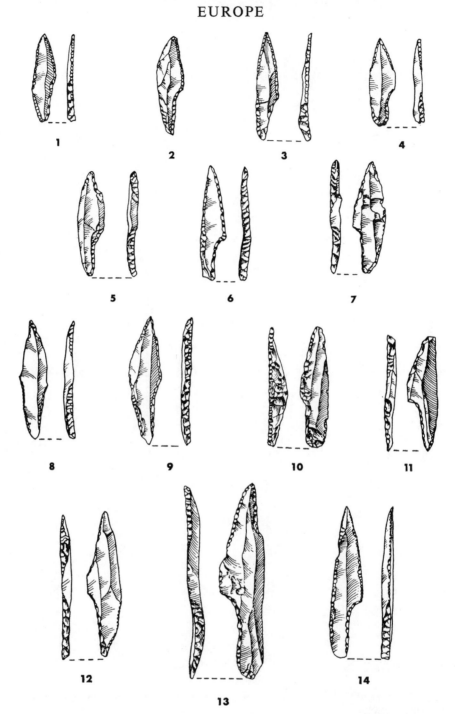

FIG. 131. Advanced Palaeolithic $\frac{1}{1}$; Kastritsa, Greece; Shouldered points and related forms

318

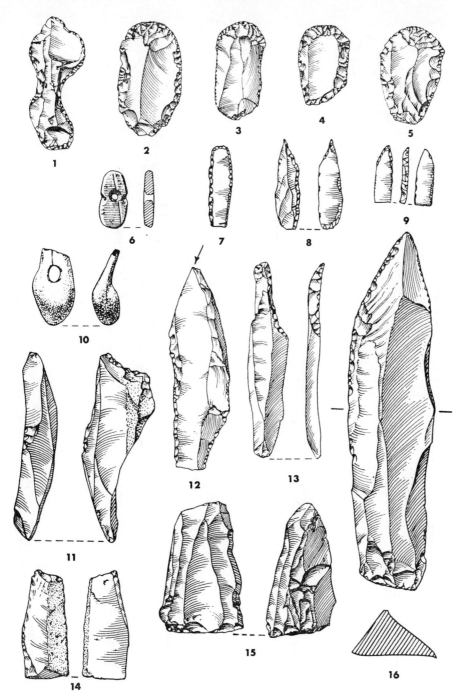

FIG. 132. Advanced Palaeolithic $\frac{1}{1}$; Kastritsa, Greece; 1 notched scraper; 2–5 scrapers; 6 perforated and incised pebble; 7–9 microliths; 10 perforated deer canine pendant; 11 burin on a core trimming flake; 12, 14 burins; 13 tanged blade; 15 core; 16 retouched blade

319

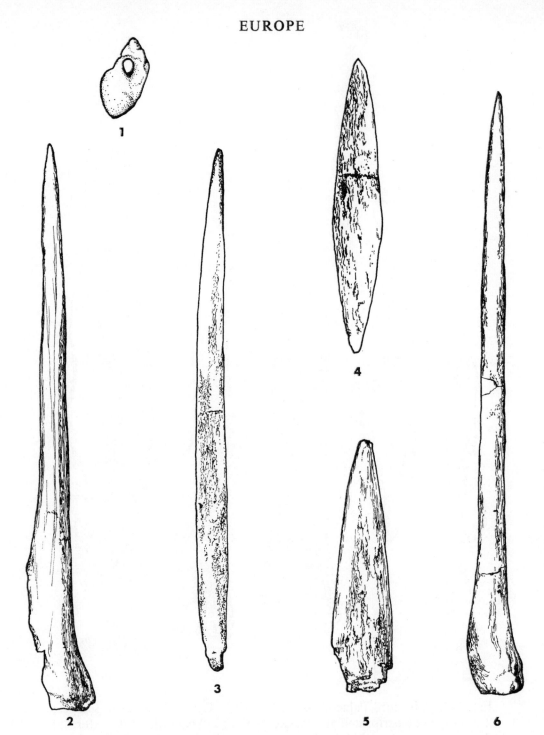

FIG. 133. Advanced Palaeolithic $\frac{1}{1}$; Kastritsa, Greece; Bone tools

ASPROCHALIKO

Asprochaliko (plate V) is a rock shelter between Arta and Ioannina in the valley of the Louros. The basal Mousterian industry (fig. 127) has a radiocarbon date of *c.* 40,000 B.P. The assemblage is in some respects different from that of the nearby site of Kokkinopilos. There are rare unifacial pieces but no bifacials. The industry contains sidescrapers (fig. 127, 1), points (fig. 127, 7), and disc cores (fig. 127, 6). In the upper Mousterian layers (fig. 128) similar techniques and tools are still present, but after *c.* 40,000 B.P. the pieces are relatively smaller. Between 40,000 B.P. and 22,000 B.P. there is an industrial change.

During the severe cold of the Last Glaciation, Greece was occupied by people making Advanced Palaeolithic industries which included, even in the early stages of their development, narrow backed blades (fig. 129, 1–10). The final industry at Asprochaliko contains triangles (fig. 130, 10–11) and crescents (fig. 130, 12, 13), shouldered points (fig. 130, 4), and microburins (fig. 130, 17).

KASTRITSA

The cave of Kastritsa gives an industrial succession from earlier than 22,000 B.P. to later than 11,000 B.P. Throughout, there are industries which have backed blades. In the upper half of the deposits there are shouldered points in quantities (fig. 131; but there is no evidence for the microlithic element which occurs in the upper layers at Asprochaliko and Romanelli. This microlithic element may be a coastal facet of the inland backed blade industries but its position in time has not yet been clearly established. Kastritsa cave also contains a number of bone points (fig. 133), perforated deer canines as pendants (fig. 132, 10), and perforated and incised pebbles (fig. 132, 6). Outside the cave there were a number of stake holes in a semicircle which indicated some form of shelter around a hearth (plate VIII).

ROMANELLI
(Blanc 1920 and 1927)

At the cave of Romanelli, near to Lecce in Italy, over a *Strombus bubonius* beach is a deposit known as the *terra rossa*, which is itself overlaid by a *terra bruna*. The *terra rossa* contains a few artefacts which have been regarded by some authorities as Mousterian and by others as of the Advanced Palaeolithic. This may represent, as elsewhere in Italy, a Mousterian industry later than a *Strombus* beach, and with the addition of a few artefacts from the *terra bruna* above. The *terra bruna* has been dated to *c.* 11,900 B.P. It contains an Advanced Palaeolithic type industry with geometric microliths (fig. 134) and is the type site of the Romanellian culture clusters. The *terra bruna* also contains a cool to temperate avifauna and *Equus hydruntinus*, the wild ass. *Equus hydruntinus* has also been found at Asprochaliko, Kastritsa and the Seidi cave.

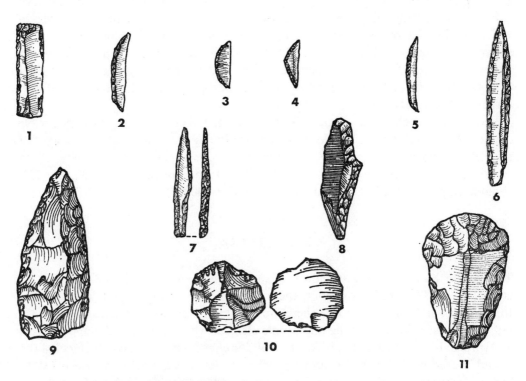

FIG. 134. Advanced Palaeolithic $\frac{1}{1}$; Romanelli, Italy; Artefacts from the upper layers. *After Blanc*

Part IV
ASIA

17

Russia, including European Russia

THE Lower Palaeolithic in eastern Europe and Russian Asia is extremely limited in its distribution and in the quantity of material. The recent finds at Vertesszöllös in Hungary have emphasized the potential problem of recognition of such early industries in gravels or similar deposits where such material is most likely to be represented.

In areas to the east, there are few attested finds of artefacts in contexts dated before Eemian times (Kernd'l 1961, 1963; Klein 1966). Handaxes and flake tools have been reported from the valleys of the Dniestr and Dniepr rivers. Typologically the material from Luká-Vrublevéckaja in the Dniestr valley has been classified as early Acheulean, but no dating evidence has been advanced, and no sites north of the Black Sea appear to represent Lower Palaeolithic activity. However, in Georgia and Armenia, concentrated to the south of the Caucasus Mountains, there are a number of sites including Sataní-Dár and Laše Balta which typologically appear to represent early occupations of this region. Sataní-Dár lies at the foot of Mt. Artin in Armenia. Sataní-Dár itself is a low hill, from the slopes of which have been recovered about 1,000 obsidian and basalt pieces classified as Chellean or Acheulean. The artefacts include handaxes, choppers, flakes with plain platforms and cores (fig. 135). The site has recently been interpreted as a workshop or factory where the obsidian source on the hill was worked. The nearest source for the doleritic basalt artefacts, however, was some 25 kilometres away.

A further group of sites on the eastern coast of the Black Sea, within the Caucasus range and south of the Kuban river, are less convincing for Acheulean occupation. By distribution alone, it is evident that this presumed early occupation of areas to the south of the Caucasus Mountains should be considered as a product of the settlement of south-western Asia. Less certain are the very few finds of typologically early material from further east, east of the Aral Sea and south of Lake Balkhash, and separated from the south-west Asian and Indian industries by the Kunlun mountain range (Kernd'l 1961). The material is too sparse for comment.

Succeeding industries in eastern Europe and Russian Asia are more widely distributed, occurring from the watershed of the Black Sea eastwards to Lake Balkhash, and northwards to the upper Volga and Dniepr. An occupation deposit in a cave at

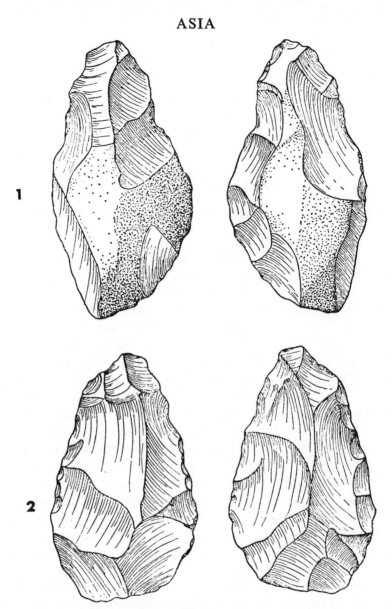

FIG. 135. Sataní-Dár, Armenia, USSR ½. *From Kernd'l 1961*

Vychvatincy in the Dniestr basin, associated with mammoth, woolly rhinoceros, *Bison priscus, Equus caballus, Cervus elaphus, Ursus spelaeus, Rangifer tarandus* and *Canis lupus*, contained a small number of flakes and several small bifacial tools which may represent a Mousteroid industry. It is uncertain whether this site should be dated to the Riss or Würm glaciation. In the same region are the sites of Molodova I and V, with a fauna indicating a coniferous forest-steppe environment. At Molodova I a house-plan measuring 10 × 7 metres was recovered, made entirely of mammoth bone

326

and ivory, and with 15 small hearths (fig. 136); associated with this house was a flake industry of Mousterian character. Molodova V yielded twelve cultural levels, the lowest levels of Mousterian character (p. 351) also containing traces of structures; one of these levels has a radiocarbon date of >40,300 B.P.

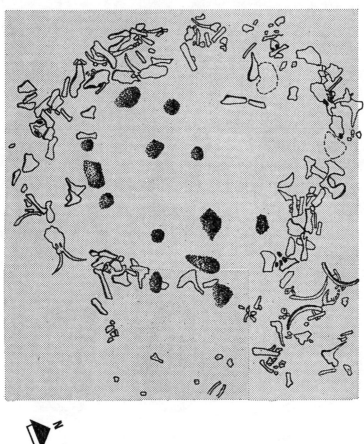

FIG. 136. Molodova I, USSR; Mousterian house plan

Further east, the Dniepr basin and its upper tributaries contains abundant evidence of occupation by the makers of flake industries. A cold fauna of mammoth, woolly rhinoceros, horse, reindeer and other forms was recovered at the site of Kodák I, some 10 km. south of Dnepropetróvsk, with a small flake industry.

In the Crimea, the Starosel'e shelter (fig. 137; p. 349) yielded an important Mousterian industry containing flake points and scrapers, some with plano-convex retouch, and bifacial leaf-shaped points; the skeleton of an infant is believed to be

327

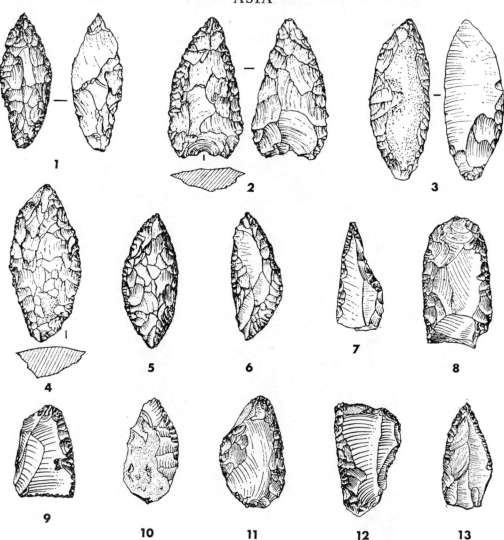

FIG. 137. Mousterian ½; Starosel'e, Ukraine, USSR. *From Müller-Karpe 1966*

associated with this industry. At Kiik-Koba in the same district, a two-level shelter site (p. 348) yielded an earlier industry of unspecialized character, with plain platform flakes and little sign of plano-convex retouch. Climatic evidence suggests a temperate period for this industry and its associated human remains consisting of some of the limbs of an adult and a child; neither skulls or jaws were found. The remains have been described as of 'primitive Neanderthal' type. The upper industry at Kiik-Koba, associated with a cold fauna, is characteristic Mousterian with plano-convex and straight-line retouch (Golomshtok 1938; Klein 1965).

Comparable industries are known from the lower Don river as well as the middle and upper Volga region. The open station at Volgográd (Stalingrád) yielded an important assemblage of Mousterian artefacts, including a few rather thick bifacially-worked points. Pollen indicates that in the region there was a steppe environment with some pine, birch, and other trees possibly in the stream valleys. The animal bones at the site consisted of aurochs, mammoth and horse, with smaller quantities of other forms.

Many sites of early Last Glacial age lie to the south, in the extreme western part of the Caucasus Mountains, and to the south of the mountains in Armenia. In the Kuban basin, the open site of Íl'skaya, on the edge of a terrace of the Íl', contained the same general proportions of animal bones (aurochs, representing 60% of the total, with mammoth and horse also present) as at Volgográd. The industry consists of points, scrapers, discoid cores, small bifacial points, leaf-shaped points with retouch on both faces and flake-blades and prismatic cores. A stone setting 5 metres in diameter with a hearth represents some form of structure. In the basin of the Kura, some of the industries also contain blades and blade-cores.

A few Mousterian sites are recorded from the western shores of the Caspian Sea, and another group lies to the east of the Caspian. In the Amu-Dar'ja basin, the site of Tešík-Táš yielded an industry of Mousterian character, containing some blade elements, and a child burial partly surrounded by a circle of five goat skulls, the horns of which had been pushed into the floor of the shelter (Okladnikov 1949). The child (plate X, reconstruction) is of *Homo sapiens* type, the postcranial bones of modern form, the skull considered to be more 'Neanderthaloid' in its features. The fauna of this site included goat, horse, deer, leopard and brown bear, and various birds. The Syr-Dar'ja basin also contains a number of Mousterian sites, in which the industries appear to contain a fairly strong flake-blade element.

In general term, flake industries which occur over the 3500 km. from west of the Black Sea to Lake Balkhash have been grouped together as east Mousterian (fig. 138). Typologically, they contain common elements in flake tools, in the bifacial working of these, and in some specific finished products, particularly the leaf-shaped points. Although certain variations exist in these industries, such as the differing forms of leaf points, and the representation of flake-blades and prismatic cores, nevertheless on typological grounds some consider that a common and basic tradition existed in industries of this character in the Ukraine and Crimea, through the western Caucasus mountains to the border regions of present-day Iran, Afghanistan and Tadzhikistan. Although this rests entirely upon typological grounds, there appears to be a significant difference between these industries and those of the south-west, in the Levant. Here the plano-convex retouch is absent, and a greater dominance on small prepared cores is observed. Between the east Mediterranean area on the one hand and the southern Caucasus and Caspian Sea regions on the other is the Kurdistan and Zagros mountains. The site of Shanidar in northern Iran, and sites in northern Iraq such as Ke Aram, appear to possess industries more in keeping with the northern

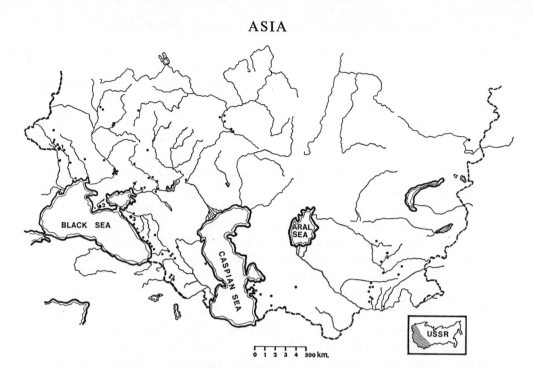

Fig. 138. Distribution of flake industries in Russia; 1 Molodova, 2 Kiik-Koba, 3 Il'skaya. *After Kernd'l 1963*

traditions, in that plano-convex retouch was employed, and the tortoise core technique was not practised (p. 371).

The Upper Palaeolithic industries of the region stretching from eastern Europe eastwards into central Russia and beyond exhibit great variation in their content (Rogachev 1957). Although much of the area was subjected to glacial conditions during the Last Glaciation, the northern ice sheets were of limited extent, so that occupation in northern Siberia was possible in full late glacial times when climatic amelioration had not yet become evident.

Stratified sites of late glacial age are not particularly well-represented in the Russian plain area, and most of the industrial sequences devised for various regions are based upon presumed typological developments. Two sites in the western area, however, have provided important stratified deposits which provide a check on this typological classification. The more famous of these two is the site of Kostienki I, in the middle Don valley (fig. 139–142; p. 349).

The stratigraphy of this site has involved the recognition of humus deposits which are believed to be capable of climatic interpretation and of correlation with other sites in the area. There is considerable doubt now about the validity of both these important aspects. Five industries have been recognized in the deposits at Kostienki I, the lowest industry (5) in a basal 'humus'. The uppermost industry (1), in loess deposits, has been considered to be in classic Gravettian tradition such as is found

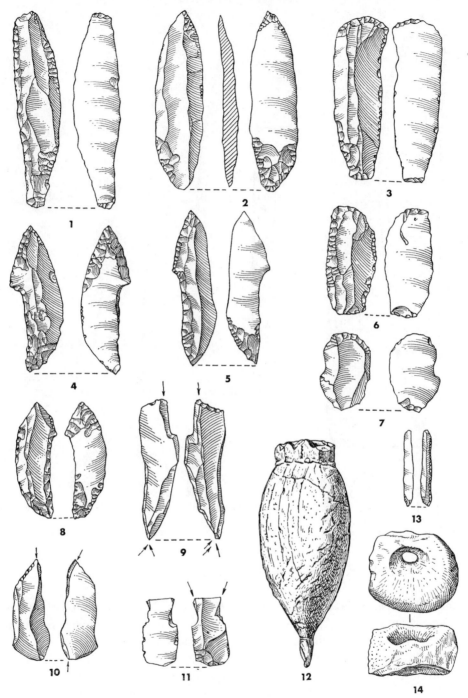

FIG. 139. Kostienki I 1, USSR ½. *After Efimenko 1958*

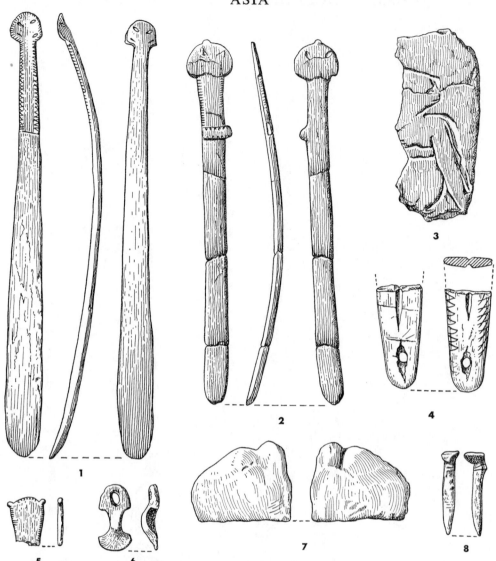

FIG. 140. Kostienki I 1, USSR $\frac{3}{4}$ (no. 2, $\frac{1}{3}$). *After Efimenko 1958*

in central Europe. A date for this industry (Kostienki I) has been recently obtained by radiocarbon analysis, *c.* 14,000 B.P., and this date is in keeping with recent inter-pretations of this site which suggest that the entire sequence of Upper Palaeolithic industries in the 20 sites at Kostienki falls within a developed phase and does not represent the initial stages of evolution of Upper Palaeolithic traditions.

The industrial succession of Kostienki I begins with an industry of flakes and flake-blades; burins, round scrapers and steep scrapers, and triangular points are charac-teristic. The blade element becomes more dominant in the succeeding industries;

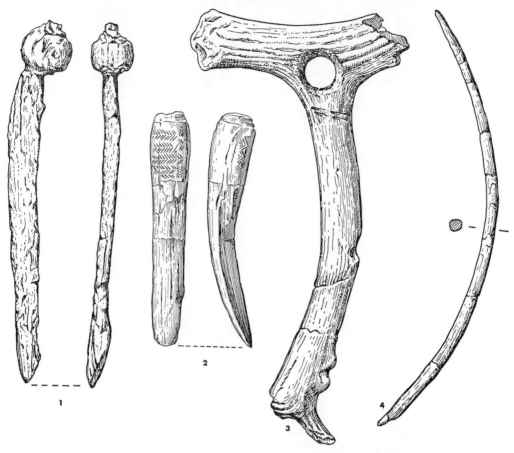

FIG. 141. Kostienki I 1, USSR ⅛. *After Efimenko 1958*

round scrapers and steep scrapers continue to appear. Smaller blade forms, including backed bladelets, occur in the middle industry, associated with longer blades with edge retouch. The uppermost industry is abundant and varied. Flint work includes backed blades, shouldered points, end scrapers and burins (fig. 139), and the bone, antler and ivory industry is remarkable in its variety (fig. 140–141). A number of female figurines were associated, including rather elongated forms with belting at the back, and more angular-shaped figurines as well. Animal figures are also represented (fig. 142). The female figurines from Gagarino in the same region (fig. 144, 1–3) may not in fact be contemporary with those from Kostienki I; one of the former is remarkably close in treatment to the Willendorf Venus (fig. 121).

The point has recently been made that the lowest industry from Kostienki I is typologically and technologically too advanced to represent a direct development from late Mousterian traditions in south Russia, such as is seen at Starosel'e for example. The transitional phase is believed to be represented at the site of Rado-

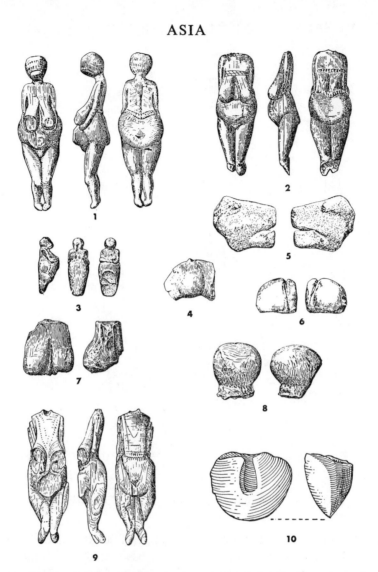

FIG. 142. Kostienki I 1, USSR; Scales: 8, $\frac{3}{8}$; 9, $\frac{1}{3}$; 10, $\frac{3}{4}$; others $\frac{1}{2}$. *From Müller-Karpe 1966, Efimenko 1958*

michle, where Mousterian points, scrapers and discs are associated with prismatic cores, blades, awls, and scrapers and burins. This industry has been compared to one from Ivanovce on the Var in Czechoslovakia where leaf-shaped points, other flake tools and discoid cores were found with prismatic cores, blades and end scrapers. Whether or not such assemblages are to be treated as demonstrating a source for the subsequent typological stages of the Upper Palaeolithic in central and eastern Europe remains to be documented.

The humus levels at Kostienki I have also been reviewed recently and it has been shown that these deposits tend to change their character over relatively small areas, so that they cannot be employed as chronological horizons. Previously the lower 'humus' at Kostienki I was believed to be of 'Göttweig' date. At Spitzina, two industries were separated by volcanic ash from Caucasian eruptions in late Pleistocene times, and at Kostienki XIV and XVII, similar ash lay beneath two 'humus' zones whereas at Kostienki VI, the ash lay above a 'humus' zone in one exposure, below it at another. The volcanic ash, potentially a most valuable correlating link, has been recognized at only four of the 20 Kostienki sites, and not at Kostienki I. Clearly the 'humus' zones are not capable of consistent interpretation. At Kostienki I 5 (the lowest level), pollen analysis indicates rather milder conditions than seem to have existed in the upper deposits.

Kostienki I is also important in showing the presence of late glacial dwellings. The site contained traces of several house plans, commencing with an oval house 4 by 5 metres in diameter associated with the basal industry. The uppermost cultural level had a line of hearths set along the central axis of a long house (fig. 143: p. 350). Other sites in the same area, such as Gagarino, have yielded house plans of small oval form.

The late glacial oval shelters range from 4 to 6 metres in diameter, and occur as individual houses at the settlements of Mezine, Gagarino and Kostienki IV (upper level, fig. 143) as well as at Pavlov and other sites in Moravia. Larger dwellings, formed by joining two round houses together, have been indicated at Pavlov and Dolni Vestonice in Moravia, and the 12 metre house at Pushkari seems to have consisted of three such round rooms joined together. The lower level at Kostienki IV yielded remains of two long houses divided into sections, according to the grouping of the hearths and soil colours. These two houses are extremely long, 22 and 34 metres (fig. 143). Attempts have been made to interpret the individual round houses and the long houses in terms of social organization in this area.

At Pushkari on the Desna, an industry was associated with an oval depression 12 by 4 metres with three hearths or postholes along the central axis; along the central line were many small pits which may have held supporting posts. A settlement at Timonovka on the same river is said to have had a number of subterranean houses probably arranged in pairs, one unheated house or storage shed to one house with hearth. It is evident that during late glacial times there was variation in house-types, and, by their nature, in the size and disposition of living units.

Among the sites at Kostienki (Boriskovsky 1963) should also be noted a number of burials. Of four burials recently described, three are said to be of Cro-Magnon type, the other of 'negroid' type. A burial at Kostienki II lay beside an oval hut and was protected by a pile of mammoth bones. Later settlements in the same complex include Kostienki XIX on a lower terrace of the river. At this site, excavation revealed the existence of a canal-like hearth leading into a hut, probably dug to provide draught for a fire. At Kostienki IV, a settlement with long houses, each divided into three sectors by ridges, lay stratified beneath several round houses; the latter were associated with an industry containing small backed blades, blade scrapers and burins,

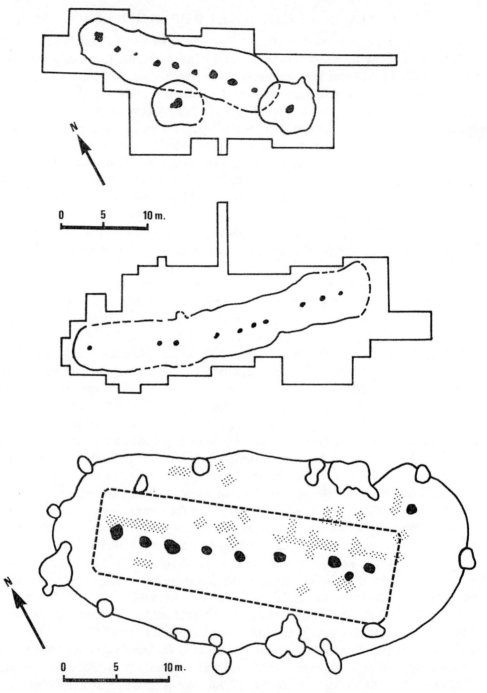

FIG. 143. House plans; upper Kostienki IV (Aleksandrovka) settlement; lower Kostienki I house. Solid line indicates excavator's estimate of house boundary: dash line indicates recent explanation of house shape; hearths are black, pits white; stipple indicates density of flints >70 per square metre over excavated area

blades with peripheral retouch, ivory and bone rods, points and figures. The early industry here had both large and small backed blades, including pointed specimens, saws, burins and scrapers, flake chisels, bone rods and perforated teeth and shells.

In the lower reaches of the Don river and along the northern shore of the sea of Azov, late glacial occupation is attested (Boriskovsky and Praslov 1964). At Amvrocievkaya, an ancient ravine holds the bones of an estimated 1000 Bison (*Bison priscus*) possibly representing a method of hunting involving ambush or blocking of an exit. The industrial equipment of the hunters, some 300 metres from the animal deposits, is in the blade and burin tradition.

Upper Palaeolithic sites in the Dniepr basin occur in the middle reaches as far north as Kiev, and sites along the Desna are also known. One of the important sites in the middle Dniepr basin is Gontsovskaya (Gontsi) which yielded two occupations of late glacial character associated with the remains of mammoth, reindeer, *Alopex lagopus* and *Lepus*. Mammoth bones were used to construct a shelter during the earlier occupation of the site. The industry consists of small scrapers, burins and backed blades, with bone points and eyed needles. The upper occupation appears to have involved the erection of a tent-like shelter, and the industry possesses some geometric forms.

Farther south is the stratified site of Osokorovka, which has yielded comparable epi-Gravettian material associated with above-ground shelters and a fauna including mammoth and reindeer in the lower level, forms which are absent from the upper level in which beaver occurs.

In the western Ukraine, along the Dniestr river, the sites at Molodova provide important evidence for the industrial succession from Mousterian through to final late glacial and early post-glacial times. The Mousterian house-plan at Molodova I, and probable house-plans from Molodova V, show that the tradition of structures made of mammoth bones and ivory was of long duration (p. 351).

At Molodova V, industries XII, XIIa and XI are of Mousterian character; XI has a radiocarbon date of >40,300 B.P. Above is a long series of blade industries, commencing with end scrapers, burins, backed bladelets, steep scrapers and long blades with edge retouch; some bifacially-worked points also occur (Occupation X; fig. 145, 8, 13–18). In a number of the Upper Palaeolithic industries here have been found representations of the human figure, as engravings or sculptures. Occupation VIII (fig. 145, 1–7) contained five separate assemblages of artefacts grouped around 18 hearths. Edge-retouched blades continue to be present; a mammoth ivory pendant represents the form of a schematic figurine. The succeeding industry (VII) is the most abundant of any at this site (fig. 146, 8–19). Blade cores, burins, end-scrapers, edge-retouched blades, awls, backed blades and shouldered blades are present. Bone and antler work includes perforated reindeer antler bâtons, of which one has an anthropomorphic engraving (fig. 148, 2).

This industry has been dated to *c.* 23,500 B.P. and in several respects has been compared to the Gravettian tradition of central Europe; it is worth noting, however,

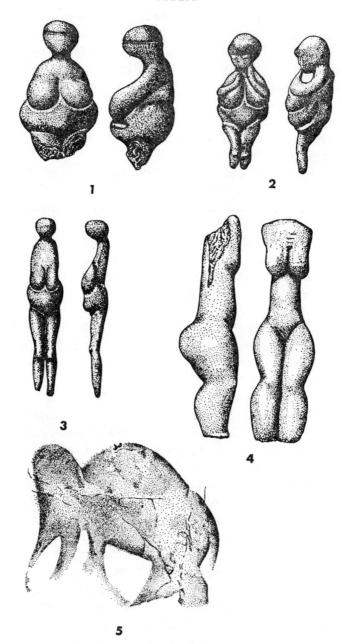

Fig. 144. 1–3 Figurines from Gagarino, Don Valley, USSR $\frac{1}{2}$; 4 figurine from Jelisejeviči, Ukraine $\frac{1}{2}$; 5 Painted representation from Šulgan-Taš (Kapova), Ural Mts. USSR. *From Müller-Karpe 1966*

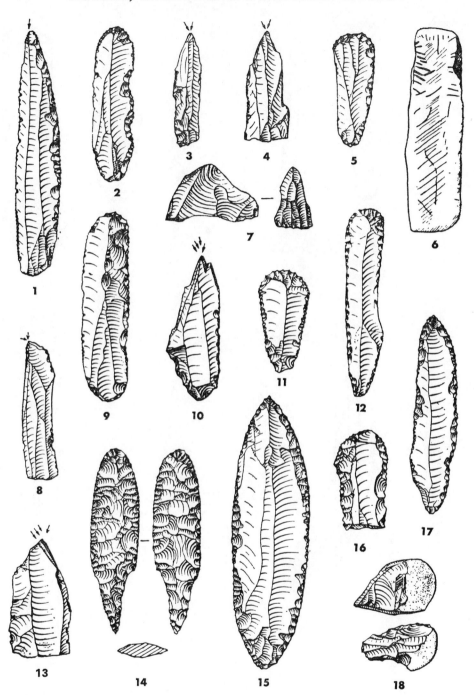

FIG. 145. Molodova V, USSR ½; 1–7 Level VIII; 9–12 Level IX; 8, 13–18 Level X. *From Chernish 1961*

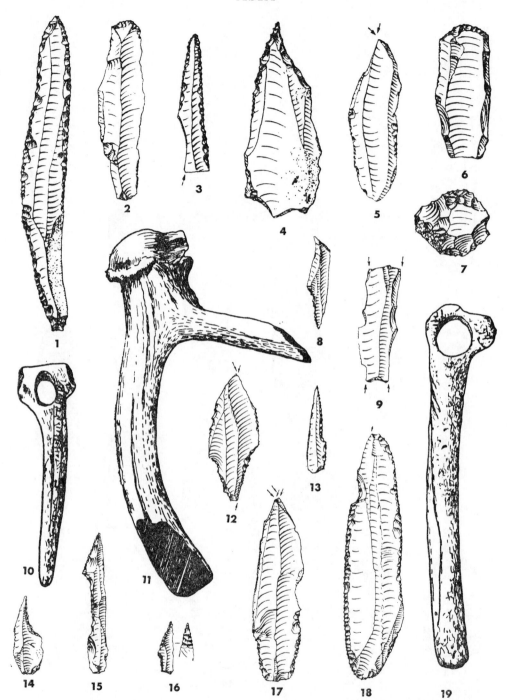

FIG. 146. Molodova V, USSR $\frac{1}{2}$; 1–7 Level VI; 8–19 Level VII. *From Chernish 1961*

that Aurignacoid elements continue to be present here in the shape of edge-retouched blades and steep scraper-like tools. It is unlikely that cultural elements over such wide areas would remain uniform, if any culture contact was in fact ever made.

The succeeding industries include associations with oval house-plans and post-holes, and are notable for the fine bone and ivory objects; among these are a number of slotted mammoth rib handles which probably held flint blades (fig. 147, 1; 149, 2). The Gravettoid industries in the upper levels are contemporary with the Magdalenian of western Europe, according to radiocarbon dates, and the uppermost industries, including Ia with a perforated harpoon head (fig. 150, 9) and antler axes (fig. 148, 3), belong to the close of the Last Glaciation.

The site of Mezine in the Ukraine is generally considered to represent another late phase of the Gravettoid industries in the area; the cultural material is remarkable in that it includes conventionalized carvings said to be of women. On this interpretation, these are decorated by schematic representation of facial and sexual features as well as other elements. Recently a circular house-plan has been recovered from this site (plate IX). In the south-west Ukraine, the site of Bolchaia Akkarja represents a late occupation of the Black Sea region in a southern steppe where *Bison* and *Bos* appear to have been the dominant fauna.

To the north, there is now evidence of Gravettoid occupation extending up to *c.* 65° North (fig. 151). North of Moscow, the site of Soungir near Vladimir has yielded an industry comparable to those in the lower levels of Kostienki I, and including a bone figure of a horse and two human burials, one of which was represented only by the head. Near Perm, the site of 'Talitsky' yielded the remains of mammoth and woolly rhinoceros with an industry containing small backed blades, including some set in a bone point.

Although many of these sites, from the Dniestr to the Yenesei, have yielded examples of sculpted and engraved figures of human and animals, only in the southern Ural area is there evidence of a tradition of decorating caves. The Kapova cave lies on the right bank of the Belaia river, and its walls bear representations of animals, including mammoth, horse and rhinoceros (fig. 144, 5). The figures are filled in yellows, reds, browns and black. In the northern Ural region, on the right bank of the Petchora river, the cave of Medvejia Pechtchera also indicates occupation in final Late Glacial times, and an open site at Byzovaia represents the most northerly Upper Palaeolithic site yet known, at 65° North; the few flints were associated with mammoth, as well as traces of reindeer and polar bear, the sole association of *Thalassarctos maritimus* with Upper Palaeolithic material (Gooselitser *et al.* 1965). In Siberia, Kokorevo on the Yenesei river yielded a bison mandible perforated by a bone point, and at Irkutsk, in eastern Siberia, flint inserts in a bone point have been found, associated with ivory figurines of humans and birds, and a rectangular house-plan. All of these sites in the north and east must represent an occupation by man near the end of the Last Glaciation.

Sites from the area between the Altai mountains and Lake Baikal are particularly

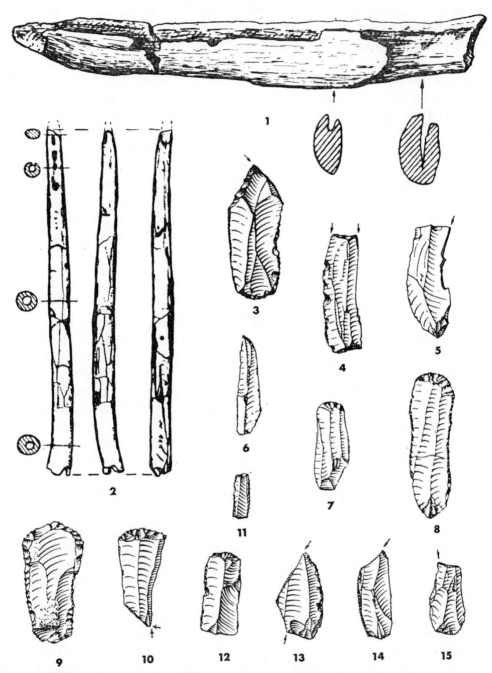

FIG. 147. Molodova V, USSR $\frac{1}{2}$; 1–8 Level IV; 9–15 Level V. *From Chernish 1961*

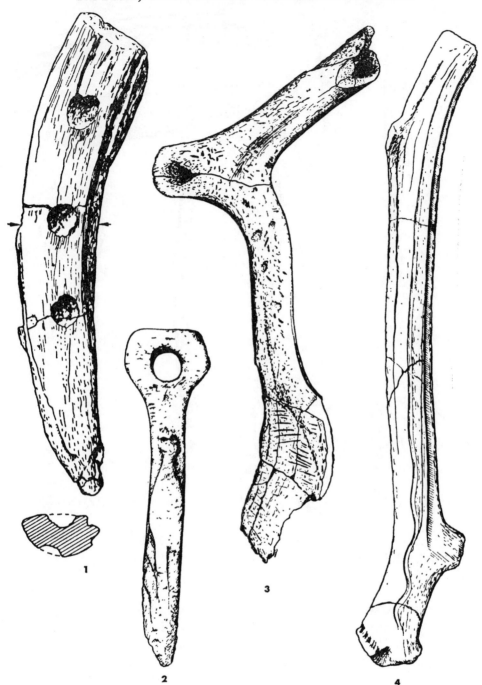

FIG. 148. Molodova V, USSR $\frac{1}{3}$; 1 level III; 2 level VII; 3 level Ia; 4 level IV. *From Chernish 1961*

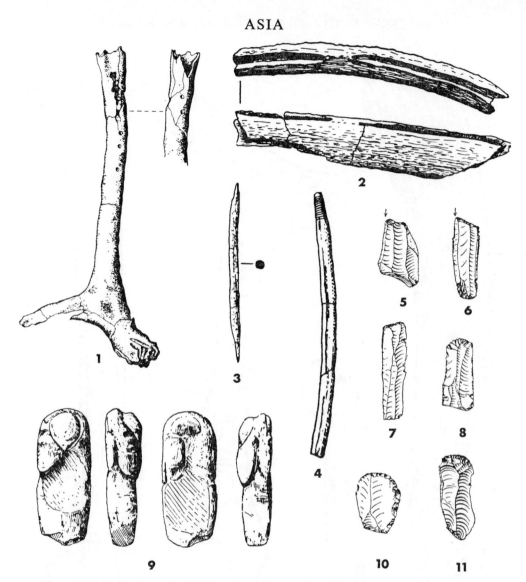

FIG. 149. Molodova V, USSR $\frac{1}{2}$; 1–4 Level II; 5–11 Level III. *From Chernish 1961*

well represented (Okladnikov 1961, 1964). One of the earliest late glacial industries from this area is represented at Ust-Kanskaia in the Altai; the industry here contains both flake and blade elements. Edge-tools, such as scrapers and knives, were made on flakes and blades, but burins are rare. Bone points occur, as well as large unretouched blades and at least one bifacially-worked leaf point. Associated with this industry is a fauna of hyena, fox, wolf, horse, woolly rhinoceros, and bear, which indicates a period of cool, not arctic, conditions.

Typologically later in this sequence are industries from Malta (fig. 152–153; p. 355)

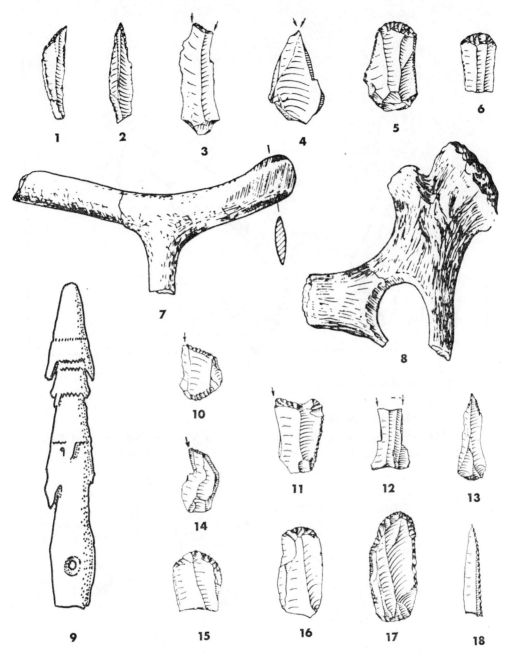

FIG. 150. Molodova V, USSR ½; 1–8 Level I; 9–18a Level Ia. *From Chernish 1961*

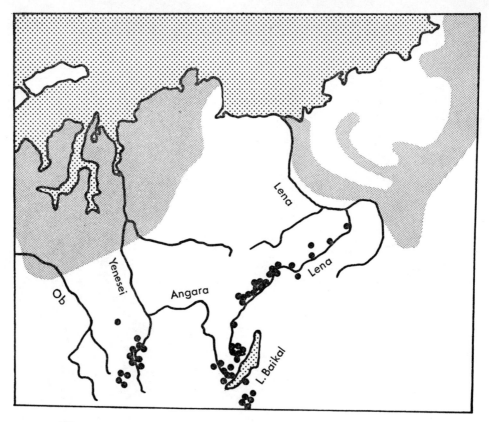

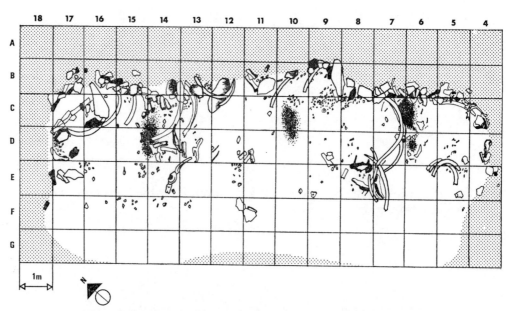

Fig. 151. Distribution of late glacial sites in Yenesei, Angara and Lena valleys, with glaciated regions indicated. *After Okladnikov 1964*

Fig. 152. Malta, Siberia; House plan. *After Gerasimov 1964*

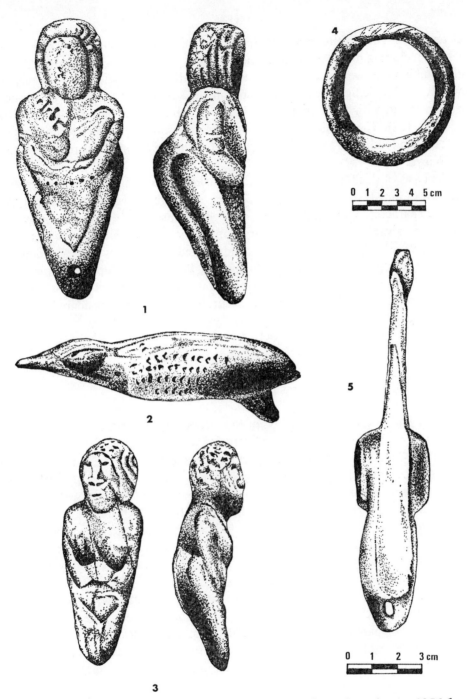

FIG. 153. Malta, Siberia; 1, 3 figurines of bone from long house 1956 $\frac{1}{1}$;
4 Ivory bracelet from long house 1956; 2 Bird figure of ivory from long
house 1956 $\frac{1}{1}$; 5 Bird figure of ivory from 9 m. by 3 m. house. *After Gerasimov
1964*

Buret and other sites in the Baikal region. The lithic material consists of blades and bladelets, including backed blades, end scrapers and burins, and awls. Points, needles and handles were made of bone and naturalistic decoration of bone pieces is known. Ivory female figurines of a rather elongated character as well as bird models have been found with these industries (fig. 153), which occur in semi-subterranean houses (fig. 152). The fauna consists of reindeer, mammoth, woolly rhinoceros and other forms and indicates that this occupation took place during full arctic conditions in late Würm.

On the basis of this fauna, these sites are considered to be earlier than occupations at Afontova Gora II and other sites in Siberia, in which the fauna is of mixed cold-temperate character. Mammoth, arctic fox, deer, moose and bear occur, but woolly rhinoceros is absent. The lithic industry contains an evolved blade element, with microliths, round and end scrapers, awls and backed blades, as well as a strong flake tradition including bifacially worked leaf points. Bone and antler was employed for points, needles, grooved hafts for mounting flints, and perforated bâtons. Beads of teeth and carved human head-like forms occur. These sites are considered to date to final Pleistocene times.

KIIK-KOBA
(Golomshtok 1938, Klein 1965)

The cave of Kiik-Koba is 25 km. east of Simferopol in the Crimea and faces south-east over the Zuya river. Six geological deposits were recognized during the excavations of 1924–26. At the top, dark ash and recent material (1) overlay an interrupted deposit of brownish, altered loam or *suglinok* (2). Yellow *suglinok* lay below this, divided into two deposits (3) and (5) by a dark brown burnt area (4), with an earlier darkened area at the base (6), resting on limestone bedrock. Industrial material was recovered in all of the five lowest levels, and was divided into two groups by the excavator, a lower industry from layers 5 and 6 (the basal dark deposit and lower yellow *suglinok*), an upper industry from layers, 2, 3 and 4. The lower industry consisted of 13,000 flints of which several thousand had retouch or utilization traces. Most of the flakes are thick and rather heavy, and there is little evidence of prepared platforms or true discoid cores. The retouch is irregular and steep. The upper industry, with nearly 5,000 flints, contains some 800 tools. The flakes are thinner, and the retouch is more regular and often directed onto the bulbar face, producing a plano-convex section. The term side-scraper has been used to describe a high proportion of the artefacts.

The fauna from the lower levels of the site, from deposits containing both groups of flints, consists of *Cervus eyriceros*, *Saiga tatarica*, *Equus caballus*, *Elephas* cf. *primigenius*, *Vulpes* and other forms less well-represented.

The decayed bedrock of the cave had been excavated, probably by the first occupants of the site, and the trench used for a burial of an adult. A child was also buried, in the debris of the earliest occupation.

STAROSEL'E
(Kernd'l 1963, Klein 1965)

The Mousterian site of Starosel'e lies in a ravine tributary of the Churuk-su-river. The rock shelter opens to the west, and was excavated from 1952–56. The deposits extend in depth to a maximum of 4 metres, which included stones from the collapsed roof of the shelter. The industrial material consists of thin flakes with fine retouch on convex or straight edges (fig. 137, 7–13). Some plano-convex retouch occurs, and bifacially worked leaf points are characteristic (fig. 137, 1–6). The associated fauna consists of *Equus hydruntinus*, with much smaller quantities of mammoth, bison, saiga antelope, red deer and reindeer. The skeleton of a child was recovered from the occupation debris.

KOSTIENKI
(Efiminko 1958)

Kostienki on the Don River provides a series of Upper Palaeolithic stratified sites which are basic for our understanding of the south Russian Stone Age, and of the origins of more widespread industrial traditions. The most important of these sites is Kostienki I because it provides the most complete sequence of industries from any one site in the area although certain other sites in the same terrace formation, such as Teleman and Kostienki XII, provide further detailed stratified industries not found at Kostienki I.

The site lies on the upper terrace of the Don River, about 15 m. above the river. The geological sequence of this terrace may be summarized as follows: at the base, over sterile gravels, is a humus deposit containing within it an intercalated pumice horizon. Above the humus is loess which is divided by a weathering horizon. The five industries recognized at Kostienki I are numbered from the top down, the lowest (5) in the lower humus, with (4) in the upper humus above the pumice. The lower loess has industry (3), and the upper two industries (2 and 1) lie in the upper part of the loess above the weathering horizon. The top industry (1) in fact is very near the top of this loessic deposit, and has been dated by radiocarbon to *c*. 14,000 B.P.

The basal industry was associated with a small oval house, 4 by 5 metres in diameter, set in the loess with an off-centre hearth. The stone tools include triangular points with slightly concave bases, finely flaked and very thin in section; these are about 6 cm. in length, and do not really appear to be of normal Middle Palaeolithic character. Round thumbnail scrapers, steep scrapers of small size, and flake scrapers occur; burins and flakes with retouched tips are also associated.

The industries above this, (4), (3) and (2), are characterized by a stronger blade element. A house with multiple hearths is claimed from (4), and the industries continue to possess the high-backed forms of scraper, as well as end-of-blade and round scrapers in (2). Microlithic backed bladelets, angle burins and lames écaillées appear in (3) along with rather long end scrapers which have side retouch in Aurignacian style. In the level above, the microlithic blades continue but now include some reverse retouch of 'Dufour' type. In very general terms this group of industries recalls some of the earlier traditions of central and western Europe.

The top level at Kostienki I has been considered to represent the classic East Gravettian industry, but its radiocarbon date (14,020 ± 60 B.P.) suggests that it may represent only a late variant industry in the Gravettian tradition of the south Russian area. One of the important features of the upper level at Kostienki I is the remains of a dwelling. The industrial material when excavated was seen to have come from an area some 37 metres by 13–17 metres, forming a roughly oblong area (fig. 143, lower). At the downslope end of this, an oval depression 8 by 6 metres was recognized. The site was reconstructed originally as an enormously long house made of clay and wood walls with wooden rafters supporting a roof of skins and earth. A small round house was believed to have been attached to the south-eastern end. The difficulty in this theoretical reconstruction was the width of roof required, some 17 metres, which far exceeded the 5 metre roof-widths of contemporary houses at Pushkari and Aleksandrovka (Kostienki IV). Recent examination of the industrial remains, and density plots, have indicated that it is more likely that the long house at Kostienki I was of the order of 27 metres by 8 metres, with pits dug well outside the walls and with a line of 9 hearths running along the centre of the house. No evidence exists that the house was subdivided by partition walls, in contrast to the Aleksandrovka houses, some 22 and 34 metres long, which appear to have been partitioned (fig. 143, upper).

The industrial material associated with the house at Kostienki is prolific. Typical, although not abundantly common, are the shouldered points, some with invasive retouch at both ends of the bulbar surface (fig. 139, 4, 5, 8). Generally the shoulder is very near the point with blunting retouch on the stem. Backed blades including narrow forms occur (fig. 139, 13) and there are also leaf-shaped blades some with retouch on the bulbar surface (fig. 139, 1–2); these are in fact shouldered points without the shoulder, and recall the pointe à face plane of western Europe. The scraping tools include end-of-blade, short end scrapers (fig. 139, 7) and some rather thick specimens although these are not truly steep scrapers. Burins of various types occur (fig. 139, 9–11), including polyhedrics, and there are retouched blades, some with chisel ends, and coarse side-retouched flake-blades, including some with terminal reverse retouch (fig. 139, 6). There are no true microlithic forms, but bladelet cores occur, which in fact recall certain steep scraper-forms. A large bifacial tool with traces of wear at the base may have been collected elsewhere and brought to the site. This flint industry exhibits a considerable range of tools, some of which probably had a part in the shaping of the very rich bone and ivory industry. The range of objects, most of them broken and incomplete, is remarkable. Ivory rods of various forms are common, including one composite object with a perforated ivory lump fitted onto a thinned rod (fig. 141, 1). Curved pieces also occur, either long and thin, or as a form of axe-adze which can be either straight or curved; these are up to 18″ long and are decorated with crisscross lines (fig. 141, 2). There is also a group of flat curved spatulate objects which have a roughly circular end decorated by 2 or 4 holes or grooves, providing a 'human' face with slanting eyes (fig. 140, 1–2). Various bone points and awls have crisscross or hatched decoration. One perforated bâton is known (fig. 141, 3), as well as a number of enigmatic objects, a funnel, pendulous objects, perforated and flat objects of various shapes, a toggle-like form (fig. 140, 6) and an elongated human figurine. Perforated chalk weights are known (fig. 139, 14), as well as sexual symbols carved in small pieces (fig. 142, 10). Several complete Venus figurines occur, and fragments of many others (fig. 142). These figurines include several elongated smoothly-curved forms, some with some evidence of narrow belting at the back and/or front, and cruder more angular versions as well. One figurine has the arms under the breasts, the feet are well-modelled, and hair or a mask is indicated on the head. At least one engraving of a figurine was found (fig. 140, 3). In addition there are many small crude carvings of animals, either whole body or head alone (fig. 140, 7; 142, 4–6).

Affinities The basal industry at Kostienki I is not unique, but is quite closely matched at a number of sites in the Don River area. The industry at Streletzki and the lower levels at Kostienki XII seem to belong to this early phase, and it is probable that less diagnostic industries from some other sites also belong to the same tradition. Although claims have been advanced for a derivation of this, the first Upper Palaeolithic industry in the area, from a form of East Mousterian as evidenced at the Crimean site of Starosel'e, of an Early Würm age, it would seem premature at the moment to consider the Starosel'e variant as the main source of the new elements in the Streletzki and related industries.

MOLODOVA V
(Chernish 1961)

The site of Molodova V lies on the Dniestr river in a locality which has several hundred Palaeolithic sites. Along the river valley is a system of terraces, the second of which has been correlated with the Eemian Interglacial. The deposits at Molodova V are on the pebble beds of this second terrace. The relation of the industries to the stratigraphy, radiocarbon dates and climatic inferences are shown in Table 1 below. This indicates that prior to 23,400 B.P. there was a series of warmer and colder, wetter and drier oscillations of the last glaciation, the details of which have not as yet been clearly established. It appears possible that two fossil soils (layers 9 and 5) were formed prior to 23,400 B.P. and that there was a further temperate period at the end of this sequence. Although it is evident that the whole of the sediments were deposited under conditions colder than they are at the present day, the mammalian fauna (Table 2) does not show any appreciable changes; the molluscan fauna, too, is interpreted as indicating cold conditions. Pollen is absent from the deposits and charcoal determinations have shown a general predominance of coniferous trees. These lines of evidence indicate an uninterrupted development of a coniferous forest-steppe environment, with cold-loving and cold-tolerating animals always comprising the whole assemblage. While the horse, the woolly rhinoceros, bison, red deer and even the mammoth are able to tolerate a wide range of environments from at least cool to cold, the reindeer is more restricted in its range and is, in fact, the dominant form throughout except for the horse in cultural levels VII–X.

Twelve major occupation horizons have been recognized at Molodova. The earliest (levels XII, XIIa and XI) consist of hearths associated with animal bones and stone artefacts. The two hearths in level XII have been interpreted as the remains of a hut, and an oval arrangement of mammoth bones in level XI has been similarly interpreted. The stone industry from these three levels is in the Mousterian tradition; industry XI is abundant, and contained numerous cores, points and side-scrapers as well as flake-blades. This industry appears to be older than 40,000 B.P.

Well above level XI, and separated from it by generally culturally sterile deposits, is level X which contains a blade and burin industry with nibbled bladelets, edge-retouched blades, and scrapers and burins, steep scrapers and a remarkable tanged flake with bifacial retouch (fig. 145, 8, 13–18). Immediately above is level IX with a blade and burin industry (fig. 145, 9–12), pestles and grindstones, colouring materials and an anthropomorphic slab. Levels X and IX are considered to represent the second stage of the Upper Palaeolithic sequence in the Dniestr. The first stage is believed to be present in the basal industry of the site at Babin I. The correlation stages of the Dniestr sequence and Molodova V are given in Table 1. The industries of level VIII were clustered around a group of hearths; the tools (fig. 145, 1–5, 7) include blades, burins, scrapers, edge-retouched blades, notched flakes, grindstones and hammer-stones, as well as a schematic statuette on mammoth ivory (fig. 145, 6).

The richest occupation level at Molodova is VII, from which over 40,000 flints were recovered. Quantities of cores, burins and end scrapers, edge-retouched blades, backed blades and rudimentary tanged points occur (fig. 146, 8–9, 12–18), associated with perforated antler bâtons (fig. 146, 10, 19), including a decorated piece (fig. 148, 2), and other artefacts of bone and antler. Colouring matter and polished stone slabs also were found. Level VII has been dated to 23,700 ± 320 and 23,000 ± 800 B.P. Level VI yielded an oval hut plan measuring 7 × 4 m., with hearths and an industry containing blades and burins, scrapers and awls (fig. 146, 1–7); bone and antler work includes a mammoth rib handle with slots for flint inserts, bone points, and an ivory schematized figure.

The succeeding industry, level V, was associated with numerous hearths. Burins, end scrapers, awls and backed blades occur (fig. 147, 9–15) with bone and antler

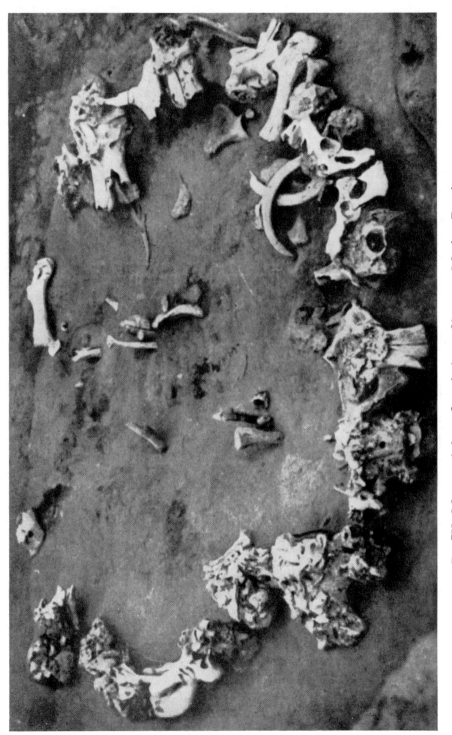

Pl. IX. Mammoth-bone foundations of house at Mezine, Russia

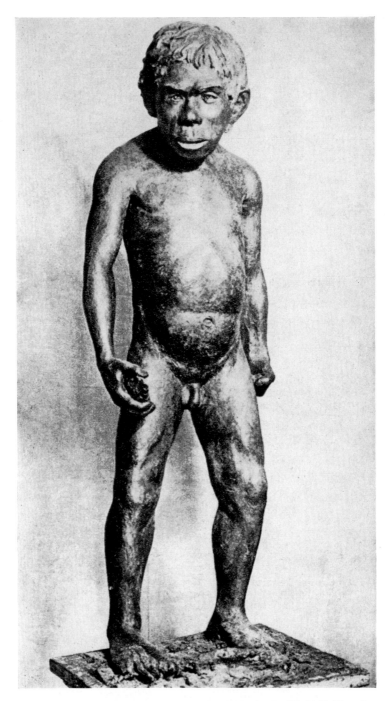

PL. X. Reconstruction of the boy buried at Tešík Táš, Russia

points, clubs and other forms, and the industry has been dated to *c.* 16,000 B.P.
Level IV also yielded many hearths and quantities of flint; the artefacts include cores,
burins of various types including parrot-beaked, end scrapers, truncated and backed
bladelets (fig. 147, 3–8). Bone and antler work (fig. 148, 4) consists of slotted rib
bones (fig. 147, 1), antler daggers and an antler flute (fig. 147, 2). No structural
remains were found on levels V and IV, but in level III a number of postholes are
presumed to indicate a dwelling. The prolific industry associated with this, and with
a series of hearths, contains blade cores, burins, scrapers, backed blades and points

TABLE 1

Layer	Sediments	Cultural Level	Dniestr Sequence	Age B.P. (approx.)	Temperature	Humidity	Russian Correlation
Top							
17	Chernozem-type soil				warm		Holocene
16	loess-loam	I	7				
	(yellow-grey)	Ia	7	10,600	temperate		Late
15	loess-loam	II	6	11,900	temperate		
	(yellow)						Glacial
14	loess-loam	III	6	13,400	cold	dry	
	(yellow-grey)	IV	6				———
		V	5	16,000	cold	wetter	Main
13	loess-loam	VI	4		cold	wetter	
	(brown)						Würm
12	loess-loam				cold	dry	
	(yellow-grey)						———
11	loam	VII	3	23,400	warmer	dry	
	(yellow-brown)						Paudorf
10	loess-loam	VIII	3		warmer	dry	
	(yellow-grey)						
9	loam	IX	2		warmer	dry	
	(dark grey, 'A' horizon)	X	2		warmer	dry	
8	loam				warmer	dry	Oscillation
	(brown, 'B' horizon)						———
7	loam				cold	humid	Middle
	(yellow-grey)						
6	loam				cold	humid	
	(yellow-brown)						
5	loam (dark)				temperate	dry	
4	loam (yellow)				cool	humid	
3	loams				cold	humid	Würm
	(blue-grey, sandy)						———
2	loam	XI		40,300	cold	humid	Brorup
	(yellow-grey)	XII			temperate	humid	
		XIIa			temperate	humid	Interstadial
1	loam (sandy)				?cold		Early Würm

TABLE 2

Cultural level	I	Ia	II	III	IV	V	VI	VII	VIII	IX	X
Reindeer	1738	219	360	369	746	343	900	476	112	63	11
	37	7	17	11	15	11	14	12	3	5	3
Horse	30	49	55	47	92	43	79	659	141	124	51
	4	6	5	4	7	4	6	10	3	5	6
Mammoth				22	76	18	161	95	19	11	8
				2	4	2	4	6	2	2	2
Woolly		4					1	4		2	5
rhino		1					1	1		1	1
Bison	5	1	10	16	21		13	2		3	7
	2	1	2	2	3		1	1		2	1
Red deer	15	8		1			9	10	2		
	1	1		1			2	1	1		
Hare				1		4	1	4	1		
				1		1	1	1	1		
Elk	1	4	1	6	3	1	59	7			
	1	1	1	2	1	1	2	1			
Aurochs			6	1				2			
			1	1				1			
Fox	2							2			
	1							1			
Wolf					3	2		1			
					1	1		1			
Deer	9	3	1	1			4	11			
	1	1	1	1			1	1			
Arctic fox				1	1			3			
				1	1			1			
Arctic hare	3										
	1										

The upper number for each species represents the number of specimens found; the lower number represents the minimum number of individuals present.

(fig. 149, 5–11). Notched mammoth ivory, schematic ivory and limestone figures (fig. 144, 4), slotted bone, horn and ivory pieces also occur (fig. 148, 1). Level III has been dated to 13,400 ± 540 B.P. This date, and the geological evidence, indicates a Late Glacial cold phase, possibly the Older Dryas.

Level II represents a scatter of industrial material and hearths, although a concentration of several hundred reindeer antlers may have been connected with a hut framework. The industry is of blade and burin character, with backed blades, as well as antler and bone points, a slotted rib bone and an unlikely antler flute (fig. 149, 1–4). Radiocarbon dates from level II, 11,900 ± 230 and 11,800 ± 200 B.P., and temperate climate indications, suggest this occupation occurred during the Allerød.

MALTA

Level Ia yielded traces of a hut and a small industry of blade and burin type with bladelets (fig. 150, 10–18), associated with a double-barbed perforated javelin point of red deer antler (fig. 150, 9) and an antler axe (fig. 148, 3) as well as other bone and antler objects. This level has a date of 10,590 ± 230 B.P. Above is level I, dated to c. 10,400 B.P. with an abundant industry containing quantities of flakes. Artefacts include burins, scrapers, notched and truncated bladelets, backed blades and geometric forms (fig. 150, 1–6). Bone and antler work contains an engraved horn, a fragment of a barbed point, a bâton and other pieces (fig. 150, 7–8).

The site of Molodova V provides a remarkably detailed picture of the major successive Upper Palaeolithic industries in the Dniestr as well as earlier flake traditions. Throughout this period of occupation, conditions appear to have been generally cold; the dominance upon reindeer of the makers of the industries of levels I to VI may be compared with the similar successful dependence of the Hamburgian-Ahrensburgian groups farther west, and with the contemporary man/animal (sheep) relationships at Shanidar in Iraq.

MALTA
(Gerasimov 1964)

The late glacial site of Malta lies in the Angara basin to the west of Lake Baikal. The site is stratified in that two occupations have been recognized, an upper one linked typologically with a late phase of the Afontova Gora group of the Yenesei basin, and a lower one yielding the classic Malta assemblage. The excavation of the deposits on the site revealed an upper loam containing a small industry of epi-Palaeolithic character; beneath was a series of sandy loams of loessic type. At a depth of over one metre was the occupation area of the Malta industry, first discovered in 1928. More extensive excavations have taken place in 1956–57, and revealed evidence of six houses set into the earth near the edge of a river terrace.

The largest of these houses seems to have been not so much a subterranean dwelling as a shelter dug partly into the slope of the terrace (fig. 152). The area within the shelter measured 14 × 6 metres, and had been walled on three sides, one of the longer sides (to the south-west) apparently remaining unprotected and open to the river. The earthen floor of the shelter sloped slightly down towards the open side; on the other three sides the shelter had been dug into the earth to a depth of $\frac{1}{2}$ metre at the back, and only $\frac{1}{10}$ metre at the front of the side walls. The shelter had been completed by walling of stone slabs, mammoth and rhinoceros bones and reindeer antler; the roof may have consisted of mammoth hide held down by stones and antlers. Ten mammoth tusks up to 2 metres long had been set along the back wall.

Near the back of the shelter were three hearths, and roof post-sockets were recognized along the central long axis of the shelter. Near the hearths, hollows had been dug into the earthen walls, and these had served to hold stone tools and ivory and

355

bone decorative pieces (fig. 153, 4). The stone industry associated with this dwelling consists of discoid cores, flakes and flake-blades, and tools made of small pebbles. High-backed scrapers, thick blades and awls are characteristic, but burins and prismatic cores are extremely rare. Bone points, awls and daggers occur, as well as beads, pendants and other ornaments of bone and ivory. Two antler handles, holding flint chisels, were found. Bone statuettes of female human figures had been recovered from earlier excavations at Malta, and several others were associated with the long house. Among these are figures with facial features and hair shown (fig. 153, 1, 3). Other statuettes represent waterfowl and partridge (fig. 153, 2).

Adjoining huts, set at the edge of the terrace deposits, were smaller and included several tent-like structures with central hearths, a semi-subterranean house probably 9 × 3 metres with ivory objects (fig. 153, 5), a structure walled with stone slabs and animal bones and containing a rhinoceros skull seat beneath which were stored many ivory objects, and a stone-built round house. The round house measured 4·5 metres in diameter, and the wall base was of vertical slabs of stone; a central hearth, ivory and bone beads, bird figures (swan and loon) and a female human figure were found near the walls.

This complex of dwellings at Malta appears to be more or less a single contemporary unit, although the variety of structures is remarkable for a one-period site. The animal bones recovered from the occupation shows a dominance of reindeer, mammoth and rhinoceros. The reindeer would provide food, sinew, skins, antler for structural material and for tools, and bone for tools and for fuel. Mammoth provided meat, ivory for ornaments and for wall supports, bone for fuel, and hide for roofing.

18

South-west Asia

THE earliest industries known from south-western Asia are pebble and flake assemblages from Ubeidiyeh in the Jordan valley, 3 kilometres south of Lake Kinnereth, Israel (Stekelis 1966). The implements were found in 12 superimposed beds of limmic origin of a total thickness of 12·9 metres which were probably formed in an ancient lake. The shores of the lake were periodically inhabited by man. The earliest tool phase is regarded as being a 'pebble' tool assemblage similar to that of Bed II at Olduvai Gorge, and it has been named IVO II Culture (Israel Variant of Oldowan II). It is suggested that IVO II has three phases. Site A contains Phase I which has chopper and chopping tools. Site B has Phase II which includes polyhedrons, spheroids and picks and Phase III which is industrially similar but is thought to be of a later date than Phase II. At Site B a Phase III industry is overlain by an assemblage of tools similar to those of Phase III but which includes some crude handaxes. This industry has been named IVA (Israel Variant of Abbevillean Culture). IVA could be regarded as a transitional industry between pebble tool and handaxe cultures. It also includes some bone specimens which may have been used as tools. The IVA deposits contained portions of a human skull and teeth, classified provisionally as *Homo sp.* At another site, Jisr Banat Yaqub, on a river terrace also in the Jordan valley, early Acheulean handaxes have been found with an extinct fauna which includes *Elephas trogontherii*, *Stegodont*, and rhinoceros. Above these are middle and upper Acheulean type handaxes which underlie a deposit which contains Levallois flakes. To the north, the site of Latamne in northern Syria has been compared with the Jisr Banat Yaqub assemblage (Clark 1966a), as well as with the industries from Sidi Abderrahman (Moroccan Acheulean IV–V). The Latamne industry is considered to be of Mindel or Hoxnian age on the basis of a fauna containing *Elephas trogontherii*, *Equus sp.*, *Dicerorhinus cf. hemitoechus* and *Hippopotamus amphibius*; such a date may compare well with the Moroccan groups.

Elsewhere there are at an early date crude flake industries which have been compared with the Tayacian of Europe. The Levallois technique occurs with these crude flake industries and a Levallois industry appears to develop locally and has been found in beach deposits at 15 metres O.D. at Adlun. Later the Levalloisian is associated with Mousterian techniques to form the widely spread Levalloiso-Mousterian industries of the caves. In some areas this industry occurs in fossil dunes which are later than the 6–8 metre shore line. The 8 metre shore line is of Last Interglacial date and therefore it is thought that this industry continued until the time of a low sea level of the Last Glaciation. Geological and faunal evidence from the caves indicates the possible presence of one, two or perhaps three wetter or colder episodes in the area, but so far there has been no general agreement as to their date or their relation to the glaciations. Radiocarbon dates are also rare. According to a radiocarbon date from Ras-el-Kelb (Lebanon) the Levalloiso-Mousterian industry occurred at least as early as 52,000 B.P.; at Geulah (Israel), a lower Levalloiso-Mousterian industry has been dated to c. 42,000 B.P.

The cave sites in south west Asia have a succession which begins with a crude Tayacian type flake industry, which is followed by a handaxe culture of Acheulean type (fig. 154, 11). The Acheulean is succeeded by the Jabrudian industries (fig. 154, 1–6, 10; 155, 1, 3, 4) which are characterized by thick scrapers on flakes with a plain platform. Sometimes bifaces are associated with them in considerable quantities. With this industry there are a number of heavy blades of Advanced Palaeolithic type. At Jabrud (Rust 1950) an assemblage, which was named pre-Aurignacian and subsequently renamed Amudian, has these blades, but the Jabrudian element is absent. It appears therefore that the pre-Aurignacian is probably a separate entity and the blade association with the Jabrudian may be due to an admixture during the excavation of the two cultural levels. This blade industry has been placed in the Last Interglacial and the Last Glaciation on geological and faunal grounds. It may be noted that at Haua Fteah in North Africa, a similar early heavy blade industry also occurred c. 70,000 B.P. (p. 186). At Adlun the pre-Aurignacian was found in and on a beach at 12 metres O.D. and it is earlier than an overlying Jabrudian industry. At Tabun the Jabrudian is succeeded by the Levalloiso-Mousterian which has been dated c. 40,000 B.P. Associated with a Levalloiso-Mousterian industry (fig. 156, 1, 2, 5–11) are the famous Neanderthal skeletons of the sites of es Skhul and et Tabun. The skeletons from these two sites may be contemporary, which raises the question of whether or not they represent a widely variable population or interbreeding between *Homo sapiens* and Neanderthal Man. Alternatively, and more probably, the two different assemblages may not be contemporary and the assemblages may belong to two different populations. The fact that the blade tools persist after the pre-Aurignacian in the Levalloiso-Mousterian, and that the Levalloiso-Mousterian tools persist in the later Advanced Palaeolithic industries, is taken, by some authorities, to indicate a slow transition from Middle Palaeolithic to Advanced Palaeolithic type industries in this area. Some think, however, that it is more likely that there were two industries in the area, the pre-Aurignacian blade industry, possibly made by *Homo sapiens*, and the Levalloiso-Mousterian industry made by Neanderthal Man.

The succeeding Advanced Palaeolithic industries in the past have been compared with various European stages. This is not now a popular approach, and a local

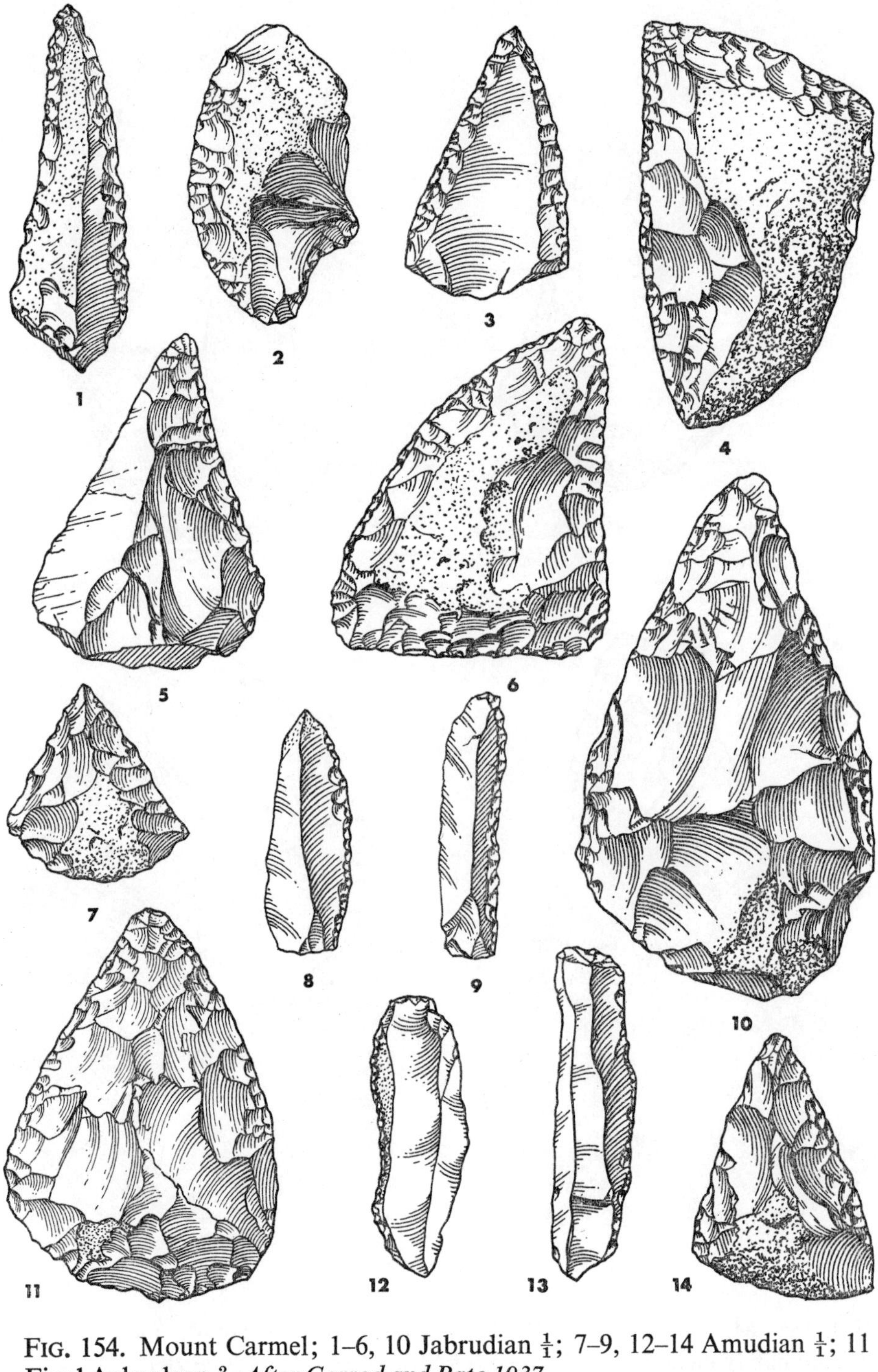

FIG. 154. Mount Carmel; 1–6, 10 Jabrudian $\frac{1}{1}$; 7–9, 12–14 Amudian $\frac{1}{1}$; 11 Final Acheulean $\frac{2}{3}$. *After Garrod and Bate 1937*

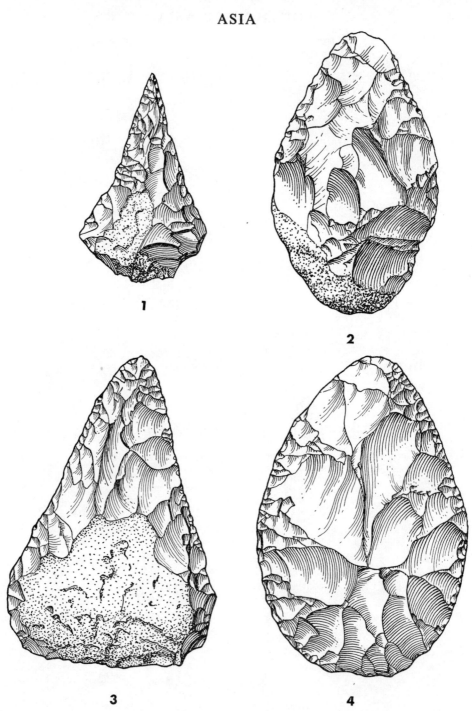

FIG. 155. Mount Carmel; 1, 3, 4, Jabrudian from et Tabun, Layer Ec ⅔; 2 Amudian from et Tabun, Layer Eb ⅓. *After Garrod and Bate 1937*

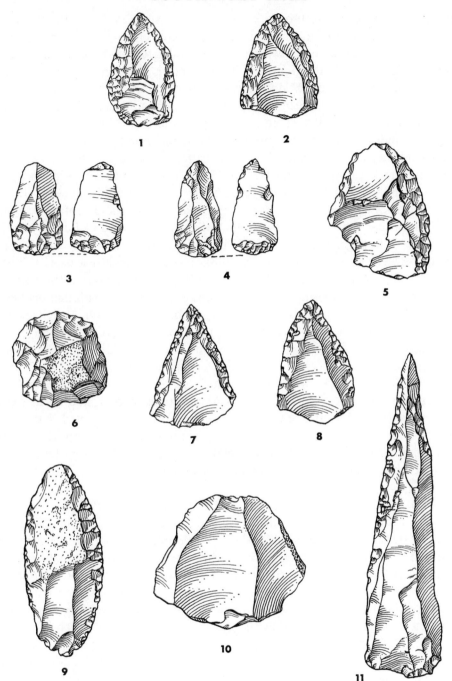

FIG. 156. Mount Carmel $\frac{2}{3}$; 1, 2, 5–11 Levalloiso-Mousterian; 3, 4 Emiran points. *After Garrod and Bate 1937*

categorization divides them into six stages. The first stage is the Emiran which has been compared in some of its aspects with the Chatelperronian of France (fig. 156, 3–4). In the absence of dating, however, it is impossible to assess with confidence even its time relationship with that industry. The Emiran is regarded by some as a transitional industry between the Middle and Advanced Palaeolithic industries and contains elements which are identical with the Levalloiso-Mousterian. There is, however, a possibility that in the caves where it has been found it was impossible to separate two different industrial layers. In support of this contention there does exist at Abou Halka an industry which includes the characteristic Emiran artefacts and which does not contain the Levallois element (Haller 1962). The second stage is not very well established but may include blunted backed blades and a Levallois element. The third and fourth stages have carinated scrapers and beaked burins and profuse peripheral retouch which has been compared with that of the Aurignacian of Europe (fig. 157, 10–24). The fifth stage, the Atlitian, is known only from two sites but has been reported elsewhere in Palestine (fig. 157, 1–8). The sixth stage is a narrow blunted blade industry which does not contain the earlier Aurignacian-like characteristics (fig. 158, 16–20). Broadly speaking the succession is comparable with that of Western Europe in that a Mousterian is succeeded by blade cultures with Aurignacian-like characteristics which are themselves succeeded by Gravettian-like industries.

In south western Iran, the earliest known industries are said to be of Mousterian character, and there is no certain evidence of occupation in the area before the Last Glaciation. This situation presents difficulties in terms of the pebble and flake industries of north eastern Africa, the east Mediterranean coast, and north western India and Pakistan. Recent work in south western Iran has indicated that climatic changes during the Last Glaciation were only moderate; snowlines in the southern Zagros mountains were lowered by only 600 metres, and pollen from Lake Zeribar shows that woodlands in the area may have been sharply reduced in extent but still survived.

The Khorramabad valley in Luristan, at 1170 metres above sea level, has yielded evidence of Mousterian and Advanced Palaeolithic occupation during this period, from > 40,000 B.P. to a suggested 12,000 B.P. (Hole and Flannery 1967). The material has been divided into Mousterian, Baradostian and Zarzian, although industrial continuity has been demonstrated for the two blade industries. The Mousterian material consists of sidescrapers and points made on flakes, with some simple burins and awls; discoid cores were used, although there is some slight evidence of the Levallois technique in Khuzistan at the head of the Persian Gulf. The succeeding industry is the Baradostian, which appears $c.$ 38,000 B.P.; the youngest dates are $c.$ 28,000 B.P. Characteristic tools are small slender points, backed blades, burins and end scrapers, and retouched rods. Bone points are common. The Zarzian industry generally resembles this material, although some of the points disappear, and are replaced by geometric microliths. The type site of the Zarzian is the Zarzi cave in Kurdistan. The industry here contained backed blades and burins and in a later stage

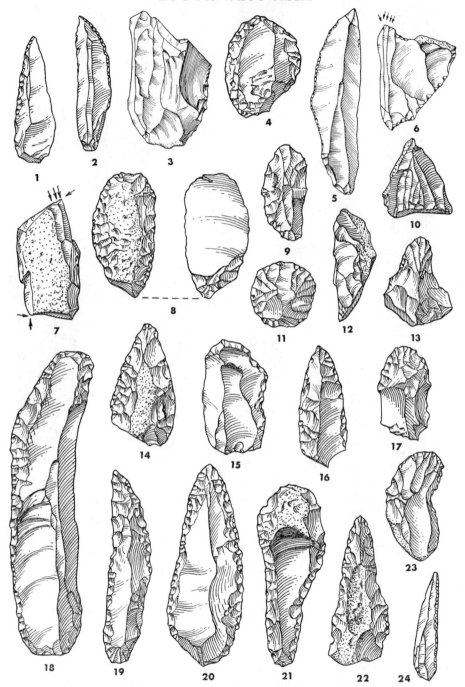

FIG. 157. Mount Carmel $\frac{2}{3}$; 1–8 Advanced Palaeolithic Stage 5; 9–24 Aurignacian type, Classes 3–4; No. 24 is said to be characteristic of Stage 3. *After Garrod and Bate 1937*

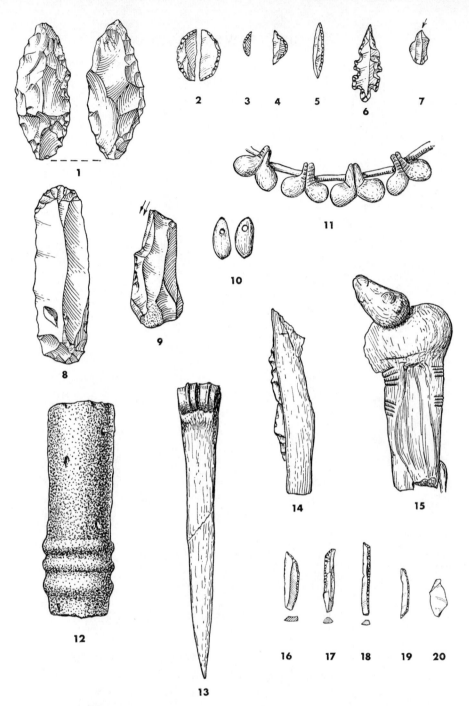

FIG. 158. Mount Carmel; 1–12, 14, 15, Natufian (1–9, $\frac{2}{3}$; 10–12, 15, $\frac{1}{2}$; 14, $\frac{1}{4}$); 11, twin bone pendant necklace; 14 hafted sickle flints; 15 animal carved in bone; 10 perforated bone pendant; 13 advanced Palaeolithic stage 3 ($\frac{3}{4}$); bone awl; 16–20 advanced Palaeolithic stage 6 ($\frac{1}{4}$); 16–19 microlithic blades; 20 microburin. *After Garrod and Bate 1937, and Garrod and Clark 1965*

microlithic triangles and lunates. The Palegawra shelter in the same area has similar geometric forms including trapezes.

The fauna associated with the industries of the Khorramabad valley sites includes *Capra hircus aegagrus* (goat), *Cervus elaphus* (red deer), *Lepus europaeus* (hare), *Vulpes vulpes* (red fox) and *Alectoris chukar* (partridge), as well as many other forms less well represented.

The sequence of industries in this area is considered to match that to the north, in northern Iraq at Shanidar where Mousterian, Baradostian and Zarzian material range in time from *c.* 50,000 B.P. to *c.* 12,000 B.P. (p. 371; pl. XI).

In parts of south western Asia there appears to have developed, before the end of the Pleistocene, a close man/animal relationship between man and gazelle similar to the relationship which existed at about the same time between man and sheep at Shanidar (pl. XI) and between man and reindeer in north temperate Europe and north of the Black Sea. To regard any one of these animals, at this time, as domesticated, and the others not, would be to read into the existing evidence an interpretation which cannot be inferred from the available evidence. There is, in fact, no line which can be drawn between domesticated and not domesticated animals except by an arbitrary taxonomic device. All that can be said is that an economic stage had been reached about this time north and south of the Black Sea which gives evidence in the archaeo-logical record of such a close relationship existing. Subsequently, probably owing to population pressures upon animal populations and therefore upon animal food supplies, some morphological changes took place in the size and perhaps the shape of the bones of some animals which indicate that a close man/animal relationship (domestication) had existed for some time.

The microlithic industries went on in some areas until 8,000 B.P. Contemporaneous with them in some areas were industries of Natufian type (p. 370; Garrod 1957; Garrod and Clark 1966) which were associated with permanent structures, houses and caves. By some authorities they are regarded as being made by a people who were in a transitional economic stage between hunting and gathering, and agriculture.

ADLUN
(Garrod and Kirkbride 1961)

The Abri Zumoffen is situated on the coast between Sidon and Tyre, about 13·8 metres above sea level. Nearby there is a large cave, Mugharet el Bazez. In the latter is a wave cut notch 18 metres above sea level, the highest level reached by the sea. Zumoffen contains a Jabrudian industry. The section shows a red earth overlying a breccia, the latter containing a Jabrudian industry overlying an Amudian (pre-Aurignacian) industry. The whole deposit rests on a beach at 12–13 metres above sea level. In another trench a breccia with an Amudian industry passed down into a consolidated *sandy* beach with a surface at 12 metres. Below was a bed of red clay overlying a pebble beach. The clay is regarded as an old land surface contemporary with a sea fluctuating at the 12 metre level. It is thought that the makers of the Amudian industry arrived when the sea was still at the 12 metre level and stayed during a regression. The shore lines of the Lebanon are at 45 metres (Tyrrhenian I, Hoxnian), 15 metres (Tyrrhenian II, Last Interglacial), and 6 metres (Tyrrhenian III) above the present level of the sea. The 6 metre shore is probably of late Last Interglacial age, but some authorities believe that it belongs to an interstadial of the Last Glaciation. The 12 metre beach is too high for the 6 metre shore line, and too low for the 15 metre shore line. It is regarded by some as having occurred during the recession of the sea from the 15 metre to the 6 metre level and by others as being a storm beach of the 6 metre level.

MOUNT CARMEL
(Garrod and Bate 1937)

The principal Palaeolithic sites of Mount Carmel consist of three sites, el Wad, et Tabun and es Skhul. At one time it was thought on faunal and typological grounds that el Wad and et Tabun provided evidence of a continuous industrial succession from at least Late Acheulean to Late Advanced Palaeolithic times. In the light of more recent evidence, however, it is thought that this is perhaps an unwise presumption. The chronological relationship of Skhul to et Tabun and el Wad is also disputed, although some authorities are of the opinion that es Skhul and et Tabun layers C and D are probably more or less contemporary. It is therefore necessary to consider the evidence from each of the caves separately.

et Tabun The fauna from this cave is regarded as more ancient than the comparatively modern fauna of el Wad. The well-known *Dama-Gazella* graph, which purported to show wet and colder or drier and warmer conditions by evaluating the fluctuations in the proportions of gazelle to fallow deer is not now considered by many authorities to have the value it was once supposed to have, although what faults it may have may be in the interpretation of the data rather than in the method of the evaluation. There is a difference of opinion as to whether or not the faunal fluctuations represent changes in hunting fashion or changes in climate. It is, however, one of the rare occasions on which some attempt has been made to evaluate faunal data numerically. If the faunal evidence is accepted as indicating climatic oscillations then Layer F at the base, with a high proportion of fallow deer, and containing the bones of a tropical bat (*Megaderma watwat*), may indicate a climate wetter than now. In contrast with this, layers C and D together have a high gazelle content and a high bovine content while the presence of gerbils also indicates drier conditions. Tabun B has again a high *Dama* content which would indicate a wetter or a colder climate than that operating during the depositions of layers C and D.

The industries of et Tabun are as follows:

Layer G at the base contains a crude flake industry. It is described as Tayacian and has been compared with Layer C of the La Micoque (p. 271). There are 464 pieces and only one carefully worked point and four steep scrapers; 338 pieces are utilized and 40 of them have faceted platforms.

Layer F yields 1233 handaxes which comprise one third of the total assemblage excluding flakes and cores (fig. 154, 11). There are a great number of racloirs and steep scrapers and some burins and blades but they are not illustrated in the report. The industry is described as Final Acheulean.

Layer Ed is now described as Jabrudian after the type site of Jabrud on the grounds that this layer has a great preponderance of scrapers. There are, in fact 11,741 racloirs (fig. 154, 4, 6). It contains 3,742 handaxes (fig. 155, 1, 3, 4) and a total assemblage of 18,783 pieces. There are said to be also 31 blades and some burins.

Layer Ec, in contrast with Ed, contains only 5,019 flints. It has 636 handaxes similar to those in Layer Ed and over 3,000 scrapers. It is also regarded as Jabrudian with a few burins and blades.

Layer Eb has an industry called the Amudian from a type site, the Wadi el Amud in Galilee. It is sometimes referred to as the pre-Aurignacian, a name which is not now used by some authorities in that it presupposes a relationship to the succeeding Aurignacian type assemblages. This layer contains again approximately 2,000 hand-axes (fig. 154, 1; 155, 2). The blades are said to be long and narrow, a distinctive characteristic of this layer (fig. 154, 12, 13).

Layer Ea is described again as Jabrudian. It contains *c*. 1,000 handaxes.

Layers D, C and B are described as Levalloiso-Mousterian. The industry contains points (fig. 156, 1, 2, 7, 8) Levallois (fig. 156, 10) and disc cores and many triangular flakes. There are a few handaxes.

The chronology of et Tabun has troubled prehistorians up to the present day. One authority places layers E, C and D in the Hoxnian, Eb in the Last Interglacial and Ea in the first cold phase of the Last Glaciation. The Jabrudian and Levalloiso-Mousterian run successively from the end of the Last Glaciation through Early Würm to a post-Würm warm oscillation. In this case layers Ec–D would have been deposited in warmer or drier times as would layer Eb, and D–B would have been deposited in colder and/or wetter times. Such a succession appears to bear little relation to the faunal succession as a whole, as is shown, for instance, in the striking difference between the faunal composition of layers D and B. It must be stated that while the larger mammalian fauna as a whole shows considerable differences, the rodent fauna of this time from other sites shows little or no change and a continuing dry climate. There appears to be no good reason for regarding the one as a more reliable indicator than the other, and the issue is, therefore, in some doubt. Both, however, may be correct in that an increase in streams which run throughout the year is not necessarily due to increased pluviation, but may also be due to decreased evaporation and/or increased vegetational cover which holds back the run-off.

The radiocarbon dates which have been collected in recent years from long standing sections are not helpful and open to question. On first runs, they came out in the reverse order of the stratigraphic succession and, further, two dates for Tabun C came out with a wide difference, 40,900 ± 1,000 years and 45,000 ± 2,000 years B.P., while Tabun B produced a date, 39,500 ± 800 years B.P. which was not appreciably younger than that of Tabun C below. Such dates, are, however, in general accord with dates elsewhere in the region for the Levalloiso-Mousterian which range from as far back as *c.* 52,000 B.P. at Ras el Kelb. The dating evidence of the multi-disciplinary approach at Haua Fteah can be interpreted as showing that there is, in the Mediterranean, evidence for a warmer oscillation between two cold phases. If that is accepted then the Tabun C and D phase might well be a warmer oscillation in between two cooler or wetter phases, Tabun B and the basal layer G. This is a conclusion which would normally be drawn from such faunal evidence. The date of this warm oscillation would either be contemporary with the Brorüp oscillation in Europe (p. 42), or with the later oscillation shown as a probability at Haua Fteah *c.* 43,000 B.P. The radiocarbon date at Tabun C would suggest that the latter interpretation is in fact the correct one.

However, consideration of other data throws further doubt on the validity of the date, and data from es Skhul and el Wad point to another possible hypothesis. Of the human skeletons, Tabun I occurred near the surface of layer C, but may have been an intrusion from layer B above. Tabun II was found 1·2 metres below the top of layer C but underlies layer A, layer B having lensed out. There are some human remains from layer A which are almost certainly included in layer C. It is clear therefore that the radiocarbon date from layer C does not necessarily date the human remains in layer C, and it may also be noted that the roots of a Carob tree which was removed by the excavators had damaged a skeleton in that layer. The danger of possible contamination of the sample is obvious. All that can be said with certainty is that the human remains from layer C are later than or as early as the deposition of layer C. Of the skeletal types found in the cave, Tabun I is of the classic Neanderthal type, without chin eminence. There is no general agreement among physical anthropologists with regard to Tabun II. Some believe that the damaged jaw shows a chin eminence and that this is sufficient to exclude it from being a true Neanderthaler. Others do not agree and suggest that there was a homogeneous type of Neanderthaler present in Palestine at that time.

es Skhul The fauna includes a warthog, *Phacochoerus garrodae*, an African species which indicates the crossing of the deserts by the African animals in wetter times. The most common animal present is a large bovine. There is a difference of opinion as to whether the presence of large bovines indicates wet or dry conditions. Owing to the hard nature of the deposits and the difficulty of collection there is not sufficient evidence upon which to base further conclusions. Rhinoceros and hippopotamus are present. As both of these animals never live far from water there must have been water within hunting distance of the cave.

If the evidence of Haua Fteah is accepted that the large bovines are indicative, in

Pl. XI. Shanidar, Iran. Photo by courtesy of Professor Solecki

PL. XII. Bushman woman and child. (Photograph by P. L. Carter)

such areas as these, of drier conditions, then es Skhul may be contemporary with the high bovine contents and dry period in layers C and D of et Tabun. On the other hand these deposits may represent a later warmer oscillation.

Layer A at the top contains mixed industries. Some are of Natufian and some Advanced Palaeolithic and Levalloiso-Mousterian in type. There are also some pottery sherds.

Layer B1 contains a Levalloiso-Mousterian industry which is similar in type to the Levalloiso-Mousterian industries of Tabun. There are no handaxes among the *c*. 5,000 specimens.

Layer B2 also contains a Levalloiso-Mousterian industry of 4,800 flints. There are 3 handaxes, and in other respects as well as the smaller size of the flint implements and in the higher proportion of prepared striking platforms, is said to resemble Tabun D.

Layer C. This is again a Levalloiso-Mousterian industry. The flints are abraded, in contrast to those from the layers above. There are 414 artefacts.

el Wad The fauna of el Wad differs from that of the other caves at Mount Carmel. It contains 'modern' species in contrast to the archaic forms found in the es Skhul and et Tabun deposits. It has been considered that the high *Dama* contents of layer D show that wetter conditions had at that time set in and that prior to that there was a drier period in the lower half of the deposits. On the other hand there is a low bovine content throughout which, by analogy with the Haua Fteah data, could indicate wetter conditions than those which had presumably prevailed during the occupation of es Skhul and Tabun C, D and E.

Layer G at the base includes a number of Mousterian forms and also Emiran points (fig. 156, 3, 4), so called from the type site of el Emireh. The industry may be regarded as either transitional between the Advanced Palaeolithic and Middle Palaeolithic type industries, as a culture contact between the two, or simply as an admixture of two separate industries. It is regarded as the first stage of the Advanced Palaeolithic of Palestine.

Layer F also contains Emireh points and Advanced Palaeolithic type blades.

Layer E is also Advanced Palaeolithic in type and Aurignacian in quality. It contains a number of nosed scrapers (fig. 157, 13), after the manner of the Aurignacian of Western Europe. It lacks, however, the characteristic split-based bone points. It is regarded as the third stage of the Advanced Palaeolithic of Palestine (fig. 157, 24, 10–23), the second stage not being clearly represented at el Wad.

Layer D is regarded as Advanced Palaeolithic 4 (fig. 157, 9–24). It has carinated and rostrate scrapers (fig. 157, 13), peripherally retouched blades are common, and the industry is regarded as having an overall similarity to the Aurignacian of Western Europe.

Layer C. This industry is called the Atlitian. It has only been found at one other site, al Khiam, and represents stage 5 of the Palestinian Advanced Palaeolithic succession, with steep scrapers and prismatic burins predominant (fig. 157, 1–8). The Advanced Palaeolithic succession is not quite complete at Mount Carmel. Elsewhere there is an industry named the Kebaran which forms with the Skiftian and the Nebekian, a group of industries of Gravettoid character (fig. 158, 16–20), earlier than the Natufian, and which may represent, with the Zarzian from the Zarzi site and layer B2 of Shanidar (dated to *c*. 12,000 B.P.), an intrusion of late Gravettoid industries into the area.

Layer B2. The industry here is the Lower Natufian. It is a geometric Mesolithic industry with crescents (fig. 158, 2, 3), triangles, backed blades (fig. 158, 5), micro-burins (fig. 158, 7), sickle blades (fig. 158, 14) and burins (fig. 158, 9).

Layer B1 is a later Natufian and contains in addition arrow heads (fig. 158, 6).

In the Natufian layers the remains of over 60 burials were found. Among the finds were basalt pestles (fig. 158, 12), headdresses of dentalian shells, bone pendants (fig. 158, 11, 10), carved figures which include a human head in calcite, carved animal figures in bone (fig. 158, 15), bone sickle hafts (fig. 158, 14), and a wide variety of other bone tools. The industry has been dated by radiocarbon to 10,900 B.P. at Jericho where it is at the base of the deposits. There is no pottery in the layers.

Mount Carmel, therefore, has a bearing upon a number of the outstanding problems of prehistory, for example:

(1) Physical types, their relation to tool types, and the origin of Modern Man (*Homo sapiens sapiens*).
(2) The origin of the blade cultures of Europe.

With regard to the physical types, there is the hypothesis that Neanderthal Man evolved and specialized to, in the end, his extinction, and that eventually he was replaced by *H. sapiens sapiens*. The absence of evidence for two clear-cut distinct human types existing at the same time is inherent in this argument, and so far such a circumstance has not yet clearly been established. The question is not whether or not the Skhul and Tabun skeletons are contemporary in a geological or archaeological sense, but were they precisely contemporary? If so, they may represent interbreeding between a Neanderthal and a *H. sapiens sapiens* population and some authorities prefer this hypothesis. On the other hand, they may represent a simple variable population existing at that time, and evolving towards *Homo sapiens*. As the time relationship of Tabun and es Skhul, however, is far from being established, it may be said that on the available evidence the Levalloiso-Mousterian at Skhul could have occurred at any time during the long duration of the Levalloiso-Mousterian in the Levant, from before 52,000 B.P. to later than 34,000 B.P.

The second problem associated with the Mount Carmel industries is the origin of the Advanced Palaeolithic industries of Europe. Authorities differ in their opinion as to whether or not the Advanced Palaeolithic developed out of underlying Mousterian assemblages in a number of areas, or whether or not they represent an intrusion into Europe of a new cultural element from the East, associated with *Homo sapiens*.

It would appear possible that the Advanced Palaeolithic-type blades associated with the pre-Aurignacian, which appear to be of very early date in the Near East, are an earlier phase or the origin of the ultimate development of the Advanced Palaeo-lithic type industries. Support for this view has been increased by finds at Shanidar in Persia where there is a radiocarbon date for an Advanced Palaeolithic type industry of *c*. 34,000 B.P., which may be earlier than the industries in Western Europe. Further, the dates of even earlier Advanced Palaeolithic industries in the Near East and North Africa are anterior to those in Western Europe (Amudian, Libyan pre-Aurignacian).

SHANIDAR
(Solecki 1963)

The cave of Shanidar is in the Zagros mountains in Northern Iraq, just south of the Turkish border. It is 765 metres above sea level (pl. XI).

A study of the pollen grains from the deposits indicates a warmer climate than now with date palms in the vicinity at the beginning of the Mousterian occupation, followed by a cooler phase with increasing fir trees. Near to the top of Mousterian Layer D there is a return to a warmer climate, *c*. 46,000 B.P. Layer C above shows a dry steppe climate at the beginning of the Advanced Palaeolithic Baradostian layer *c*. 36,000 B.P. and a wetter and colder phase near to the end *c*. 27,000 B.P. There is then a hiatus in the occupation of the site of about 15,000 years to the base of Layer B. In B the pollen shows a cooler climate changing to a warmer one *c*. 12,000 B.P. In general these oscillations are in agreement with the climatic oscillations at Haua Fteah.

The greater part of the faunal remains have not yet been published; the main species represented, sheep, goat and deer, are not highly sensitive to climatic change and the faunal fluctuations may be due to changing economies rather than to climatic oscillation.

Layer D at the base of the deposits contains a Mousterian industry and seven Neanderthal skeletons which were thought in part at least to have been killed by a roof fall. They are said to be of the classic Neanderthal type similar to those of et Tabun. The industry contains the typical Mousterian points and racloirs, but differs from the Mount Carmel Mousterian in the absence of the Levallois technique. Layer D, from a sample taken from above one of the skeletons and near to the top of the layer, is radiocarbon dated to *c*. 50,000 B.P.

Layer C is variously dated by radiocarbon from 28,500 to 29,500 B.P. at the top and 33,300 to 35,000 B.P. below. It contains an industry known as the Baradostian. This is a crude industry with faint Aurignacian characters and is said to be advanced Palaeolithic in character. The main characteristic is said to be a number of burins with a number of blade facets and blade-like cores. It is generally different in type from the industry in Layer D.

Above the Baradostian layer (C), there is a Mesolithic industry, layer B2 which underlies a proto-Neolithic level B1; on the top of the succession there are Neolithic to recent artefacts.

Layer B2 contains a number of triangles, crescents and backed blades of Gravettian type and is dated by radiocarbon *c.* 12,000 B.P. The proto-Neolithic assemblage includes a number of bone, slate and stone tools with incised decoration and is dated by radiocarbon to *c.* 12,000 B.P. The neighbouring site of Zawi Chemi Shanidar is thought to have the earliest known 'domesticated' animal, the sheep, and is dated to 10,870 ± 300 years B.P.

The early date of the Baradostian suggests a possible link in this area between these Advanced Palaeolithic industries and the Amudian; however from the published data it is not clear that the Baradostian is to be considered as a true Advanced Palaeolithic type industry.

Recently a study of the floral remains associated with one of the Neanderthal skeletons at Shanidar suggests that the body was covered with flowers at the time of its interment (Leroi-Gourham 1968).

19

India and Pakistan

THE earliest evidence for the presence of man in Pakistan and India is in the Soan valley of the northern Punjab (Movius 1948). Here the raw material available for tool manufacture is a fine-grained quartzite and Panjal trap, both of which are available in limitless quantities. Near Rawalpindi have been recovered quantities of large quartzite flakes, percussion-struck but heavily rolled. The flakes have inclined platforms and generally show cortex on their dorsal face; no true secondary flaking has been recognized, nor is there much evidence of preliminary work on the parent rock. Battered edges are in all probability due to rolling by natural agencies. These flakes occur in fan-gravels of a boulder conglomerate associated with the moraine of the Second Himalayan glaciation, and it is uncertain therefore whether or not this 'Punjab Flake Industry' can be accepted as of human manufacture.

The first unequivocable evidence for early man occurs in deposits of the succeeding climatic phase, the 'Second Interglacial', in the Soan Valley. The geological evidence for this date is that the cultural material occurs with terrace gravels on the surface of a boulder conglomerate linked with the Second Himalayan glaciation, and in a rolled state with gravels connected with the third glaciation. This material, grouped together under the cultural term Soan, consists of river pebbles flaked along one edge to produce a series of sharp intersections. Some of the quartzite or lava lumps flaked in this way are basically Oldowan in type, and these 'choppers', as they are called, are different from the Soan 'chopping-tool', which in theory consists of a flat pebble flaked on both faces along one edge or peripherally to form a discoid. Typologically, the Soan has been divided into various phases, in the same way as Acheulean material has been grouped, but this need not indicate any progressive passage of time. In general terms, smaller-sized Soan industries (fig. 159, 8–11) occur in geologically later phases, but typology alone here, as elsewhere, is no guide to chronology. 'Early Soan' industries, which have been recognized from a number of sites in the Indus watershed, contain choppers made on water-worn pebbles flaked either from a natural cleavage surface or from the original surface of the pebble itself (fig. 159, 4), chopping-tools with alternate flaked edges (bifacial) and irregular wavy cutting edges, discoidal cores (fig. 159, 2) and flakes (fig. 159, 1, 3). The flakes bear little signs of secondary

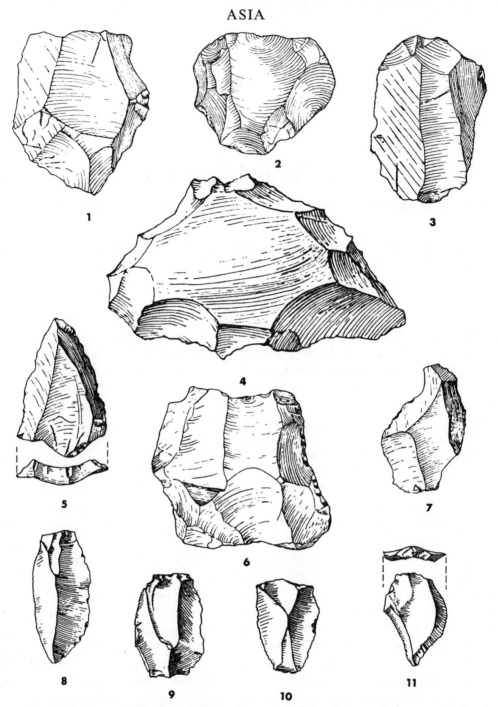

FIG. 159. Soan, India ½; 1–4 Early Soan. 1, 3 flake; 2 core; 4 chopper; 5–7 Late Soan A. 5 prepared flake; 6 core; 7 flake; 8–11 Late Soan B. 8–10 flakes; 11 prepared flake. *From Movius 1948*

retouch, although utilization has left blunted edges, and often cortex remains on the dorsal face. A small number of flakes show greater preparation of the core prior to flake detachment, and some examples of rudimentary prepared platforms have been reported. 'Late Soan' industries occur in gravels correlated with the Third glacial phase of the Himalayan sequence, and some evidence suggests that Soan-like industries were being practised as late as Third Interglacial times. The pebble tool element is reduced and flake artefacts make up a major part of these assemblages (fig. 159, 5–11); prepared cores with faceted platforms occur and their flakes (fig. 159, 5, 11) are associated with greater quantities of plain flakes with inclined platforms (fig. 159, 7–10). Little secondary retouch has been recorded, but utilization traces are present.

Soan industries in the northern Punjab appear to be typologically indistinguishable from assemblages in northern India near Rawalpindi, and it may be that this area, immediately south of the Himalayan glacial belt, represents a culture-province entirely distinct from the contemporaneous Acheulean traditions to the south. Soan-like artefacts (fig. 160, 3) are claimed from many of these Acheulean industries, but these are unlikely to indicate little more than a common method of preparing pebbles for work.

All of the lithic industries of the Indian sub-continent have been broadly grouped under the terms Early, Middle and Late Stone Age. The Early Stone Age industries appear to consist of at least two traditions, the Soan (described above) and the Acheulean. The Acheulean industries, characterized by bifacial handaxes, are found principally in central and southern India, extending as far south as Madras province; the early recognition of such industries in Madras has led to the term Madrasian for this material. However, these industries in the sub-continent are very clearly aligned in their typology to those of western Asia, Africa and western Europe, and might therefore be classified under the general name Acheulean.

Quartzite was the major source of material for the handaxe industries (fig. 160), in which flake cleavers are an important element (fig. 160, 4). Both the use of quartzite and the production of cleavers have been considered to demonstrate a close relationship between the Indian Acheulean and the Acheulean of central and southern Africa, presumably via western Asia. Some of the typologically developed Acheulean industries of India contain a prepared core element with faceted-platform flakes, as well as ovate handaxes with twisted cutting edges; the latter feature, and the presence of flake cleavers, may indicate a comparable functional relationship with those from Bed IV at the Olduvai Gorge, East Africa. The Indian industries do not, however, contain much evidence of stone balls which have on occasion been considered as bolas stones in Africa. Other typological differences include local Indian production in advanced Acheulean industries of finely flaked discoid (fig. 160, 2) and ovoid tools, and beaked tools which may have served as borers and hollow scrapers.

Our knowledge of these industries is far from complete because of the absence of full description of living or factory sites. A high proportion of the material has been

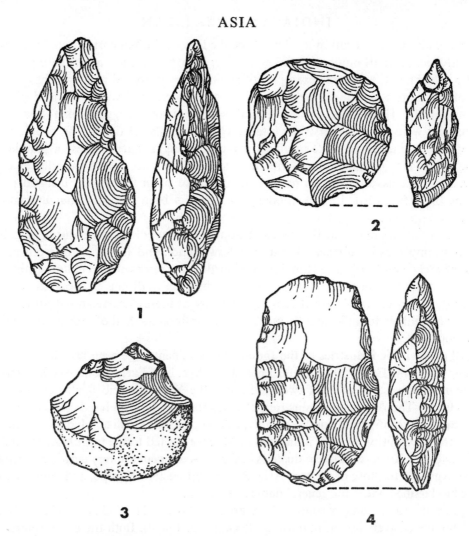

FIG. 160. Madrasian (Acheulean); Attirampakkam, India ½. *After Allchin 1963*

obtained from river terrace gravels, and although these occurrences may assist in the establishment of a relative chronology and typological development, they can tell us little about the life of the makers.

Quantities of Acheulean quartzite material has been recovered from river terraces near Madras. The deposits consist of riverine sands and silts, and redeposited laterites. At Vadamaduri, rolled typologically early handaxes in a conglomerate with sand-gravel were stratigraphically succeeded by finer Acheulean axes of ovate or pointed forms deposited in detrital laterite and associated with retouched flakes. At Attirampakkam, fine Acheulean artefacts occur in a basal laterite gravel of the Kortalayar 20-foot river terrace (fig. 160). In southern India, there is evidence of alternating phases of aggradation and erosion by rivers, but correlations of these with the glacial phases of the north are uncertain, and the Attirampakkam industry cannot therefore be assumed to be contemporaneous with the third, or any, Himalayan glaciation.

An important stratified site with Acheulean material is in the Narbada valley of central India. The Pleistocene sequence here commences with a laterite deposition during a tropical climatic period with much rain and hot dry seasons. The top of this deposit is weathered, and is covered by a coarse conglomerate containing Acheulean handaxes and cleavers with associated Middle Pleistocene fauna of *Elephas namadicus* and *Hexaprotodon namadicus* (hippo). The conglomerate is sealed by sands and silt which are separated from overlying gravels, sands and silt by an unconformity. These uppermost deposits have yielded Soan material associated with a fauna comparable to that of the conglomerate. Climatic evidence suggests that the Acheulean here is to be correlated with a period of at least seasonal drying, following a wet phase.

In northern India and Pakistan, rolled bifacial handaxes occur in gravels correlated with the Second Interglacial and Third Glacial of the Himalayan sequence. Certain of the forms recovered are heavy and coarse bifaces, but other sites have yielded finer handaxes of lanceolate, ovate and cordiform shapes. Cleavers, discoidal cores and retouched flakes are associated with these more evolved axes. At Chauntra in the Soan valley a series of artefacts were incorporated in gravels believed to be of Third Glacial age. The assemblage consists of rolled heavy handaxes, less rolled handaxes of more developed forms, and unrolled ovate and pointed handaxes, faceted platform flakes and discoidal cores. The developed handaxe industry here has been compared with Madrasian assemblages. The belief that both Soan and Acheulean traditions were separate entities in the northern Punjab, coalescing only in developed stages, is hardly tenable on the evidence available; nevertheless, the distributional and chronological evidence from India and eastern Asia does tend to indicate that the overall pebble and flake tradition became well established early in the Middle Pleistocene, and that handaxe industries only appeared as a minor episode in central and southern India. Two distinct movements appear to be indicated.

The Ratnapura industries of south-western Ceylon, which occur at varying levels in the Gem sands, also illustrate the tradition of unspecialized production of functionally efficient tools which is dominant throughout much of south and eastern Africa. The artefacts, on pebbles of chert, jasper and quartz, are associated with *Hexaprotodon*, and indicate the penetration of this territory by hunters during a phase of low sea-level; a drop of the order of 60 feet would allow an easy passage.

From these industries of the Early Stone Age developed, seemingly without external influences, the Middle Stone Age traditions which are characterized and defined by a dominance of tools made on flakes (Allchin 1959). Quartz is rarely employed in these industries and chert types were selected for the production of suitable flakes, using either a discoidal core technique for round flakes or more oblong cores for long flakes and flake-blades; in both cases preparation of the platform was sometimes carried out. The discoidal method involved careful preparation of the cores, in Levallois-Mousterian fashion (fig. 161, 4); the other class of cores are less well-prepared, but careful flaking was done to control the fracture and obtain more lengthy flakes from the flat river pebbles often used for raw material. The cores so produced, either by discoidal or other methods, were often used as choppers or scrapers, and formed a heavy element in an otherwise light industry. The flakes themselves were occasionally retouched steeply, or were utilized without retouch, and wear marks were evident. Some flakes were trimmed into beaked or hollow scrapers (fig. 161, 5), and re-trimming was often carried out on dulled edges. The hollow scrapers appear to have been a popular element in the equipment of the Middle Stone Age, and in double form results in a flaked tool probably used as a scraper or an awl. It has been suggested that this beaked tool was a functional substitute for the burin, the latter being extremely rare in India. Stone points too are rather uncommon, and possibly indicate the use of bone or wood for projectile-heads. In total, the Middle Stone Age assemblages appear to represent wood-working activities, and it is probable that the essential tools of these industries have perished.

At Pandav Falls, in central India, a small factory site of the Middle Stone Age yielded an industry of flake tools and cores (fig. 161, 1–4). This site lies on the northern edge of an extension of the Vindhya hills, where the Central Indian uplands fall away to the low-lying alluvium of the Ganges — Jamuna Doab. The industry is unrolled, although it appears to have been heavily weathered through exposure and erosion of the containing soil and underlying sandstone. The flakes from Pandav were struck from prepared cores (fig. 161, 4), including some with faceted platforms. Retouched flakes are rare, but a few concave edges as well as convex edges had been prepared. Tortoise cores and discoidal cores are present, as well as small pebble choppers and a bifacially-flaked quartz handaxe. Of the large quantity of flakes, some are core-preparation flakes, others were utilized as tools. The association here, and elsewhere, of handaxes and flake industries probably represents nothing more than a developing tradition based on a greater importance for the flake element which was always present in the Acheulean of Africa, Europe and western Asia. It would in fact be surprising if handaxes were never found with Middle Stone Age industries. A more interesting problem is the relationship of these industries to the Late Soan tradition of the north (see below).

Flake industries have been recovered from widespread areas of peninsular India, and various regional groups have been distinguished. Again, it would be surprising if industrial features were uniform over a territory which contains varying environmental situations. In western India, the flake industries of the Middle Stone Age are apparently restricted to areas of higher rainfall, and excluded through climatic reasons from the Sind desert and adjacent regions. In north-east India, little trace has been found in the Gangetic plains, or the eastern foothills of the mountains. To the north-west, in the western foothills of the Himalayan chain, Late Soan material appears to fall typologically within the variability range of Middle Stone Age industries, and provides the earliest dating evidence for the latter, with associations in the second phase of

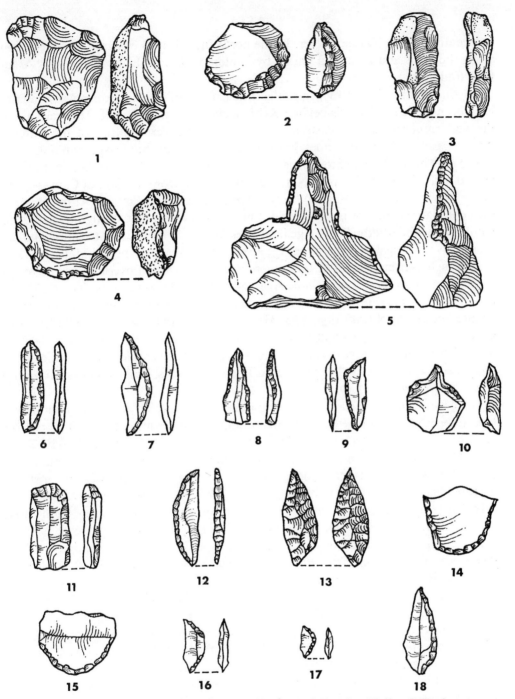

FIG. 161. 1–5 Middle Stone Age, India $\frac{3}{5}$; 1–4 Pandav Falls; 5 Keslapur, North Deccan; 6–18 Late Stone Age, India and Ceylon *c*. $\frac{1}{1}$; 6–11 Bara-simla, India; 12–14 Bandarawela, Ceylon; 15–18 Bombay region, India. *After Allchin 1963*

aggradation of the Narbada river. In the north there is also evidence of penetration along the Oxus and mountain passes by hunters with knowledge of the west Asian flake traditions.

On the central plateau of peninsular India, finds of Middle Stone Age material have been made southwards beyond Krishna river, but there is still little trace along the western coasts, and in eastern central India. The Teri industry of the extreme southern part of the country does, however, contain Middle Stone Age material.

The date of the Middle Stone Age flake industries rests upon correlations between aggradation phases of the upper Narmada river inland from the Gulf of Cambay, and of the Pravara river near Bombay, with external climatic oscillations. At the moment such correlations are not possible, and it may only be said that stratigraphically and typologically the Middle Stone Age industries follow the Acheulean tradition and are eventually succeeded by Late Stone Age assemblages (Wainwright and Malik 1967).

Although over large areas of India there is little evidence of overlapping and merging Middle Stone Age — Late Stone Age traditions, in the west, in the central Deccan and in the extreme south, sites have been found which suggest continuity of material culture and geographical siting. Near Hyderabad, and in the Krishna valley, factory sites of Late Stone Age hunters were positioned immediately adjacent to Middle Stone Age occupation areas; south of Madras, typological considerations indicate the presence of what can only be called transitional industries. The intimate relationship is even more marked in Ceylon.

The generally post-glacial lithic assemblages of India which are grouped under the term Late Stone Age range from fine microlithic industries in central India to coarser variants in the west and Deccan and to southern industries with strong Middle Stone Age affinities (Allchin 1963). The deliberate choice of raw materials may have contributed to some of the basic dissimilarities. To the north and west of northern Mysore, fine-grained rocks were used as raw material, including jasper, agate and cornelian; the resultant tools must have been a source of visual pleasure to the user. To the south, including Ceylon, quartz was deliberately chosen for artefacts.

In central India, numerous caves and shelters as well as open sites have yielded quantities of lithic material, ranging from factory sites to short-lived occupation areas. At Barasimla near Jabalpur a large workshop area yielded cores, primary flakes and blades, core-rejuvenation flakes and other debris with relatively few finished tools; the latter included end and thumbnail scrapers, small points, microlithic triangles and crescents, small backed blades and points and awls (fig. 161, 6–11). This and the other industries in this region are in the blade tradition, using cylindrical or conical cores. Blunting retouch formed knives or points, and geometric forms are common. Flake knives or scrapers were obtained from small prepared cores, but in this area there is little evidence of the relationship between the Middle and Late Stone Age traditions. Little evidence of bone work has survived, but there is reason to suppose that this played an important part in the industry. There is also presumptive evidence that the paintings in some of the occupied caves and shelters were the product of Late Stone Age activities. These paintings tend to represent events rather than isolated objects, and are drawn in a simple but suggestive style; the scenes include herds of deer or antelope, hunters with spear, shield, bow and arrow, dancing figures, and disguised or totemic human figures with animal heads.

The Late Stone Age industries of western India in general are considered to represent an intrusive tradition, supplanting the Middle Stone Age material culture. A general contrast has been made between the geometric microlithic assemblages of the west, with typological affinities to Zarzian-like material in Iraq, and the non-geometric assemblages of the south and east which may stem entirely from indigenous sources.

In northern Gujarat the late Stone Age lithic tradition is comparable to that of central India, and represents probably the first occupation of this marginal area during a time when sufficient water was available. There is some evidence that occupation continued through a phase of wetter climate until and after the knowledge of pottery-making had been carried into the region.

To the south, near Bombay, sites on peninsulas or small islands have yielded coastal variants in Late Stone Age tradition. Some implements tend to be larger, but the same small elements occur, geometric forms, backed blades and points (fig. 161, 15–18). Other regional variants are known from eastern central India, where the use of quartz as raw material contributes to the contrast between these industries and those of the west. In the south, on the Mysore plateau, quartz was also used extensively but here the industries are remarkably similar to those on finer-grained rock from the Krishna valley.

Another group of coastal sites in the south have been recognized at Tinnevelly, Madras, where they are associated with sand dunes of former shore lines, at 6–9 metres and 16 metres above the present sea level. The higher industries, on chert, are of essentially Middle Stone Age character, and the lower material consists of finely-prepared microlithic industries utilizing small prepared cores and prismatic blade cores of quartz and chert. The flakes were retouched into lunates, transverse arrow-heads and points. Also present are bifacially-flaked quartz points. These Teri sites are linked industrially with the Late Stone Age of Ceylon, particularly in the south-east where inland caves and shelters have yielded lithic material, on quartz, of this general character associated with shell, bone and antler objects (Allchin 1958). Perforated shells probably served as wood-planes or as utensils for peeling fruit and vegetables. The quartz implements exhibit a highly developed technique of production, and many of the forms are extremely small. Bifacial points, lunates and backed blades, scrapers and arrowheads are characteristic types (fig. 161, 12–14). The sites of this group include small settlements and large factory areas; a factory site at Bandarawela yielded quantities of preparation material. It is possible that quartz was broken up at this site by a method of heating the rock and then shattering it by percussion. Up until recent times some of the caves containing Late Stone Age material, sometimes called the Bandarawelian industry, were occupied by the Veddas, a nomadic hunting people, and it is possible that a direct line from the Stone Age to modern groups will be demonstrated here.

A midden of the Bandarawelian industry at Bellan Bandi Palassa yielded food remains of deer, pig, monkey, squirrel, elephant and lizard, as well as quantities of snails and mussels. Broken human bones also occurred in the debris, distinct in their treatment from intact flexed burials also laid in the midden. These human remains have been termed the Balangodese people. A late Bandarawelian industry at Udupi-yan, in Balangoda district, contained sun-baked and fired pottery, and appears to have been associated with ground stone axes.

As in parts of sub-Saharan Africa, there can be no doubt that certain Late Stone Age groups of India and Ceylon maintained their traditional methods of existence to a time well after that when agriculture first began in these regions. Stratified sites exist where microlithic industries occur beneath Neolithic occupation, and there is little tangible evidence of any considerable overlap, but nevertheless the existence in the recent past of hunting communities in remote areas of central India and in both the western and eastern Ghats, as in Ceylon, must indicate a long continuance of Late Stone Age traditions.

20

South and East Asia

THE distribution of the Soan pebble and flake industries of India and Pakistan appears to fall conveniently between the early industries of the west (north-east Africa and south-west Asia) and the pebble and flake industries of Burma, Malaya and other regions of south-east Asia. The distribution of these industries in Asia suggests a relatively rapid and direct penetration south of the Himalayas into Burma and beyond (fig. 162). Although the distances involved in this postulated movement are enormous, and typological similarities between industries of this character may be considered suspect, it is likely that some relationship exists in terms of human penetration and endeavour between the Soan and the other pebble and flake industries to the south and east. Such industries represent the first evidence for the presence of man in this region, and indicate a colonization of areas linked by accessible land-bridges during periods of low sea-levels, bridges which may have allowed relatively easy movement between areas inaccessible to one another through extensive and impenetrable vegetation. The lowering of the sea during a glacial episode would expose areas of muds and sands along the previous shore which might be suitable for population drift or deliberate movement.

Although separated from the Soan industrial province by some 1200 km, the industrial material from the terrace system of the Irrawaddy in Burma represents the closest geographical neighbour of the Soan area (Movius 1948). This material has been called Anyathian (fig. 163–164). In the upper Irrawaddy river, a series of terrace gravels has been dated to a period from the Second Himalayan glaciation to near the end of the Pleistocene, although such correlations rest upon a proposed relationship between the glaciations and pluvial episodes. The earliest Anyathian material is associated in the valley with lateritic gravels and conglomerates which are believed to represent heavy rainfall conditions, and which are correlated with the Second Himalayan glaciation. There followed a dry period with terrace gravel deposition, succeeded by an episode of heavy rainfall and red earth deposition which is correlated with the Third Himalayan glaciation. Anyathian material is associated with deposits both of the dry and wet phases.

The artefacts are made on pebbles of silicified tuff and on pieces of fossil wood. The

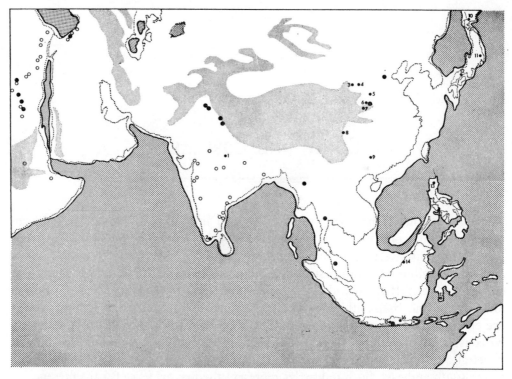

FIG. 162. Distribution of important Pleistocene sites in Southern Asia.
● Pebble and flake industries ('chopper-chopping tools'); ○ Handaxe
industries; • Other sites mentioned in text: 1. Pandav Falls, India;
2. Tinnevelly, India; 3. Shui-tung-kou, China; 4. Sjara-osso-gol, China;
5. Ting-ts'un, China; 6. Sha-yuan, China; 7. Lantian county, China;
8. Tzu-yang, China; 9. Lai-pin, China; 10. Shirataki, Japan; 11. Gongenyama, Japan; 12. Ishima, Japan; 13. Cabalwan, Philippines; 14. Niah,
Sarawak; 15. Ngandong, Java; 16. Trinil, Java; 17. Tjabenge, Celebes.
Shoreline drawn at c. −200 metres to indicate presumed exposure of
Sunda shelf in south-east Asia. Shaded areas +2000 metres

latter occurs in Tertiary formations in Burma from the Upper Chindwin to the Gulf of
Wartaban, and was available in abundance to Pleistocene man. Such material controlled to a certain extent the manner in which flaking could be successfully applied,
because the longitudional grain of the wood allowed flaking only in one plane. Many
of the pieces therefore have been flaked at one end to form an irregular but effective
cutting edge. The Anyathian artefacts on tuff followed this tradition, although tuff
could have been flaked in different planes.

The tools of the Anyathian have been grouped into various categories of implement, categories which have been applied to the stone industries of the Soan,
Tampanian, Fingnoian, Patjitanian and Choukoutienian (Movius 1948). The

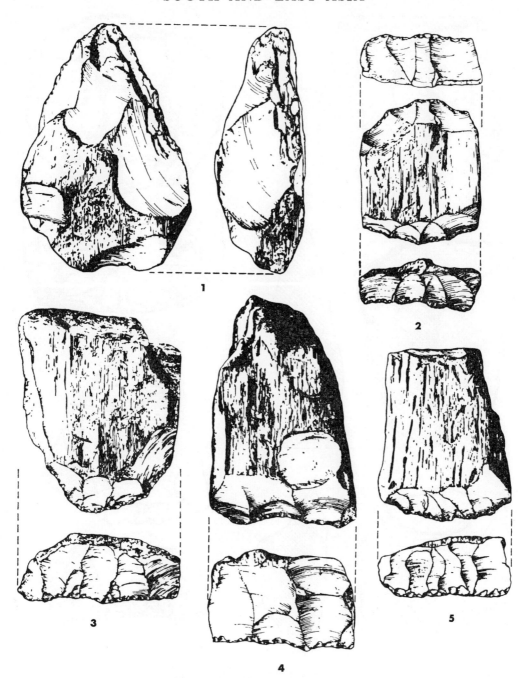

FIG. 163. Anyathian, Burma ½; Fossil wood. 1 proto handaxe; 2–5 hand-adzes. *From Movius 1948*

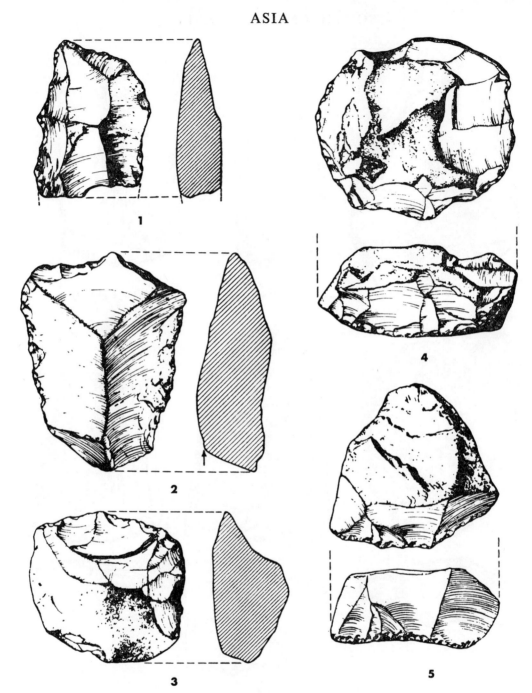

FIG. 164. Anyathian, Burma ½; Silicified tuff. 1–2 flakes; 3 pick; 4 chopper; 5 hand-adze. *From Movius 1948*

Anyathian 'chopper' consists of a pebble or block with one curved or straight working edge; secondary work has been confined to one face of the tool, so this implement may be termed unifacial (fig. 164, 4). The cutting edge may be convex, straight or even concave, and utilization traces are abundant. These choppers may be as large as 23 cm. in length. The 'chopping-tool' of this industry is bifacial, with the cutting edge produced by the intersection of flake scars on both faces of the pebble or block. These tools form an important element in the Anyathian industries. A third category is the 'hand-adze', which is a flattened elongated block of material with unifacial retouch at one end; the Anyathian use of fossil wood as raw material contributes to the shape of this tool, and for this reason a very high proportion of the artefacts in the Anyathian industries on fossil wood are 'hand-adzes', which may be single (fig. 163, 3–5) or double-ended (fig. 163, 2). The angle of retouch on these varies between 45° and 75°, and some examples of reverse retouch occur. The cutting edge of these tools may be convex, straight or concave. The fourth category of implement in the pebble or flake industries of south-eastern Asia is the 'proto-handaxe', which is rare in the Anyathian (fig. 163, 1); this tool was made on a flake or a pebble, with unifacial retouch assisting to form a sharp point; cortex remains on the rounded butt. Flake tools do not appear to have formed a basic element in the Anyathian; those that are present have plain inclined platforms, and only a few have been re-touched (fig. 164, 1–2). Cores with roughly prepared platforms occur, and were used for the detachment of small flakes and flake-blades; few of these have been recognized in the rolled industries of the Anyathian.

Typologically the Anyathian industries, which occur in four terrace gravels of the Irrawaddy River, have been divided into Early and Late, but there are few essential differences between these except perhaps in the smaller quantities of 'hand-adzes' in the later assemblages. The lower terrace gravels appear to be of late Pleistocene age, and in fact there is evidence to suggest that the Anyathian tradition was still in force until and after agriculturists had entered the area.

This pebble and flake tradition in Burma has also been recognized in Thailand, in gravels of the Kwae Noi River near the Burmese border (Heider 1958). The artefacts occur in terrace gravels approximately 6–11 metres above the present river, and were made on quartzites, sandstone and other rocks. These pebble-tools, which have been called Fingnoian, are unifacially-flaked and there is no evidence of bifacial work; most of the retouch consists of a series of flakes removed from one edge or end of the pebble. Some peripheral retouch occurs on flat pebbles. A flake element is present but there is little evidence of secondary retouch. Nor is there much material suitable for dating purposes.

A related industry farther south, the Tampanian of Malaya, represents a further geographical element in the pebble and flake traditions. The type site for this industry is at Kota Tampan in north-western Malaya (Walker and Sieveking 1962). In western Malaya alluvial material lies consistently at about 230 feet above mean sea-level. The absence of evidence for isostatic changes, and other geological observations, have prompted the view that these represent deposition under an eustatic sea some 230 feet higher than that of today. Three high sea levels have been recognized in Java and Sumatra, and the Kota Tampan alluvium is correlated with the highest of these. At Kota Tampan, coarse water-worn gravels occur at this level, and have been interpreted as deriving from an early period in the recession of the high sea, when the Perak river was rejuvenated and enabled to carry coarse material. The deposition of the gravels would not have occurred at this level after the sea level had fallen appreciably, and so a date early in a glacial period is indicated. It has been suggested that this period may be early Mindel.

At Kota Tampan the gravels contained, generally in their lower part, a series of chipped pebbles and flakes. These are rolled, but in many cases only slightly, and are therefore believed to be almost contemporary with the gravel deposition. Most of the artefacts are of quartzite, but quartz pebbles and hornfels were also employed. The problem of core or flake preferences is unimportant here, as it should be in most studies of industrial material; pebbles or tabular lumps were used as raw sources for choppers, and smaller tools such as scrapers were made on flakes. The flakes in the industry are often thin and regular, exhibiting primary scars on the back, but there is no evidence of faceted platforms. The retouch on these flakes is rather coarse and steep. The tools as a whole appear to fall into functional categories, such as points (fig. 165, 1–4), cleavers, picks, and scrapers (fig. 165, 5–7), although there is little doubt that such terms mask a variety of other functions and multiple-use artefacts.

Pebble picks, with several flake scars at one end either on one face only or on both faces, are present in the Kota Tampan industry, and these, as well as pointed tools made on small river pebbles (fig. 165, 1–3), are generally on quartz. Larger pointed artefacts (or proto-handaxes) were made by flaking pebbles on the converging edges of one face only. Flake tools (fig. 165, 4–7) include pointed forms, and scrapers or knives; few of these are retouched, and represent convenient and standardized flake shapes presumably used at the pointed end or along a naturally sharp edge.

Pebbles were also flaked on one surface to form a steep convex edge, and these cleaver-like tools (choppers) show little difference from a few bifacially-worked pebbles (chopping-tools) which have also been classified as cleavers. The remainder of the industry consists of flakes lacking any recognizable typological features, pebbles of uncertain validity as artefacts, and oblong flakes which, although they might be considered as hand-adzes, are perhaps entirely fortuitous. Quartzite hammerstones are also present.

The Tampanian industry of Malaya is of considerable importance in that it represents an occupation in the Far East of a group using a pebble and flake industry at a time when the great handaxe tradition of the western Old World had only recently been developed. The correlation dates of the Tampanian with those of the west and north suggest that man was present in Malaya, and without doubt elsewhere in the Far East, early in the Middle Pleistocene. The movement of man in these areas may have been facilitated by expanses of land linking the mainland of Thailand, Vietnam

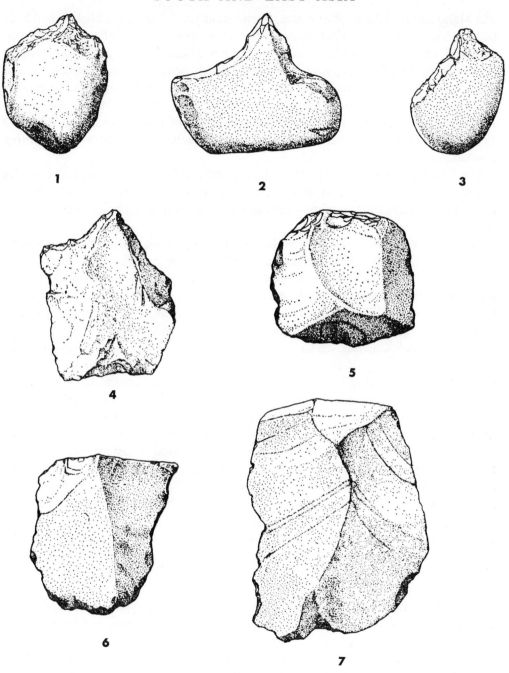

FIG. 165. Tampanian, Malaya $\frac{1}{1}$; Kota Tampan. 1–3 pebble points; 4 flake point; 5–7 flake scrapers. *From Walker and Sieveking 1962*

and Malaya to the islands of Sumatra, Borneo and Java. The Sunda Shelf would have been at least partially exposed during Pleistocene low sea-levels (fig. 162), and was exploited early in the Pleistocene by a faunal assemblage called Siva-Malayan, considered to be of Villafranchian affinities, which penetrated through Burma and Malaya into Java. Elements of this early fauna have been recognized in the Irrawaddy deposits of Burma, but not in any association with artefacts. The Middle Pleistocene faunal assemblage, Sino-Malayan, also occupied parts of Burma, southern China and Java, indicating a further period when the Sunda Shelf was accessible for migrating animals.

The Celebes almost alone appear to have remained isolated during these episodes of low sea-level, the Macassar Strait proving an effective barrier, although here too there is some later evidence of man's persistence in extending his range of distribution (p. 393).

Java, however, was reached in Middle Pleistocene times, and a pebble and flake tradition was established (van Heekeren 1957). A large quantity of stone artefacts has been recovered from southern central Java, and this has been called Patjitanian after the type site. Most of the objects are of silicified tuff, but limestone and fossil wood was also used. The large pebbles of raw material were shattered by percussion, and the resulting flakes were used or modified. Some of the flakes are enormous, over 30 cm. long and weighing up to 7 pounds. Other flakes are small and have been retouched. A majority of the flake artefacts are ordinary flakes with little sign of preliminary work, and although some evidence of faceted platform flakes exist (fig. 166, 1–2), there is no evidence of a true tortoise core element; discoidal cores are conspicuously absent. Nevertheless, the presence of flake-blades (fig. 166, 6–7) in an industry otherwise noted for its heavy elements is important, and represents a lithic tradition as advanced in this respect as any other yet found in eastern Asia in Middle Pleistocene contexts. Some of these flakes have irregular retouch on edges and ends (fig. 166, 1–3) and utilization traces. The basic tools of the Patjitanian, however, are large flakes or pebbles retouched on one face or on both faces to form choppers and chopping-tools. Choppers form the largest element in heavy equipment; most of these have convex working-edges formed by unifacial retouch of the step variety. Chopping-tools on water-worn pebbles are comparable in appearance to Anyathian forms. Hand-adzes, with single-end retouch on oblong flakes, were sharpened by unifacial trimming. Large flakes with flaking over much of the dorsal surface, and with a rounded butt, are classed as 'proto-handaxes' although the typological relationship between these and hand-adzes appears to be one of difference only in degree and not in intent. Nevertheless, a small number of Patjitanian artefacts might well be described as handaxes in African contexts; these pointed tools have been retouched from the pointed end, the flake scars running roughly parallel to the longer axis of the implement. Cortex often remains on the butt. The fact that most of these categories grade into one another does not allow of the opinion that the Patjitanian industry possesses true handaxes in western Old World fashion.

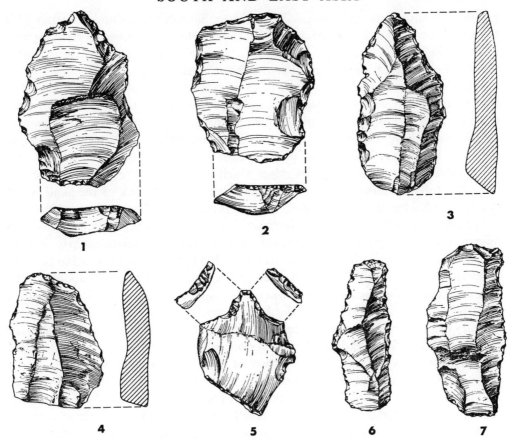

FIG. 166. Patjitanian, Java ½. *From Movius 1948*

The stratigraphical position of the Patjitanian is not well-established, because much of this material is in a derived state in recent gravels of the Basoka River; some rolled artefacts are reported from late Pleistocene gravels of the same river. The industry is often considered to have been manufactured at a time when the Upper Trinil Beds were being deposited. No certain evidence of this industry has been recovered from the Lower Trinil Beds, wherein the various remains of *Homo erectus* (formerly *Pithecanthropus*) have been found.

The detailed stratigraphy of the Middle Pleistocene deposits in this area may be reduced to two major series, the lower and earlier Putjangan Beds containing a Djetis fauna with *Cervus zwaani*, *Antilope modjokertensis* and *Leptobos cosijni*, and yielding remains of *Homo erectus* (*Homo modjokertensis*, *Pithecanthropus* IV and recent finds). The upper series, of Kabuh Beds with a Trinil fauna of *Stegodon*, *Elephas namadicus* and *Bos palaeosondaicus*, have yielded other remains of *Homo erectus* (*Pithecanthropus* I–III and recent finds). The sites from which these and the earlier finds have been made include Modjokerto, Sangiran and Trinil. The mandible from Kedung Brubus is now considered not to be certainly classified as *Homo erectus* (Tobias 1966). Potassium-argon dates within the geological sequence have indicated that *Homo erectus* was present in the area *c.* 500,000 years ago.

The *Homo erectus* finds from Java in their general morphological characteristics may be compared with the Choukoutien fossils from north China, and with finds recently made at Lantian in Shensi province, China. The Chinese representatives of *Homo erectus* have a cranial capacity ranging from 850 to 1300 c.c., the Javanese from 775 to 900 c.c. The average of all known *H. erectus* skulls is about 1000 c.c. The skull itself has prominent brow ridges which form a shelf-like projection over the face. The forehead slopes away from these ridges and the back of the skull is not evenly rounded but is rather pointed. The jaw is massive and projecting and the chin is receding. The teeth are large and the canine is massive, but overall they are basically human. The limbs bones of *H. erectus* demonstrate quite a close relationship to those of modern man, and, as in the Australopithecines, they have been considered to be more 'modern' than the skull. The height of *H. erectus* seems to have been about 5 feet.

A later occupation of Java is indicated by a flake industry on chalcedony which was found in the upper gravels of the Notopoero Beds at Sangiran. A comparable industry has been recovered from a terrace in the Solo valley at Korsono. The industry consists of flakes, flake-blades and cores of chalcedony, some of which were retouched into scrapers, knives, points and awls. Most of the flakes are small, less than 7 cm. in length. Bone and antler artefacts also occur. At Ngandong in the Solo valley, some 20 miles downstream from Trinil, a number of fragmentary human skulls have been found; all of the remains come from a small area some 50 by 100 metres, and are associated with some antler picks, sting-ray fragments, stone balls of andesite and small jasper and chalcedony flakes. The fluviatile beds at Ngandong are considered to be of the late Upper Pleistocene, and associated fauna here and with the Sangiran industries contains a number of extinct forms. The presumed maker of these industries, *Homo sapiens soloensis*, possessed a skull with thick cranial wall, a visor-like supra-orbital ridge, a receding flat forehead and strong occipital ridges; the average cranial capacity was 1250 c.c.

The exposure of the Sunda Shelf during Pleistocene low sea levels has been noted previously, and the point made that such a sea would allow relatively easy movement between Thailand, Malaya and the islands of Sumatra, Borneo and Java. Little evidence of Pleistocene human occupation in Sumatra has been recorded, but early man was present in Borneo during the latter part of the Pleistocene. In Sarawak, excavations in the Great Cave of Niah have yielded abundant material with radio-carbon dates extending back to approximately 40,000 years ago (Harrison 1957). The cave itself is enormous, 800 feet wide at its mouth, 200 feet high in places and enclosing some 26 acres; near the mouth of the cave the archaeological material extends in depth to over 12 feet, with a sterile deposit at 66 to 72 inches below the surface.

The industry below this marker bed consists of pebble and flake elements, with a radiocarbon date of 39,600 ± 1000 B.P. at 100 inches depth. Above the sterile deposit are industries containing pebble choppers, bone objects, large unretouched flakes and smaller flakes also generally without retouch. The pebble tools are unifacially-flaked. Radiocarbon dates straddling these occupations, between 42 and 72 inches below the surface, are 19,570 ± 190 and 32,630 ± 700 B.P. At a depth of 100 inches a skull of *Homo sapiens sapiens* was discovered. The associated fauna appears to be largely extant except for an extinct pangolin, *Manis palaeojavanica*. In view of the skull and this faunal assemblage, further evidence and samples for radiocarbon dating are required before the high antiquity of *Homo sapiens sapiens* in this area is accepted without reserve.

The Sunda Shelf does not extend to the Celebes, and the 1800 metre-deep Macassar Strait, separating the islands from the Borneo and Java and Malayan landmass, always presented a barrier at least 40 kilometres wide during the Pleistocene. Nevertheless, an occupation in the southern part of the Celebes, associated with an extinct fauna, has indicated the presence of man here in late Pleistocene times (van Heekeren 1958). The fauna includes a pygmy form of *Archidiskodon*, giant tortoise, and a pig (*Celebochoerus*), an assemblage different from that of Java, just as the modern faunas are different.

The industrial material and the fauna have been recovered from a terrace 40 metres above the present Walanae river near Tjabengè. The artefacts are on chalcedony, jasper and other siliceous rocks, and consist of short thick flakes retouched into points and edge-tools; most of the flakes have plain platforms, but faceted platforms occur. The assemblage has been compared with the Sangiran of Java and with industries in the Philippines; the evidence of the Macassar barrier, and the suggestion of near-physical connections between the Philippines and North Celebes along the Sangihe islands (not shown on the map (fig. 162)) may point to a northern source for the Tjabengè industry.

In the Philippines there is evidence of a quartzite pebble industry, called Cabalwanian, in northern Luzon, which is believed to be associated with *Stegodon*; in addition, flake assemblages recalling the Tjabengè have been reported in deposits with pygmy elephants, and a theory has been advanced which suggests, on the basis of connections between the Celebes, the Philippines, the Babuyan and Batan islands. Formosa and the Asiatic mainland, that the stone industries of the Philippines and Celebes had origins ultimately in China. For this there is little proof, but the theory is ingenious and attractive.

Without doubt the pebble and flake industries of south-eastern Asia underwent development and change through the millennia of the closing phases of the Pleistocene, but the point has been made that this region was not subjected to extreme climatic and environmental alterations in late Pleistocene times, and that there may have been less stimulus to man to adapt and alter his material culture in response. Although the principle of environmental determinism cannot be accepted as the sole source of cultural change, the pebble and flake industries in south-east Asia represent one of the longest-lived lithic traditions in the world, exceeded in time perhaps only by the hand-axe industries of the sub-Saharan Africa.

The final phase of the pebble and flake industries in Asia is the Hoabinhian tradition which appears to have been practised in post-Pleistocene times in an area from south China through Vietnam, Laos, Cambodia, Thailand and Malaya to Sumatra. The Hoabinhian sites are generally recognized as middens, either in caves or in the open, and may be positioned by marine- or fresh-water. In Sumatra, middens of marine shells occur 10 km. inland, and must represent a relative withdrawal of the sea from these areas.

The stone industry is in the pebble and flake tradition, with large flakes, unifacially- or bifacially-worked pebbles, and stone pounders and mortars. Long flat oval pebbles of sandstone, flaked on one face, have been termed Sumatraliths. In Vietnam and Laos, stones with paired grooves occur in Hoabinhian industries, and were probably used to smooth and sharpen split bamboo lanceheads. Contracted inhumation was practised, with red ochre sprinkled in the grave. At Gua Gha in Malaya, in addition to burials, evidence of cannibalism was found. The burials are of a physical type called Palaeo-Melanesian.

Another lithic tradition of relatively recent date is the Toalian of the Celebes which was associated with a different group of people, smaller than the Hoabinhians. The industrial remains consist of stone arrowheads, edge-tools and microlithic forms, and comparable material has been recognized in Java and Sumatra; by this time, man in south-east Asia must have been well able to cope with difficult sea crossings from island to island.

21

China and Japan

THE abundant evidence from northern China of pebble and flake industries is important not only for the association of industry and fossil man, but also for distribution of Middle Pleistocene occupation. There is little doubt that these industries represent a tradition related to those of northern India, Burma and the Sunda Shelf territories, but at the moment it is not possible to explain the degree of relationship except in theoretical terms. A convenient and economical explanation of the north Chinese occupation is that it represents an offshoot from a main stream of cultural movement flowing from northern India and Pakistan through Burma and southwards. This explanation, however, rests entirely on a presumed source relationship between the Soan-Anyathian on the one hand and, on the other, the pebble and flake industries of the late Villafranchian in eastern Africa, with the potential intermediate find of Ubeidiyeh in the Near East which appears to be of the early Middle Pleistocene (p. 357). The Ubeidiyeh industry, of spheroids, unifacially and bifacially retouched pebbles and flakes, and pointed flakes, is not in its range outside the variability limits of the Asian pebble and flake traditions. Although this theory is attractive, involving only one source of tool-making, there is no proof of industrial connections between Africa and Asia, and there is little against the alternative theory of indigenous invention of tool-making in each area except in the realm of the human types associated. It must be considered more likely that *Homo erectus* of Africa and Asia had a common ancestor than that he developed independently in each area.

The geological deposits of Pleistocene China are exceedingly complex, and although broad correlations can be made between widely-separated regions, there are considerable difficulties in attempting a more detailed survey of contemporary events through the middle and upper Pleistocene (Cheng 1959). In North China, where many of the significant finds of Pleistocene man have been made, the deposits of the Middle Pleistocene are reddish conglomerates and clays, called *Terra Rossa* on occasion. In limestone areas, many underground cavities were exposed through erosion, and these were gradually filled with sub-aerial deposits and mammalian, including human, remains through deliberate occupation. The succeeding deposits, overlying the red earths, include gravels at the base of the loess, or yellow earth, and which mark the onset of cold, steppe-like conditions. Contemporary deposits in regions other than the loessic Kansu, Shensi and Shansi include consolidated dunes in the Ordos desert, silts in dessicated lakes in Singkiang and Mongolia, brown loams in Manchuria, the Hopei plains and the Yangtse basin.

The table provides a very schematic guide to these deposits and their correlation with archaeological sites and finds of fossil man.

Principal archaeological sites and fossil finds in China

	Middle Pleistocene	Upper Pleistocene	
		earlier	later
Industry	Choukoutien (Loc. 13–1–15) Kê-hê	Shui-tung-kou Hou-kê-ta-fêng	Choukoutien Up. Cave Sjara-osso-gol Ting-Ts'un Hsaio-nan-hai Gobi
Fossil man	*Homo erectus* (*Sinanthropus pekinensis*, *S. lantianensis*)	Ti-shao-kou Ch'ang-yang Ma-pa-hsaing	Ting-ts'un Sjaro-osso-gol Tzŭ-yang Lai-pin Liu-chiang Choukoutien Up. Cave
Geology	—*Terra Rossa*—	Basal — Loess — Gravels	

(based on Cheng 1966)

The Choukoutienian industries belong to the pebble flake tradition of eastern Asia. A number of sites near Peking have yielded quantities of lithic material, but the most important assemblages are from localities 1 and 15. The Choukoutien sites consist of fissure deposits in limestone, which range in time, on the basis of fauna, from the Pliocene to the end of the Pleistocene or into the Holocene. The industrial material occurs first in Middle Pleistocene deposits.

The earliest evidence for human occupation is at Locality 13, where sub-aerial red clays in a shallow fissure yielded a patinated chert chipping-tool (fig. 167), apparently associated with an early middle Pleistocene fauna considered by some authorities to be of Cromerian affinities; in our opinion this dating seems premature. At Locality 1, collapsed cave deposits are stratified with successive occupation debris yielding hearths, abundant stone tools and the bones of animals and *Homo erectus* ('*Sinan-*

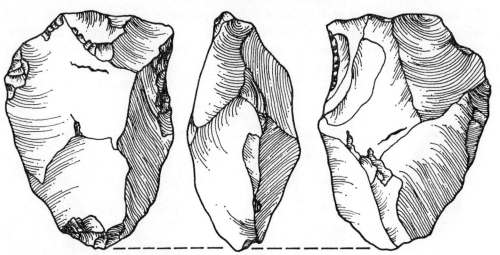

FIG. 167. Choukoutienian *c.* ½; Choukoutien Locality 13. *After Movius 1948*

thropus'). The original cave, opening to the north-east, appears to have undergone a series of phases of collapse over much of Middle Pleistocene times, and man continued to occupy the cave following most of these phases when angular material fell from the roof. The site when excavated was 175 metres by 50 metres in diameter, and the deposits of earth, stone, sand and clay, reached a depth of over 50 metres. Two major stages of filling have been recognized, an upper Zone I with extensive layers of ash, limestone fragments, animal bones and industrial material with human remains near an underlying stalagmite, and the whole Zone sealed by stalagmite at the top. Zone II consists of sandy clays with limestone debris, lithic material, animal and human bones. The basal part of Zone II is a fissure filled with concreted sands and loams also containing human material. There is little evidence in the fauna or human remains that the two Zones are appreciably separated in time. The fauna includes *Siphneus wongi*, *Machairodus inexpectatus*, *Euryceros pachyosteus*, *Pseudaxis*, *Bubalus teilhardi*, *Rhinoceros merckii* and *R. tichorhinus*, *Ursus spelaeus*, *Felis youngi*, and this *Sino-Malayan* assemblage as a whole, taken with some floral evidence, is considered to indicate a climate rather milder and damper than that of today. The relationship of this fauna, with its micro-mammalian elements, to European faunal stages is considered to be not well established, and it is uncertain if the occupation at Locality I should be correlated with an early Mindel phase or a later episode. In terms of hunting preferences, almost 70% of the animal bones are of a type of fallow deer *Euryceros pachyosteus* or another deer, *Pseudaxis grayi*. It is also likely that elephant, rhinoceros, camel, buffalo, horse, boar, sheep and musk-ox were brought to the cave as game, and that some at least of the predatory beasts, lion, tiger, leopard, cave bear, hyena, were killed by Choukoutien man and are not present by entirely natural causes.

The industrial material at Locality 1 consists primarily of unworked flakes and pebbles. The raw material employed is varied, sandstone, quartz, chert and limestone, with smaller quantities of quartzite and flint. All of this was available within a few miles of the site. The implements include choppers and chopping-tools made on pebbles (fig. 168, 3–4), and numerous flake tools with rather irregular retouch. The

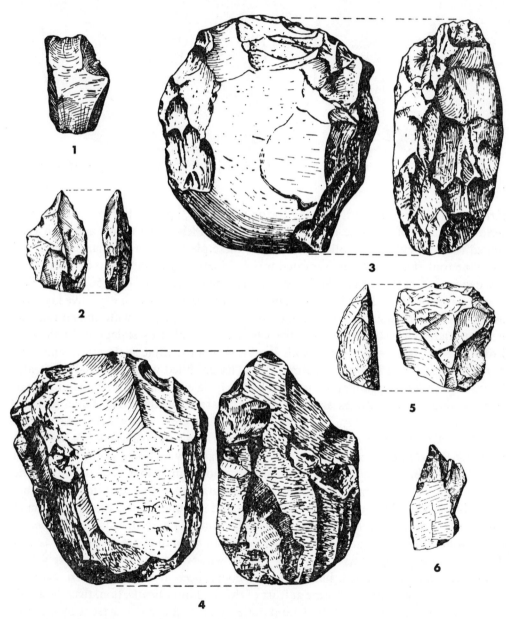

FIG. 168. Choukoutienian ½; Choukoutien Locality 1. *From Movius 1948*

bipolar technique of fracturing quartz was in common practice (fig. 168, 1). Other flakes indicate the free anvil method of percussion, with inclined platforms; very little evidence of core preparation has been found. Secondary retouch is rare and, when present, of irregular form (fig. 168, 5–6). On the other hand, traces of utilization on retouched flakes are abundantly represented (fig. 168, 2). The retouch present appears to have been designed to produce edge tools, suitable for use as scrapers or knives, and roughly pointed tools. Cores are not particularly abundant, those surviving being small (diameters 4–8 cm.) and either discoidal or conical. The evidence of bone and antler artefacts is not conclusive, and at the moment there seems to be relatively few recognizable objects of organic material that were fashioned into tools.

Although the depth of deposit in Locality 1 is considerable, there is very little acceptable evidence of industrial evolution throughout the successive occupation levels, other than a general agreement that the chert tools from the stalagmite layers high in Zone I typologically are more 'advanced' than the majority of lithic material from the many metres of deposits below.

The significance of Locality 1 at Choukoutien rests with the association of *Homo erectus*, pebble and flake industries and evidence of controlled fire. The use of fire at Choukoutien is one of the earliest records of this important element in man's control over his environment. In Europe, fire is attested in the Mindel period at Vertess-zöllös, but there is little trace of this in similar time contexts in Africa.

Locality 15 lies only some 70 metres away from Locality 1. The deposits lie in a fissure, and have yielded abundant stone artefacts and animal bones, but no human remains. The fauna includes an evolved form of *Euryceros, Equus hemionus, Rhinoceros tichorhinus, Gazella prjewalski, Cervus canadensis, Siphneus* cf. *wongi*, with Jerboa and Ostrich. The loamy deposits also contain materials in their upper part which indicate deposition under a cool rather than dry climate, and some of the fauna such as Jerboa and Ostrich are unlikely to have been present in north China under more temperate conditions.

The industry from Locality 15 was made on quartz, sandstone, chert, flint, slate, limestone and volcanic rock. Recognizable tools are much more abundant here than at Locality 1. Choppers on rounded or flat pebbles (fig. 169, 2), chopping-tools with bifacial retouch (fig. 169, 10) and massive flake cleavers occur, along with quantities of smaller flake tools (fig. 169, 1, 3–7). The bipolar technique is not evident, but there is some evidence of core preparation before flake detachment (fig. 169, 1). Although deliberate retouch on flakes is again relatively rare, those finished tools that are present exhibit both flat and steep retouch carried out to produce edge and point tools. Utilized flakes are abundant, and discoidal cores were also employed as scrapers or knives. Both industrially and on faunal grounds, the industry from Locality 15 is believed to represent a younger phase of human activity at Choukoutien.

An occupation in southern Shansi contemporary with Locality 1 at Choukoutien has recently been indicated by excavations at Kê-hê, where stream erosion has yielded a sequence of deposits of Middle Pleistocene age (Cheng 1966). Resting on an erosion

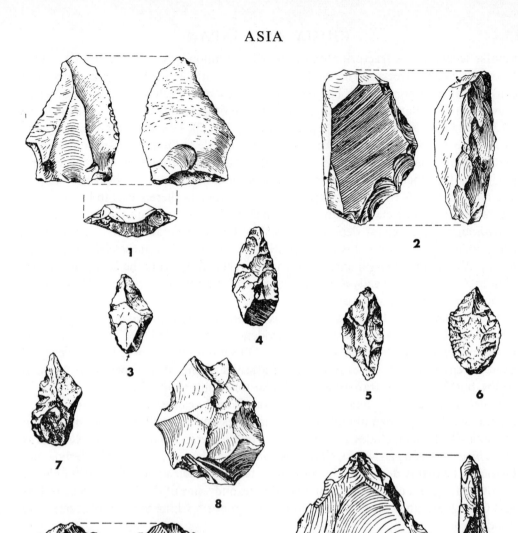

FIG. 169. Choukoutienian ½; Choukoutien Locality 15. *From Movius 1948*

surface is a gravel deposit containing stone artefacts and animal remains, and which is sealed by sands and red clays. The clays have been correlated with the Choukou-tienian occupation. The artefacts are on quartzite pebbles, and choppers, cores, and round stone balls form the major heavy elements. Flakes including pointed forms are also represented. There is little evidence of secondary retouch. The associated fauna is believed to be early Middle Pleistocene in its general character; *Stegodon zdanski*, an elephant, suggests a time prior to that of the Choukoutien occupation, but *Euryceros flabellatus* and *E. pachyostus* have been reported from the early sites near Peking.

Other sites in Shansi, and in Shensi and Honan, have yielded artefacts of pebble and flake character from reddish clays which are considered to be of Choukoutienian age and affinities.

The Choukoutienian industries, the Kê-hê industry, hominid remains from Lantian, and the numerous industrial sites in the basin of the Huangho are all considered to be of Middle Pleistocene age according to their stratigraphical relationship with the Lower Reddish Clays which were deposited sub-aerially in north China. The industry from Locality 15 at Choukoutien represents a period of activity relatively later in this sequence, and may be considered as only slightly earlier than other industries in the Upper Reddish Clays and the basal gravels of the loess. At Yang-chuang and Hou-kê-ta-fêng in northern Shansi, basal gravels of the loess have yielded lithic material clearly related in tradition to the Choukoutienian industries; at Hou-kê-ta-fêng, pebbles of quartz were used to produce artefacts with edge retouch in the form of points, scrapers and knives.

These finds are considered to date in general terms to the earlier part of the Upper Pleistocene, which stratigraphically infers a geological position in north China within the basal gravel or the lower part of the loess. Several recent finds of fossil man have been considered to be of this age, and to represent a type of man emergent from the *Homo erectus* form of the Middle Pleistocene.

The human remains, which are believed to be contemporary with the industries of developed pebble and flake tradition, have been found at Ti-shao-kou in the Huangho valley of Inner Mongolia, at Ch'ang-yang in the Yangtse valley of Hupei, and at Ma-pa-hsaing in the Sinkiang valley of Kwang-tung. Geological and faunal evidence suggests that the Ma-pa-hsaing skull is the earliest of these finds, all of which are believed to be of potential sapient stock.

Industrially there follows in north China, in the valley system of the Huangho and the Fenho rivers, the appearance of flake industries containing both heavier elements of presumed ancient ancestry, and smaller elements which may indicate an establish-ment of connections to the north.

In Shansi, along the banks of the Fenho river, a number of industries have been recovered from terraced deposits at Ting-ts'un (fig. 170–171; Pei Wên-chung *et al.* 1958). The third and lowest terrace of the river here consists of sands and gravels rising some 20–30 metres above the present river level. The uppermost deposit of this

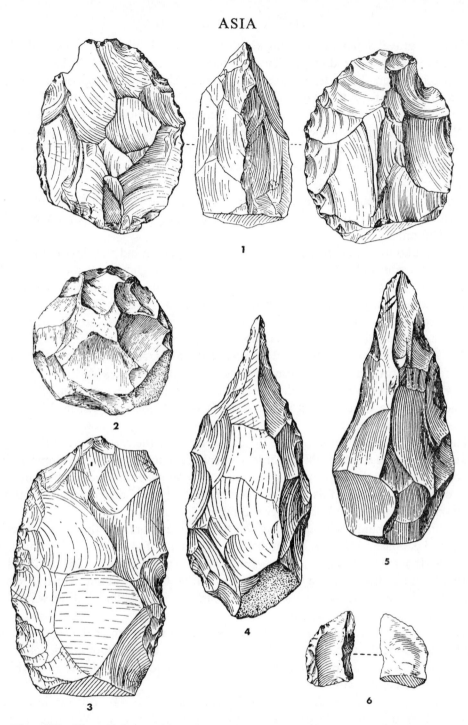

FIG. 170. Ting Ts'un, China $\frac{1}{2}$; 1 chopper; 2 bolas; 3 unifacial flake; 4–5 picks; 6 plain platform flake. *From Pei* et al. *1958*

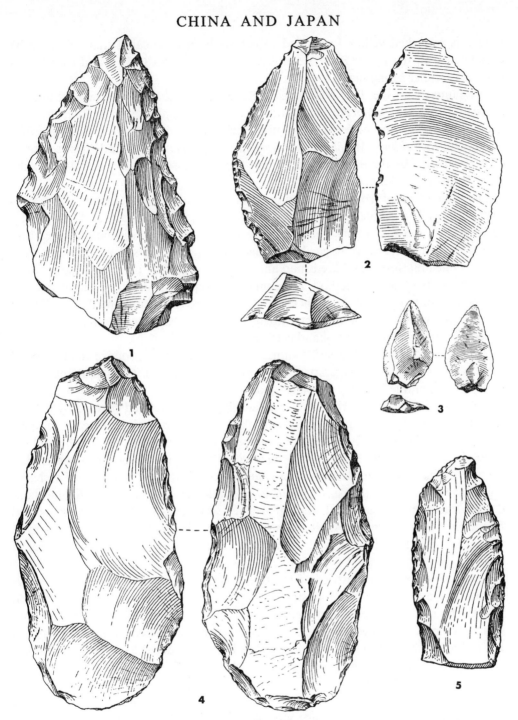

FIG. 171. Ting Ts'un, China $\frac{1}{2}$; 1 unifacial point; 2–3 prepared platform flakes; 4 bifacial flake; 5 unifacial flake. *From Pei* et al. *1958*

terrace is rewashed yellow loess, and recent study has indicated that this may be correlated with the upper Pleistocene yellow loess of north China, and with Sjara-osso-gol in Inner Mongolia.

The fauna from the Ting-ts'un sites include forms believed to represent archaic survivals, such as *Rhinoceros merckii*, *Coelodonta antiquitatis* and *Palaeoloxodon tokunagai*, and forms of loessic affinities such as *Equus hemionus*, *E. prjewalski*, *Rhinoceros tichorhinus*, *Mammuthus primigenius*, *Bos primigenius* and *Sinomegaceros* cf. *ordosianus*. The three associated human teeth are also said to be related to the tooth from Sjara-osso-gol.

The lithic material from Ting-ts'un is on black hornfels pebbles from hills 7 kilo-metres away. The pebble and flake industry is typologically archaic, and led initially to the suggestion that it was contemporary with the Choukoutienian, a suggestion now discarded by recent geological and palaeontological studies. The flakes generally have inclined platforms and are broad and thick (figs. 170, 6; 171, 5). Angular cores, the biproducts of such a method, are abundantly represented, as are hammerstones and bolas stones (fig. 170, 2). Bifacial implements are well represented (figs. 170, 1; 171, 4), and include handaxe forms which in the entire south-east Asian region are called 'chopping-tools', 'proto-handaxes' or 'picks' (fig. 170, 4, 5).

Retouch, probably with a soft hammer, was employed to produce thick pointed tools and edge-tools such as scrapers and knives (fig. 171, 1, 5). At Li-ts'un, near Ting ts'un, a comparable industry on black quartzite has been recovered from a stratified terrace deposit of a former river. The artefacts lay in a gravel bed covered by reddish clay and loess. Types include bifacially-flaked core tools, flake and core scrapers and points, and stone balls. In the same region, but lying between the Fen-ho and the Huangho rivers, sites in the Chiao-ch'eng area have also yielded industrial material of Ting-ts'un character, but these, as at Li-ts'un, are considered by a number of archaeo-logists to be older than the period of the loess, while the Ting-ts'un material has been described as of the loess period. Several artefacts at Cheng-chia Chuang were located on the basal Gravels, intermediate in time. The industries of all these sites appear to be related in basic tradition, with an initial source perhaps in the Kê-hê industries of Shansi.

The earliest known industries of the Ordos region in Inner Mongolia are repre-sented by the Shui-tung-kou industry from the upper Huangho valley (Boule *et al.* 1928). The industry is on quartzite and limestone, and flakes were retouched into points, scrapers and knives (fig. 172, 1–8). Heavy artefacts include unifacial choppers, but a third element is the blade; this site has been considered as representative of a widespread tradition in Inner Mongolia which contains heavy material of possible Choukoutienian derivation, flakes of indigenous development, and blades of an intrusive industry which has potential connections with Siberian material (p. 348). The blades may represent an introduction of Upper Palaeolithic traditions into northern China during the final glacial period, when loess was being extensively deposited.

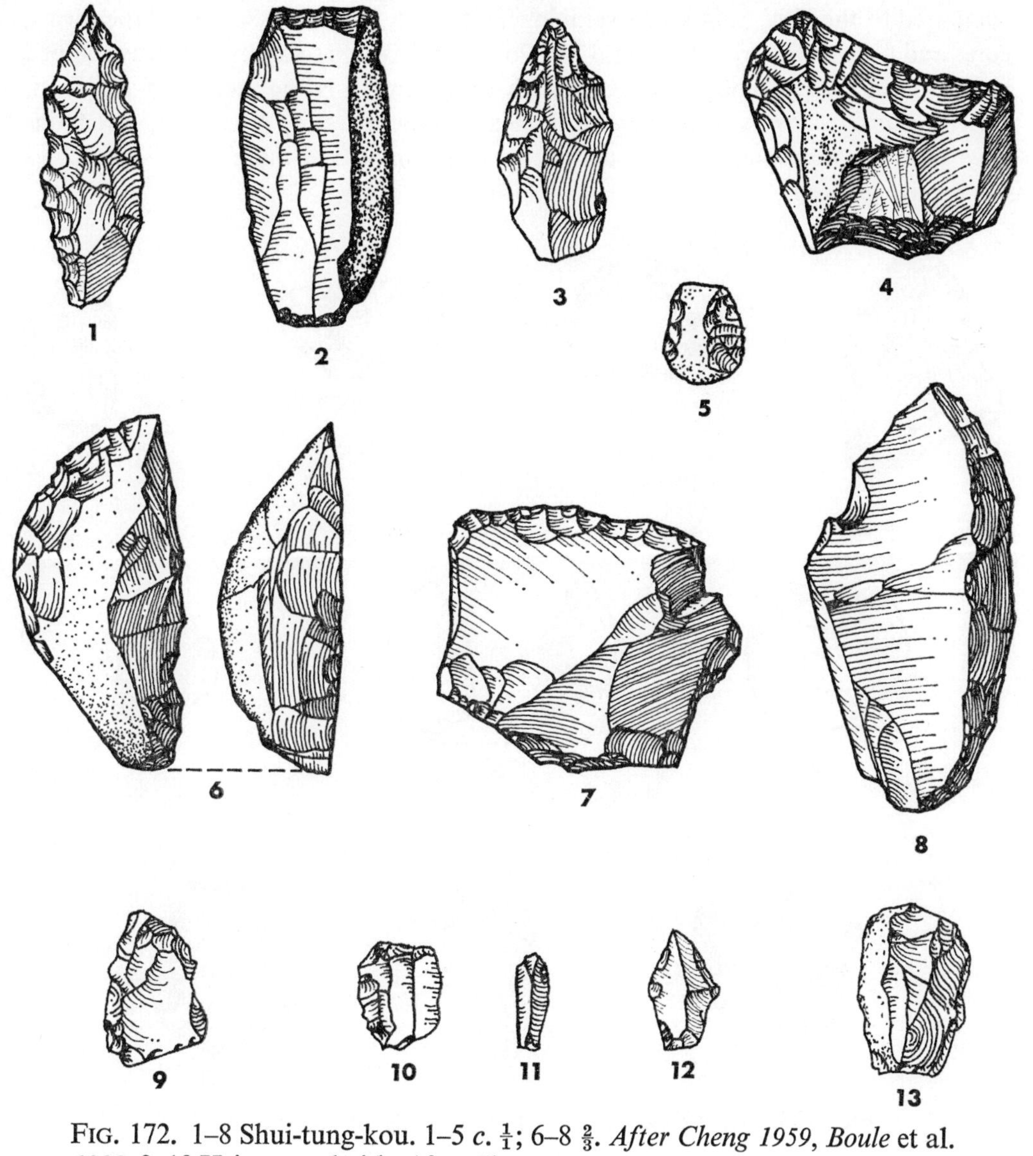

FIG. 172. 1–8 Shui-tung-kou. 1–5 *c*. $\frac{1}{1}$; 6–8 $\frac{2}{3}$. *After Cheng 1959, Boule* et al. *1928*. 9–13 Hsiao-nan-hai $\frac{1}{2}$. *After Cheng 1966*

Of later date than the Shui-tung-kou industry in the Ordos is the site of Sjara-osso-gol which lies at the southern border of the Ordos desert in Suiyuan, where a lake existed in late Pleistocene times. In the sands and muds of alternating lacustrine and dune deposition has been found lithic material associated with an abundant mammalian fauna. The latter includes animals of the steppe, horse, ass, camel, woolly rhinoceros, mammoth, and other forms including the giant ostrich.

The industry was made on black siliceous stones, and in character has been compared to the Shui-tung-kou assemblage, although at Sjara-osso-gol all the forms, cores and flakes, are very small (fig. 173). Points, knives and scrapers as well as chipped pebbles occur. Apparently associated with this industry is the incisor of *Homo* cf. *sapiens neanderthalensis*. Elsewhere in the Sjara-osso-gol valley other human remains have been reported but their association with this industrial material in some cases has been disproved.

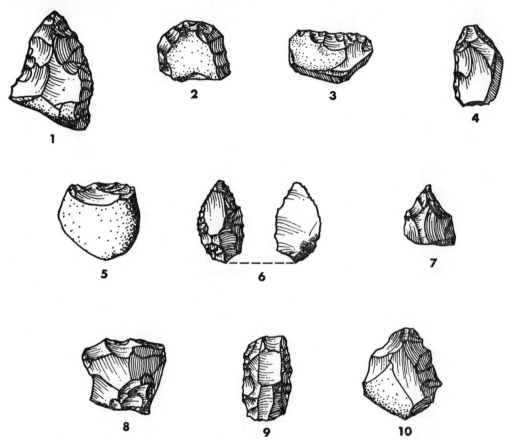

FIG. 173. Sjara-osso-gol; 1–7 $\frac{1}{1}$; 8–10 $\frac{2}{3}$. *After Boule* et al. *1928*

An occupation contemporary with the lakeside site of Sjara-osso-gol is at Chou-koutien, where a high-level cave became accessible to man through erosion. This Upper Cave was filled by deposits containing a fauna mostly of modern species but including the extinct *Ursus spelaeus*. The human remains included an elderly male and two adult females, all of whom seem to have met death by violence; all are of *Homo sapiens* character but are said to possess differing racial characteristics. Several thin industrial horizons yielded pebbles and flakes of quartzite and chert, shaped into choppers, scrapers and knives. Other equipment consisted of a long bone needle with perforation, as well as beads of bone, tooth, shell and stone; the stone beads, with hour-glass perforation, were painted red. There is also evidence of deliberate burial of the dead in the cave, and the use of ochre in the grave rite. The materials employed by Upper Cave man are believed to represent a variety of sources, the marine shells 200 km. to the south-east, oolitic haematite 150 km. to the north, and unionid shells 350 km. to the south.

Another occupation in north China at Hsiao-nan-hai in Anyang, Honan, indicates the presence of microlithic traditions in late glacial times. The cave site was filled with yellow earth deposits yielding a fauna of *Rhinoceros tichorhinus* and the ostrich *Struthiolithus* and an industry on flint and quartz. The artefacts include microlithic flakes and flake-blades struck from small cores and retouched into small points and edge tools (fig. 172, 9–13). A comparable industry has been found at Ku-lung in Shansi, also in loess, and these sites are considered to represent an extension of a tradition previously established in the Gobi desert in late glacial times.

The Gobi desert, particularly in the regions east of the Shara Murum river, has yielded abundant evidence for the presence of man in the Pleistocene. This occupation apparently took place in wind-scooped areas of consolidated sand dunes near lakes; the industries, on jasper, are microlithic in character, with small points, scrapers and knives, and is non-geometric.

Many human finds of late glacial age have been made in China. The Ting-ts'un teeth, the Upper Cave finds at Choukoutien, and the Sjara-osso-gol teeth have been noted previously. At Tzu-yang, Szechwan, a skull of an adult female was recovered from a deposit underlying loessic and sandy material and was associated with a fauna containing *Mammuthus primigenius*. The human skull has been recorded as *Homo sapiens*, and is comparable to finds from Lai-pin and Lui-chiang, Kwangsi. All are considered to represent potential ancestral forms of the Mongoloid race.

In Shensi, a number of industries have been recovered from sand-dunes at Sha-yüan (Chang 1958). The material consists of flint, sandstone, agate and jade cores leaf-shaped points, scrapers, awls and other small forms, and a larger flake element retouched into edge-tools and points. These Sha-yüan industries may represent the activities of hunters and gatherers in immediately pre-Neolithic times; typologically the material has been considered as a derivation from the Sjara-osso-gol tradition of the upper Huangho.

Pre-neolithic material from Japan has also been recognized, and relatively recent research has indicated that these islands were occupied first during late glacial times, when mainland connections were established during a low sea level (Serizawa and Ikawa 1958). At Tarukishi in Hokkaido, and at many other sites, blade industries have been recovered; these appear to represent a variety of assemblages which may indicate seasonal or functional variations in a basic blade tradition. Radiocarbon dates for blade industries in Japan appear to cluster around 13–12,000 B.P., although some hint of earlier dates has recently been made.

In northern Hokkaido, the sites at Shirataki provide a stratified sequence of

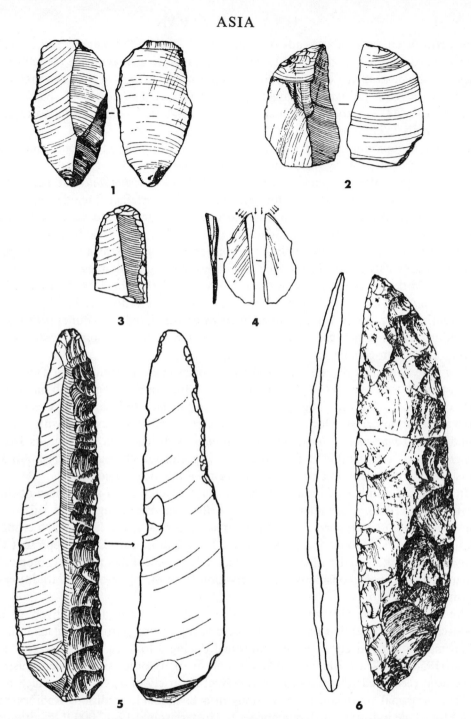

FIG. 174. Shirataki, Japan; obsidian; 1–2 Shirataki 27 ½; 3, 5 Shirataki 13 ⅔; 4, 6 Shirataki 33 ⅔. *From Serizawa and Ikawa 1958*

industries on obsidian contained within a terrace system of the Yubetsu valley. The earliest material consists of broad blades with little retouch (fig. 174, 1–2); a later stage contains long and short blades with edge or end retouch (fig. 174, 3, 5). Burins and small blade-cores occur in succeeding assemblages (fig. 174, 4), where bifacial retouch appears on leaf-shaped points (fig. 174, 6). A late coastal variant in northern Hokkaido contains points with reverse retouch, burins, blades and ground-stone tools and pendants (fig. 175, 4, 5, 8).

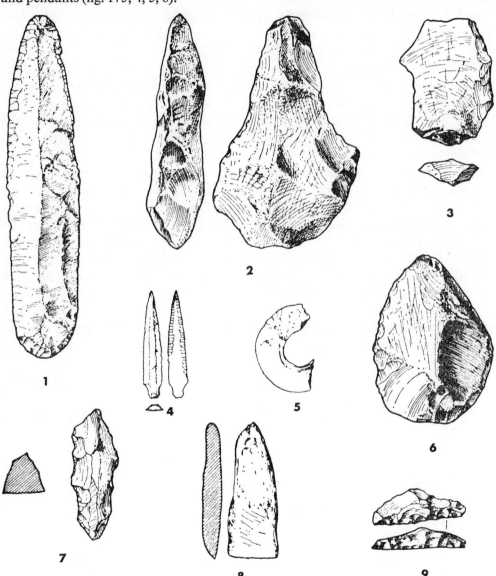

FIG. 175. Japan; 1, 7 Tarukishi $\frac{3}{5}$; 2, 3, 6, Gongenyama $\frac{3}{5}$; 4, 5, 8 Shimo-Yubetsu $\frac{1}{2}$; 9 Ishima $\frac{3}{5}$. *From Serizawa and Ikawa 1958*

Southern Hokkaido contains the Tarukishi site with a shale industry of long blades with edge retouch (fig. 175, 1), blade cores, end scrapers and steep scrapers (fig. 175, 7).

In Honshu, comparable blade and burin industries on shale have been found; at Araya, a pit had been dug in which part of an abundant industry occurred. The material included burins, end scrapers, steep scrapers, and heavier pebble elements. In the Kanto Plain, typologically earlier forms were found at Gongenyama; pear-shaped axes with large flakes (fig. 175, 2, 3, 6) and flake-blades occurred beneath a smaller flake industry. In the south, at Ishima, microlithic flakes and cores were associated with steeply-retouched flakes (fig. 175, 9).

Of the many blade and burin sites known in Japan, most are located on slopes overlooking rivers or lakes or the sea. On stratigraphical grounds, the large blade industries are perhaps the earliest manifestation of industrial activity in Japan, although there is nothing inherently difficult about accepting the typologically earlier material from Gongenyama which could be taken to represent an early penetration from mainland China.

Support for this potentially early occupation has recently been obtained from Sozudai, Kyushu, where an industry on vein quartz and quartz rhyolite was found on a 25–30 metre coastal terrace (Serizawa 1965). The industry consists of flake tools struck from prepared cores, and artefacts made on blocks or pebbles. Some bifacially-flaked tools have been called proto-ovates and proto-handaxes; chopping tools with alternate retouch, choppers with unifacial retouch, thick flakes with retouch to a well-defined point, and other irregular forms occur. Typologically, this industry has been compared with those from Choukoutien and Kê-hê, and with the Patjitanian of Java. The gravel deposit on the coastal terrace is believed to be of early Last Glacial age, but correlations with other areas are difficult, and another view suggests that the terrace may be of Hoxnian age.

Part V
THE NEW WORLDS

22

Australia

ARCHAEOLOGY developed late in Australia partly because informed opinion considered that the arrival of man in that continent was of a late date. A stimulus to excavation was thereby lacking.

Early man, however, has been shown to have been present in Southern Queensland as early as *c.* 16,000 B.P., and there is a radiocarbon date of *c.* 18,200 B.P. from Koonalda on the Nullabor Plain; other dates from Arnhem Land, Northern Territory, appear to be as early as 22,000 B.P. It may be suspected, however, that the Wallace Divide, an ocean bed depression between Borneo and the Celebes, acted as a barrier to very early migration for a land bridge could not have been formed even at the times of low sea levels during glaciations. From these presumed early beginnings, the Stone Age of Australia continued until the entry of the Europeans (Mulvaney 1961, 1966) and indeed in some areas to the present day.

Perhaps fortunately, there has not been sufficient evidence to group industries into 'culture' clusters after the European fashion. Pioneer attempts, which were made on European models current at the time, have been discarded. Australia, however, has an advantage in that written records of the behaviour of aboriginal populations exist, and these may form a basis for future archaeological work in interpreting the meaning of clusters of artefactual traits. The artefactual assemblages have been divided on original lines into admittedly hypothetical 'non-hafted' and 'hafted' phases. Tools too small to have been used other than by hafting are regarded as 'hafted' tools. The 'non-hafted' phase is the earlier. Although it is impossible to state that the earlier larger tools were not hafted, it may be that there was at least a change in hafting technique. The early phase consists of different kinds of assemblages, characterized by high domed scrapers, flat curved edge scrapers and retouched cores and pebbles, differences being due to cultural, functional or other factors. At Seelands, Curracurang and Capertee (fig. 176), tools of the early phase are overlain by tools of the late phase, and the same situation possibly exists at Noola and at Laura in the Northern Territory. There is a strong similarity with the stone tools of Tasmania. The early phase terminated, at least in southern Queensland, *c.* 5,000 B.P., and was succeeded there by pirri points (fig. 178, 1, 2), backed blades (fig. 178, 4), small geometric pieces

413

(fig. 178, 5, 6, 7) and ground stone axes. The widely-spread pirri point (fig. 177) is dated, for example, at The Tombs to between *c.* 3,700 and *c.* 3,500 B.P. The equally widely-spread microlithic industries with pirris are dated at Fromm's Landing to between 3,550–5,050 B.P. Elsewhere the pirris are again dated to *c.* 4300 ± 140 B.P. Pirri points are confined chiefly to South Australia and the Darling drainage area.

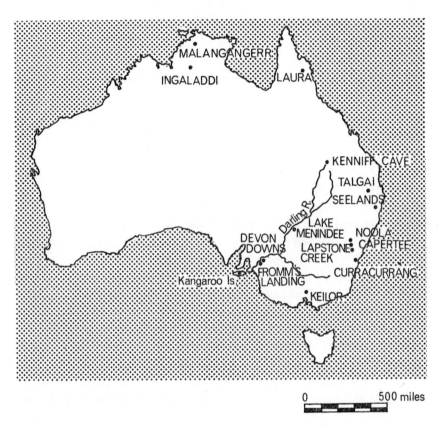

FIG. 176. Distribution of important Australian sites

They are thought by some to be related to similar forms in the Middle Toalian industries of the Southern Celebes (p. 394).

The human groups which made the tools of the 'early' phase hunted such extinct animals as *Diprotodon, Nototherium,* the giant kangaroos *Palorchestes* and *Procoptodon,* and the flightless birds *Genyornis* and *Dryormornis. Diprotodon* has been found in Southern Australia in late glacial times. *Sarcophilus* (Tasmanian Devil) and *Thylacinus* (Tasmanian Wolf) probably became extinct in the Fromm's Landing area during the second millennium B.C. The dingo, possibly a feral dog, introduced from elsewhere, may have been a contributory cause of the extinction of an archaic fauna which had become only marginally viable in less suitable post-glacial climates.

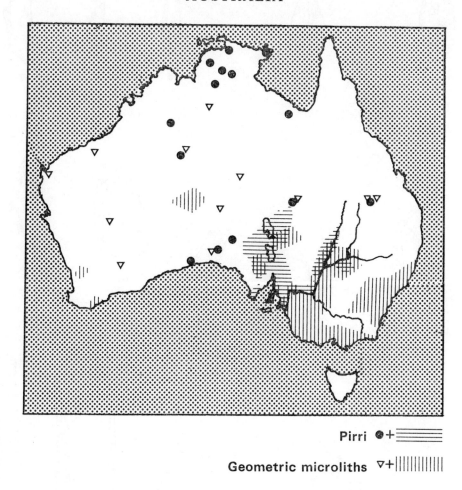

Pirri ●+▤

Geometric microliths ▽+||||||||||||

FIG. 177. The distribution of pirri points and microlithic industries

KENNIFF CAVE
(Mulvaney and Joyce 1965)

The Moffatt Cattle Station is 150 miles north east of Charleville in Southern Queensland. It has on it numerous small caves and the well-known Kenniff Cave and The Tombs. Kenniff Cave faces north, and contains a horizontally bedded sequence of sandy deposits up to 11 feet in depth. The sands are coarse down to $3\frac{1}{2}$ feet below the surface, between $3\frac{1}{2}$–$4\frac{1}{2}$ feet they are of a medium grade, and below they are of fine sand. A sedimentation analysis suggests that before 12,000 B.P. the climate was drying. From then until 7,000 B.P. there was an arid period during which deposition almost ceased and the cave was not occupied. Such differences however may be due

415

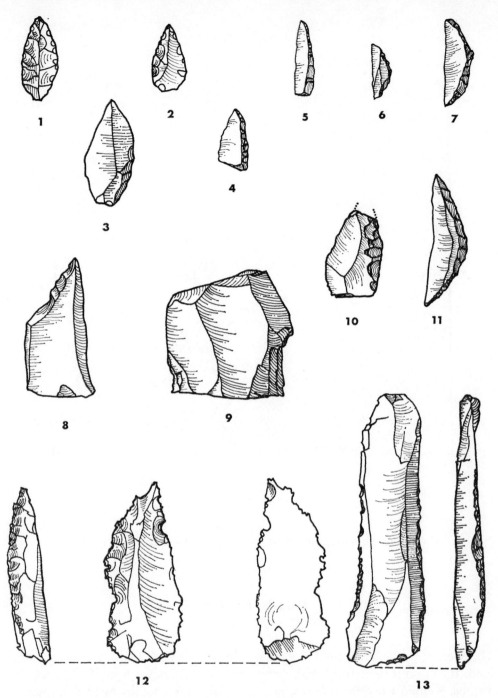

FIG. 178. Australian Hafted and Non-hafted tools. The Tombs and Kenniff Cave; 1–3 The Tombs, $\frac{1}{1}$. 1, 2, Pirri points; 3 retouched flake. 4–13 Kenniff's cave. 4–11 hafted phase, $\frac{1}{1}$; 12, 13 non-hafted phase, $\frac{1}{2}$; 3 retouched flake; 4 backed blade; 5 Bondi point, 6 crescent; 7 geometric microlith; 8 obliquely blunted point; 9 core; 11 geometric microlith; 12 Juan knife; 13 blade. *After Mulvaney 1961, Mulvaney and Joyce 1965*

to the presence or absence of human occupation. The cave was again inhabited after 7,000 B.P., during which period deposition increased.

From 4 feet below the surface to bedrock, scrapers are 100% of the classifiable artefacts. From 4 feet to 2 feet scrapers are rare, and above 4 feet microlithic artefacts are present. These small tools are dated from 5,000–3,000 B.P. The industrial artefacts do not fall into the European type of classification. In general the cave assemblage is said to consist of layers of flake industries with a blade element at the top. Figure 178 illustrates the presumed non-hafted and hafted artefacts. Essentially, Kenniff Cave shows a similar situation to that which has been found in a number of excavations in Australia, the microlithic industry stratified above the earlier phase. *The Tombs* is a rock face in which there is a cave and an adjacent shelter. The evidence from the excavation helps to confirm the conclusions drawn from the Kenniff Cave excavations. The earliest traces of human occupation have a radiocarbon date of 9,510 ±93 B.P. The artefacts are few but in accord with the early phases noted at Kenniff Cave. Between *c.* 3,700 and 3,500 B.P. microlithic and unifacial pirri points were present and the microliths extended upwards to a later date.

At both The Tombs and Kenniff Cave there is extensive wall art.

FROMM'S LANDING

The cave yielded a number of stratified hearths and occupation layers. The radiocarbon dates run from 3,240 ±80 B.P. to 4,850 ±100 B.P. Pirri points occur in layer 8, 3,881 ±85 B.P. and layer 10, 4,850 ±100 B.P. A further date of 3,756 ±85 B.P. was determined from charcoal which was deposited after the last pirri point. Fromm's Landing is only 10 miles from the site of Devon Downs excavated some 35 years ago. At Devon Downs, deposits in a cave, which contained 34 pirri points, were dated by radiocarbon to 4,290 ±140 B.P.

THE KEILOR SKULL

The Keilor Skull, discovered in 1940 in a river terrace 10 miles north of Melbourne, was found by a workman and its provenance is uncertain. A lens of charcoal and bones has recently given a radiocarbon date of 18,000 ±500 B.P. The lens, however, is not certainly associated with the skull. Nevertheless this site is regarded by some as probably an early record of human occupation in Australia.

MALANGANGERR

Malangangerr is a rock shelter on the coastal plain of Arnhem Land, Northern Territory. A coastal plain extends 30–60 miles from the sea, to the foot of the Arnhem

Land plateau. The cave contains 80–120 cm. of unstratified basal sands and above them interdigitating lenses of shell, bone, ash and charcoal within a shell midden 40–100 cm. in depth. Within the sands there is an industry which consists largely of scrapers, utilized flakes and edge ground axes. Radiocarbon dates are from 24,900–18,000 B.P. The overlying deposits contain points, small rectangular scrapers and edge ground axes. Radiocarbon dates range from $5,980 \pm 140$ B.P. at the base to 370 ± 80 B.P. towards the top of the deposits. The industrial succession and the radiocarbon dates are confirmed by evidence from two other sites in the same area, Nawamoyn and Tyimede II. This evidence conflicts with that from elsewhere in Australia, but the check dates from the other two sites appear to confirm the earlier results (White 1967).

TASMANIA

Tasmanian stone assemblages bear a strong typological resemblance to the older phase recovered on the mainland. It is likely that man arrived on the island during late glacial times when it was connected to the mainland by a land bridge. In north west Tasmania, a sequence has been established extending over the past 8,000 years (Jones, Rhys 1966, 1967). In the coastal cave of Rocky Cape, with a basal date of $8,120 \pm 165$ B.P., the first inhabitants relied almost completely on the sea shore for their protein food. Shell fish, seals and parrot fish were eaten, together with a variety of vegetable foods. Crudely retouched flakes and cores were made from locally available rocks, and bone points were used. This phase continued until about 4,000 B.P., after which until modern times, there was an increased exploitation of land animals, particularly marsupials and birds, and a decline in the importance of seals. Fish remains and bone tools are absent from these levels, the stone tools include circular scrapers, high domed scrapers and concave retouched pieces made from excellent raw materials brought from limited sources up to sixty miles away.

23

America

As no Neanderthal remains have so far been found in America it is presumed that the earliest human beings in that continent were *Homo sapiens*. The arrival of *Homo sapiens* from Asia is therefore considered to have been later than the Neanderthal/Mousterian–*Homo sapiens*/Advanced Palaeolithic transition which occurred in Europe and Asia *c.* 45–35,000 years ago.

The earliest known industries in America are those which are characterized by the Clovis point (fig. 179, 1). Equally early may be the industries associated with the Sandia point (fig. 179, 2–4). Together they form the probable basis of the American projectile point industrial succession. Other early forms are the leaf-shaped Cascade point of the North West Pacific coast (fig. 179, 19), the early assemblages of the Desert tradition of the Great Basin, and some unfluted points.

The Clovis industries have been dated by radiocarbon to as early as 11,000 B.P., contemporary with the Two Creeks interstadial which is the equivalent of the Alleröd oscillation in north temperate Europe. There is no certain earlier evidence for human occupation. In many areas, however, there are a number of crude assemblages without projectile points which are undated, and so far efforts to date them have been unsuccessful. Nevertheless, it is believed by some authorities that ancestral to the projectile point succession was a pre-projectile phase which had its origins in the late Middle Palaeolithic industrial tradition in Asia and which arrived in America some 20,000–40,000 years ago. Others are of the opinion that there were no human beings in America before the Two Creeks (Alleröd) oscillation, and that the origin of the projectile succession is with similar industries in Asia at that time.

A first consideration is, of course, at which periods human beings could have crossed from Asia to Alaska. A land bridge is regarded as being the first necessity and it must have been contemporary with a period when the Continental Ice Sheets themselves would not have formed an effective barrier to migration farther south, which they did at some periods of the Last Glaciation. If this is so, then the crossing must have taken place either before or after the glacial maximum. Radiocarbon dates indicate that there was a low sea level between *c.* 26,000 and *c.* 11,000 B.P. and probably no ice sheet barrier existed until 20,000 B.P. or after 12,000 B.P. (Wendorf 1966).

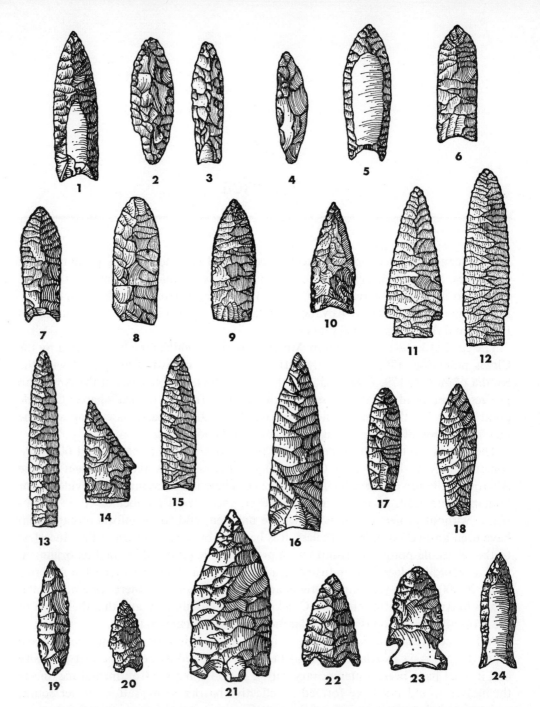

FIG. 179. Projectile points, America; 1 Clovis fluted point; 2–4 Sandia points; 5 Folsom point; 6 Plainview point; 7–8 Midland points; 9 Milnesand point; 10 Meserve point; 11–16 Parallel flake points; 11, 12 Scottsbluff points; 13 Eden point; 14 Cody knife; 15 Angostura point; 16 Frederick point; 17 Agate point; 18 Hell Gap point; 19 Cascade point; 20 Old Cordillera tradition, Pinto Basin; 21–23 Archaic points, Early Middle and Late; 24 Cumberland point. Scales: 1–7, 9–10, 17–18, 20–23: $\frac{1}{2}$, 8, 11–16, 19, 24: $\frac{2}{3}$. *After Willey 1966, and Sellards 1952*

The crossing, therefore, *on this hypothesis*, would be certainly later than 37,000 B.P. and probably between 26,000 and 20,000 B.P. when there was both a land bridge and an open corridor leading southwards, or between 12,000 B.P. and *c*. 11,000 B.P. when a similar situation existed. The problem then is to find Asian industries which are typologically similar to the American industries of a date *c*. 26,000–20,000 B.P. or *c*. 12,000–11,000 B.P. If Clovis and Sandia industries and the other early forms are contemporary with one another and not far removed in time from the first immigration, then one would expect to find in Asia, at about the same time, an industry or industries which have similar points, and which are largely composed of flakes, side and end scrapers, rare blades, little bone and no microliths. However, there are no industries in Siberia which are obviously like the American industries, and particularly dissimilar are the Asian industries which are known to be of 'Two Creeks' age. Only a full-scale multivariant analysis of artefactual assemblages on both sides of the Bering Straits is likely to offer more than tentative suggestions. Some authorities prefer the industry of the Siberian Late Palaeolithic Stage I at Ust-Kanskaia and traditions which are believed to be related, such as at Malta (p. 355), for a comparison, and suggest that the Middle Palaeolithic/Advanced Palaeolithic transitional industries of Siberia are the most likely source. However, the transitional stage in Siberia remains as yet undated.

Other authorities prefer a date of *c*. 40,000 B.P. as the most likely date for such a migration, and associate the supposed earliest but undated crude industries of America with the Middle Palaeolithic industrial traditions of Europe and Africa. This opinion is based on the heavy flake nature of the industries involved and the bifacially worked pieces. It must be remembered however, that bifacial leaf-shaped tools recur from time to time and in various localities in the Old World from the Middle Palaeolithic to the Neolithic and their recurrence is by no means always clearly associated with earlier evolving forms. They may represent a recurring need met by the application of a similar technique widely known from Acheulean times onwards. Further, isolated from cultural developments elsewhere, there is no need to suppose that the early American industries, related as they were to the different kind of biotope, needed any great period of time to elapse before they developed their own individuality. Another view of this problem of migration dates and industrial relations involves the existence of some form of sea-going craft in Palaeolithic times, but this view seems less likely than the others, difficult as they are.

The Palaeo-Indian Tradition Both the early dates for assemblages of artefacts from levels which contain Clovis, Sandia and Folsom points, and their association with the High Plains (fig. 183), the most likely route for migration from the north, suggest that they underlie the later developments of the American succession. The technological tradition of these projectile points was associated with the hunting of big game such as elephants and large bison in the grassland areas. It must be remembered that most American sites are kill sites or transit sites, where animals have been killed and dismembered, or where a brief halt was made by hunting bands; such sites

421

are different from the home-base type of cave site which provides the basis of the European succession. There is little doubt that the discovery of cave sites with long industrial successions in America, and closer attention to the open sites of Europe, would add greatly to our overall understanding of the behaviour of prehistoric man.

This Palaeo-Indian tradition, as it has been called, is known to have existed as early as 12,000 B.P. and lasted until 10,000–9,000 B.P. The earliest of the tool assemblages is the Llano Complex which contains Clovis points. The name Llano is taken from the Llano Estacado or Staked Plains of Texas and New Mexico. Clovis points (fig. 179, 1) are fluted and are up to 12 cm. in length and 4 cm. at the base. The base is ground at the edges and the tool is said to have been formed by percussion rather than pressure-flaking. Clovis points have been dated by radiocarbon to as early as 11,150 B.P. and possibly as late as 10,450 years ago. Their distribution is concentrated on the High Plains, the south-western deserts and Texas, but they have been found over the greater part of the United States, Canada, Alaska, Mexico and central America. With the Clovis points there are also a number of unfluted points, hammerstones, scrapers and some bone tools (Wormington 1957).

Assemblages with Sandia points may be contemporary regional variants possibly as old as or even older than the Llano complex. The Sandia projectile point is named after the Sandia cave in the Sandia mountains in New Mexico. Here they underlie Folsom points. They have been dated to around the 'Two Creeks'/Valders advance, c. 11,000–10,000 B.P. They are of two types (fig. 179, 2, 3).

Folsom points (fig. 179, 5) are believed to be a development from the Clovis type and to be associated with a change from mammoth to bison hunting. They occur most frequently in the plains east of the Rocky mountains, in New Mexico, eastern Colorado, eastern Wyoming and the adjoining territories. They are smaller than the Clovis points, widest in the middle and have a concave base with pointed projections. The fluting runs almost the whole length on both sides of the point. Radiocarbon dates have placed them between 11,000–10,000 B.P. and contemporary with the Valders ice advance. Unfluted points are also found associated with Folsom points.

After c. 10,000 B.P., numerous other types of large lanceolate points were made in the High Plains. They are thought to have been derived from the earlier forms, and are described as plano-projectile points which have been sub-divided into two groups, the Plainview group and the Parallel flaked group. The Plainview category includes non-fluted points such as Plainview, Midland, Milnesand and Merserve types (fig. 179, 6, 7, 8, 10 resp.). Plainview and Midland points have been dated from 9,750–7,050 B.P. Plainview points, probably contemporary in some areas with the Folsom points, are concentrated on the southern high plains but also extend as far as Canada and Mexico. The parallel flaked group include Scottsbluff, Eden, Cody knife, Angostura or Frederick, and Agate Basin points (fig. 179, 11–17). The Milnesand point has been dated to around 6,500 B.P. and has been found over an area from Texas to

Canada. Of the parallel sided group, Agate Basin points have been dated to *c.* 8,000 B.P. The Agate Basin points were followed at the Hell Gap site by Hell Gap points (fig. 179, 18), and later in the sequence were Alberta points. The Alberta points are followed by the Cody complex of Scottsbluff and Eden points and Cody knives *c.* 8,500 B.P. Finally, this was followed by the Frederick complex. At the Blackwater Draw site, Clovis and Folsom points were followed by Agate Basin, Cody and Frederick complex material. A correlation between the projectile points succession and the fossil bison succession in the High Plains has been suggested, along the lines of *Bison antiquus* with Folsom, Folsom and Plainview with *B. antiquus figginsi*, Plainview and Scottsbluff and Eden with *B. occidentalis*, and the later types with *Bison bison* (the modern descendant).

In eastern North America fluted points similar to Clovis points have been found over a wide area but have not been well dated. Their appearance there may be as early as it was in the High Plains. In the east the Palaeo-Indian tradition was succeeded by another tradition known as the Archaic. On the Plains the Palaeo-Indian tradition continued until 7,000–6,000 B.P. In southern Arizona and the West it was replaced by an expansion of what have been termed the Desert Cultures.

The Old Cordilleran Tradition   The north-west Pacific coastal areas and the hinterland have assemblages which are characterized by the leaf-shaped Cascade point (fig. 179, 19). Associated with it are various forms of 'knives', bolas stones and chopper tools. The assemblages are believed to be as early as or earlier than the assemblages of the Desert tradition. There is a radiocarbon date of 9,750 B.P., but these industries are thought to have occurred also at a much earlier date, estimated as 11,000–10,000 B.P. The leaf points have been found in desert areas in Oregon with the characteristic organic remains of the Desert cultures, sandals and cord. In California, with somewhat different associations, the leaf-shaped points also occur with characteristic artefacts of the Desert tradition. The Old Cordilleran tradition seems to have gone on from perhaps 11,000–7,000 B.P., and elements in it continue down to historic times. The Cascade or similar points have also been found in Middle and South America.

The Desert Tradition is important in that it can be traced as a way of life down to historic times. The Paiuté indians of the nineteenth century A.D. are regarded as practising an economy similar to that of the prehistoric people of the desert cultures. The mode consisted of a mobile economy, based, as with the Palaeolithic hunters of Epirus (p. 71), on the exploitation of the uneven seasonal distribution of natural resources. Like the Epirus bands they exploited a region systematically, moved seasonally from valley to upland and used the caves as home bases to exploit their home ranges. The prehistoric cultures, like the Piauté indians, used the basket and milling stones. The early centre of the Desert tradition was the Great Basin, an area which includes parts of eastern California, Nevada, Utah, Oregon, Wyoming and Idaho. In Utah it has been dated to *c.* 11,000 B.P. in so far as the leaf point is concerned, and *c.* 9,500 B.P. basketwork has been found. In Nevada both home base sites (caves) and transit sites have been found *c.* 8,750–7,000 B.P. A different facies, the Humboldt cultures, from the Humboldt lake region, include spear throwers and shell beads and cord, while the south-eastern Californian desert cultures have a characteristic triangular point with a narrowed base (fig. 179, 20). In southern Arizona, the Cochise culture, a facies of the Desert tradition, begins as early as *c.* 9,000 B.P. and continued until the beginning of the South-west tradition with agriculture and pottery. In the South-west region, gourd and amaranth may have been in an early form of domestication as early as 6,000 B.P.

The Eastern Woodland The Palaeo-Indian tradition was followed by the Archaic tradition. Characterized by large broad points and ground and polished stone tools, the Archaic lasted from 10,000–3,000 B.P. (fig. 179, 21 early, 22 middle, 23 middle and late). In the south-east, as in the Old World shell middens, seasonal sites of inland groups were accumulated adjacent to rivers, and a variety of small mammals as well as deer, elk and bear were hunted. In this environment, agriculture does not appear to have developed until relatively late. Weapons included a throwing stone, the atlatl or banner stone, and throwing sticks, as well as stone and antler projectile points. There were also awls and bodkins, bone fish-hooks and beads. Pottery appeared about 4,000 B.P.

In the north-east there are two variants of the Archaic tradition, the Early and Late Coastal variants and the Boreal variants of the forest. The latter had tools for working wood, banner stones and grooved axes. In general the people using the Archaic tradition of tools showed a tendency towards sedentism in favourable food situations, as at the Modoc cave (p. 426).

In the plains, the Archaic tradition lasted from 6,000 B.P. to recent times. In arid areas a number of variants of the Desert culture were eventually replaced by other forms, but in the Great Basin, they continued down to historic times. A limited but necessary technology based on the restricted raw materials and food supplies available was common over a large area but a number of idiosyncratic traits distinguish economic or cultural influences from each other.

Middle America In Middle America the traditions at the base of the succession are Palaeo-Indian and Old Cordilleran and date to *c.* 9,000 B.P. Fluted points have been recorded from northern Mexico and Costa Rica. The desert cultures are believed to have developed the cultivation of plants over a period between 9,000 and 4,000 B.P. In Tehuacan during the Coxcatlan phase from 7,000–5,350 B.P. the bands had a close relationship with corn (*Zea mays*), beans (*Phaseolus vulgaris*), gourds (*Lagenaria*), chile (*Capsicum annuum*), amaranth (*Amaranthus leucocarpus*) and other forms (MacNeish 1965).

South America Some authorities believe that the Palaeo-Indian hunting bands passed along the whole of the Andean range in South America (Lynch 1967). Palaeo-Indian type points have been found in Venezuela, Ecuador, Patagonia and Tierra del Fuego (fig. 183). In western South America the succeeding forms may have been derived from this tradition. The Stone Age in this area is believed to have lasted from *c.* 12,000 B.P. until, in the south, the extinction of the Yahgan and Ona Indians in recent times (Pl. I). The succession has been divided in the north into 4 periods; I, 12,000–10,000 B.P. as at the site of El Inga in Ecuador; Period II, 10,000–8,000 B.P. as in the earliest levels at the site of Lauricocha; Period III, 8,000–5,000 B.P. with willow leaves and bifacial knives; Period IV with shouldered points down to the introduction of pottery. However only two horizons have been clearly established, the willow leaf horizon *c.* 9,000–8,000 B.P. and a later horizon with smaller points *c.* 5,000–4,000 B.P. Coastal Peru, the Tehuacan, southern Tamaulipas have long records of developing agriculture. In Peru, gourds and lima beans appear to have been in close association with human groups *c.* 6,000 B.P.

Arctic regions In the Arctic areas after 8,000–7,000 B.P., as in post-glacial times in the Old World, a hafted tool phase (after the Australian fashion) took place and consisted basically in the production of small microlithic blades. A micro-blade tradition continued until *c.* 5,500 B.P. in Alaska and in other areas until *c.* 3,000 B.P. In the north-west the microlithic blade tradition appears to have been associated with coniferous forests. An Arctic Small Tool tradition appears to develop *c.* 6,000–5,000 B.P., and continues until *c.* 3,000 B.P. It extended as far as Greenland, and some of its tool elements survive with the Eskimo. These Small Tools appear to have been made by people practising an economy based on marine animals and caribou. The Eskimo cultures begin 4,000–3,000 B.P. and the recently domesticated musk ox represents the first change from a purely hunting-fishing-gathering economy.

The prehistoric record of the Americas is therefore over a very short period of time relative to that of the Old World, in fact, the shortest record of all the continents. It is, however, unique in that it has an abundance of literary evidence relating to the behaviour of hunter and hunter-gatherer and early agricultural peoples. It is therefore surprising that more use of this evidence has not, up to the present, been made the basis of considerations of archaeological data of the Old World.

BLACKWATER NO. 1 LOCALITY, ROOSEVELT COUNTY, NEW MEXICO
(fig. 181–182)

At this site, 15 miles south-west of the town of Clovis, the depression of an ancient lake or marsh eventually became filled by deposition. The stratigraphy is illustrated in fig. 180. Above bedrock begins the grey sand, a lake fill. It contained a number of complete skeletons of elephant, horse, bison and other animals, and artefacts including points were found in association with the elephant bones. In the overlying brown sand no artefacts have been found but in the diatomaceous earth above there was a great quantity of bison remains and Folsom artefacts. A radiocarbon date suggests an age of *c.* 10,000 years B.P. for this deposit. The Folsom horizon is therefore later

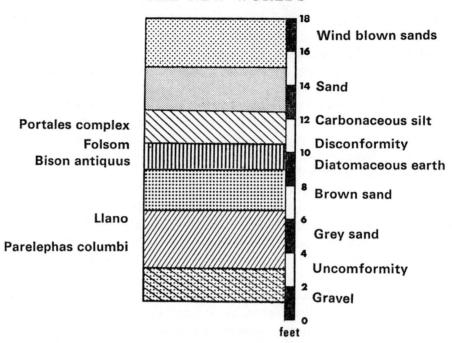

FIG. 180. Section, Blackwater Draw, Locality No. 1. *After Sellards 1952*

than the Llano artefacts and the Clovis point in the grey sand, but how much later is uncertain. Above the diatomaceous earth layer there is a carbonaceous silt which again contains bison bones and a variety of points, some of which resemble the Eden, Scottsbluff and Plainview types.

THE MODOC ROCK SHELTER
(Fowler 1959)

The Modoc rock shelter is at the foot of one of the bluffs at the edge of the flood plain of the Mississippi, and is associated with a number of ecological zones, a high-level prairie, a transitional prairie-forest zone, and an oak/hickory highland forested area.

Radiocarbon determinations show that the shelter was occupied from before 10,000 B.P. to after 4,000 B.P. The data recovered from the site has been considered in relation to the use of the shelter as a habitation, rather than for an analysis of tool types. All the factors involved, sediments, mammalian remains, molluscs, etc. have been studied quantitatively by taking a unit of volume of the deposits 1 ft. × 5 ft. square and considering them against time. The different graphs show considerable agreement and similar trends. The conclusions are that the shelter was occupied *c.* 10,000 B.P. by a human group which utilized a wide variety of natural resources. The

426

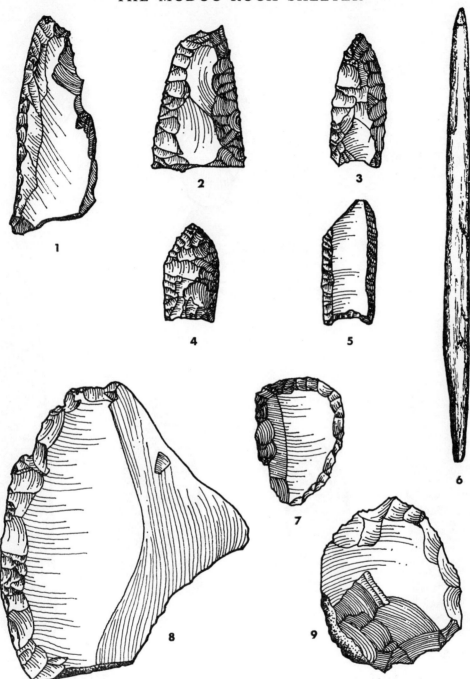

FIG. 181. Artefacts from Blackwater Draw; 1 scraper; 2, 3 projectile points; 6 bone artefact in the basal grey sand, $\frac{7}{12}$; 4, 5 projectile points; 7–9 scrapers from the Folsom horizon. *After Sellards 1952*

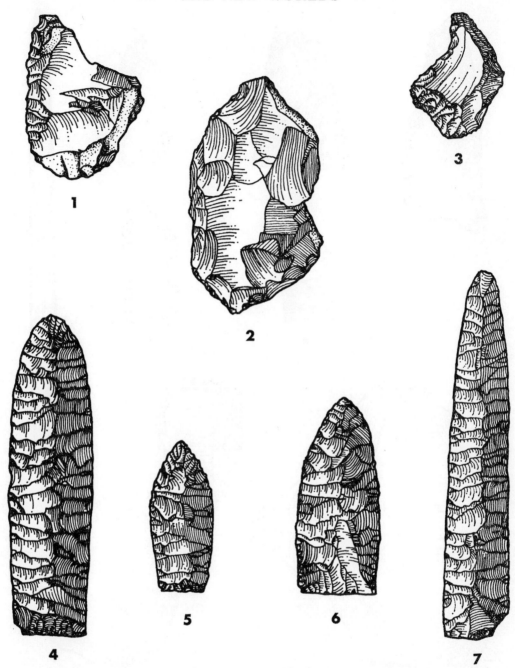

FIG. 182. Artefacts from Portales horizon, Blackwater Draw $\frac{1}{1}$; 1–3 crude scrapers; 4–7 projectile points. *After Sellards 1952*

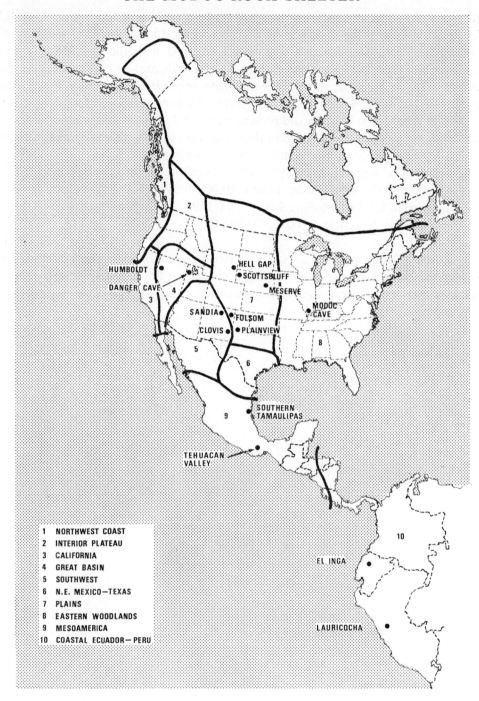

FIG. 183. Culture areas of north and middle America, and north-western South America. *After Willey 1966*

site was at that time a transit site, occupied for brief periods of time. After 9,000 B.P. the site continued to be occupied by a group whose tools showed elements of the Archaic tradition. The group was mainly concerned with the utilization of local resources and there is a wide variety of tools which indicates an occupation period or periods of longer duration. At this time the shelter might be considered as a home base or one of a number of home bases. The greatest intensity of occupation was *c.* 6,000–5,500 B.P. After 5,500 B.P. the site became a seasonal autumn and winter home base as the inhabitants concentrated upon deer and waterfowl, with equipment including projectile points rather than domestic or manufacturing tools.

The occupation is therefore thought to have been divided into three phases:

1. An initial Archaic occupation from *c.* 10,000–9,000 B.P.
2. A period of local adaptation, 9,000–5,500 B.P.
3. Specialized adaptation, 5,500–4,000 B.P.

A number of contemporary sites in the same area have also been considered. They may be habitations of individual groups, each one exploiting a particular ecological niche, or they may represent an economic entity, a single group exploiting economically complementary ecological zones.

24

New Zealand

NEW ZEALAND was possibly the last major area of the World to have been settled by Stone Age man. Its closest neighbouring landmass is Australia, over a thousand miles to the West, but archaeological evidence indicates that it was from eastwards, two thousand miles distant in Eastern Polynesia, that the first settlers came. The earliest settlements are found round the extensive coastline, throughout the whole length of the islands and are radiocarbon dated to about a thousand years ago, though it would seem probable that the original settlement was some hundreds of years earlier. These early sites were commonly located at river or harbour mouths where it would have been possible to exploit the open sea as well as the shore and inland waters and also have access inland. They show evidence for intensive line fishing and sea mammal hunting, but the most distinctive discoveries in the middens are the bones of various species of extinct, giant, flightless birds, the moas. The assemblages of these moa-hunters were classified by R. S. Duff as distinct from and earlier than those of the Maoris observed by Captain Cook and other early explorers. For example, they had necklaces instead of pendant ornaments, varieties of tanged adzes instead of simple ones, bait and lure hooks closely resembling the fishing gear of tropical Polynesia instead of the distinctive Maori forms and, finally, they seem not to have developed the warfare so characteristic of the Maori (Golson & Gathercole 1962). It has also been supposed that the moa-hunters lacked agriculture. This idea however is not based on specific evidence but rather on the belief that hunters would not be cultivators. Between the fourteenth and seventeenth centuries A.D. the moa became extinct and this change is assumed to have coincided with the appearance of traits recognizable as Maori from ethnological sources, though there is surprisingly little documentation of how the alteration took place, whether through internal development or by later introductions. Some authorities have argued that the transition was accompanied by a great increase in agricultural production, particularly of the sweet potato. But recent investigations into the economic evidence on later sites suggest no such dramatic change (Shawcross 1967). Instead, the basic pattern of the exploitation of a variety of environments by means of a seasonal cycle, which probably began with the earliest settlers, was retained. The population dispersed in small units round the coastline in early summer, exploiting marine resources and storing food, and then reforming into larger groups later in the year to obtain vegetable foods, usually inland. As in other areas of the World this social and economic equilibrium was shifted by the advent of European technology, the first development being a dramatic application of the new introductions to Maori ends, yet within a century much was submerged or lost.

Bibliography

Allchin, B. (1958) 'The Late Stone Age of Ceylon', *J. R. Anth. Inst.* 88, 179.

Allchin, B. (1959) 'The Indian Middle Stone Age: Some new sites in Central and Southern India, and their implications', *U. of London Bull. Inst. of Arch.* 2, 1.

Allchin, B. (1963) 'The Indian Stone Age Sequence', *J. R. Anth. Inst.* 93, 210.

Almagro Basch, M. (1962) 'Cronologia del arte rupestre mesolitico', *Atti del VI Congresso Internazionale delle Scienze Preistoriche e Protostoriche. I. Relazioni Generali.*

Ardrey, R. (1961) *African Genesis.*

Armstrong, A. L. (1931) 'Rhodesian Archaeological Expedition (1929): Excavations in Bambata Cave and Researches on prehistoric sites in Southern Rhodesia', *J. R. Anth. Inst.* 61, 239.

Balout, L. (1955) *Préhistoire de l'Afrique du Nord.*

Bandi, H. G. (1961) 'Rock Art of the Spanish Levant' in Bandi *et al., The Art of the Stone Age.*

Behm-Blancke, G. (1960) 'Altsteinzeitliche Rastpltäze in Travertinggebiet von Taubach, Weimar, Ehringsdorf', *Alt-Thüringen*, 4.

Biberson, P. (1961) *Le Paléolithique inférieur du Maroc Atlantique. Service des Antiquités du Maroc*, 17.

Biberson, P. (1967) 'Stratigraphical details of the Quaternary of Northwest Africa' in Bishop and Clark, 1967, 359.

Bishop, W. W. and Clark, J. D. (1967) *Background to Evolution in Africa.*

Blanc, G. A. (1920 and 1927) 'Grotta Romanelli I and II', *Archivo per Antropologia e Etnologia*, 50 and 58.

Bohmers, A. (1951) 'Die Höhlen von Mauern', *Palaeohistoria*, 1, 1.

Bond, G. (1967) 'River valley morphology, stratigraphy and palaeoclimatology in southern Africa', in Bishop and Clark, 1967, 303.

Bonifay, F. (1962) 'Quaternaire et préhistoire des régions mediterranéennes françaises', *Quaternaria*, 6, 343.

Bordes, F. (1956) 'Some observations on the Pleistocene succession in the Somme Valley', *P.P.S.* 22, 1.

Bordes, F. (1961) 'Mousterian Cultures in France', *Science*, 134, 803.

Bordes, F. (1961a) *Typologie du Paléolithique ancien et moyen. Pub. de l'Institut de Préhistoire de l'Université de Bordeaux*, I.

Bordes, F. (1968) *The Old Stone Age.*

Bordes, F. and Fitte, P. (1953) 'L'atelier Commont', *L'Anthropologie*, 57, 1.

Bordes, F. and Prat, F. (1965) 'Observations sur les faunes du Riss et du Würm en Dordogne', *L'Anthropologie*, 69, 31.

Boriskovsky, P. I. (1963) 'Ocherki Po Paleolitu Basseyna Dona', *Materialy i Issledovaniya po Arkeologii S.S.S.R.* 121.

BIBLIOGRAPHY

Boriskovsky, P. I. and Praslov, N. (1964) *Paleolit Basseyna Dnepra i Priazovya.*

Boule, M., Breuil, H., Licent, E. and Teilhard, P. (1928) 'Le Paléolithique de la Chine', *A.I.P.H.* 4.

Bourgon, M. (1957) 'Les industries moustériennes et prémoustériennes du Périgord', *A.I.P.H.* 27.

Brain, C. K. (1958) *The Transvaal Ape-Man Bearing Deposits. Trans. Mus. Mem.* 11.

Breuil, H. (1912) 'Les Subdivisions du Paléolithique supérieur et leur signification', *C. R. Cong. Intern. d'Anth. et d'Arch. Préhist.* 14, 165.

Breuil, H. (1932) 'Les Industries à éclats du paléolithique ancien: Le Clactonien', *Préhistoire*, 1–2, 125.

Breuil, H. (1939) 'The Pleistocene Succession in the Somme Valley', *P.P.S.* 5, 33.

Breuil, H. (1952) *Four Hundred Centuries of Cave Art.*

Breuil, H. and Lantier, R. (1965) *The Men of the Old Stone Age.*

Brothwell, D. and Higgs, E. S. (1969) *Science in Archaeology.*

Burkitt, M. C. (1933) *The Old Stone Age.*

Butzer, K. W. (1964) *Environment and Archaeology.*

Capitan, L. and Peyrony, D. (1928) *La Madeleine, Son Gisement — Son Industrie — Ses Oeuvres d'Art.*

Caton-Thompson, G. (1946) 'The Levalloisian Industries of Egypt', *P.P.S.* 12, 57.

Caton-Thompson, G. and Gardner, E. W. (1952) *Kharga Oasis in Prehistory.*

Chang, K. (1958) 'New Light on Early Man in China', *Asian Perspectives*, 2, 41.

Charlesworth, J. K. (1957) *The Quaternary Era.*

Chavaillon, J. (1967) 'Un australopithèque africain', *B.S.P.F. comptes rendus des séances mensuelles*, CXCVI.

Cheng Te-K'un (1959) *Archaeology in China I. Prehistoric China.*

Cheng Te-K'un (1966) *New Light on Prehistoric China.*

Chernish, O. P. (1961) *Palaeolitigina stoanka Molodova V.*

Chiappella, V. (1964) 'Il Palaeolitico inferiore di Venosa', *Bull. Di Paletnologia Italiana*, n.s. 15, 73.

Clark, J. D. (1950) *The Stone Age Cultures of Northern Rhodesia.*

Clark, J. D. (1950a) 'The Newly Discovered Nachikufu Culture of Northern Rhodesia', *S.A.A.B.* 5, 2.

Clark, J. D. (1954) *The Prehistoric Cultures of the Horn of Africa.*

Clark, J. D. (1957) 'A Re-examination of the Industry from the type site of Magosi, Uganda', *Proceedings of the Third Pan-African Congress on Prehistory, Livingstone, 1955.*

Clark, J. D. (1958) 'The Chifubwa Stream Rock Shelter, Solwezi, Northern Rhodesia', *S.A.A.B.* 13, 21.

Clark, J. D. (1959) *The Prehistory of Southern Africa.*

Clark, J. D. (1962) 'The Problem of the Pebble Cultures', *Atti del VI Congresso Internazionale delle Scienze Preistoriche e Protostoriche. I. Relazioni Generali.*

Clark, J. D. (1963) *Prehistoric Cultures of north-east Angola and their significance in tropical Africa.*

Clark, J. D. (1964) 'The Sangoan Culture of Equatoria: the implication of its stone equipment'. *Diputacíon provincial de Barcelona. Instituto de Prehistoria y Arquelogiá. Monografías*, 9, 309.

Clark, J. D. (1966) *The Distribution of Prehistoric Culture in Angola.*

Clark, J. D. (1966a) 'Acheulian Occupation Sites in the Middle East and Africa: a study of Cultural Variability', *Amer. Anth.* 68, 202.

Clark, J. D. (1967) *Atlas of African Prehistory.*

BIBLIOGRAPHY

Clark, J. G. D. (1952) *Prehistoric Europe. The Economic Basis.*

Clark, J. G. D. (1954) *Excavations at Star Carr: an early Mesolithic Site at Seamer near Scarborough, Yorkshire.*

Clark, J. G. D. (1958) 'Blade and Trapeze Industries of the European Stone Age', *P.P.S.* 24, 24.

Clark, J. G. D. (1962) 'A Survey of the Mesolithic Phase in the Pre-history of Europe and South-west Asia', *Atti del VI Congresso Internazionale delle Scienze Preistoriche e Protostoriche. I. Relazioni Generali*, 97.

Clarke, D. L. (1968) *Analytical Archaeology.*

Cole, S. (1963) *The Prehistory of East Africa.*

Coles, J. M. (1968) 'Ancient Man in Europe' in Coles, J. M. and Simpson, D. D. A. (eds.) *Studies in Ancient Europe.*

Cooke, H. B. S. (1967) 'The Pleistocene sequence in South Africa and problems of correlation', in Bishop and Clark 1967, 175.

Coulonges, L. (1935) 'Les Gisements Préhistoriques de Sauveterre-la-Lémance', *A.I.P.H.* 14.

Dakaris, S. I., Higgs, E. S. and Hey, R. W. (1964) 'The Climate, Environment and Industries of Stone Age Greece, Part I', *P.P.S.* 30, 199.

Dart, R. A. (1957) *The osteodontokeratic culture of Australopithecus promethus. Trans. Mus. Mem.* 10.

Davies, O. (1964) *The Quaternary in the Coastlands of Guinea.*

Day, M. (1965) *Guide to Fossil Man.*

Deacon, J. (1966) 'An annotated list of Radiocarbon dates for sub-Saharan Africa', *Annals of the Cape Provincial Museum*, 5.

Efimenko, P. P. (1958) *Kostienki I.*

Emiliani, C. (1955) 'Pleistocene temperature variations in the Mediterranean', *Quaternaria*, 2, 87.

Emiliani, C. (1966) 'Isotopic Palaeotemperatures', *Science*, 154, 851.

Felgenhauer, F. (1956–9) 'Willendorf in der Wachau', *Mit. Praehist. Komm. Osterr. Akad. Wiss.* 8/9.

Fowler, M. L. (1959) 'Summary Report of the Modoc Rock Shelter', *Illinois State Museum Report of Investigations*, 8.

Freund, F. (1952) *Die Blattspitzen des Paläolithikums in Europa.*

Gabori, M. (1953) 'La Solutréen en Hongrie', *Acta Arch. Hung.* 3, 1.

Garrod, D. A. E. (1955) 'Palaeolithic Spear Throwers', *P.P.S.* 21, 21.

Garrod, D. A. E. (1957) 'The Natufian Culture: The Life and Economy of a Mesolithic People in the Near East', *Proc. Brit. Acad.* 43, 211.

Garrod, D. A. E. and Bate, D. M. A. (1937) *The Stone Age of Mount Carmel.*

Garrod, D. A. E. and Clark, J. G. D. (1965) 'Primitive Man in Egypt, Western Asia and Europe', *The Cambridge Ancient History*, I.

Garrod, D. A. E. and Kirkbride, D. (1961) 'Excavations of the abri Zumoffen, a palaeolithic rock shelter near Adlun, South Lebanon', *Bull. Mus. Beyrouth*, 16, 7.

Gerasimov, M. M. (1964) 'The Palaeolithic Site Malta. Excavations of 1956–57', in Michael, H. N. (ed.), *The Archaeology and Geomorphology of Northern Asia: Selected Works*, 3.

Golomshtok, E. A. (1938) 'The Old Stone Age in European Russia', *Trans. Amer. Phil. Soc.* 39, 189.

Golson, J. and Gathercole, P. W. (1962) 'The Last Decade in New Zealand Archaeology', *Antiquity*, 36, 168.

Gooselitser, B., Kaniviets, V. and Timofeev, E. (1965) 'The Bizovia Station — a Palaeolithic Site in The Arctic Circle', *Sovetskaya Arkheologiya.*

Gorjanovic-Kramberger, K. (1906) *Der diluviale Mensch von Krapina in Kroatien.*

BIBLIOGRAPHY

Graziosi, P. (1960) *Palaeolithic Art*.

Haller, J. (1942) 'L'Abri de Abou-Halka (Tripoli)', *Bull. Mus. Beyrouth*, 6.

Harrison, T. (1957) 'The Great Cave of Niah', *Man*, 57, No. 211.

Hay, R. L. (1967) 'Revised stratigraphy of Olduvai Gorge', in Bishop and Clark 1967, 221.

van Heekeren, H. R. (1957) *The Stone Age of Indonesia*.

van Heekeren, H. R. (1958) 'The Tjabengè Flake Industry from South Celebes', *Asian Perspectives*, 2, 77.

Heider, K. G. (1958) 'A Pebble-Tool Complex in Thailand', *Asian Perspectives*, 2, 63.

Henri-Martin, F. (1957) 'La Grotte de Fontéchevade', *A.I.P.H.* 28.

Higgs, E. S. (1967) 'Faunal Fluctuations and Climate in Libya', in Bishop and Clark 1967, 149.

Higgs, E. S. and Jarman, M. (1969) 'The origins of agriculture: a reconsideration', *Antiquity*, 43.

Higgs, E. S. and Vita-Finzi, C. (1966) 'The Climate, Environment and Industries of Stone Age Greece, Part II', *P.P.S.* 32, 1.

Higgs, E. S., Vita-Finzi, C., Harris, D. and Fagg, A. (1967) 'The Climate, Environment and Industries of Stone Age Greece, Part III', *P.P.S.* 33, 1.

Hole, F. and Flannery, K. V. (1967) 'The Prehistory of Southwestern Iran: a Preliminary Report', *P.P.S.* 33, 147.

Howell, F. C. (1966) 'Observations on the Earlier Phases of the European Lower Palaeolithic', *Amer. Anth.* 68, 88.

Howell, F. C. and Clark, J. D. (1964) 'Acheulian Hunter Gatherers of sub-Saharan Africa' in Bourlière, F. and Howell, F. C. (eds.), *African Ecology and Human Evolution*, 458.

Hugot, H. J. (1967) 'Le Paléolithique terminal dans l'Afrique de l'Ouest', in Bishop and Clark, 1967, 529.

Inskeep, R. R. (1967) 'The Late Stone Age in Southern Africa', in Bishop and Clark, 1967, 557.

Isaac, G. (1966) 'New Evidence from Olorgesailie relating to the character of Acheulean occupation sites', *Actes du Ve Congrès Panafricain de Préhistoire*.

Jewell, R. A. (1966) *Play, Exploration and Territory in Animals*.

Jones, N. (1940) 'Bambata: a Reorientation', *Occ. Pap. Nat. Mus. S. Rhod.* 2, 11.

Jones, N. (1949) *The Prehistory of Southern Rhodesia*.

Jones, Rhys (1964–5) 'Archaeological Reconnaissance in Tasmania, Summer 1963–64', *Oceania*, 35, 191.

Jones, Rhys (1966) 'A speculative archaeological sequence for north-west Tasmania', *Records of the Queen Victoria Museum*, 25.

Jones, Rhys (1967) 'Middens and man in Tasmania', *Australian Natural History*, September 1961.

Kernd'l, A. (1961, 1963) 'Übersicht über ein Forschungsstand der Ur- und Frühgeschichte in der Sowjetunion — I–II', *Berliner Jahrbuch für Vor- und Frühgeschichte*, 1 (1961) 172; 3 (1963) 112.

King, W. B. R. and Oakley, K. P. (1966) 'The Pleistocene Succession in the Lower Parts of the Thames Valley', *P.P.S.* 2, 52.

Klein, R. G. (1965) 'The Middle Palaeolithic of the Crimea', *Arctic Anthropology*, 3, 34.

Klein, R. G. (1966) 'Chellean and Acheulian in the Territory of the Soviet Union; a critical review of the evidence as presented in the literature', *Amer. Anth.* 68, 1.

Klima, A. (1963) *Dolní Vestonice*.

Kretzoi, M. and Vertes, L. (1965) 'Upper Biharian (Intermindel) Pebble-industry occupation site in Western Hungary', *Current Anthropology*, 6, 74.

BIBLIOGRAPHY

Kurten, B. (1968) *Pleistocene Mammals of Europe.*

Lacam, R., Niederlender, A. and Vallois, H. V. (1944) 'Le Gisement mésolithique du Cuzoul de Gramat', *A.I.P.H.* 21.

Leakey, L. S. B. (1931) *The Stone Age Cultures of Kenya Colony.*

Leakey, L. S. B. (1951) *Olduvai Gorge.*

Leakey, L. S. B. (1965) *Olduvai Gorge 1951–1961. A Preliminary Report on the Geology and Fauna.*

Leakey, M. D. (1967) 'Preliminary survey of the cultural material from Beds I and II, Olduvai Gorge, Tanzania', in Bishop and Clark 1967, 417.

Leeson, P. A. (1939) 'A New View of the Western European Group of Quaternary Cave Art', *P.P.S.* 5, 51.

Leroi-Gourhan, A. (1967) *The Art of Prehistoric Man in Western Europe.*

Leroi-Gourhan, A. (1968) 'Le Neanderthalien IV de Shanidar', *Centre Nationale des Researches Scientifiques.*

Lotka, A. J. (1924) *Elements of Mathematical Biology.*

de Lumley, H., Gugnère, S., Barral, L. and Pascal, R. (1963). 'La Grotte du Vallonet Roquebrune Cap-Martin (A-M)', *Bull. du Musée d'Anthropologie préhistorique de Monaco,* 10.

Lynch, T. F. (1967) 'The Nature of the Central Andean Preceramic', *Occ. Pap. Idaho State University Museum,* 21.

Lynch, T. F. (1967a) 'Quishqui Puncu: A Preceramic Site in Highland Peru', *Science,* 158, No. 3802.

Malan, B. D. (1955) 'The Archaeology of the Tunnel Cave and Skildergat Kop, Fish Hoek, Cape of Good Hope', *S.A.A.B.* 10, 3.

Mason, R. (1962) *Prehistory of the Transvaal.*

Mason, R. J. (1965) 'Makapansgat Limeworks fractured stone objects and natural fracture in Africa', *S.A.A.B.* 20, 3.

McBurney, C. B. M. (1950) 'The Geographical Study of the Older Palaeolithic Stages in Europe', *P.P.S.* 16, 163.

McBurney, C. B. M. (1960) *The Stone Age in Northern Africa.*

McBurney, C. B. M. (1967) *The Haua Fteah (Cyrenaica) and the Stone Age of the south-east Mediterranean.*

MacNeish, R. S. (1964) 'Ancient Mesoamerican Civilisations', *Science* 143, No. 3606, 531.

MacNeish, R. S. (1965) 'The Origins of American Agriculture', *Antiquity,* 39, 87.

Megaw, J. V. S. (1960) 'Penny Whistles and Prehistory', *Antiquity,* 34, 6.

Mellars, P. (1965) 'Sequence and Development of Mousterian Traditions in South-western France', *Nature,* 205, 626.

Movius, H. L. (1948) 'The Lower Palaeolithic Culture of Southern and Eastern Asia', *Trans. Amer. Phil. Soc.* 38, 329.

Müller-Karpe, H. (1966) *Handbuch der Vorgeschichte. I. Altsteinzeit.*

Mulvaney, D. J. (1961) 'The Stone Age of Australia', *P.P.S.* 27, 56.

Mulvaney, D. J. (1966) 'The Prehistory of the Australian Aborigine', *Scientific American,* 214, 3.

Mulvaney, D. J. and Joyce, E. B. (1965) 'Archaeological and Geomorphological Investigations on Mount Moffatt Station, Queensland, Australia', *P.P.S.* 31, 147.

Nash, M. (1966) *Primitive and Peasant Economic Systems.*

Nenquin, J. (1967) *Contributions to the Study of Prehistoric Cultures of Rwanda and Burundi.*

BIBLIOGRAPHY

Oakley, K. P. (1964) *Frameworks for Dating Fossil Man.*

Oakley, K. P. and Leakey, M. (1937) 'Report on Excavations at Jaywick Sands, Essex (1934) . . .', *P.P.S.* 3, 217.

Okladnikov, A. P. (1949) *Tešík-Táš.*

Okladnikov, A. P. (1961) 'The Palaeolithic of Trans-Baikal', *Amer. Antiquity*, 26, 486.

Okladnikov, A. P. (1964) 'Palaeolithic Remains in the Lena River Basin', in Michael, H. N. (ed.), *The Archaeology and Geomorphology of Northern Asia: Selected Works*, 33.

Ovey, C. D. (1964) *The Swanscombe Skull. Roy. Anth. Inst. Occ. Paper* 20.

Pei Wên-chung *et al.* (1958) *Report on the excavations of Palaeolithic sites at Ting-ts'un, Hsiang-fên-Lsien, Shansi province, China.*

Pericot Garcia, L. *La Cueva del Parpallo.*

Peters, E. (1930) *Die altsteinzeitliche Kulturstätte Petersfels.*

Peyrony, D. (1930) 'Le Moustier, Ses Gisements, Ses Industries, Ses Couches Géologiques', *Revue Anth.* 14.

Peyrony, D. (1934) 'La Ferrassie', *Préhistoire*, 3.

Peyrony, D. (1936) 'L'abri de Villepin', *Bull. Soc. Préh. Fran.* 33, 253.

Peyrony, D. and E. (1938) 'Laugerie Haute près des Eyzies (Dordogne)', *A.I.P.H.* 19.

Piggott, S. (1959) *Approach to Archaeology.*

Radley, J. and Mellars, P. (1964) 'A Mesolithic Structure at Deepcar, Yorkshire, England, and the Affinities of its associated Flint Industries', *P.P.S.* 30, 1.

Riek, G. (1934) *Die Eiszeitjägerstation am Vogelherd im Lonetal.*

Robinson, J. T. and Mason, R. J. (1962) 'Australopithecines and Artefacts at Sterkfontein', *S.A.A.B.* 17, 87.

Roche, J. (1963–4) *L'épipaléolithique Marocain.*

Roe, D. A. (1964) 'The British Lower and Middle Palaeolithic. Some problems, methods of study and preliminary results', *P.P.S.* 30, 245.

Rogachev, A. N. (1957) 'Palaeolit y Neolit S.S.S.R.', *Materialy i Issledovaniya po Arkeologii S.S.S.R.* 59.

Rosholt, J. N., Emiliani, C. *et al.* (1961) 'Absolute dating of deep-sea cores by the Pa^{231}/Th^{230} method', *J. Geol.* 69, 162.

Rust, A. (1937) *Das Altsteinzeitliche Rentierjägerlager Meiendorf.*

Rust, A. (1943) *Die alt- und mittelsteinzeitlichen Funde von Stellmoor.*

Rust, A. (1950) *Die Hohlenfunde von Jabrud (Syrien).*

Sampson, G. G. (1967) 'Excavations at Zaayfontein Shelter, Norvalspont, Northern Cape', *Researches of the National Museum, Bloemfontein*, 2. No. 4.

Sampson G. and M. (1967) 'Riversmead Shelter: Excavations and Analysis', *Nat. Mus. Bloemfontein Mem.* 3.

Schmidt, R. (1912) *Die diluviale Vorzeit Deutschlands.*

Schmidt, E. (1965) 'Die Seidi-Hoehle. Eine Jung Palaeolithische Station in Griechenland'. Extrait du *Compte Rendu du Colloque.* Athens.

Schwabedissen, H. (1954) *Die Federmesser-Gruppen in des Nordwesteuropäischen Flachlandes.*

Sellards, E. H. (1952) *Early Man in America: a study in prehistory.*

Semenov, S. A. (1964) *Prehistoric Technology.*

Serizawa, C. (1965) 'A Lower Palaeolithic Industry from the Sozudai site, Oita Prefecture, Japan', *Reports of the Research Inst. for Japanese Culture*, 1.

Serizawa, C. and Ikawa, F. (1958) 'The Oldest Archaeological Materials from Japan' *Asian Perspectives*, 2, 1.

BIBLIOGRAPHY

Shackleton, N. (1967) 'Oxygen Isotope Analyses and Pleistocene Temperatures Re-assessed', *Nature*, 215, 5096.

Shawcross, W. (1967) 'An Investigation of Prehistoric Diet and Economy on a Coastal Site at Galatea Bay, New Zealand', *P.P.S.* 33, 107.

Singer, R. and Crawford, J. E. (1958) 'The significance of the archaeological discoveries at Hopefield, South Africa', *J. R. Anth. Inst.* 88, 11.

Smith, P. E. L. (1965) 'Some Solutrean problems and suggestions for further research', *Diputacíon provincial de Barcelona. Instituto de Prehistoria y Arquelogia. Monografias* 18, 389.

Smith, P. E. L. (1966) *Le Solutréen en France*.

Smith, P. E. L. (1966a) 'The Late Palaeolithic of Northeast Africa in the Light of Recent Research', *Amer. Anth.* 68, 326.

Sokal, R. R. and Sneath, P. H. A. (1963) *Principles of Numerical Taxonomy*.

Solecki, R. S. (1963) 'Prehistory in Shanidar Valley, Northern Iraq', *Science*, 139, 179.

de Sonneville-Bordes, D. (1960) *Le Paléolithique Supérieur en Périgord*.

Stekelis, M. (1966) *Archaeological Excavations at Ubeidiya 1960–1963. Israel Acad. of Sciences and Humanities*

Tauber, H. (1967) 'Differential Pollen Dispersion and the Interpretation of Pollen diagrams', *Danmarks Geologiske Undersøeelse*, 2. ser. 89.

Taute, W. (1963) 'Funde der spätpaläolithischen Federmesser-Gruppen aus dem Raum zwischen mittlerer Elbe and Weichsel', *Berliner Jahrbuch für Vor- und Frühgeschichte* 3, 62.

Tchernov, E. (1968) 'Succession of rodent faunas during the Upper Pleistocene of Israel,' *Mammalia Depicta*.

Thompson, M. W. (1954) 'Azilian Harpoons', *P.P.S.* 20, 193.

Tixier, J. (1961) 'Les Pièces pedonculées de L'Atérien', *Libyia*, 6–7.

Tixier, J. (1963) *Typologie de l'Épipaléolithique du Maghreb. Mémoires du Centre de Recherches Anthropologiques, Préhistoriques et Ethnographiques, Alger*.

Tobias, P. V. (1965) 'Australopithecus, Homo habilis, tool-using and tool-making', *S.A.A.B.* 20, 167.

Tobias, P. V. (1966) 'A Re-examination of the Kedung Brubus mandible', *Zoologische Mededelingen* 41. No. 22, 307.

Tobias, P. V. (1967) *Olduvai Gorge. 2. The Cranium and Maxillary Dentition of Australopithecus (Zinjanthropus) Boisei*.

Tobias, P. V. (1967a) 'Cultural Hominisation among the earliest African Pleistocene Hominids', *P.P.S.* 33, 367.

Tobias, P. V. (1967b) 'General Questions arising from some Lower and Middle Pleistocene Hominids of the Olduvai Gorge, Tanzania', *S. Af. J. Sci.* 63, 41.

Tobias, P. V. (1968) 'Middle and Early Upper Pleistocene Members of the Genus *Homo* in Africa' in Kurth, G. (ed.), *Evolution and Hominisation*.

Tode, A. *et al.* (1953) 'Die Untersuchung der palaeolithischen Freilands- station von Salzgitter-Lebenstedt', *Eiszeitalter und Gegenwart* 3, 144.

Treacher, M. S., Arkell, W. J. and Oakley, K. P. (1948) 'On the Ancient Channel between Caversham and Henley, Oxfordshire, and its contained Flint Implements', *P.P.S.* 14, 126.

Ucko, P. J. and Rosenfeld, A. (1967) *Palaeolithic Cave Art*.

Van Zinderen Bakker, E. M. (1967) *Palaeoecology of Africa and of the Surrounding Islands and Antarctica*, II.

Van Zinderen Bakker, 'Palynology and Stratigraphy in sub-Saharan Africa' in Bishop and Clark, 1967, 371.

BIBLIOGRAPHY

Vaufrey, R. (1936) *Préhistoire de l'Afrique. I. Le Maghreb.*

Wainwright, G. J. and Malik, S. C. (1967) 'Problems of Archaeology and Pleistocene Chronology in India', *P.P.S.* 33, 132.

Walker, D. and Sieveking, A. (1962) 'The Palaeolithic Industry of Kota Tampan, Malaya', *P.P.S.* 28, 103.

Wendorf, F. (1966) 'Early Man in the New World: Problems of Migration', *The Amer. Naturalist*, 100, 253.

West, R. G. (1956) 'The Quaternary Deposits at Hoxne, Suffolk', *Phil. Trans. Roy. Soc. London*, 665, 239.

West, R. G. (1968) *Pleistocene Geology and Biology.*

West, R. G. and McBurney, C. B. M. (1954) 'The Quaternary deposits at Hoxne, Suffolk, and their archaeology', *P.P.S.* 20, 131.

White, C. (1967) 'Early Stone Axes in Arnhem Land', *Antiquity*, 41, 149.

Willcox, A. R. (1956) *Rock Paintings of the Drakensberg.*

Willcox, A. R. (1963) *The Rock Art of South Africa.*

Willey, G. R. (1966) *An Introduction to American Archaeology*, Vol. I.

Wormington, H. M. (1957) *Ancient Man in North America.*

Wymer, J. (1961) 'The Lower Palaeolithic Succession in the Thames Valley and the date of the Ancient Channel between Caversham and Henley, Oxon.', *P.P.S.* 27, 1.

Wynne-Edwards, V. C. (1962) *Animal Dispersion in relation to Social Behavior.*

Zeuner, F. E. (1959) *The Pleistocene Period.*

Zotz, L. (1955) *Das Paläolithikum in dem Weinberghöhlen bei Mauern.*

Author Index

441

Site Index

SITE INDEX

SITE INDEX

General Index